SUSTAINABILITY AND POLICY

FUNDAMENTAL QUESTIONS PROGRAM

This book is published as an outcome of the Fundamental Questions Program of the Centre for Resource and Environmental Studies, The Australian National University. The Program began in 1988, focusing interdisciplinary research efforts on the problem of achieving ecological sustainability. It promoted research and systematic discussion of the problems involved in attaining sustainability. An aim of the Program was to present the research outcomes to a wider audience. This book seeks to fulfil this aim in relation to economic policy.

Information about the Fundamental Questions Program and publications arising from it can be obtained from the Centre for Resource and Environmental Studies, Australian National University, ACT 0200.

SUSTAINABILITY AND POLICY
Limits to Economics

MICHAEL COMMON

Centre for Resource and Environmental Studies,
Australian National University

Department of Environmental Economics
and Environmental Management,
University of York

CAMBRIDGE
UNIVERSITY PRESS

Published by the Press Syndicate of the University of Cambridge
The Pitt Building, Trumpington Street, Cambridge CB2 1RP, UK
40 West 20th Street, New York, NY 10011–4211, USA
10 Stamford Road, Oakleigh, Melbourne 3166, Australia

Printed in Hong Kong by Colorcraft

National Library of Australia cataloguing-in-publication data

Common, Michael S. (Michael Stuart)
Sustainability and policy: limits to economics.
Bibliography.
Includes index.
1. Sustainable development. 2. Environmental protection
– Economic aspects. 3. Environmental policy – Economic
aspects. 4. Economic development – Environmental
aspects. 5. Natural resources – Government policy.
I. Title.
338.9

Library of Congress cataloguing-in-publication data

Common, Michael S.
Sustainability and policy: limits to economics/Michael Common.
Includes bibliographical references and index.
1. Sustainable development. 2. Economic development –
Environmental aspects. I. Title.
HD75.6.C6454 1995
333.7 – dc20   94–34142

A catalogue record for this book is available from the British Library.

ISBN 0 521 43001 1 Hardback
ISBN 0 521 43605 2 Paperback

Contents

Tables

Figures

Preface

This book is about sustainability, policies to address threats to it, and the role of economics in the debate about such matters in industrial nations. Because I believe it is important that these matters are widely debated, I have kept the arguments as non-technical as possible. There are no equations. It has been necessary, however, to use some formal economic analysis, so that the policy prescriptions based upon it can be properly assessed.

Much of the impetus for writing the book has come from interaction with participants in the policy process in Canberra, in the context of efforts to examine the implications of a national commitment to sustainable development. Another stimulus was participation in the Fundamental Questions Programme, established in the Centre for Resource and Environmental Studies by Stephen Boyden, intended to promote consideration of the sustainability problem. Both of these experiences suggested that the contributions and limitations of economics in this area were not always properly appreciated.

The Institute of Advanced Studies at the Australian National University is unusual in that its staff are largely free of day-to-day teaching responsibilities. This greatly facilitates research, and involvement with policy makers and their advisers. The Centre for Resource and Environmental Studies, part of the Institute, has staff from the social and natural sciences and its rationale is the transdisciplinary analysis of environmental management. Most of the work on this book was done in this highly appropriate academic environment. I also worked on the book while in the Department of Environmental Economics and Environmental Management at the University of York, which is also committed to a transdisciplinary approach, in teaching as well as research. Some of the material here was presented to first year students there, and useful feedback was obtained.

As well as these two institutions, I should thank a number of individuals. Umme Salma compiled a number of the tables in Chapter 2. Fay Goddard, Sue Kelo and Ettie Oakman helped with manuscript production. Kevin Cowan drew the figures. A number of colleagues in Australia and England were very generous with their time, offering constructive advice as well as correcting my errors. The book was improved as a result: I take full responsibility for any faults that remain. I particularly thank Stephen Boyden, Stephen Dovers, Chris Nobbs, Charles Perrings, John Proops, David Stern, and John Taylor. I also thank Branwen Common for her tolerance and support.

MICHAEL COMMON
Canberra

CHAPTER 1

Introduction

This chapter provides some background to the emergence of sustainability as a problem for policy. It outlines the major themes to be explored and developed in subsequent chapters and it describes how the book is organised.

Background

To sustain is to support without collapse. Sustenance is that which supports life. Currently, humans are unequally provided with sustenance, and many suffer actual deprivation. It is widely believed that addressing these problems requires that levels of economic activity be increased worldwide. It is also generally accepted that increased levels of economic activity would potentially damage the natural environment and impair its ability to sustain humanity although some believe that current levels of economic activity are already unsustainable. Here, the sustainability problem is taken to be: how to address problems of inequality and poverty in ways that do not affect the environment so as to reduce humanity's future prospects.

This is a global problem, which is now an important item on political agendas throughout the world. The high political profile for the sustainability problem is a relatively recent phenomenon. Arguably, it emerged in political and public arenas in 1972, with the publication of the book *The limits to growth* and the United Nations Conference on the Human Environment in Stockholm in June of that year.[1] It explicitly linked concerns for the natural environment to the problem of economic development in poor countries. Among the 26 principles adopted were a group that stated that:

1

Development and environmental concern should go together, and less developed countries should be given every assistance and incentive to promote rational environmental management.

This characterisation is by McCormick(1989) who notes that they were 'designed to reassure LDCs'. Many of the less developed countries (LDCs) saw concern for the environment on the part of the rich nations as likely to lead to the blocking of the LDCs' development in the interests of conservation.

The limits to growth, TLTG (Meadows et al. 1972) reported results from a computer model of the world economy which included a representation of the economic system's extractions from the environment, its use of natural resources of various kinds, and its insertions into it, in the form of waste discharges. The first TLTG conclusion was that the finite nature of the natural environment meant that, in terms of material throughput, the world economic system could not expand indefinitely. There were environmental limits to growth. It was not asserted, as was widely claimed, that global economic collapse was inevitable. The second major conclusion was that if actions were taken to modify current trends, the world economic system could move into a configuration that would be 'sustainable far into the future'.[2]

TLTG generated considerable debate and controversy. Prominent among its detractors were economists. Very few economists were prepared to see any merit at all in TLTG.[3] The TLTG proposition that economic growth could not continue indefinitely, elicited an entirely predictable response from economists, who have a strong attachment to the objective of economic growth. Commitment to the growth objective is not confined to economists. It is widely diffused throughout society.[4] Interestingly, TLTG had no discernible impact on government policies.

Economic growth is widely seen as the only feasible way to alleviate poverty. In this context the general reaction to TLTG is understandable. It appeared to be saying that what was considered the only feasible way to eliminate poverty was, in fact, infeasible. Economic growth in the world system had to cease if that system was not to collapse. TLTG claimed that collapse was avoidable consistent with the satisfaction of the basic material needs of each person on earth. The obvious implication of this claim was a major redistribution of wealth and income from rich to poor as between, and within, nations. While few of the critics focused explicitly on this implication, it clearly influenced much of the reaction to TLTG. The prospect of sustainability offered in TLTG was widely unappealing.

The concept of **sustainable development** gained prominence in 1987 with the publication of the so-called Brundtland Report, according to which:

> Sustainable development seeks to meet the needs and aspirations of the present without compromising the ability to meet those of the future.[5]

This report was produced by the World Commission on Environment and Development (WCED) set up by a resolution of the United Nations General Assembly in 1983. The report derives its popular title from the name of the Chairman of the Commission, Gro Harlem Brundtland, a former Minister for the Environment, and Prime Minister, of Norway. The official title of the report is *Our common future* (World Commission on Environment and Development 1987). The Brundtland Report is a brilliant political document. It has been widely praised and little criticised, evoking positive responses from many governments, as well as non-governmental organisations (NGOs) concerned with the environment and development, and industry and labour organisations around the world. Sustainable development is now on political agendas throughout the world.

The different reactions to the Brundtland Report and TLTG are interesting. In fact, both tell very similar stories and reach somewhat similar conclusions. In both cases, environmental constraints on growth/development are identified and discussed. In both cases, it is argued that it is impossible to conceive that current trends can be continued far into the future. In both cases it is concluded that radical changes are called for in the way the world economy is run. The reception accorded the later Brundtland Report was no doubt influenced by an increased public awareness of a systemic relationship between economic activity and environmental conditions. This increased awareness was due partly to publications such as TLTG, and also to a number of widely publicised environmental problems, and severe economic problems, particularly famines, related to environmental conditions. The role of the media, and particularly television, was undoubtedly important in focusing public awareness on these issues in the more developed nations.

Undoubtedly, another factor was the difference in the bottom line conclusions of the two documents. What TLTG explicitly offers, given the necessary changes, is sustainability in the sense of a constant level of total world output which can be maintained into the indefinite future. Implicit is the continuing existence of pressure for redistribution from rich to poor nations. What the Brundtland Report offers, if policy changes are adopted, is quite different:

Far from requiring the cessation of economic growth, it (i.e. sustainable development) recognises that the problems of poverty and underdevelopment cannot be solved unless we have a new era of growth in which developing countries play a large role and reap large benefits (World Commission on Environment and Development 1987, p.40, parenthesis added).

The rich industrial nations are not told that they must abandon the growth objective. On the contrary:

Growth must be revived in developing countries because that is where the links between economic growth, the alleviation of poverty, and environmental conditions operate most directly. Yet developing countries are part of an interdependent world economy; their prospects also depend on the levels and patterns of growth in industrialised nations. The medium-term prospects for industrial countries are for growth of 3-4 per cent, the minimum that international financial institutions consider necessary if these countries are going to play a part in expanding the world economy. Such growth rates could be environmentally sustainable if industrialised nations can continue the recent shifts in the content of their growth towards less material- and energy-intensive activities and the improvement of their efficiency in using materials and energy (World Commission on Environment and Development 1987, p.51).

Major themes

This section identifies the five major themes running through the book.

Interconnectedness

The sustainability problem arises from the nexus between economic activity and the natural environment. Economic activity impacts on the natural environment: the state of the natural environment affects economic activity. Responses to the sustainability problem must also recognise a second dimension of this linkage, that between humans, which operates both at the individual and social levels. Actions by an individual/society affect the natural environment with implications for individuals/societies displaced in time and space. For many actions the resulting implications are trivial. But, the number of actions involving non-trivial implications increases with human numbers and the level of economic activity. The level of human impact on the natural environment is now such that its capacity to support future economic activity at the level required by the expected human population and its aspirations is questionable. The issues arising are characterised by ignorance and uncertainty. The human impact on the environment is now such that global responses are necessary. The sustainability problem is extremely complex.

Poverty

There are now many humans suffering material deprivation, and there is much inequality in human conditions. Poverty alleviation is generally taken to be desirable and to require output growth as well as, or instead of, the redistribution of the existing level of output by the world economy. Attempts at redistribution on any significant scale imply the potential for social conflict. But, if the current level of world economic activity is threatening the environment, output growth now implies less output in the future. This, in turn, implies future social conflict, as well as a failure to alleviate future poverty. The question arising is whether those currently better off can come to see it as in the interests of themselves and their descendants to act in the interests of the poor. This is not so much a matter of aid flows, as of reducing the environmental impact of the affluent so as to make 'environmental room' for the poor.

Affluence

Currently the industrial nations do not appear to be disposed toward significant redistribution in favour of the developing world. The pursuit of further economic growth and higher material living standards remains a primary policy objective for these nations. The connection between material living standards and human well-being is much less clear than is generally taken to be the case, leaving aside actual deprivation. Generally the industrial nations are democracies, where voters apparently remain convinced that their interests require the continuance of national economic growth. A more widespread appreciation of the complex and somewhat tenuous relationships between economic growth and individual welfare is needed if there is to be informed public debate.

Economics

Sustainability is an economic problem, in so far as economics is the study of the ways in which human beings satisfy their material needs and aspirations. Sustainability is not, however, a problem that falls exclusively within the domain of economics. Nor is economics, as it is currently taught, particularly well suited to analysing the problem. In terms of the nature of the sustainability problem, economics suffers from being ahistorical, amaterial, and apsychological. Economics, that is, largely ignores: history; the material laws of nature; and the study of the nature of man. Despite this, economics has much to say about the means of achieving sustainability-related social goals that is important and useful, but which is often ignored in the process of policy formation. The point is not that economists have nothing of interest to say, but rather, that their expert status relates to questions about means rather than ends. With regard to the debate on the ultimate goals of policy, economists should not be accorded the privileged status that they frequently appear to claim for themselves.

Solutions

There is no blueprint for a sustainable society waiting to be discovered. The problem itself changes over time as the result of economy–environment linkages, and their repercussions in human societies. In so far as there is any solution to the sustainability problem, it is successful adaptation to changing circumstances. The notion of success in this regard is, itself, somewhat ambiguous. In terms of policy relevant analysis, it is a matter of addressing current and prospective threats to sustainability, rather than preparing and implementing the blueprint for a sustainable system.

Reader's guide

The linkages outlined above are dealt with in Chapters 2 and 3. Chapter 2 is concerned with interconnections between human societies, describing aspects of the world economy relevant to the sustainability problem. Chapter 3 considers the economy–environment nexus, and discusses the different conceptualisations of the sustainability problem that arise from economics and ecology.

Poverty and affluence are dealt with in Chapters 2 and 4. Chapter 2 considers poverty and inequality in the world economy today. Chapter 4 reviews some relevant aspects of human history, and looks at the connection between material affluence and individual well-being. Chapter 5 is about thinking about the future. This involves both technical assessments of economy–environment linkages and views about the determinants of human well-being.

Chapters 6, 7 and 8 are about economics. Chapter 6 is a brief, and selective, overview of the subject as a whole, designed to provide some insight into the mental equipment with which economists approach policy analysis. Given this background, Chapter 7 deals with the subdiscipline of resource and environmental economics, which is the part of the subject usually seen as directly relevant to the sustainability problem. Chapter 8 looks at some new developments in economic thinking.

Chapters 9 and 10 are concerned with solutions. The reader should not be looking here for the blueprint for a sustainable world system. Rather, these chapters consider policies to address threats to sustainability. In Chapter 9 this is undertaken from the perspective of an industrial economy, and a broad strategy is outlined. This chapter primarily uses Australian data to illustrate the arguments simply because these were the most accessible. The arguments are, in general terms, applicable to all advanced industrial economies. In Chapter 10 an international perspective is adopted, i.e. recognising the existence of many trading economies, and the global climate change problem is discussed.

Consideration of the sustainability problem does not lend itself to a neat linear progression from beginning to end. Virtually every chapter touches on all of the themes. The final chapter, 11, restates the basic ideas and arguments, and reviews some recent institutional developments.

This is not an economics textbook. However, part of the purpose is to expose the economist's way of thinking. Hence, in some places it has seemed useful to employ diagrammatic analysis. In these instances I have kept the analysis to the minimum necessary for the purposes of the exercise. This has required the use of some concepts and jargon from economics and the natural sciences that cannot be fully explained here. I have tried to include enough explanation to make the book intelligible in its own right, and to provide references to more detailed explanations. Where a definition is included in the text it is in bold type. The first entry in each section of the Index gives the page where it appears in bold type. Subsequent index entries are by page number sequence in the usual way.

I have not attempted to provide precise definitions where this is unnecessary for the purpose at hand. The book covers many areas where I lack expertise. This is a necessary feature of the sustainability problem. It requires either many books written by experts, or one book where many areas are treated in a non-expert way. I believe there is a role for the latter.

CHAPTER 2

The world economy: north and south

The previous chapter identified the constituent elements of the sustainability problem and provided some background to its current position on political agendas. This chapter is concerned with the world economy, particularly in relation to the differences between the industrial north and the developing south, and the question of poverty. The chapter is primarily descriptive and draws heavily on the *Human development report* (United Nations Development Programme 1992), hereafter HDR.[1]

Demography

Table 2.1 gives the estimated total world population for 1960 and 1990, and a projected level for the year 2000, together with the estimated world average population density for 1990. It also provides corresponding data for **developing nations** and **industrial nations**. As used by HDR, these terms are approximately synonymous with the terms 'south' and 'north' as widely used in discussions of the world economy.

The north-south terminology was employed in the Brandt Report (Independent Commission on International Development Issues 1980) and its usage became widespread. Previously the north had widely been referred to as 'advanced' and the south as 'under' or 'less developed', giving rise to the acronyms UDC and LDC.

The industrial nations comprise the nations of Europe, the United States, Canada, Israel, Australia, New Zealand, Japan, and the former USSR. The remaining nations of the world comprise the developing group. On average, developing nations are more crowded than industrial nations (see Table 2.1). Over the period 1960 to 2000 the proportion of the world's population resident in developing nations is projected to increase from 68.5 per cent to 79.7 per cent.

Table 2.1 *Population levels and densities*

	Population size millions			Population density persons per 1000 h.a.
	1960	1990	2000	1990
Industrial nations	950	1210	1270	225
Developing nations	2070	4070	4980	541
World	3020	5280	6250	409

Note: h.a.–hectare
Source: HDR (1992), Table 22.

Table 2.2 gives historical and projected population growth rates. Both are higher for the developing nations. For both groups of nations, the growth rates are projected to fall in the 1990s compared with those in the 1960–90 period. The world's population growth rate is slowing. However, this trend does not apply throughout the world. For the least developed nations (a subset of the developing nations as defined by the UN General Assembly, see HDR p.208), the average annual growth rates are 2.5 per cent for 1960–90 and 3.0 per cent for 1990–2000. For sub-Saharan Africa, they are 2.8 per cent and 3.2 per cent.

Table 2.2 *Population growth rates*

	Annual percentage rates	
	1960–90	1990–2000
Industrial nations	0.8	0.5
Developing nations	2.3	2.0
World	1.8	1.7

Source: HDR (1992), Table 22.

Within each of the industrial and developing groups there is consider-able diversity between nations. This is illustrated in Table 2.3, where the selection of nations used throughout this chapter requires some expla-nation. The selection derives from HDR which uses a threefold classifi-cation whereby nations are assigned to the categories **high, medium and low human development**. Assignment of a nation is according to its score for HDR's human development index, discussed later in this chapter in the section on inequality and deprivation. It is an attempt to provide a quantitative measure of relative development across nations. Canada, Australia and Mexico are in the high category (47 nations); Mauritius and Algeria in the medium category (48 nations); and El Salvador, Bangladesh and Guinea are in the low category (65 nations). From each category we consider the nations with the highest and lowest index scores. Actually Mexico is the second lowest ranking nation from the high development category. The lowest is Qatar, which, as a very small oil exporting nation is anomalous. Also included are Australia, which ranks seventh in the high category, and Bangladesh, which ranks thirtieth in the low category. Of these eight nations, only Australia and Canada are members of the group of industrial nations.

Australia and Canada are large nations with small populations. Their population densities (persons per hectare) are very low by some industrial nation standards: the United States, 272; the United Kingdom, 2357; and Japan, 3280. However, Canada and Australia have high population growth rates compared with the United States, the United Kingdom and Japan, for example (their 1960–90 annual population growth rates were 1.1, 0.3 and 0.9 per cent respectively). The important point to note is that while developing nations typically have higher population growth rates than industrial nations, there is substantial variation within both groups.

Table 2.3 *Demographic data for selected nations*

	Population millions 1990	Annual growth rate % 1960–1990	Population density persons per h.a. 1990
Canada	26.5	1.3	29
Australia	16.9	1.7	22
Mexico	88.6	2.9	461
Mauritius	1.1	1.7	5963
Algeria	25.0	2.8	106
El Salvador	5.3	2.4	2535
Bangladesh	115.6	2.7	8632
Guinea	5.8	2.0	280

Source: HDR (1992), Tables 22, 43 and 44.

National economies

In order to consider some comparative economic data for industrial and developing countries it is necessary to introduce some terminology used in national income accounting, which is discussed more fully in Chapter 8. A country's national product is the value of the total output of goods and services that pass through markets or are supplied by government. The conventions for this accounting are such that this value is the same as the total of the personal incomes earned in production in the country, so that national product is also known as national income. National income/product is divided by its population size to derive **per capita national income.**

Table 2.4 gives data on per capita national income. For present purposes the difference between gross national product (GNP) and gross domestic product (GDP) is not important: this and the significance of 'gross', will be explained in Chapter 8.

Given that total output value is the same as total incomes earned, per capita national income can be interpreted as average individual income, as normally understood. Few economists would claim that per capita national income is a totally satisfactory measure of the average welfare of an individual in an economy. Most would argue, however, that higher per capita national income is better than lower and that large differences in per capita national income do reflect differences in welfare.

Table 2.4 *Per capita national income: north and south*

	Real GDP PPP$ 1989	GNP US$ 1989
Industrial nations	15043	17017
Developing nations	2296	770
World	4622	3836

Note: PPP–purchasing power parity (defined below).
Source: HDR (1992), Table 17.

The north-south differences shown in Table 2.4 are large. In both columns, the developing nations average is less than half the world average, while the industrial nations average is more than three times the world average. The figures in the second column are derived by converting local currency national income data to US dollars using official exchange rates. This can be very misleading as to the relative domestic purchasing power of per capita national income, due to differing price structures between the domestic and US economies. For example, a unit of domestic currency may exchange for one US dollar while purchasing a basket of goods in the domestic economy that would cost two dollars if bought in the United States. The figures in the first column of Table 2.4 are calculated to take account of this. This involves valuing the quantities of the goods and services produced in each country using a common set of prices.[2] This procedure is intended to measure total output in currency units which have **purchasing power parity** across all countries. The units are expressed as US dollars, hence PPP$ in Table 2.4. Generally, the effect of going from measures using official exchange rates to PPP$ is to reduce the size of differences in per capita national income. In Table 2.4 this effect reduces inequality, measured as the ratio of industrial to developing nations' per capita national income, from 22 to 7.

The first two columns of Table 2.5 present the same data for selected countries. The averages of Table 2.4 conceal considerable variation within each group, and mask the extent of the differences between per capita national incomes. Thus, for example, in PPP$ Canada's GDP per capita is three times that for Mexico, and 31 times that for Guinea. The figures in the third column are measured on the same basis as those in the second. They represent the average income of the individuals in the lowest 40 per cent of households in income terms. Clearly, while there is substantial inequality within nations it is not as great as that between nations.

Table 2.5 *Per capita national income: selected countries*

	Real GDP PPP$ 1989	GNP US$ 1989	Lowest 40% of Households
Canada	18635	19030	6480
Australia	15266	14360	4270
Mexico	5691	2010	450
Mauritius	5375	1990	430
Algeria	3088	2230	n.a.
El Salvador	1879	1070	330
Bangladesh	820	180	70
Guinea	602	430	n.a.

Source: HDR (1992), Tables 1, 17 and 38.

Clearly, the developing nations are poor, in terms of per capita national income, relative to the industrial nations. Table 2.6, however, shows that, on average, they are growing faster than the industrial nations. To gain some insight into the implications of compound growth rates let's assume the current per capita income levels for the industrial and developing nations are 100 and 20, respectively. Then, after 100 years of growth at the rates shown in Table 2.6, per capita national income would be 566 for the developing nations and 881 for the industrial nations. The measure of inequality i.e. the ratio of industrial to developing country per capita income would have been reduced from five to 1.6.

Table 2.6 shows, again, that comparisons between industrial and developing nations as groups mask substantial within-group variation. The determinants of a nation's growth rate are many and their interaction is complex. Economic theory emphasises the role of capital accumulation by saving and investment. Table 2.6 gives data on saving and investment for the selected countries. Where saving and investment differ, this is because of net inflows from abroad: see the following section on international trade and capital movements. As shown in Table 2.6, the correlation between rates of saving/investment and growth is not high. While this is partly due to the effects of comparing the latter over a decade with the former for a single year at the end of that decade, it is now recognised that the growth process involves more than just capital accumulation, i.e. it is necessary but not sufficient for growth.

Table 2.6 *Savings, investment and growth*

	Investment % of GDP 1989	Savings % of GDP 1989	Growth GNP per cap. % per annum 1980–89
Canada	23	23	2.6
Australia	26	23	1.8
Mexico	17	18	−1.5
Mauritius	29	21	5.3
Algeria	31	31	0.0
El Salvador	16	6	−1.1
Bangladesh	12	1	0.7
Guinea	18	19	n.a.
Developing nations	25	26	3.4
Industrial nations	22	22	2.2

Source: HDR (1992), Tables 24 and 46.

The process of economic growth is often distinguished from the process of economic development. The basis for the distinction is that whereas growth is expansion without qualitative change, development involves qualitative change. Indeed, for many commentators qualitative change in their social and economic structures is precisely what poor countries must achieve in order to have growth. For example, the extension of market relationships in production and exchange, at the expense of relationships based on custom and reciprocal obligations, is widely seen as necessary to lift rates of saving and investment. On this view, growth in poor countries is inhibited by their social and economic structures. Development, as qualitative change of a certain kind, will reduce this inhibition, promoting growth, which in turn, induces further development. This view tends to see development proceeding until economic maturity is reached, after which growth takes over. Growth and development are seen as distinct problems for distinct kinds of economies.

At one level this distinction has little merit. In the past four decades, growth in industrial economies has been accompanied by structural change, socially and economically. This is the everyday experience of most adults in these economies. At another level, the industrial economy of, say, the United Kingdom in 1990 was more like that of the United Kingdom in 1950 than either was like the economy of, say, Guinea in either year.

One way of describing economic structure is in terms of the allocation of the labour force between broadly defined economic sectors, as in Table 2.7. The transfer of labour from agriculture to industry is widely regarded as an essential feature of the process of economic development. Apart from El Salvador, all the countries have much higher proportions of their labour force in agriculture than do Australia and Canada. However, some of the countries classified as developing have larger proportions in industry than do Australia and Canada. According to some commentators, many of the countries which HDR calls 'industrial' would more properly be called 'post-industrial'. This arises from the observation that many of the HDR industrial economies have, in the past two or three decades, experienced a second major reallocation of labour. The first was from agriculture, or primary industry, to manufacturing, or secondary industry. The second was from secondary to tertiary industry, the services sector. Canada and Australia conform to this pattern. However, although Table 2.7 shows that Algeria and El Salvador have similar proportions of their labour force in services to Canada and Australia, this sector is quite heterogeneous. It includes, for example, persons employed in international banking and in pavement shoe shining. The point about post-industrial economies is not so much that they have large tertiary sectors, but rather the nature of those sectors.

Table 2.7 *Labour force allocation*

	Agriculture %	Industry %	Services %
Canada	3.4	19.4	77.2
Australia	5.3	16.4	78.3
Mexico	22.9	20.1	57.0
Mauritius	19.0	31.1	49.9
Algeria	13.9	10.9	75.2
El Salvador	8.2	21.8	70.0
Bangladesh	56.5	9.8	33.7
Guinea	78.1	1.3	20.6

Source: HDR (1992), Tables 16 and 36.

International trade and capital movements

A central feature of recent economic history has been the internationalisation of the world economy. National economies have become more interconnected by international trade in goods and services. Over the period 1960 to 1988 world exports grew by a factor of over four, while world output grew by a factor of three, i.e. the proportion of output entering international trade grew.[3] The trade data on which this statement is based exclude international trade in services, or 'invisibles' as they are sometimes called. Historically, services have been traded less than commodities: until quite recently national trade statistics gave very little useful information on services trade. In many cases international services trade is simply impossible: having a haircut or a medical consultation requires physical proximity. However, modern technological developments are expanding the range of services in which trade is possible. Between 1970 and 1987 trade in services, measured by value, grew by 13 per cent per annum on average, with the fastest growth in telecommunications and financial services. Most of the trade in services is between industrial nations. In 1989 the industrial nations were responsible for 79.5 per cent of world exports and 77.2 per cent of world imports of services.[4] The following discussion of world trade refers to trade in commodities only, owing to the scarcity of data on trade in services.

Table 2.8 gives data on changes in the commodity composition of trade. 'Primary' products are unprocessed raw materials, such as iron ore for example. The data refer to shares of total world exports in value terms. Hence, the declines shown for 'food' and 'primary' do not imply that either the value or the physical volumes of trade in these products declined. In fact, their value and volumes (as well as that of total trade) increased between 1965 and 1990.

Table 2.8 *Commodity shares in world trade*

	1965 %	1990 %
Food	0.18	0.09
Primary	0.13	0.05
Energy	0.10	0.10
Manufactures	0.60	0.77

Source: International Economic Data Bank, Australian National University.

Data such as that shown in Table 2.8 are often cited to support the proposition that participation in international trade has had differential benefits between industrial and developing nations. The point made is that the latter are mainly in the business of exporting food and primary commodities, where relative opportunities are declining. Data in Tables 2.9 and 2.10 (see pp. 17 and 18) show that this characterisation of the position of developing economies is broadly correct, but involves some oversimplification. Before looking at these data, two further points relevant to the developing nations' relative specialisation in food and primary commodities should be noted. First, the prices for these types of commodities in world markets are generally volatile, changing sharply over short periods of time. This causes instability in the domestic economies of the exporters. Second, long-term trends in world prices for food and primary commodities compared with manufactures mean that the **terms of trade** have generally moved against food and primary exporters. The terms of trade are the volume of exports that can be exchanged for a given volume of imports. Over the period from 1960 to 1988 the average prices of consumer goods in the industrial nations increased by a factor of approximately 4.5, while the prices of primary products (defined to include foodstuffs) in developing countries rose by a factor of approximately three.[5] Leaving aside exchange rate movements, and assuming that all trade between industrial and developing nations involves the former shipping consumer goods to the latter in exchange for primary products, this means that in 1988, developing countries had to ship 50 per cent more exports in volume terms than in 1960 to obtain the same volume of imports. This simple and approximate calculation illustrates a real problem which has faced many developing nations in recent decades.[6]

The data in Table 2.9 show the 1990 commodity trade patterns for four broad groupings of nations. The developed economies are those previously treated here as the industrial nations excluding the centrally planned economies (Albania, Bulgaria, Czechoslovakia, East Germany, Hungary, Poland, Romania), and Norway. All other nations go into the category of developing economies, except for those which earned 5 per cent or more of their export revenues from oil exports, which are the oil economies. On this basis, in addition to the commonly known oil producing nations, the USSR, Norway, Mexico and Egypt are also categorised as oil economies in 1990. **Balance of Trade** (BOT) is the excess of commodity export receipts over commodity import expenditures. The value totals shown for exports and imports for each group of countries are reported in the same units as BOT, i.e. billions of US dollars. The export and import shares refer to these value totals.

The trade pattern for the oil economies is such that energy dominates exports and manufactures dominate imports. These economies run BOT surpluses on energy and deficits on manufactures, and are in BOT surplus overall. For the developed economies, a BOT surplus on manufactures only partially offsets deficits on all of the other commodity groups. Manufactures comprise 84 per cent of exports, and 76 per cent of imports. The developing economies have BOT deficits on energy and manufactures, surpluses on food and primary, and an overall deficit. Note that while for the latter two commodity groups export shares exceed import shares, for energy the shares are approximately equal. While the import share is greater than the export share for manufactures, the latter share is 74 per cent. The main feature of the trade

Table 2.9 *Trade patterns by commodity: 1990*

	Share of total exports	Share of total imports	Balance of trade US$ billions
Oil economies			
Food	0.05	0.12	−14.81
Primary	0.04	0.04	1.60
Energy	0.66	0.02	178.90
Manufactures	0.25	0.82	−114.29
Value	*277.63*	*226.22*	*51.41*
Developed economies			
Food	0.09	0.09	−15.72
Primary	0.04	0.05	−13.22
Energy	0.04	0.11	−173.77
Manufactures	0.84	0.76	151.62
Value	*2377.32*	*2428.40*	*−51.08*
Developing economies			
Food	0.13	0.07	28.72
Primary	0.07	0.05	11.16
Energy	0.07	0.08	−5.88
Manufactures	0.74	0.80	−37.42
Value	*521.32*	*524.73*	*−3.42*
Centrally planned economies			
Food	0.14	0.10	1.81
Primary	0.06	0.06	0.45
Energy	0.07	0.06	0.73
Manufactures	0.73	0.79	0.09
Value	*37.68*	*34.60*	*3.08*

Source: International Economic Data Bank, Australian National University.

pattern of the centrally planned economies is that they have engaged in very little trade with the rest of the world. Most of their trade has been in manufactures. The view that developing nations are predominantly exporters of primary products and importers of manufactures, and vice versa for the industrial nations, is not supported by this data. However, treating the developing nations as a single entity in relation to manufacturing exports is misleading. A small group of nations classified as developing account for a very large proportion of total developing country manufactured exports. The spectacular rates of growth of manufactured exports recently achieved by Taiwan, Singapore, Hong Kong, and South Korea have been widely noted. In 1989, these countries accounted for the following percentage shares of world manufactured exports: 2.1, 1.4, 2.4, 2.0. China, also, has grown rapidly as a manufacturing exporter, with a 1989 world share of 1.7 per cent. The 1989 shares of Mexico and Brazil were 1.2 per cent and 1.1 per cent respectively.[7]

From Table 2.9, the developing countries share of world total exports of manufactures is 16 per cent. The combined shares cited above for seven developing countries total 11.9 per cent. For the purposes of comparison, Mexico must be excluded as in Table 2.9 it is an oil economy, so that six developing countries account for 67 per cent of total developing country manufacturing exports by value. This leaves the remaining 33 per cent to be spread over some 100 developing countries.

The data in Table 2.10 are for total commodity trade flows between the four country groupings shown in Table 2.9. Exports are read across rows, and imports down columns. For the oil economies, 82 per cent of exports go to the developed economies, and 81 per cent of imports into oil economies come from developed economies. For the developed economies, trade is dominantly within the group itself. Of the export total, 77 per cent is to other developed economies. Of the import total, 76 per cent is intragroup. Most of this intragroup trade is in manufactures. The developing economies export mainly to the developed economies, 65 per cent, and import mainly from them as well, 64 per cent. Intragroup trade for these economies is 28 per cent for both exports and imports.

Table 2.10 *World trade flows: 1990 (US$ billions)*

	1	2	3	4	World
1	6.41	227.46	39.63	4.13	277.63
2	183.70	1834.89	334.18	24.55	2377.32
3	30.71	340.27	147.85	2.49	521.32
4	5.40	25.78	3.07	3.43	37.68
World	226.22	2428.40	524.73	34.60	3213.95

Notes: 1 Oil economies.
2 Developed economies
3 Developing economies.
4 Centrally planned economies.
Source: International Economic Data Bank, Australian National University.

It is widely understood that developing nations are more heavily dependent on international trade than industrial nations, and that this creates problems for them. In Table 2.11, the figures shown under trade dependence are for the ratio of the sum of the values of exports and imports to GDP, expressed as a percentage. On this definition, developing nations as a group are more trade dependent, but the group averages conceal considerable within-group variation. As to whether this is a problem, recall that developing nations tend to be exporters of food and primary commodities and importers of manufactures, that the terms of trade have moved against the former, and also that the prices of the former are more volatile.

Table 2.11 *Trade and debt: 1989*

	Trade dependence %	Total debt/GNP %	Debt service %
Canada	47	n.a.	n.a.
Australia	26	n.a.	n.a.
Mexico	22	51	39.6
Mauritius	133	41	9.8
Algeria	43	57	68.9
El Salvador	30	32	16.6
Bangladesh	24	53	19.9
Guinea	33	85	15.2
All developing nations	41	43	23.2
All industrial nations	31	n.a.	n.a.

Note: n.a.–not available.
Source: HDR (1992), Tables 18, 19, 39 and 40.

Most developing nations are net debtors, and there is much commentary on the problems that this, together with their dependence on foreign trade, gives rise to (for example, George 1988). In Table 2.11 total debt/GNP represents overseas debt as a percentage of GNP, and debt service is the sum of interest charges and principal repayments as a percentage of export revenues. It should be noted that export revenues used for debt service are thereby not available for payment for imports of goods and services.

Table 2.12 gives data on capital flows to all developing nations throughout the 1980s. Capital flows are transfers of finance which are not payments for goods and services received. Official development finance (ODF) refers to capital flows originating with the governments of industrial nations, as opposed to the private sectors of industrial nations. It comprises both loans and gifts, with the latter referred to as overseas development assistance (ODA). ODF includes both bilateral flows, from one nation direct to another, and multilateral flows, channelled through international organisations such as United Nations' agencies.[8] Export credits (EC) are governmental payments to assist the financing of import requirements, usually on a bilateral basis. Private direct investment (PDI) involves flows from the private sector to create, or acquire, assets in the developing nations: returns arising and paid overseas are dividend payments. Private lending (PL) is lending by private sector banks at commercial interest rates. The figures shown against interest and dividend payments (I&D) include not only dividends and interest on private loans, but also interest on governmental loans (usually at concessionary rates). The International Monetary Fund (IMF) is an organisation which makes loans to developing nations on a short-term basis in order to provide temporary assistance in the financing of import requirements.

Table 2.12 *Capital flows to developing nations (US$ billions)*

	1981	1983	1985	1987	1989
ODF	45.5	42.4	48.9	61.6	69.0
EC	17.6	4.6	4.0	−2.6	1.2
PDI	17.2	9.3	6.6	21.0	22.0
PL	55.1	36.3	21.9	10.0	14.0
NGO	2.0	2.3	2.9	3.5	4.2
Total	137.4	94.9	84.3	93.5	110.4
(in 1988 dollars)	(201.9)	(143.0)	(128.3)	(100.3)	(111.5)
I&D	−86.4	−84.2	−95.6	−79.0	−107.7
IMF	6.6	12.5	0.8	−4.7	−3.2
Net inflow	57.6	23.2	−10.5	9.8	−0.5

Notes: ODF–official development finance.
EC–export credits.
PDI–private direct investment.
PL–private lending.
NGO–non-government organisation grants.
I&D–interest and dividend payments.
IMF–International Monetary Fund credits.
Source: Mendez (1992), Table 2.2.

As shown in Table 2.12, private lending declined substantially during the 1980s, though private investment increased. As ODF, government originating flows increased sharply at the end of the decade although, taken together with export credits, the increase of 1989 over 1981 is considerably smaller than if ODF only is examined. The flows which were grants from non-government organisations (NGO), essentially private charitable donations, doubled from 1981 to 1989. The total capital flows are net capital flows from developing to industrial nations, in that repayments of principal, for example, against private loans have been subtracted. During the 1980s inflation occurred worldwide so that each dollar bought less over time. The figures shown in parenthesis are calculated using 1988 exchange rates and expressed in terms of 1988 US dollars. On this basis, the real value of the total net capital inflows to developing countries, from all sources, declined substantially over the decade. The next two rows in Table 2.12 show, in current US dollars based on current exchange rates, offsets against the inflows arising as a result of payments of interest and dividends and new credit from the IMF. The final row shows these items subtracted from total capital inflow. Whereas in 1981 the net flow to developing countries was positive, it was negative in 1989.

Table 2.13 gives data on official development assistance, that is gifts, as opposed to loans, from industrial country governments to developing nations. For the industrial nations as a group, and for Canada and Australia, the figures represent payments: for the developing nations, they are receipts. OECD stands for the Organisation for Economic Cooperation and Development, established in 1961 with the objectives of encouraging trade between its members, increasing their national incomes, and coordinating their aid to developing countries. Its membership is essentially the industrial nations as defined in HDR less the former centrally planned economies.

The data in column one are in terms of US dollars per capita. These figures can be compared with the per capita income figures from Tables 2.4 and 2.5. In 1970, the General Assembly of the United Nations adopted a resolution calling upon the industrial economies to set the figure of 0.7 per cent of GNP as a target for the level of their ODA. The second column in Table 2.13 shows ODA outgoings and receipts as percentages of GNP in 1990. The industrial nations on average were halfway towards that target. Note that for Bangladesh and Guinea, ODA amounts to more than 10 per cent of GNP.

Table 2.13 *Official development assistance*

	ODA per capita US$ 1989	ODA, % of GNP 1990
Canada	9.3	0.44
Australia	5.7	0.34
Mexico	1.0	0.10
Mauritius	79.0	4.20
Algeria	9.0	0.40
El Salvador	65.0	6.40
Bangladesh	18.0	10.50
Guinea	48.0	11.60
Developing nations	11.0	1.50
Industrial nations	7.0[a]	0.35[a]

Notes: [a]–OECD countries.
Source: HDR (1992), Tables 18, 19, 39 and 40.

Energy production and use

Industrial and developing nations differ markedly in their use of energy. Historically, a central feature of the process of industrialisation has been a transformation in human energy use. Table 2.14 gives data on energy use for industrial and developing nations. The industrial nations use approximately 10 times as much energy per capita as the developing nations. They account for 23 per cent of the world's population, but 74 per cent of world energy use. With energy use, as with other matters, there is considerable variation within the two groups of nations. This means that the differences between high energy use industrial nations and low energy use developing nations are very great. In Table 2.14, Canada's per capita energy use is 195 times that of Bangladesh.

Table 2.14 *Energy use and carbon release*

	Energy per capita 1989[a]	Energy total 1989[b]	Greenhouse index 1988/89[c]
Canada	9959	263914	4.9
Australia	5291	89418	5.2
Mexico	1288	114117	1.5
Mauritius	369	406	0.2
Algeria	1906	47650	0.8
El Salvador	226	1198	0.3
Bangladesh	51	5896	0.3
Guinea	71	412	1.3
Industrial nations	4930	5965300	3.5
Developing nations	505	2055350	0.9
World	1331	8020650	1.5

Notes: [a]–kilograms of oil equivalent.
   [b]–kilograms oil equivalent x 10^6.
   [c]–carbon heating equivalents in metric tons per capita.
Source: HDR (1992), Tables 23 and 44.

In most industrial and many developing nations the dominant source of energy for commercial use is the combustion of fossil fuels, i.e. coal, oil and natural gas. This combustion releases carbon dioxide, which is the major greenhouse gas. Greenhouse gases reduce the reflected radiation passing from the earth's atmosphere into space, and increasing concentrations of such gases in the atmosphere are expected to lead to global warming: see Chapter 10. The final column of Table 2.14 shows the estimated per capita emissions of all greenhouse gases, expressed in equivalent carbon heating units. These figures indicate that the industrial nations are contributing four times as much in per capita terms as the developing nations to the build-up of greenhouse gas concentrations in the atmosphere. The per capita contribution of Australia is 26 times that of Mauritius.

Energy use is a reasonably good proxy for general environmental impact, in so far as it is the use of energy that permits the large-scale movement and transformation of matter. Fossil fuels are exhaustible resources in that an increase in current use means that less is available for future use. On the basis of the data shown in Table 2.14, each individual resident in the industrial nations has a much larger impact on the environment, both in terms of resource depletion and in terms of environmental impact, than does an individual resident in the developing nations.

Table 2.15 shows the patterns of energy use in Australia. These are reasonably representative of those in industrial nations. The units are petajoules (PJs) where a joule is the energy conveyed by one watt of power during one second. This is a very small unit for accounting for energy use at the level of national economies, and the prefix peta, accordingly, refers to a multiple of 10^{15}. The data refer to commercial energy use. **Primary energy** refers to the energy content of fuels extracted from the environment domestically, or imported. The first four primary fuels distinguished are coal, oil, natural gas, and hydro-electricity. The major renewable primary input is biomass: solar and the other renewables contribute only 2 per cent of total renewable primary energy.

Conversion uses refer to the use of primary fuels to produce fuels for end use. While crude oil requires processing before it is suitable for combustion, natural gas and coal do not, but are burned to produce electricity. In Australia, this use accounts for 88 per cent of the primary input of coal: only 12 per cent of the coal used in Australia is used in its original form by final energy consumers. In Table 2.15 the negative sign on electricity in terms of conversion uses gives the amount of electricity generated by means of primary fuel combustion. The supplies available after conversion uses are known as **secondary fuels**. One way of looking at the way economies use energy is via the ratio of secondary fuel availability to primary fuel input. For Australia this ratio is 0.68. Such ratios reflect both the efficiencies of the processes for converting primary to secondary fuels, and the mix of processes. In terms of energy use, electricity is inefficient in that the energy content of electricity produced by fossil fuel combustion is considerably less than the energy content of the fossil fuel burned. The thermal efficiency of fossil fuel electricity production varies from around 20 per cent to around 35 per cent.

The lower part of Table 2.15 shows how secondary fuels are used. Residential refers to use by households that actually takes place in the household, and thus excludes personal transport use, which appears under transport. It includes heating and cooling, lighting and power for domestic appliances. Note that 75.7 per cent of the end use of oil is for transport. Agricultural uses are included in industry. Commercial corresponds to the services sector. Non-energy uses include feedstocks for the petro-chemicals industry, the manufacture of asphalt, and lubricating oils etc.

Table 2.15 *Energy balance for Australia: 1990/91*

	Coal	Gas	Oil	Elec.	Renewable	Total
Primary energy	1664.0	695.8	1493.9	57.7	184.1	4095.5
Conversion uses	1462.9	157.2	124.6	−428.1		1316.6
End use	201.1	538.6	1369.3	485.8	184.1	2778.9
of which percentage shares are:						
Residential	0.3	16.5	1.2	28.9	43.1	11.7
Industry	94.7	76.7	18.4	49.9	56.5	43.2
Commercial	2.8	6.5	0.8	19.7	0.3	5.3
Transport	2.1	0.2	75.7	1.4		37.8
Non-energy			3.9			1.9

Source: ABARE (1991).

An **energy balance**, as shown in Table 2.15, is the standard way of reporting data on the total inputs of primary fuels and their uses. This approach shows explicitly what is involved in conversions from primary to secondary fuels. However, for many purposes this accounting for fuels use is not very helpful, and it can be misleading. Take the question of electricity production and use. On the basis of accounts such as those in Table 2.15, it is frequently stated that electricity is responsible for 1462.9/1664.0 = 88 per cent of coal combustion in Australia, which is 1462.9/4095.5 = 36 per cent of total primary energy use.[9] This statement is true. However, as shown in the lower part of the table, 28.9 per cent of the electricity is delivered to households for heating, lighting and appliance power, while 71.1 per cent is delivered to industry, commerce and transport where it is used to produce other goods and services. This proportion of electricity is not produced for the direct meeting of household wants for electricity. It is produced to be used in the production of other goods and services. Since household consumption is seen as the purpose of productive activity, a useful accounting for energy uses would assign 71.1 per cent of electricity use to the goods and services produced using it. The use of coal in producing that electricity would then be assigned to those goods and services.

Consider the production of, say, refrigerators, and the assignment to that production of the use of fuels in the economy. On the accounting basis used in Table 2.15, the assignment would only pick up purchases of fuels by the factory in which the refrigerators were manufactured. However, this is an incomplete accounting for the claims made on primary fuels inputs by this production. As well as purchasing fuels, the factory purchases many other inputs – steel, rubber, plastics, wiring etc.– the production of which involved the use of fuels. A complete accounting for the energy use for which refrigerator production is responsible requires that such indirect fuel use be included, together with direct use.

Figures 2.1 and 2.2 give the results arising when indirect as well as direct energy uses are accounted for, for Australia in 1986/7, for 27 industries/commodities.[10] Table 9.3 (see p. 236) lists the sectors corresponding to the numerical identification used in these figures. The **energy intensities** shown in Figure 2.1 have the following interpretation. They give the total amount of primary fuels, expressed as PJ, which were used indirectly as well as directly to produce A$1 million worth of each commodity for consumption by households.[11] Thus, for example, consider agriculture, forestry and fishing. The use of energy shown per unit of output by this sector, 1, includes not only its purchases of fuels to run its machinery and equipment, but also the energy used in producing its other inputs, such as fertiliser. Note that this sector ranks seventh in energy intensity, ahead of, for example, 13, 14, 15 and 16 which are fabricated metals and three different manufacturing sectors. This counterintuitive result arises because indirect as well as direct energy uses are accounted for – the production of fertiliser uses large amounts of fuel. Sectors 10, 17 and 18 are petroleum and coal products, electricity, and gas, respectively.

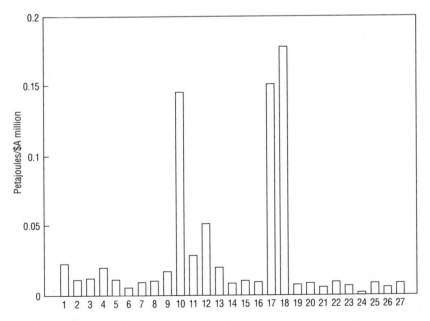

Figure 2.1 Energy intensities.

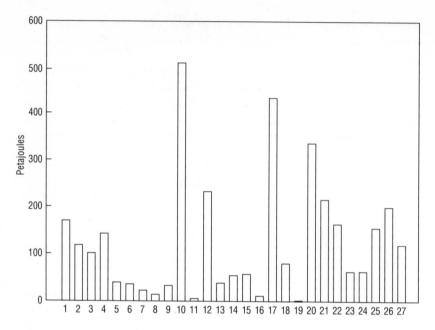

Figure 2.2 Energy use levels.

The data illustrated in Figure 2.2 refer to the actual amounts of energy used directly and indirectly in each of the 27 sectors to produce their outputs. The sector output concerned is that which is delivered to final consumption: deliveries to other producing sectors are not counted as part of a sector's output here.[12] The data in Figure 2.2 are derived from multiplying the energy intensities by the corresponding sectoral output levels. The first point to note is that 17, electricity, accounts for 420 PJs which is some 11 per cent of total primary energy use. On this basis, the energy use attributed to electricity is just that associated with primary fuel use by electricity generated for delivery to final consumption. The primary fuel use involved in generating electricity which was used in other productive sectors, directly and indirectly, is attributed to those other sectors. The second point to note is that 20, construction, is a relatively low ranking sector in terms of energy intensity, but ranks third by total use, on account of its large size. Third, note also that a similar point applies in respect of 21, 25, 26 and 27, which are all services sectors.

These data show the way in which energy use permeates an industrial economy when account is taken of its indirect as well as its direct use. Sectors, such as the services sector, which would normally, on the basis of their direct use, be regarded as minor in regard to energy use – see commercial in Table 2.15, for example – turn out to be major users when indirect use is also considered.

Inequality and deprivation

Many argue that differences in human welfare between nations are not properly reflected by per capita national income data. Economists would agree with this. They take the objective of economic activity to be consumption rather than production. However, many economists take the view that looking at per capita national income represents a good first cut at the problem.

The United Nations Development Programme, in HDR (1992), makes the distinction between means and ends in the development process. GNP growth is seen as a means to ends to be defined in terms of people's needs and aspirations. The **human development index** (HDI) is intended to give 'a composite measure of human progress' and to 'ensure that development planning is directed to people's needs' (p.19). While noting that for these purposes any single index must be inadequate, HDR (1992) argues that the HDI is nonetheless useful:

> Indices such as the HDI ... cannot hope to reflect the breadth and complexity of the questions they cover. But they can help stimulate and clarify debate on subjects whose difficult and frequently controversial nature often permits them to escape full national and international attention (p.3).

The HDI is an index of relative performance, which takes account of income (Y), longevity (L), and a measure of educational attainment (E), which is constructed from data on the adult literacy rate (R), and years of school attendance (S). For Y, L and E a country is given a score which is its relative performance on that subindex. The highest score possible is 0, the lowest 1. For each country, the three scores are added, then divided by three and the result subtracted from one. Thus, if a country did best in all of Y, L and E its HDI would be one. If it did worst on all three, its HDI would be zero. The income measure used, Y, is derived from per capita national income measured in PPP\$ such that dollars above a poverty line are given progressively less weight as that income increases. The measure Y is called **adjusted income**. A comparison of the last column of Table 2.16 with the first column in Table 2.5 shows the effect of the adjustment. The poverty line is \$4829 in PPP\$.

Table 2.16 gives the values of the variables used in the calculation of the HDI for the selected countries considered in this chapter. Table 2.17 gives the HDI values arising for these countries, together with data for GNP per capita, and the country rankings according to these two indices. The figures in Table 2.16 require little comment. By the standards of the north, the situation in regard to life expectancy, education and income in countries in the low human development category is extremely poor.

Table 2.16 *Components of the human development index*

	L 1990	R 1990	S 1990	Y 1989
High human development				
Canada	77.0	99.0	12.1	5051
Australia	76.5	99.0	11.5	5040
Mexico	69.7	87.3	4.7	4888
Medium human development				
Mauritius	69.6	86.0	4.1	4876
Algeria	65.1	57.4	2.6	3088
Low human development				
El Salvador	64.4	73.0	4.1	1897
Bangladesh	51.8	35.3	2.0	820
Guinea	43.5	24.0	0.8	602

Notes: L–longevity.
 R–adult literacy rate.
 S–years of school attendance.
 Y–income.
Source: HDR (1992), Table 1.

Table 2.17 *Income and the human development index*

	GNP per capita	HDI	HDI rank	GNP rank
Canada	18365	0.982	1	11
Australia	15266	0.971	7	22
Mexico	5691	0.804	46	61
Mauritius	5375	0.793	48	63
Algeria	3088	0.533	95	58
El Salvador	1897	0.498	96	83
Bangladesh	820	0.185	135	150
Guinea	602	0.052	160	119

Source: HDR (1992), Table 1.

A question to be considered here is the relationship between per capita national income and relative performance as measured by the HDI. In Table 2.17 the per capita national income measure reported is for GNP converted to US dollars at official exchange rates. The deficiencies of this measure were noted earlier. Given that it is this measure which is most readily available and most widely used, it is instructive to take this per capita income measure (given its limitations), and compare the rankings by it with those by HDI. As Table 2.17 shows, for an individual country the rankings may differ considerably. However, if we compute the rank correlation coefficient for all 160 countries it takes the value 0.91.[13] The highest value that a rank correlation coefficient can take is one, the lowest is minus one. Therefore, overall, the GNP per capita ranking is quite a good predictor for the HDI ranking. However, it is instructive to compute the rank correlation coefficient for high, medium and low human development groupings separately. We then get the following results: high, 0.45; medium, –0.44; low, 0.46. In the high and low groups, the coefficient indicates a low positive association between the two rankings, while for the medium group the association is negative. In the high group, countries on average have a lower HDI rank than their GNP per capita rank, whereas in the other two groups the HDI rank is the higher of the two.

Table 2.18 *North-South gaps*

	1960	1990
Narrowing gaps		
Life expectancy at birth	67	84
Child mortality rate	80	90
Daily calorie supply	73	81
Adult literacy	48	66
School enrolment	63	74
Widening gaps		
PPP$ GDP per capita	17	15
Mean years of schooling	38	36
Population per nurse	15	8
Population per doctor, 1984:	10	
Tertiary enrolment, 1988/89:	22	
Scientists and technicians, 1985–89:	11	
Radios, 1988/9:	17	
Daily newspaper circulation, 1988/89:	13	
Telephones, 1988/89:	6	

Source: HDR (1992), Tables, 6, 7, and 8.

The data on which the HDI is based, see Table 2.16, illustrate north-south differences. Further data relating to this are given in Tables 2.18 and 2.19. Again these require little comment, beyond some explanation of terminology. In Table 2.18 all the data are expressed as index numbers where for each year in question the industrial nations average takes the value of 100. Thus, for example, whereas in 1960 average life expectancy at birth in the developing nations was 67 per cent of average life expectancy at birth in industrial nations, in 1990 the ratio was 84 per cent. The indices are all constructed so that the smaller is the number, the larger is the gap. A population per doctor figure of 10 means that there were 10 times as many people per doctor in developing nations as in industrial nations, on average. These data thus refer to relativities and inequalities. Nonetheless, many would see them as indicative of actual deprivation in the developing nations.

Table 2.19 provides data directly relevant to actual deprivation in the developing nations. In considering these data it should be noted that they refer to national averages only. Some in these countries will be better off than these data suggest, and others worse off. According to the standards of the north, many of the inhabitants of the nations of the south must be considered deprived in an absolute sense.

Table 2.19 *Nutrition and child mortality*

	Calorie intake 1988[a]	Children malnourished 1980–90[b]	Child mortality 1990[c]
Mexico	135	14	49
Mauritius	118	24	28
Algeria	112	10	98
El Salvador	105	15	87
Bangladesh	83	66	180
Guinea	88	n.a.	237
All developing nations	109	35	112
Least developed nations[d]	87	45	189

Notes: [a] Daily calorie supply per capita as a percentage of the per capita requirement. Requirement: the average number of daily calories needed to sustain a person at normal levels of activity and health, taking into account the distribution of the population by age, sex, body weight and environmental temperature. Supply: the calorie equivalent of the net food supplies in a country, divided by the population, per day.
[b] The percentage of children under five who are underweight.
[c] The under-five mortality rate per thousand live births.
[d] As defined by the United Nations (UN). Most suffer from one or more of the following: GNP per capita of $300 or less, land-locked, remote, desertification, exposure to natural disasters.
n.a.–not available
Source: HDR (1992) Tables 2 and 11.

CHAPTER 3

Sustainability

The sustainability problem is that of managing economic activity so as to address inequality and poverty in ways that do not undermine the base for future economic activity. The problem has two dimensions. The previous chapter considered the human dimension in terms of the world economy. In this chapter we look at economy–environment interconnections, and ways of analysing this dimension of the sustainability problem.

The economy and the environment

Economic activity takes place within, and is part of, the system which is the earth and its atmosphere. This system will be referred to here as the **natural environment**, or more briefly as the **environment**. This system, itself, has an environment, which is the rest of the universe. The **biosphere** is:

> The region of the earth and its atmosphere in which life exists. It is an envelope extending from up to 6000 metres above to 10 000 metres below sea level and embraces alpine plant life and the ocean deeps. The special conditions which exist in the biosphere to support life are: a supply of water; a supply of useable energy; the existence of interfaces, i.e. areas where the liquid, solid and gaseous states meet; the presence of nitrogen, phosphorous, potassium and other essential nutrients and trace elements; a suitable temperature range; and a supply of air (although there are anaerobic forms of life).[1]

Figure 3.1 is a schematic representation of economy–environment interconnections.[2] The heavy black-lined box represents the environment, which is a thermodynamically closed system in that it exchanges energy but not matter with its environment. The biosphere receives inputs of solar radiation. Some of that radiation is absorbed and drives biospheric processes. Some is reflected back into space. This is

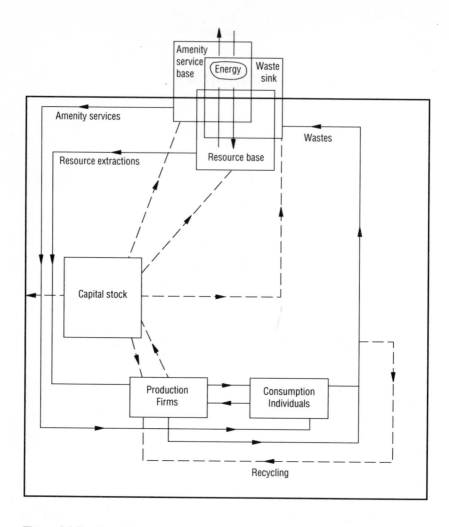

Figure 3.1 Economic activity in the natural environment.

represented by the arrows crossing the heavy black line at the top of
Figure 3.1. Matter does not cross the heavy black line at all, meteorites
and spacecraft aside. The balance between energy absorption and
reflection determines the way the global climate system functions: see
Chapter 10. The energy in and out arrows are shown passing through
three boxes, which represent three of the functions that the
environment performs in relation to economic activity. This is to indicate
that it is energetic openness which drives these three functions. It also

drives the fourth function, represented by the heavy black-lined box itself, which is the provision of the life support services which hold the whole system together. Note that the three boxes intersect one with another and that the heavy black line passes through them. This is to indicate that the four functions interact with one another.

Focusing on the essentials, economic activity involves production by firms, and consumption by individuals. There are two complementary flows between firms and individuals. The former supply the latter with produced goods and services, the latter supply the former with labour services for use in production. Not all of production is consumed. Some of the output from production is added to the **capital stock**, the services of which are used, together with labour services, in production. Figure 3.1 also shows production using a third type of input, resources extracted from the environment. It also shows a flow of amenity services passing from the environment to individuals without the intermediation of productive activity. Both production by firms and consumption by individuals involve the generation of wastes which are discharged into the environment.

We now discuss these four functions in more detail, and the interactions between them.[3]

Resource base

Natural resources used in production are of several types. One distinguishing characteristic is whether the resource exists as a stock or a flow. The difference lies in whether the level of current use affects future availability. **Flow resources** have the characteristic that the current rate of use has no implications for future availability. An example is solar radiation used to heat water via a solar panel on the roof of a house. The amount of heating done today has no effect on the amount that can be done tomorrow. There is, however, an upper limit to the amount of heating that can be done today, set by the amount of radiation incident to the panel. This limit can vary from day-to-day, according to season and weather. **Stock resources** have the characteristic that future availability is affected by current use.

A second standard distinction concerns the nature of the link between current use and future availability. **Renewable resources** are biotic populations – flora and fauna. **Non-renewable resources** are minerals, including the fossil fuels. In the former case, the stock existing at a point in time has the potential to grow by means of natural reproduction. If in any period use of the resource is less than natural growth, stock size grows. If use, or harvest, is always the same as natural growth, the resource can be used indefinitely. Such a harvest rate is often referred to as a sustainable yield. Harvest rates in excess of sustainable yield imply declining stock size. For non-renewable resources there is no natural reproduction, except on geological timescales. Consequently, more use now necessarily implies less future use. For this reason these resources are sometimes known as **exhaustible**, or **depletable**, **resources**. This is somewhat misleading as renewable resources can also be exhaustible. Continual harvesting at levels in excess of the sustainable yield will eventually exhaust the resource. All stock resources are potentially exhaustible. The point here is that whereas with non-renewables there is no positive constant rate of use that can avoid eventual exhaustion, with renewables there is.

Some argue that in the case of non-fuel minerals eventual exhaustion is not inevitable, given the possibilities for recycling and mining successively lower grade ore down to crustal abundance. (See, for example, Simon 1981.) While these considerations are relevant, it seems simply perverse to argue that they repeal the exhaustibility of non-renewable resources. First, recycling can never be complete. Second, as the ore grade declines so the energy required to produce useable metal increases at a greater than proportional rate. Third, the volume of waste production increases as the ore grade declines. Non-renewable resource lifetimes can be stretched, but not to infinity.

Within the class of non-renewables the distinction between fossil fuels and the other minerals is important. First, the use of fossil fuels is pervasive in an industrial economy. Second, fossil fuel combustion is an irreversible process in that there is no way that the input fuel can be even partially recovered after combustion. In so far as coal, oil, and gas are used to produce heat, rather than as inputs to chemical processes, they cannot be recycled. Minerals used as inputs to production can be recycled. This means that whereas in the case of minerals there exists the possibility of delaying, for a given use rate, the date of exhaustion of a given initial stock, in the case of fossil fuels there does not. Given their key role in industrial economies, this is clearly important. Among other things, it has led to an interest in nuclear fission and nuclear fusion as energy sources.[4]

The flow energy resources comprise: solar radiation, wave power, wind power, hydro power, and tidal power. The so-called energy crisis of 1973/74 drew attention to the advantages of such energy sources in terms of their non-depletable characteristic, and as an alternative to nuclear fission.[5] More recently they have come to be seen as also having advantages in that they avoid the atmospheric emissions associated with fossil fuel combustion, especially of carbon dioxide. There are offsetting features to be taken into account. With the exception of tidal power, their availability is neither continuous nor assured at any particular time. Tidal and hydro power, and to a lesser extent wave and wind power, are feasible only at a limited number of locations.

Solar radiation differs from the other flow resources in several ways. Most importantly, it is what drives all of the life processes in the biosphere. As an alternative energy source, the use of solar radiation to generate electricity could be competitive with its use in driving life processes. Solar radiation is not used by economic activity only when it is captured by solar panels and used to generate heat and/or electricity. If an area of land is covered with solar panels the incident solar radiation is not then available to the photosynthetic process. Solar radiation is, ultimately, what gives rise to growth in renewable stock resources. Further, even when attention is restricted to solar radiation as a source of energy inputs to economic activity, it is wrong to think solely in terms of solar panels. Solar radiation can be used by means of biomass fuel, most familiarly as wood.

Waste sink

The activities of production and consumption give rise to waste products, or residuals, to be discharged into the natural environment. Indeed, such injections into the environment are the necessary corollary of the extraction of material resources from it. Matter can neither be created nor destroyed by human activity. It is merely transformed from one state to another. This is variously known as the **law of conservation of mass**, or the **materials balance principle**. The mass of material extracted as resources from the environment in any period is necessarily returned to it. The return is not generally instantaneous, and may be much delayed. At one extreme we have a return period which is effectively instantaneous, as when, for example, a tree is felled for immediate use as fuel. At the other extreme consider the case of iron ore extracted and transformed into structural steel. The building involved may stand for hundreds of years, and after its collapse or destruction, the disintegration of the structural steel may take many more years. An intermediate case would be iron ore used to make steel for use in automobile manufacture.

In terms of Figure 3.1 (p. 32), the flow of wastes going into the environment is simply a continuation of the flow of resources coming out of it. Human economic activity involves only delay and physiochemical transformation. The 'only' refers to matters seen from the perspective of the long-term functioning of the environment. From the human perspective 'only' is a completely inappropriate adjective. The delay/transformation is what economic activity is essentially about. One dimension of the sustainability problem is the concern that some transformations may generate irreversible damage to environmental functions.

Questions relating to the consequences of waste discharge into the environment are generally discussed under the heading of **pollution**. To the extent, and only to the extent, that waste discharge gives rise to problems perceived by humans, economists say that there is a pollution problem.

This definition of pollution is entirely in keeping with the general approach of economics to the environment, which is entirely anthropocentric. In the environmental sciences pollution is seen instead as that which damages system function. Thus, for example: 'A pollutant is a resource which is available in concentrations far in excess of a sufficient or optimal level' (Watt 1973, p.24). It is clear from the context that 'sufficient or optimal' refers to system function.

The pollution problem can be conceptualised in two ways. One, which finds favour with economists, sees pollution as a stock of material resident in the natural environment. The other, which ecologists favour, sees pollution as a flow which affects the natural environment. In the former case, pollution is treated in the same way as a stock resource, except that the stock has negative value. Residual flows into the environment add to the stock. There is a parallel also to the distinction between renewable and non-renewable stock resources. For some pollutants, the stock existing in the environment will decrease over time in the absence of further flows of the residual involved. Such decrease may be due to either biochemical processes that transform the pollutant into some other substance, or to physical transport out of the particular area of concern. If the area of concern is the whole of the environment, such transport is impossible. Where natural processes work to reduce stock size, a positive residuals flow rate is consistent with a non-increasing pollutant stock size, so long as the flow is less than the natural rate of stock reduction. In such cases, pollutant accumulation is, potentially, a reversible process. If the residual flow is stopped, the stock of pollutant will decline over time. For some pollutants, biochemical decay processes may be non-existent (heavy metals), or so slow as to be effectively non-existent (long-lived nuclear wastes).

The flow model treats the environment as having an **assimilative capacity**, defined in terms of a rate of residual flow. Pollution is then the result of a residual flow rate in excess of assimilative capacity. There is no pollution if the residual flow rate is equal to, or less than, assimilative capacity. If the residual flow rate is persistently in excess of assimilative capacity, the latter declines over time, and may eventually go to zero, in which case the amount of pollution in every period is the same as the residual flow. By reducing the residual flow rate, declining assimilative capacity can be halted but not reversed. Once assimilative capacity is reduced, the effect is permanent.

These models are not to be understood as mutually exclusive. Rather, they focus on different perceptions of the key feature of the problem. In the stock model, the focus is on the reversible accumulation of some residual perceived as harmful to human interests. In the flow model, the focus is on an irreversible process of damage to the environment, where one manifestation of damage is a reduced ability to assimilate wastes from economic activity. One model will be more appropriate thinking about some pollution problems, the other for other problems.

Amenity base

In Figure 3.1 amenity services flow direct from the environment to individuals. The biosphere provides humans with recreational facilities and other sources of pleasure and stimulation. Swimming from an ocean beach does not require productive activity to transform an environmental resource into a source of human satisfaction, for example. Wilderness recreation is defined by the absence of other human activity. Many people enjoy simply lying out of doors in the sunshine. The role of the natural environment in relation to amenity services can be appreciated by imagining its absence.

In many cases the flow of amenity services to individuals does not directly involve any consumptive material flow. Wilderness recreation, for example, is not primarily about exploiting resources in the wilderness area, though it may involve this in the use of wood for fires, the capture of game for food, etc. A day on the beach does not involve any consumption of the beach in the way that the use of oil involves its consumption. This is not to say that flows of amenity services never impact physically on the natural environment. Excessive use of a beach area can lead to changes in its character, as with the erosion of sand dunes following vegetation loss caused by human visitation. The point is rather that, as distinct from resource use, in many cases amenity services use does not necessarily affect the environment. Indeed, in the context of amenity services we frequently refer to over-use when consequential changes in the environment are observed.

In some cases the direct enjoyment of environmental services by individuals does intentionally affect the biosphere. Hunting as recreation is an example. In other cases the impact is ancillary to the enjoyment of the amenity service, as with the development of facilities for tourists. Again, such development may itself impair the flow of services for at least some individuals, as when a beach once accessible only by a long journey on foot is transformed by the construction of an access road and a holiday resort.

The matter of amenity service flows is complex, and it is not possible to capture what is generally involved with simple formulations. This should not obscure the fact that this is an important environmental function in relation to human interests.

Life support system

The fourth environmental function is also difficult to represent in a simple and concise way. Over and above serving as the resource base, waste sink and amenity base, the biosphere currently provides the basic life support functions for humans. While the range of environmental conditions that humans are biologically equipped to cope with is greater than for most other species, there are limits to the tolerable. We have, for example, quite specific requirements in terms of breathable air. The range of temperatures in which we can exist is wide in relation to conditions on earth, but narrow in relation to the range on other planets in the solar system. Humans have minimum requirements for water input. And so on. The biosphere functions now in such a manner that humans can exist in it.[6] Rather than try to provide an exhaustive account of the life support functions of the biosphere, we will consider two aspects of the matter, which illustrate the differentiation of this function from the three already discussed, and the interconnections involved.

Consider first solar radiation. We have already noted the role of this as one element of the resource base, and the fact that, for some people at least, sunbathing is an environmental amenity service. In fact, solar radiation as it arrives at the earth's atmosphere is harmful to humans. There it includes the ultraviolet wavelength UV-B, which causes skin cancer, adversely affects the immune system, and can cause eye cataracts. UV-B radiation affects other living things as well. Very small organisms are likely to be particularly affected, as UV-B can only penetrate a few layers of cells. This could be a serious problem for marine systems, where the base of the food chain is very small organisms living in the surface layers of the ocean, which UV-B reaches. UV-B radiation also adversely affects photosynthesis in green plants.

Solar radiation arriving at the surface of the earth has much less UV-B than it does arriving at the atmosphere. Ozone in the stratosphere absorbs UV-B, performing a life support function by filtering solar radiation. The stratosphere is the portion of the earth's atmosphere above the troposphere, which extends up from the surface about 80 kilometres. In the absence of stratospheric ozone, it is questionable whether human life could exist. Currently, stratospheric ozone is being depleted by the release into the atmosphere of chlorofluorocarbons

(CFCs), compounds which exist only by virtue of human economic activity. They have been in use since the 1940s. Their ozone-depleting properties were recognised in the 1980s, and policy to reduce this form of pollution is now in place. Notwithstanding this, it is anticipated that human skin cancer rates will increase substantially, and adverse effects on the growth of organisms at the base of food chains are possible.[7]

Consider next biodiversity. Biota are relevant to the three functions discussed above. Many species of flora and fauna are exploited as renewable resource inputs to production. Many species are involved in the transformation of the wastes that are discharged into the environment, and contribute to its assimilative capacities. The amenity services that individuals derive from the environment are dependent on the existence in it of flora and fauna. The number of species currently existing is unknown, but is certainly much larger than the number of species that can be identified as being directly involved in resource base, waste assimilation and amenity service provision. This does not mean that the species not thus identifiable are, from the human perspective, redundant.

The current functioning of the biosphere involves all extant species. Some may be more important than others, but rather little is known about this. It should be presumed that the extinction of any species will change the way the biosphere functions. Such changes may, considered separately, be beneficial or harmful to human interests, in terms of the environmental functions which are resource base, waste assimilation and amenity service provision. Again, very little is known about this. What is clear is that the extinction of any species reduces the pool of genetic material in existence. Such reduction can be presumed deleterious to human interests on two counts. First, a species not currently regarded as directly useful may turn out to be regarded as directly useful in the future. Second, genetic diversity is the basis on which natural selection works to produce evolution. Evolutionary processes can be regarded as part of the life support function of the biosphere. We can be reasonably certain that the environment will change over time. To keep it functioning in human interests may require the emergence of new species. The potential for such emergence is reduced to the extent that the size of the currently existing gene pool is reduced.

Function interactions

The linkages between economic activity and the environment are pervasive and complex. The complexity is increased by the recognition that the four classes of function each interact one with another. In Figure 3.1 (p. 32) this is indicated by having the three boxes intersect one with another, and jointly with the heavy black line representing the life support function. What is involved can be illustrated with two examples on very different scales.

Consider first a river estuary. It serves as the resource base for the local economy in that a commercial fishery operates in it. It serves as the waste sink in that urban sewage is discharged into it. It serves as the amenity base in that it is used for recreational purposes such as swimming and boating. It contributes to life support functions in so far as it is a breeding ground for marine species which are not commercially exploited, but which play a role in the operation of the marine ecosystem. At rates of sewage discharge equal to or below the assimilative capacity of the estuary, all four functions can coexist. If, however, the rate of sewage discharge exceeds assimilative capacity, not only does a pollution problem emerge, but the other estuarine functions are impaired. Pollution will interfere with the reproductive capacity of the commercially exploited fish stocks, and may lead to the closure of the fishery. This does not necessarily mean its biological extinction. The fishery may be closed on the grounds of the danger to public health. Pollution will reduce the capacity of the estuary to support recreational activity and, in some respects, such as swimming, may drive it to zero. Pollution will also impact on the non-commercial marine species, and may lead to their extinction with implications for marine ecosystem function.

Consider next the global climate system and the emission into the atmosphere of greenhouse gases. The major greenhouse gas is carbon dioxide, and here we will assume for simplicity that it is the only greenhouse gas. Carbon dioxide is a natural constituent of the earth's atmosphere. In the past two centuries carbon dioxide concentrations in the atmosphere have been increasing as a result of human activities, notably fossil fuel combustion. The majority view amongst competent scientific commentators is that it should be assumed that this will lead to increasing average global temperatures, with the rate of increase greater than anything that the global system has experienced in the past 10 000 years, and rapid by the standards of the past 1 000 000 years.

The anticipated consequences of global warming are a matter of uncertainty, and some dispute. However, if global warming does occur at the rate envisaged by majority scientific opinion, some of the broad features of responses in terms of the functions of the biosphere are reasonably clear. In terms of resource availability, there would firstly be losses in low lying coastal areas due to sea level rise. Changes in regional climates would mean changes in the crops that could be grown there. Some crops and wild species in some areas would grow faster with higher temperatures and carbon dioxide concentrations. Others would grow more slowly. The interactive effects on species, of increased ultraviolet radiation with higher temperatures and increased carbon dioxide concentrations, are largely unknown. Matters are further complicated by the fact that global warming would likely be accompanied by increased cloud cover. About all that can reliably be said is that the geographical patterns of availability of renewable resources and agricultural crops would change.

In terms of waste assimilative functions there is also little that can be said definitively other than that changes would occur. To take one example, the assimilative capacity of a river for organic sewage decreases as water temperature increases. On the other hand, it is expected that higher temperatures would generally be accompanied by increased rainfall, which would suggest greater rates of stream flow and hence increased assimilative capacity in river systems. But again, it is expected that while average rainfall would increase this would, in many areas, be accompanied by greater variability over time. Increased average rainfall is not inconsistent with increased incidence of periods without rain. To the extent that this occurred there would be an increased temporal variability in the assimilative capacity of a river.

As regards amenity services, the direct implications of global warming might be thought to depend fairly closely on where one lives. Whereas the inhabitants of Siberia might welcome warmer winters, the inhabitants of, say, Athens might not welcome warmer summers. Assessment of the overall impact would also be expected to depend on ones' inclinations. In Australia, it would be expected that opportunities for skiing would diminish, while opportunities for sunbathing would increase (leaving aside the UV-B problem!).

For some commentators, it is in the area of what are here called life support services that the possible implications of global warming are seen as most worrying. This worry arises via the prospects for biodiversity in relation to the anticipated rate of climate change. As noted above, this anticipated rate is greater than is thought to have occurred in the past 10 000 years. Most species of flora have quite narrow ranges of climatic tolerance. Adaptation to climate change would involve genetic evolution and/or migration. The rates at which either of these processes can occur is slow relative to that anticipated for climate change, and the prospect envisaged is one of the extinction of many species of flora. This would, in turn, have implications for species of fauna which have evolved to be dependent on particular species of flora. Reductions in biodiversity resulting from climate change would have implications for amenity services as well as life support functions. The natural recreational facilities available in particular areas would change.

All of this is inconclusive. It is not certain that the earth will warm, and even if it did the consequences could not be forecast with any certainty.

This, in itself, is a particular example of an important general feature of the interconnections between the natural environment and economic activity. They are characterised by uncertainty.

Substituting for environmental services

One feature of Figure 3.1 remains to be considered. We have so far discussed the interconnections represented in Figure 3.1 by solid lines. The dashed lines represent possibilities of substitutions for environmental services.

Consider first **recycling**. This involves interception of the waste stream prior to it reaching the natural environment, and the return of some part of it to production. Recycling substitutes for environmental functions in two ways. First, it reduces the demands made upon the waste sink function. Second, it reduces the demands made upon the resource base function, in so far as recycled materials are substituted for extractions from the environment.

Recycling is usually thought about in the context of non-renewable resources where it is particularly pertinent given the absence of reproductive growth of the stock existing in the environment. Residuals from renewable resource use can be used as inputs to production. Vegetable and animal wastes can be used as fertilisers, as fuel, and as animal fodder. The extent to which this kind of recycling occurs in agriculture varies greatly, and is generally less in industrialised economies where agricultural wastes are often a major problem. Paper recycling is now often regarded as important in relation to reducing the demands on forest resources.

The extent to which recycling is possible varies across resource types, and with the nature of the transformation involved in the production process. Fossil fuel combustion is an irreversible process such that no recycling at all is possible. The recycling of other natural resources is a process which itself requires inputs of energy and labour. Generally, the complete recycling of any mineral resource extracted from the environment is impossible.[8]

Also shown in Figure 3.1 are four dashed lines from the box for capital stock running to the three boxes and the heavy black line representing environmental functions. These lines are to represent possibilities for substituting the services of capital for environmental services.

Consider first the waste sink function. **Capital equipment** can be used to augment assimilative capacity. To illustrate, consider again the discharge of sewage into a river estuary. Various levels of treatment of the sewage prior to its discharge into the river are possible. According to the level of treatment, the demand made upon the assimilative capacity of the estuary is reduced for a given level of sewage. The sewage treatment plant substitutes for the natural environmental function of the waste sink to an extent dependent on the level of treatment that the plant provides. The higher the level of treatment the more capital equipment is needed. The operation of the capital equipment would require inputs of labour and, if mechanised, of energy. Note also that the construction of the capital equipment itself requires the extraction of resources from the environment.

An example from the field of energy conservation illustrates the substitution of capital for resource base functions. For a given level of human comfort, the energy use of a house can be reduced by the installation of insulation and control systems. These add to that part of the total stock of capital equipment which is the house and all of its fittings, and thus to the total capital stock. Note again, however, that the insulation and control systems are themselves material structures and their production involves extractions, including energy, from the environment. Similar fuel-saving substitution possibilities exist in productive activities.

Consider next some examples in the context of amenity services. An individual who likes swimming can either do this in a river or lake, or from an ocean beach, or in a man-made swimming pool. The experiences involved are not identical, of course, but given the existence of swimming pools, recreational swimming is still a possibility for individuals without access to natural facilities. Similarly, it is not now necessary to actually go into a natural environment to derive pleasure from seeing it. The capital equipment in the entertainment industry means that it is possible to see wild flora and fauna without leaving an urban environment. Apparently it is envisaged that computer technology will, via virtual reality devices, make it possible to experience most of the sensations of actual use of the natural environment without actual use of it.

It appears that in the context of the life support function many regard the substitution possibilities as severely limited. However, from a technical point of view, it is not clear that this is the case. Artificial environments capable of supporting human life have already been created, and in the form of space vehicles and associated equipment have already enabled humans to live outside the biosphere, albeit for limited periods.[9] It would apparently be possible, if expensive, to create conditions capable of sustaining human life on the moon, given some suitable energy source. Equally, human life could apparently survive on a biologically dead planet earth. To make this point is not to downgrade the importance of the life support functions provided by the biosphere in its present form.

It is to put the matter into perspective. This involves two points. The first is that the quantity of human life that could be sustained in the absence of natural life support functions would appear to be quite small. It is not that those functions are absolutely irreplaceable, but that they are irreplaceable on the scale at which they currently operate. The second point concerns the quality of life. One might reasonably take the view that while human life on a biologically dead earth is feasible, it would not be in the least desirable. It appears that what is at issue even in the worst case scenarios about environmental damage is not the end of human life, but the end of human life as we know it.

The possibilities for substituting for environmental services have been discussed in terms of capital equipment. Capital is accumulated when output from current production is not used for current consumption. Current production is not solely of material structures, and capital does not only comprise equipment–machines, buildings, roads etc. Economists recognise **human capital** as well as material capital. Human capital is increased when current production is used to add to the stock of knowledge, and this is what forms the basis for technical change. However, in order for technical change to impact on economic activity, it generally requires embodiment in new equipment. Knowledge that could reduce the demands made upon environmental functions does not actually do so until it is incorporated into equipment that substitutes for environmental functions.

Capital for environmental service substitution is not the only form of substitution that is relevant to economy–environment interconnections. In Figure 3.1 environment–economy flows are shown as single lines. These single lines each represent many different physical flows. Thus, for example, the resource input flow comprises flows of stock and flow resources, where the former comprises flows of renewable and non-renewable resources, and where the latter comprises oil, iron ore, copper ore etc. With respect to each of the flows shown in Figure 3.1, substitutions between components of the flow are possible and affect the demands made upon environmental functions. The implications of any given substitution may extend beyond the environmental function directly affected. For example, a switch from fossil fuel use to hydro-electric power reduces fossil fuel depletion and waste generation in fossil fuel combustion, and impacts on the amenity service flow in so far as a natural recreation area is flooded.

Limits to growth?

According to *The limits to growth* (Meadows et al. 1972, and see also Meadows et al. 1992) economic expansion must soon come to an end, because of environmental limits. It is then necessary to plan for dealing with poverty and inequality in a no-growth world economy. *Our common future* (World Commission on Environment and Development 1987) starts from an essentially similar understanding of the nature of economy–environment interconnections, but draws the conclusion that growth can and should continue, so as to deal with poverty and inequality. However, this growth would take a different form from past growth, and would be sustainable development.

The difference between these positions really turns on the substitution possibilities discussed above. Essentially, the limits to growth position follows from the view that the potential for reducing the demands on environmental functions by such substitutions is quite limited. The sustainable development position takes the view that by virtue of such substitutions it is possible for the world economy to continue growing without increasing the demands made upon the environment beyond limits that it can tolerate.

Which view is correct? No-one really knows. Reasonable people may reasonably differ on the question. There are several dimensions to an answer, and they are not all 'scientific'.

Views differ about the nature of the limits that should be considered. At one extreme the limit would be set by the possibility of human life. Quality of life considerations aside, this limit may well not exist. At the opposite extreme, some appear to take the view that any change in biospheric functioning from the current state, or even some prior state, represents passing the limits. One alternative approach is to think in terms of rates of change. The situation is to be deemed intolerable when the rate of environmental change exceeds the rate at which humans can adapt. We have little idea what the latter rate is, so this approach does not define limits at all precisely.

Leaving this aside, there remain great uncertainties regarding substitution possibilities. Experts differ over the purely technical dimensions in particular instances. The case of nuclear fission is instructive. At its inception it was asserted, and widely believed, that it would mean that electricity would be so abundant that it would not be worth metering and charging for it. However, it now appears that very few fission reactors would be built on purely commercial criteria. The electricity that they produce is generally more expensive than that based on fossil fuel combustion.

In some cases while there may be a reasonable consensus on the technology itself, its systemic implications are poorly understood and disputed. Thus, to continue with the nuclear fission example, much of the disputation concerning its ability to substitute for fossil fuels on a large scale stems from different understandings of the problems of waste disposal and risk management. On one view these are amenable to technical solutions, on another they are not. Disagreements here derive from different subjective attitudes to the risks involved as much as from differing technical assessments of costs and risks. If some people find a given level of risk acceptable while others do not, there is no objective basis for arguing that one group is 'wrong' and the other 'right'.

Another difficulty is the fact that we do not know which are the critical areas where substitution is required. Within less than 20 years, the perceived fossil fuel problem has changed from one of scarcity to one of overabundance. In the 1970s the critical problem with fossil fuels was widely considered to be the fact that they were non-renewable resources, which would be exhausted within relatively short time horizons. The wastes arising from fossil fuel combustion were noted, but not regarded as of major concern. An announcement that world fossil fuel reserves were 10 times as high as previously understood would then have been regarded as a matter for general congratulation. In the 1990s the critical problem associated with fossil fuels is widely seen as being the atmospheric emissions arising from their combustion, especially carbon dioxide. The scarcity considered most pressing now is the assimilative capacity of the atmosphere for carbon dioxide.

The economic conceptualisation of sustainability

Standard economic thinking about sustainability has at its core a very simple representation of the physical and human elements of the problem. This focuses attention on some of the key issues. These are the substitution possibilities discussed above. It does not and cannot empirically resolve the question of the extent of those substitution possibilities. Rather, it makes clear that this is a central issue. It also generates an important insight into one dimension of the question of policy in regard to sustainability. This is the matter of the adequacy of capital accumulation.

The core of standard economic thinking about sustainability is the **Hartwick model**.[10] The point of departure for this model is another model, often known as the **cake-eating model**. The origin of this appellation is in the analogy with the problem of dividing up a cake between a large number of would-be cake eaters. Suppose that the only natural resource available is a finite stock of a non-renewable resource, and that recycling is impossible. Suppose that humans directly live off this resource, which is essential to life. To simplify even further, suppose that the human population size is constant across generations. The question then is: what is the largest constant rate of per capita consumption that can be maintained indefinitely? What is the maximum sustainable rate of consumption?

The answer to this question is clearly zero. There is no positive use rate for a finite non-renewable resource stock that can be maintained indefinitely. A cake of finite size cannot be divided into an infinite number of pieces of equal size. In a cake-eating world, sustainability is impossible.

Economists, at least in their formal models, generally do consider infinite time horizons. This is basically because it avoids the problem of deciding what the time horizon should otherwise be. Suppose some non-infinite time horizon, T years hence, is adopted. Then, the plan would involve the cake/resource being exhausted within T years, so that in the year T+1 consumption would be zero. If it were known that human life would anyway cease in the year T, this would be a very sensible plan. But this is not known. If human life is not to cease in year T, planning with a time horizon of T means that it will. Hence, T is set at infinity, to be understood as an indefinitely large number.

Now we turn to the Hartwick model itself. Suppose, as in Figure 3.1 (p.32), that the non-renewable resource is not directly consumed, but is used in the production of output which can either be consumed or added to the stock of capital, which stock is itself an input to production. To focus on the essentials, the assumption of constant population size is retained. Is sustainability now possible? Is there some constant level of consumption that can be maintained indefinitely? The answer turns upon what is assumed about the substitution possibilities between the resource and capital in production. If it is assumed that the resource is absolutely essential in production, in the sense that capital cannot substitute for it and without some input of it production goes to zero, then sustainability is impossible, as in the cake-eating model. If it is assumed that the resource is inessential, in the sense that production is possible without inputs of the resource, then there is no problem in continuing to produce after the resource stock is exhausted, and sustainability is possible. However, in this case, the problem is not very interesting, since it assumes that production and consumption are possible without any extractions from the natural environment. This is, of course, an incorrect assumption.

It turns out that it is possible to make assumptions about the substitution possibilities in production such that the resource is not inessential, but sustainability is possible.[11] The assumptions are that with no resource input there is no output, but that as the resource input gets very small so its contribution to output gets indefinitely large. In this case, while sustainability is possible, it is realised only if a particular form of behaviour in relation to capital accumulation is adopted, and a particular time path for the extraction of the resource is followed. The form of savings behaviour required is that involved in following the **Hartwick rule**. This rule specifies how much output can be consumed in each period, and how much must be saved and added to the capital stock. Once stated, the rule has considerable intuitive appeal. It says that in each period the amount to be saved is the amount by which the use of the resource contributed to production over and above the costs of extracting the resource. This contribution to production arising from use of the resource is known as rent. The Hartwick savings rule, invest the rent from resource extraction, applies to the rent arising in each period when the efficient time path for extraction of the resource is followed.[12] Given that the resource is extracted according to an efficient depletion plan and that in every period the rent arising is not consumed but added to the capital stock, sustainability is attained.

While the Hartwick rule was originally derived in the context of a model with just one non-renewable resource, it has been shown that it extends to situations where many different resources are used in production. Given that resources are exploited efficiently, investing the rents arising will give constant consumption indefinitely if the substitution possibilities are such that this is feasible. Following the rule is necessary but not sufficient for sustainability. The rule only works if the required substitution possibilities exist. We have already noted that in fact little is actually known about these possibilities. It should also be noted that even where it is assumed that the substitution possibilities are favourable, the rule only works as stated for a constant population. If it is assumed that the population is growing, then the feasibility of constant per capita consumption requires some additional assumptions about technical progress.[13]

The Hartwick rule is to be regarded as a mathematical parable, rather than an empirical proposition about the world we live in. The question which then arises is: why is the rule interesting? There are three answers to this question.

First, discussing the rule is a convenient way of demonstrating how economics conceptualises the sustainability problem. The approach is totally anthropocentric. Sustainability is constant consumption by humans. The state of the biosphere is of concern only in so far as it is relevant to human interests. Further, ultimate human interests in relation to the environment are conceived solely in terms of consumption. The state of the environment *per se* is of only instrumental concern. Humans are seen as feeding off the biosphere, albeit in rather complex and possibly immaterial ways, rather then being part of it. The natural environment exists for humans, and alternative states of the environment are to be ranked according to individual preferences.

Second, the main point is the identification of the key role of substitution possibilities. Curiously, having made this identification, mainstream economics has not really regarded empirical investigation of the matters arising as an important priority. This is not to say that economists have completely ignored such matters. In the 1970s there was a lot of empirical work done, in the light of a perceived energy crisis, on substitution possibilities as between inputs of energy and inputs of capital and labour. We discuss some implications of this work in Chapter 9. It is to say that they have not yet impinged much on the way economists in general think.

It is also true to say that where economists have specifically addressed such matters it has typically been on the basis of extrapolating past trends in the availability of resource inputs. It is not too much of a caricature to say that most empirical research in this area has involved looking at historical time series for resource prices, noting that they have generally been downward, and concluding that resource scarcities in the future can be assumed away. Having identified the question of substitution possibilities as critical, economists have shown rather little interest in the relevance of the laws of nature to the actual possibilities.

Third, the Hartwick rule does make good intuitive sense as a guide to prudent behaviour. Stripping away the mathematical formalism and the consequent air of precision, it says that if consumption involves depleting one asset it is wise to build up another asset to replace it. Thus, for example, a country largely dependent on extracting and selling oil would be prudent to invest some of the proceeds, rather than using them entirely to finance current consumption. This does not guarantee that the accustomed level of consumption can continue after the oil has run out. The particular investment might turn out to be unsuccessful. But clearly if the oil revenues are entirely used for current consumption, the level of consumption will definitely fall when the oil is exhausted. This intuitive content to the Hartwick rule has prompted interest in incorporating into national accounting procedures measurement of the depletion of natural assets.[14]

An ecological conceptualisation of sustainability

Whereas economists start with human interests, defined as consumption, ecologists start with the properties of the system of which humans are a part. This is not to say that the ecological approach ignores human interests. It does not. But it identifies them with the continuing existence of a functioning biospheric system, rather than defining them as consumption. It follows from this that the ecological approach pays more attention to the properties and behaviour patterns of ecological systems than does the economic approach.

We need first to distinguish between stability and resilience.[15] **Stability** refers to a propensity for return to an equilibrium level following a disturbance. In Figure 3.2 the vertical axis measures the size of some population in an ecosystem, and the horizontal axis measures time. At time 0 the ecosystem is subjected to some disturbance. The population in panel (a) is more stable than that in panel (b).

Resilience is a property of an ecosystem rather than a population within an ecosystem. It is the ability of a system to maintain its structure and patterns of behaviour in the face of disturbance. Resilience of a system is consistent with low stability for some of the component popu-

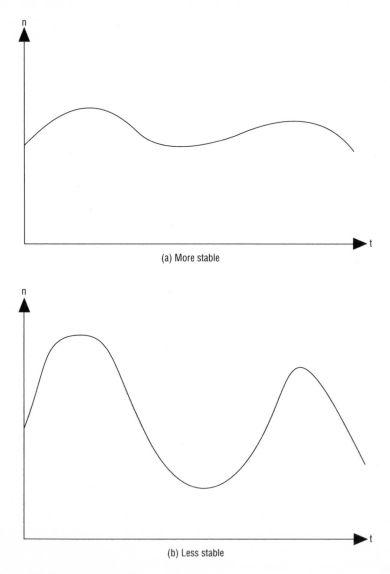

(a) More stable

(b) Less stable

Figure 3.2 Population stability.

lations of the system. A resilient system is one that stays in existence, functioning in the same essential way, in the face of a major shock to it. A system that is not resilient collapses in the face of a major shock to it. Note that resilience means the system remains in being. It is not necessary that all of the populations existing prior to the disturbance survive. It is necessary that the system continue to function in the way that it did prior to disturbance, as indicated, for example, by the total amount of incident solar radiation captured by its photosynthetic processes. A system is sustainable in the ecological sense if it is resilient.

In this sense, sustainability is a system property the presence or absence of which can only be determined with hindsight by observation of its behaviour in the face of disturbance. An important research topic in ecology is the question of whether there are indicators of resilience, such that by looking at them it would be possible to say prior to a disturbance whether or not the system would prove to be resilient. At the present time, it would appear that there are no agreed resilience indicators available. Further, a system that has proved resilient to one type/size of disturbance may not prove resilient in the face of a shock of a different type/size.

At one time it was understood that more complex ecosystems were more stable, so that population sizes fluctuated less. Complexity was taken to be good for ecosystem persistence in the face of a shock. Complexity is measured by the number of species in an ecosystem, and the interactions, such as links in the food chain, between them. A system with more species each of which feeds off many others is a more complex system. The basic idea was that with more linkages, the removal of any one linkage would be less damaging to the system. It is now understood that matters are much more complicated. First, it has been shown that increased complexity does not necessarily increase stability (May 1973). Second, system resilience has been distinguished from population stability and it has been established that systems characterised by low stability can demonstrate high resilience. The measure of complexity relevant to resilience would be one defined over those species contributing to the physical structure and dynamic behaviour of the ecosystem. From a resilience perspective, some species may be redundant. The identification of such species is, however, problematical.

Existing ecosystems are the result of evolutionary processes. They are adapted to the disturbances to which they have been subjected. This does yield some general insights. Tropical ecosystems experience low variability in temperature and precipitation, and are characterised by stable population sizes but low resilience. They are vulnerable in the face of large disturbances, such as those consequent upon large-scale forest clearing by humans. Temperate ecosystems have evolved in the

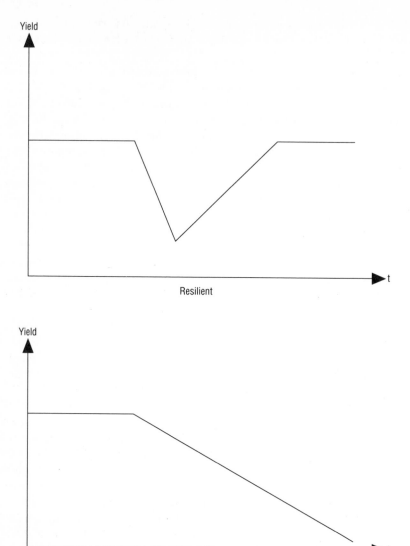

Figure 3.3 System resilience.

face of larger climatic variability and exhibit less stability in population sizes but greater resilience, and are more robust in the face of large-scale human disturbance. Ecologists see such considerations as an argument for regarding the conservation of biodiversity as an important goal. Evolution operates by selecting from existing biotic entities those most fitted to current conditions. Conditions change. The range over which selection under new conditions can operate is reduced to the extent that genetic diversity is now reduced. Reductions in current biodiversity reduce evolutionary potential and therefore the potential for keeping functioning ecosystems in being as environmental change takes place.

While it is clear that the concept of resilience is what characterises an ecological approach to sustainability, there are no precise definitions arising, as there are in the case of the economic approach. The idea of resilience has been used, and explicitly related to a definition of sustainability in terms of human interests, in the analysis of agricultural systems. Conway (1985) defines productivity in an agricultural system as 'the yield or net income per unit of resource'.[16] He then defines stability as: 'the degree to which productivity is constant in the face of small disturbances caused by the normal fluctuations of climate and other environmental variables'(p.35). Sustainability is defined as: 'the ability of the system to maintain productivity in spite of a major disturbance' the incidence of which is essentially unpredictable, such as a rare drought or a new pest(p.35). Clearly, this sustainability concept is a resilience concept. It does not refer to the size of variations about an equilibrium in the face of normal shocks to the system, but to the ability of the system to keep going in the face of a major and unpredictable shock. Figure 3.3 shows Conway's distinction between a sustainable and an unsustainable system. Note that on Conway's definition of yield, it is not necessary that exactly the same crops are produced after the shock as prior to it. What matters is the ability to produce comparable yield, in physical and/or financial terms.

Conway (1985) discusses stability and sustainability in the context of agroecosystems in 'Less Developed Countries' (LDCs). He notes that, given rapidly increasing populations, increased productivity has been the major goal in that context. Since World War II there has been an agricultural revolution, sometimes known as the **Green Revolution**, in many LDCs based mainly on the introduction of new crop varieties and the greatly increased use of irrigation and fertilisers. Conway notes that notwithstanding substantial productivity gains, 'the incremental returns to the varieties and inputs on which the revolution depends are beginning to diminish' (p.32). After noting some of the barriers to the spread of the new methods, some of the problems attending the methods are cited:

> The new technologies have also been accompanied by a number of serious short- and medium-term problems. These include increasing incidence of pest, disease and weed problems, sometimes aggravated by pesticide use, deterioration in soil structure and fertility, increased indebtedness and inequity (Conway 1985, p.32).

In relation to these problems it is noted that:

> One answer has been to tackle these various issues individually as they arise. However, there has been a growing realisation that many, if not all, of the problems are essentially systemic in nature. They are linked to each other and to the performance of the system as a whole. As a consequence problems that were initially viewed as side-effects often, it turns out, threaten directly the main objectives of development. Moreover, even where agricultural production is increased, this success may be short lived if attention is not diverted to side effects which threaten other equally important development goals (p.32).

The point being made is that the productivity levels of the new agricultural systems may turn out to be unsustainable. Conway's hope is that given recognition of this possibility and appropriate responses, it will be avoidable.

No simple prescription for sustainability is offered. It is noted that:

> Satisfactory methods of measuring sustainability still need to be found, however. Lack of sustainability may be indicated by declining productivity but, equally, collapse may come suddenly and without warning (p.35).

It is not that there are no indicators that are relevant to sustainability.[17] The point is that there is no indicator, or group of indicators, against which adequate performance guarantees sustainability in the face of all conceivable shocks to the system.

Ecological sustainability is, then, not a well-defined state to be attained by following some simple rules. We can say that it is the requirement that the resilience of the system be maintained through time. There is not a set of indicators such that performance against them can be said to demonstrate that resilience is, or is not, being maintained. In this, ecological sustainability might seem to contrast with economic sustainability, where there is an unambiguous definition, constant consumption, and a clear indicator for its attainment, the saving and investment of resource rents. However, the greater precision of the economic approach is more apparent than real. It arises because the complexities of the way that the total system functions are largely ignored, as are the complexities of human interests in relation to system performance.

A synthetic and operational approach?

The economic approach to sustainability yields a precise definition and a rule that is necessary, but not sufficient, for its realisation. The attainment of this kind of sustainability could be consistent with massive environmental degradation as normally understood. This does not, on the economics approach, matter so long as consumption is constant. Economics tends to assume that the degree of possible substitution between environmental services and economic services which would permit consumption to remain constant, if the Hartwick rule were followed, does actually exist.

The concept of ecological sustainability is imprecise beyond the injunction to maintain the functioning of the ecosystems, i.e. the biosphere in total, that support life. The notion of functioning itself is imprecise and not identifiable from a set of indicators in any well-defined way. One could, though apparently ecologists have not, extend Conway's definition for agroecosystems to the biospheric level, and define global ecological sustainability as constant total biomass. **Biomass** is simply the total mass of living tissue. From a human perspective this might not be an appealing definition, since it does not differentiate between types of tissue. It does not accord privileged status to human tissue. Biomass could remain constant with plant tissue substituting for human tissue. Further, it is not clear what rules for human conduct it would imply, since the functioning of ecosystems is poorly understood.

Economists emphasise human management in human interests, narrowly conceived, and neglect considerations relating to the functioning of the biosphere and its constituent systems. Ecologists emphasise system function considerations, but cannot relate those to human interests in any direct and simple way. The question which arises is whether there can exist a synthetic approach, which can operationally inform the analysis of human behaviour and debate over how human society should behave.[18]

The position taken here is that there is such an approach but it necessarily involves imprecision. The sustainability problem can be stated as that of managing human affairs so as to address the problems of poverty and inequality while also minimising threats to ecological sustainability. There is no 'solution' to this problem, in the sense of a blueprint for a sustainable society. The stated formulation of the problem is intended to indicate this. On this view, rather than attempting to prescribe a general solution, the appropriate approach is to address particular problems in the light of such knowledge as is available on how the total system functions, and in explicit recognition of the fact that such knowledge is necessarily incomplete, imperfect and changing over time.

This approach is anthropocentric. The resilience of the biosphere is not understood as the only objective. Human interests are pre-eminent. It is difficult to see how any different understanding of the nature of the problem can be operational. Equally, it is taken as given that threats to biospheric resilience are to be avoided, in human interests, to the extent that they are known to exist. It is taken as given that human interests would be better served by a biosphere functioning much as now than by a radically different system in which human life was possible.

This approach focuses on addressing poverty and inequality, and on policies to address threats to ecological sustainability. We now discuss the attributes of environmental problems in relation to threats to ecological sustainability. We can distinguish six attributes, as follows:[19]

1. **Spatial extent** refers to the geographical range of the problem–does it affect a large or a small area of the earth's surface?
2. **Temporal extent** refers to the duration of the problem through time–is this a matter of hours, days, weeks, months, years, centuries?
3. **Impact size** refers to the effect on each individual and the number of individuals affected–are a small number affected a little, or many greatly? Clearly, in terms of the number of affected individuals, impact size is related to spatial and temporal extent – the larger the area and the longer the duration the larger the number of individuals affected.
4. **Complexity** refers to the number and nature of the cause and effect relationships involved in the problem – does it have one source or are there many interrelated origins and pathways to the human impact?
5. **Ignorance** refers to human awareness and understanding of the nature of the problem – is the problem recognised and well understood, recognised but poorly understood, or unrecognised? In principle, a complex problem may be well understood while we may be quite unaware of a problem that is simple in its nature. In practice we would expect ignorance to increase with complexity.
6. **Intractability** refers to the difficulty of devising and implementing a response to the problem–is an appropriate and generally acceptable response readily apparent, is there a readily apparent technical response that is not generally acceptable, or is there no obviously appropriate response? Acceptability will, in part, reflect the costs that individuals perceive themselves incurring.

In each of the two panels of Figure 3.4 there are three axes corresponding to one of the above attributes. A rough scoring of an environmental problem according to each attribute can then be used to place it in each of the three dimensional spaces. This helps us to think about environmental problems as threats to ecological sustainability. In Figure 3.4 we use the examples of carbon dioxide and its role in global climate change, and the use of lead as an additive in petrol. The former was briefly discussed above: see Chapter 10 for more detail.

As shown in Figure 3.4, the climate change problem gets a high score according to all of the attributes distinguished here. It is global in its spatial extent, and the temporal displacement between cause and effect is measured in units which are decades and centuries. Given this, very many individuals will be impacted. The severity of individual impacts will

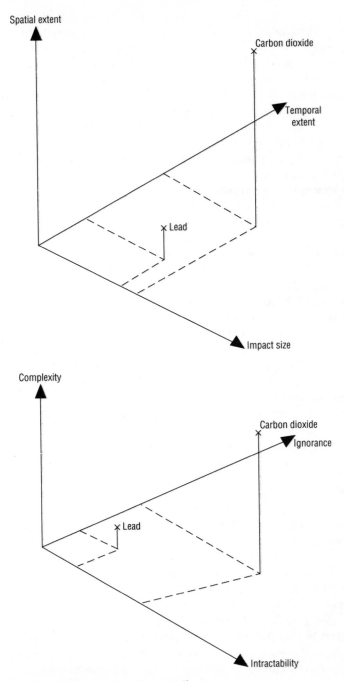

Figure 3.4 Environmental problem attributes.

vary, across time and space, and is, in any case, the matter of some disagreement. The climate change problem involves natural systems at the
global level, such as the carbon cycle, and the world economic system. It
is, therefore, very complex. Many of the systems involved are poorly
understood, so that there is a high level of ignorance. This is the source
of uncertainty and disagreement. Finally, this problem is highly intractable. At the technical level the appropriate responses are reasonably
clear – reduce greenhouse gas emissions. However, the implications of
doing this are not generally acceptable. In part, this follows from complexity and uncertainty, and from ignorance about the effects of climate
change, but it also involves cost. Fossil fuel combustion is fundamental
to the operation of advanced industrial economies, and is the major
source of carbon dioxide, the most important greenhouse gas. The
developing economies see increased fossil fuel use as essential to their
development.

The problem of atmospheric lead pollution arising from the use of
lead as an additive to motor vehicle fuel has attracted a lot of attention
in recent years. This pollution is generally accepted as being damaging
to human health in several ways. The impairment of brain function for
children with high lead content in their bloodstreams has received a
great deal of attention. This problem is spatially extensive in that it
occurs in many places, but it is not in that the lead does not travel far
from the point of emission. It is limited in its temporal extent. Lead
levels in the bloodstream can be reduced with suitable treatment. If the
use of lead in petrol ceased, the impact would vanish with the death of
the last affected individual. The impact size is great for directly affected
individuals, but otherwise very limited. The problem is not very complex, and is generally well understood, notwithstanding disagreements
among 'experts' as to the precise roles of other sources of bloodstream
lead and the quantitative relationship between its level and various
effects on mental and physical health. The problem is relatively tractable
in that motor vehicle engines which do not require the use of leaded
petrol can be produced at little extra cost. Action on this problem has
already been taken in most industrial countries.

This is all somewhat imprecise, but a rough scoring against each of
these attributes is a useful way to examine and categorise environmental
problems. Among some environmentalists there is a tendency to treat
all environmental impacts as sustainability relevant, and a reluctance
to determine priorities. Given the number of environmental impact
problems that can be identified, some prioritisation according to
sustainability-relevant criteria is necessary for effective policy analysis.
The approach of Figure 3.4 can assist in this. Thus, for example, we can
say that while the problem of climate change clearly does represent a

threat to sustainability, the lead problem apparently does not. This does not, of course, mean that we are saying either that the latter problem is unimportant on other criteria, or that nothing should be done about it.

Space does not permit an exhaustive discussion of environmental problems against the six attributes. What we can say is that threats to ecological sustainability will generally be characterised by being extensive in space and time, implying a large impact, and that such threats will be more difficult to address to the extent that they are complex, involve ignorance, and are intractable. Environmental impacts which are localised and short-lived will not generally be threats to sustainability, however serious they may be to those individuals affected. Such impacts may be complex, intractable, and involve ignorance. They may well attract more media attention than genuine threats to sustainability, partly on the basis of their localisation.

Climate change obviously qualifies as a sustainability threat. We now briefly mention some other obvious qualifiers. The list is not exhaustive. Biodiversity loss is irreversible and hence extensive in time, and its spatial extent is global in that it reduces evolutionary potential. The size of impact in terms of human interests is uncertain in any particular case. While the problem is, in general terms, well understood in regard to causes – mainly habitat destruction – it is intractable by virtue of the low general acceptability of measures to reduce habitat destruction. Depletion of the stratospheric ozone layer scores highly according to spatial and temporal extent and impact size. It is fairly complex, but is considered to be well understood. It has proved tractable largely because the technical solution is simple and widely acceptable because of the understanding of the consequences of not acting on the problem.

The depletion of non-renewable resources, particularly the fossil fuels, scores highly on temporal extensiveness, being irreversible. It is also globally extensive. The question of impact size depends crucially on substitution possibilities. Nobody cares about, for example, oil deposits *per se*. What they care about is the availability of an energy source with certain characteristics, the availability of lubricants, and of inputs to the chemical industry. This problem is relatively simple, though there is uncertainty about both the size of stocks of these resources and the substitution possibilities. The tractability of the problem depends primarily on the substitution possibilities.

CHAPTER 4

History and perspective

We have looked at some aspects of the world economy, and considered its relationship with the natural environment. In subsequent chapters we will discuss alternative views of the future prospects for humanity, and some policy issues arising from them. In this chapter the objective is to provide some background to, and perspective on, the subsequent discussion. We first look at a very broad overview of human history, focusing on aspects of the interconnections between human activity and the natural environment. The connections between the material standard of living and human welfare are then discussed. Finally, we consider one approach to measuring economic performance with allowance for environmental impact.

Human history

The timing of the beginning of human history is not self-evident. Our species shares 98.4 per cent of its genetic endowment with chimpanzees: genetically we are closer to chimpanzees than they are to apes. The evolutionary divergence of humans and chimpanzees is estimated to have taken place between six and eight million years ago. The species *Homo erectus*, a precursor of ours, is estimated to have appeared about 1.7 million years ago, *Homo sapiens* about 500 000 years ago, and *Homo sapiens sapiens*, ourselves, about 100 000 years ago (Diamond 1992). It is widely understood that we differ from other Homo species, now extinct, primarily in the extent of our aptitude for culture, where this involves the ability to invent symbols and use them for communication, and a propensity toward technological innovation (Boyden 1987; Boyden et al. 1990).

Humans are omnivorous and evolved as a species for which food acquisition involved hunting animals and gathering plants. We evolved, that is, as **hunter–gatherers**. As such, we were constrained in terms of potential numbers by the same constraints faced by other animals. Competition with other species following similar food acquisition strategies occurred within constraints set by the energy input to the biosphere, and the efficiencies with which it is captured and transformed into living tissue.

Figure 4.1 shows the general pattern of movement for energy and minerals in ecosystems. An **ecosystem** is an interconnected biotic assemblage of plants, animals and microbes, together with its abiotic physiochemical environment.[1] **Producers** are plants which transform solar radiation into tissue by means of the process of **photosynthesis**. **Herbivores** are animals that obtain the energy which they require for life by eating plants. **Carnivores** eat herbivores, and in some cases other carnivores. **Omnivorous animals** eat plants and animals. The photosynthetic process requires the availability of minerals, also known in this context as nutrients, as do the life processes of animals which feed, directly and indirectly, off plants to get their energy inputs. As shown in Figure 4.1, minerals flow around an ecosystem in a closed cycle, they are recycled. The flow of useful energy, by contrast, is unidirectional.

Figure 4.2 shows how the amount of energy available decreases as it passes from photosynthetic plants to the various types of animal. This **trophic pyramid** is constructed in energy units, but if the amount of biomass were measured and plotted the result would look much the same. By mass, the quantity of plants greatly exceeds that of herbivores, which exceeds the quantity of carnivores. Table 4.1 gives some data for a particular ecosystem, in energy terms. Note that of the incident solar

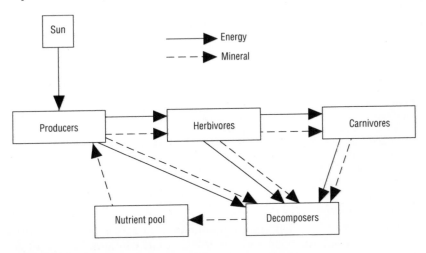

Figure 4.1 Energy and mineral movement in ecosystems.

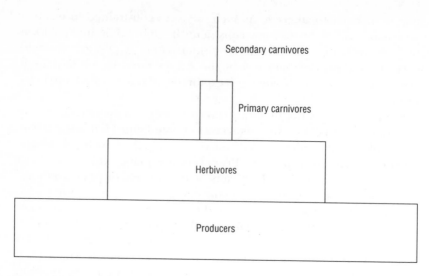

Figure 4.2 A trophic pyramid.

radiation, only 1.2 per cent is converted into plant tissue by photosynthesis. This is a representative figure for the efficiency of photosynthesis: it never exceeds 5 per cent. The efficiency with which herbivores capture plant energy, by eating plants, is even lower. Not all of the energy captured at each stage is converted to tissue, with the respiratory loss being the proportion of energy captured that is used in maintaining life processes, rather than converted into tissue. Respiratory loss is greater higher up the trophic pyramid, or food chain.

Table 4.1 *Energy flow in a terrestrial community*

	Energy[a]	Efficiency	Respiratory loss[b]
Incident solar radiation	47.1×10^8		
Photosynthetic production	58.3×10^6	0.012	0.15
Herbivore consumption	250×10^3	0.004	0.68
Carnivore consumption	5824	0.023	0.933

Notes: [a] Calories per hectare per year.
[b] Respiration ÷ Production/Consumption.
Source: Watt (1973), Table 2.1.

The amount of living tissue that can exist at each level is determined by the amount of incident solar radiation and the efficiencies of capture and conversion. At each level of the trophic pyramid, competition between species determines the amount of energy capture by each species. Species at a given level vary in their photosynthetic efficiency (plants) and the energy efficiency of their food acquisition strategies (animals). Species which are more energy efficient will tend to displace those which are less energy efficient, so that at the ecosystem level, the efficiencies for transfers between levels are, in part, determined by the outcome of competitive processes. Human hunter–gatherers were a species with a relatively non-specialised food acquisition strategy, which enabled them to spread throughout most of the world. In many of the ecosystems in which they participated they were a relatively successful species in terms of competition in energy capture.

Two economic transitions

Human hunter–gatherer numbers were necessarily limited by these energetic constraints. The **agricultural revolution** changed the nature of the energetic constraints on human behaviour and numbers. Agriculture involves the domestication of some animals and plants, the manipulation of their reproductive behaviour, and the control (in some cases eradication) of the plants and animals not domesticated.[2] The overall effect is to increase the amount of energy available to humans, and hence the potential size of the human population. The agricultural revolution did not involve the sudden conversion of all humans from hunter–gatherers to agriculturalists. The exact date of the first adoption of agriculture by a human group is unknown. Here we put it at 10 000 BC or 12 000 BP where BP stands for 'before the present'. To indicate the approximate nature of all numbers and dates here, we take the present as the year 2000 AD.

Agriculture spread slowly. Ponting (1992) puts the beginnings of agriculture at 10 000 BP, and describes its spread over several thousand years. At one time it was thought that it spread from a single innovating human group, but the current understanding is that it emerged independently in several centres. According to Boyden et al. (1990) agriculture 'began in some regions of the world 10 000–12 000 years ago' (p.12). As late as 1788 AD, all of the human inhabitants of the continent of Australia were hunter-gatherers. Estimates of human numbers prior to the introduction of agriculture are necessarily speculative. For the purposes of Figure 4.3 we take the size of the human population at the start of the agricultural revolution to be four million. Except as noted, all population size estimates here are taken from Ponting (1992), Chapter 6.

Given greater access to the products of photosynthesis, human numbers grew as agriculture spread. By 2500 BP, the estimated human population size was 100 million. In Figure 4.3 we have simply drawn a straight

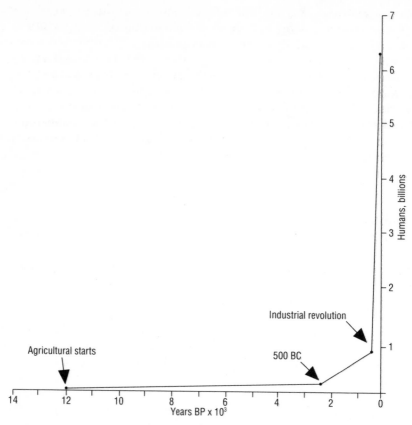

Figure 4.3 The history of human numbers.
Source: Ponting (1992), United Nations Development Programme (1992).

line from the horizontal axis at 12 000 BP to 0.1 billion at 2500 BP, and another straight line from that point to 0.9 billion for 200 BP (1800 AD). The growth in numbers over these two time intervals was definitely not smooth and uninterrupted, nor do the two line segments reflect with any accuracy relative growth rates over time. We are interested here in the broad picture, not details.

While agriculture improved human access to the products of photo-synthesis, human beings still operated within the limits set by incident solar radiation and life processes based upon it. By 1800, most human societies had the knowledge to utilise energy derived from wind and water. However, the processes behind these energy sources are them-selves ultimately driven by solar radiation: see Cipolla (1962). This changed with the **industrial revolution**. The exact date at which this began is a matter of dispute among historians. The matter turns, in part, on what are taken to be the distinguishing characteristics of the industrial revolution. We take the distinguishing characteristic of the industrial phase of human history to be the general use of fossil fuels in production and transport. Initially the relevant fossil fuel was coal, and the industrial phase first appeared in England. We date the onset of the industrial revolution, in round terms, at 1800 AD, or 200 BP. The systematic exploitation of fossil fuel meant that humans were not energetically constrained as they had been previously. In effect, for humans, solar radiation was supplemented by energy from fossil fuels. This affected the production of food in many ways, direct and indirect, as well as what we normally think of as 'industry'. Fossil fuel use increased potential food production, and hence the potential growth of human numbers.

From 200 BP to the present, 2000 AD, the human population increased in size from 0.9 billion to 6.25 billion. The latter figure is a projection rather than an historical fact (see Table 2.1, p. 9). However, catastrophe apart, a human population of around six billion in 2000 is now inevitable. By previous historical standards, the growth rate for human numbers in the last 200 years has been very high, and the population is now five times as large as it was 200 years ago.

We can, then, divide human history into the hunter–gatherer phase, the agricultural phase, and the industrial phase, each distinguished by the human position in regard to the exploitation of solar energy. In the first phase, humans operated on essentially the same basis as other animal species. In the second, they adopted a novel evolutionary strategy, but remained totally dependent on solar radiation as the ultimate source of energy. In the third phase, they removed themselves from the constraints set by the solar energy flux. Throughout most of their history, humans were hunter–gatherers and it is this mode of existence for which evolution had found them to be fitted. The length of the hunter–gatherer phase greatly exceeds that of the other two combined.

For a long time, the life of hunter–gatherers was understood to be 'nasty, brutish and short'. Recently, this appreciation has undergone substantial revision. It is now understood that hunter–gatherer life circumstances varied greatly with environmental conditions. In favourable conditions, hunter–gatherers appear to have had a nutritionally adequate diet and enjoyed more leisure than is the norm in modern industrial societies. Life expectancy at birth was, by the current industrial standards, low. However, while alive, hunter–gatherers appear to have been generally healthy.[3]

A revised appreciation of the conditions of hunter–gatherer life has been accompanied by increasing awareness of the limited impact that this phase of human history had on the biosphere, in comparison with that of the later phases. Given their duration, many hunter–gatherer economic systems have to be regarded as having been sustainable. The Australian Aboriginals, for example, had a history of some 50 000 years prior to the European invasion of 1788 (see Blainey 1975 for a general account, and Dingle 1988 for an economic history). However, it is not true that hunter–gatherers had no impact on their environments. There is evidence of the widespread use of fire to alter vegetation, to favour those plant species edible by humans and those favoured by hunted herbivores. These practices indicate that a sharp distinction between agriculture and hunting and gathering is somewhat artificial. Hunting is taken to have been one of the contributory factors in the extinction of a number of animal species during the hunter–gatherer phase of human history. Some hunter–gatherer societies did have cultural practices which had the effect of protecting the exploited food sources from over-use. However, it would appear that the major reason for the relatively limited environmental impact of humans in this phase of their history was the small number of humans. Population densities were everywhere low by subsequent standards. There is evidence of social practices which had the effect of limiting human numbers, such as infanticide and prolonged breastfeeding of infants.[4]

The transition from hunting and gathering to agriculture is regarded as a revolution because of its consequences – population growth, the emergence of cities, and social stratification – rather than because it was a dramatic and sudden event. As noted, the transition took place over millennia. Revolution also carries the implication of purposeful intent. At one time the view was that humans set out to invent agriculture as the means to a better life, perceived as possible before it was actual, and having invented it, adopted it as a complete new system. This view is not now widely held:

> Rather a series of marginal changes were made gradually in existing ways of obtaining food as a result of particular local circumstances … Adjustments in subsistence methods to a more intensive form enabled a larger population to be supported but meant that it became impossible to go back to a gathering and hunting way of life … there was no straight line of development from 'gathering and hunting' to 'agriculture'. Many different ways of obtaining food from plants and animals would have been tried in various permutations and with changing balances between plant and animal foods. Some of these strategies would have failed and others would have been only partially successful. Only slowly and unconsciously did a radically new solution to the human problem of extracting food from different ecosystems emerge (Ponting 1992, p.38).

The question then arises as to why some human societies produced the innovations that eventually made up the agricultural revolution. As noted, the view that humans purposely sought 'progress' has now largely been abandoned. Rather, the innovations are now widely seen as adaptive responses to changing circumstances.[5] In some areas climatic change may well have been an important factor. More generally, population size in relation to the food that could be made available by hunting and gathering is now seen as important. The use of population control practices by hunter–gatherers has been noted. In some cases these may not have existed, in others existing practices may have broken down. In yet other cases one group in an area may have experienced competitive pressure from a migratory group, forcing it into areas less productive with hunter-gatherer technology (Ponting 1992; Cohen 1977). While there is disagreement over the details, it appears now to be widely accepted that the main driving force in the transition to agriculture was adaptation to deteriorating circumstances.

In comparison with hunter–gatherer societies, the environmental impact of agricultural societies was relatively large. This follows from the greater share of the available solar energy captured by humans. Agriculture involved clearing natural vegetation, and hence the destruction of habitat for wild plants and animals. Settled human populations at high densities gave rise to local problems of waste disposal, and pollution. Technology was not static during the agricultural phase. Not all agricultural societies were sustainable. Population growth was, in general, faster in the agricultural phase than in the hunter–gatherer phase, and in some agricultural societies a mismatch between population size and the production available from the resource base, given the existing technology, emerged. Responses varied. In some cases, societies simply collapsed (Ponting 1992). In others, outward migration occurred, which impacted on other societies. In others, the response involved technological innovation. Migration and technological innovation are not mutually exclusive.

It is generally agreed that an industrial revolution occurred first in England. There is less agreement about why and when it occurred. We have characterised industrial societies by their widespread use of fossil fuel. Coal use in England was well established by the sixteenth century, and by the end of the seventeenth it was widespread in industry. The transition from wood to coal as fuel appears to have been driven by an increasing scarcity of wood, rather than an appreciation of the superiority of coal. In fact, there is a good deal of evidence that contemporaries saw wood as superior to coal. However, during the sixteenth and seventeenth centuries, the price of wood was rising steadily and rapidly (Wilkinson 1973, 1988). This reflected increasing scarcity arising from population growth. On the one hand population growth increased the demand for fuel, on the other it reduced the land available for wood production as more land was taken for food production. The increasing demand for coal led to problems in its mining with existing technology. Iron production in the first half of the eighteenth century still required wood as fuel, making iron, and hence machinery, expensive. Transport was a problem both as far as coal was concerned and in moving food to the growing urban areas.

The decisive steps in the transition to an industrial system in England appear to have been the use of coal in iron making, and in transport. The former began in the latter half of the eighteenth century, the latter in the early nineteenth century. Hence, our dating of the start of the industrial revolution at 1800 AD, or 200 BP. In nineteenth century England, coal production and the human population grew rapidly. The United Kingdom became the dominant economy in the world. The industrial revolution spread to much of the world, and affected all of it. This would not have been possible without the developments in transport consequent upon fossil fuel exploitation. In the nineteenth century, the only fossil fuel used on any significant scale was coal. In the twentieth century, oil became the dominant fossil fuel, especially in relation to transport.

Complexity and specialisation

The **somatic energy** used by an average adult human leading a moderately active life, 10 MJ per day, is a useful unit of measurement, the **human energy equivalent**, HEE. It is estimated that whereas per capita energy use in the hunter–gatherer phase varied between one and two HEE, in the agricultural phase it was some four HEE, and that in the industrial phase it has reached 100 HEE in some societies (Boyden et al. 1990). The excesses over one HEE are by virtue of the use of **extra-somatic energy**, i.e. energy from sources other than human muscles, such as biomass combustion (in the hunter–gatherer phase), wind, or animal muscles (in the agricultural phase), or fossil fuels (in the industrial phase).

These figures for energy use are consistent with increasing per capita environmental impact through the course of human history to date. Associated with this has been increasing complexity of the economic system, and occupational specialisation. The production processes by which environmental extractions become consumption goods have become longer, involving more intermediate stages and greater use of capital equipment. This historical development has been called a 'technological treadmill' (Pezzey 1992). Consider food consumption, for example. For hunter–gatherers the intermediate stages between production and consumption are few and simple, and the time distance is very short. Most adults are directly involved in food production.[6] Consumption may occur at the same location as production, and involve no delay at all in time. For agriculturalists, the time distance between production and consumption may be considerable – crops are sown now for consumption next year. Similarly, the spatial distance may be considerable, with farmers producing for consumption in urban areas. The proportion of the labour force directly employed in agriculture varies, but generally is below 50 per cent. Of course, much of the rest of the workforce is indirectly involved in food production, providing tools and administrative services, for example. A widely noted feature of the transition to agriculture is the emergence of occupational specialisation, and of manufacturing.

In the industrial phase, temporal and spatial distancing of production and consumption is taken further, based on the use of fossil fuels in transport. Occupational specialisation increases, and the proportion of the labour force directly employed in agriculture drops. However, looking at employment in agriculture as the indicator of employment in food production is misleading. A substantial part of employment elsewhere in the economy is related to the production of inputs to food production – equipment and machinery, fertilisers etc. – and to the transport of food from farms to consumers. Associated with the displacements in time and space of food production and consumption is the processing of food as an industrial activity, so that consumers do not purchase the output of agriculture but rather the output of 'the food industry'. Table 4.2 illustrates this in the case of bread in the United

Table 4.2 *Energy inputs to bread production – United Kingdom*

	MJ	%
Tractors, etc.	1.47	7.3
Fertilisers	2.34	11.6
Other	0.08	0.4
Total, farming	*3.89*	*19.3*
Direct fuel use	1.49	7.4
Packaging	0.44	2.2
Transport	0.28	1.4
Other	0.40	2.0
Total, milling	*2.61*	*13.0*
Direct fuel use	4.76	23.6
Packaging	1.67	8.3
Other	2.90	14.4
Total, baking	*9.33*	*46.3*
Heating and lighting	1.73	8.6
Transport	2.46	12.2
Total, retail distribution	*4.19*	*20.8*

Source: Chapman (1975), Figure 8.

Kingdom, in terms of (mainly extrasomatic) energy inputs at the various stages involved in getting a standard loaf onto the shelf in a shop. An account in terms of labour input would tell essentially the same story. Note that less than 20 per cent of total energy input actually arises on the farm, whereas slightly more than 20 per cent arises in retail distribution. We should note that Table 4.2 does not tell the whole story. It remains for the loaf to reach a consumer's home, which involves the expenditure of time and energy by the consumer. In some industrial nations the trend away from small neighbourhood shops to large supermarkets has shifted some of the production involved in getting food into homes from what is conventionally regarded as the production sector into the household sector.

Work and leisure

In hunter–gatherer societies the distinction between work and leisure is typically not a sharp one. Circumstances differed widely among hunter–gatherer societies, and we have access to data on the workload for but a small sample of all such societies that have existed. On the basis of the available evidence, it appears that by modern industrial standards the workload in hunter–gatherer societies was not great. Sahlins (1974) reviews some of the evidence and calls the typical hunter–gatherer society 'the original affluent society' on the basis that physiological and psychological needs were satisfied for a low expenditure of effort.[7] In the case of Australian Aboriginals at the time of the European invasion, for example, Dingle (1988) notes that they were typically well nourished, and remarks:

> Nor was a great deal of time and energy required to find food ... the acquisition and preparation of food took four to five hours daily. This included frequent rests, and there was no sense of urgency in the food quest except when an animal had been located and a hunt was in progress. Not everyone went out daily ... Earlier observers reported that two to four hours intermittent effort provided enough food for the day ... It is interesting that some Aboriginal languages did not possess words which distinguished work from play. We are looking at an economy which was enjoying a thirty to thirty-five hour week at the time when European labourers worked almost twice as long to sustain themselves.

Over a 52-week year, a 35-hour week is 1820 hours per annum. Figure 4.4 shows estimates of annual working hours for the agricultural and industrial phases. On these necessarily imprecise figures, the initial effect of the transition to industry was an increase in the workload. By the 1980s, some 200 years after the beginning of that transition, the workload was about where it was toward the end of the agricultural phase, which was itself comparable with the workload in hunter–gatherer societies.[8]

Annual workloads are not, of course, the whole story. Individuals do not work for every year of their lives, and the extent to which this is the case varies between societies, as does longevity. A measure which picks up these considerations is lifetime hours of leisure, where leisure is simply time not spent working. Comparing, for example, modern Australians with pre-invasion Australian Aboriginals on this basis, a necessarily very rough calculation suggests that the former are, in this respect, of the order of 50 per cent better off than the latter. Whereas the latter used at most one HEE of extrasomatic energy, the former use some 99 HEE. The modern Australian is using about 100 times as much extrasomatic energy to increase lifetime leisure by 50 per cent. These numbers are very rough. Halve the first and double the second. The modern Australian is still using 50 times as much extrasomatic energy to double lifetime leisure. We have argued that extrasomatic energy use is a good first approximation proxy for environmental impact. We might also note that while the history of the Australian Aboriginals is at least

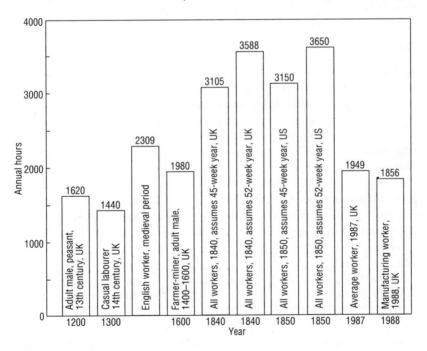

Figure 4.4 Annual hours of work.
Source: Schor (1991) Figure 3.1.

50 000 years, that of modern Australians almost exactly coincides with the length to date of the industrial phase – some 200 years.

Affluence and welfare

Industrial economies are affluent in the sense of having high average levels of consumption of produced goods and services. It is a major objective of policy in all such economies to increase affluence by economic growth. There are a number of reasons why economic growth is a major objective of policy, but one central idea is that growth will make the representative citizen more affluent and thus improve her welfare, making her happier. Policies to address threats to sustainability are judged, among other criteria, on the basis of their perceived implications for economic growth. The fact that such policies are generally seen as harming the prospects for growth is a powerful force working against their adoption. In this section we argue that in advanced industrial economies the connection between the average level of affluence and welfare is tenuous. If this were more widely appreciated, policies to address threats to sustainability would face less resistance.

Growth scarcity and subsistence

Writing in 1930, the most famous economist of the twentieth century, J.M. Keynes, saw in economic growth the prospect of the abolition of the problem that economics studied – scarcity.[9] Keynes was concerned to put in perspective the waste involved in the non-use of available resources, notably labour, that the Great Depression of the interwar years entailed. If the means to avoid such waste could be found, Keynes claimed that growth at 2 per cent per annum would be easily attainable. He noted that this implied that over 100 years, output would grow more than sevenfold. Hence the abolition of scarcity, and a situation in which economics, and economists, would not be seen as interesting or important. In the big picture then, Keynes' view of the eventual status of economics was that:

> It should be a matter for specialists – like dentistry. If economists could manage to get themselves thought of as humble, competent people, on a level with dentists, that would be splendid.

With growth, economic concerns would become less central and the status accorded to the views of economists on big social issues would be reduced. While it is only 60-odd years since this was written, it is clear that on this matter Keynes was wrong. The details can be disputed, but we can safely say that in those 60 years the economies of North America and Western Europe, and Australia, have experienced average annual growth of the magnitude envisaged by Keynes. We are about halfway to Keynes' sevenfold increase in per capita national income. The perceived importance of economics and economists has increased, not diminished. There is now a Nobel prize in economics. The number of professional economists has increased enormously: in the 1930s there were hardly any, whereas in 1993 there were 100 000 of them in the United States alone.[10] Citizens are now told that they need to be economically literate for effective participation in the political process. The media gives a high priority to economic matters. Politicians routinely talk to electorates about the major economic problems facing their nation, and the scarcity of resources for worthy causes, such as the alleviation of poverty at home and overseas.

Economic growth has not apparently been very effective in diminishing scarcity. We can look at recent history in the United States for one illustration of the general point, and take an assessment from a journal not known to undersell the benefits of economic growth, *The Economist*. In its 10 November 1990 issue, it ran a special feature 'American Living Standards: Running to Stand Still'. This noted that while national income per head had been rising since 1973, there was a perception that living standards had actually remained constant or fallen for middle-class Americans. It found the perception to be based on reality:

> The stagnation or even decline in middle-class living standards since 1973 is a reality affecting most Americans, not a fiction of the statisticians.

The point is not that less is being consumed. On the contrary, the article cites the increasing consumption of the services of lawyers, real estate agents and doctors, for example. The point being made is that the increasing consumption makes no contribution to welfare.[11]

This article is noted here because it is exceptional in standard economics. The standard view is that individual welfare increases in line with consumption. Taking this view, the welfare of the representative individual has been improving over the course of the development process with the growth of production and consumption. The polar opposite view is that there is no connection between the welfare of the representative individual in a society and that of society's level of consumption. On this view, all that any successful economic system does is to deliver subsistence needs to its representative individual. An economic system that cannot do this cannot replicate itself, and will cease to exist. On this view, the association in history of increasing consumption with economic development is to be understood as involving increasing subsistence requirements for the representative individual, rather than increasing welfare for the representative individual (Wilkinson 1973; Common 1988b). Given that subsistence continues to be satisfied, the representative individual's welfare is unchanging. Her consumption increases because subsistence needs increase with changing technology and economic organisation.

There are two ways in which the consumption which corresponds to subsistence can change with development. First, an unchanging physical or psychological need may be met in different ways. Second, as the economic system changes, so the physical or psychological nature of subsistence requirements may change. As examples of the first case, consider dietary change with the transition from hunter–gathering to agriculture, and the different ways in which physical and mental stimulation are provided as between agricultural and advanced industrial economies. As an example of the second case, consider transport needs in an industrial as compared with a hunter–gatherer society. **Subsistence needs** for the representative individual are the requirements for full participation as a member of society. Such needs are determined by economic structure and cultural norms, which, of course, are related.

It is not necessary to consider the long sweep of human history to see the force of the idea that subsistence needs increase with economic development. Such changes are part of the common experience of people in industrial societies. For example, given the changes in the methods of food production and distribution over 1950 to 1990, the use of a refrigerator was not a subsistence requirement in 1950 but was in 1980. Telephones were not a subsistence requirement in 1950, but are now in industrial societies, because most people have one. It seems plausible that by the end of the century a home computer, or computer terminal, will be a subsistence requirement. The article from *The Economist* noted above cited increasing consumption of legal services, for example, as not delivering increased welfare. The puzzle is solved when it is recognised that, for middle-class Americans, subsistence as understood here has required such increasing consumption.

The observation that development is, in fact, accompanied by an increasing level and a changing pattern of consumption for the representative individual is not inconsistent with the proposition that at all times the productive system is delivering subsistence requirements. Nor is this inconsistent with increasing per capita national income. The assumption, for the purposes of understanding economic history, that the economy always delivers subsistence may be no more extreme than the more common assumption that welfare increases everywhere and always with increasing income and consumption. The view that the course of human history to date has not been one of steadily improving social and individual welfare strikes many as absurd, and/or repugnant. However, it is difficult to see how the standard assumption could be justified on strictly economic grounds, as this would require that the consumption patterns of periods widely separated in history be judged according to a common set of representative individual preferences. Given that preferences are culturally determined, this is an impossible requirement. Consider the question of whether the consumption pattern and lifestyle typical in Australia prior to the European invasion represents a higher or lower welfare level than that typical in Australia today. Clearly, the answer would depend upon whether the preferences of a pre-invasion Aboriginal Australian or the preferences of a current inhabitant were to be used for evaluation.

It is possible to reconcile the idea that all the economy ever does is to deliver subsistence with the idea of economic development as progress by taking the view that some subsistence patterns are preferable to others, on non-economic grounds, and that preferable succeed less preferable patterns as development proceeds. The criteria here could be philosophical, religious or aesthetic. A single example will indicate what is involved here, that of education and knowledge. It might be conceded that as development proceeds, so the increasing complexity of the productive system required to deliver subsistence necessitates that individuals have more education and that nature is more fully understood. Higher levels of education and knowledge are, that is, new subsistence and production needs and do not imply higher levels of welfare. However, it might be argued that more education and knowledge mean greater self-awareness for individuals, and that increasing self-awareness represents progress on philosophical grounds. It is, of course, possible to take an opposite view. There are those who see the hunter–gatherer state as a desirable one from which humanity has fallen.

Finally here, note that this view of the relationship between consumption and welfare has implications for an understanding of poverty in an affluent society. Subsistence is understood not in terms of physiological needs, but as what is needed for effective participation in society. Those whose needs so defined are not met can be said to be in poverty. The argument here is that these needs increase with social affluence as measured by per capita national income. Increasing per capita national income as such will not reduce poverty so defined. Poverty is relative to a changing standard defined in terms of consumption. The standard is the consumption of the representative individual. Those who consume less are poor. To revert to examples cited above, in 1950 to lack a refrigerator or telephone was not to be poor, in 1990 it is. We return to this in Chapter 9.

Welfare well-being and utility

We have used 'affluence' as a convenient shorthand for consumption of produced goods and services. This is fairly standard and widespread usage, which, despite imprecision, appears to give rise to little difficulty. The term 'welfare' is more problematic. However, welfare is widely identified with some general notion of well-being and it is considered meaningful to talk about increases or decreases in welfare/well-being, though not to try to express such changes in quantitative terms.

Economists make extensive use of the term welfare. There is a branch of the subject called **welfare economics.** Individuals are taken to have preferences over all of the alternative states that they might experience. Each possible state corresponds to a particular level of **utility** for the individual, and states can be ranked by the corresponding utility levels. A change that moves an individual from a lower to a higher level of utility increases the individual's welfare, and vice versa. At the level of individuals, utility and welfare are synonymous in economics. Economists do not inquire into the nature of individual preferences, nor how they are determined. They do assume that an individual's preferences are stable over time. Individuals thus conceived are often referred to as consumers, as the apparatus of utility theory was originally developed for the analysis of consumption behaviour in relation to marketed goods and services. However, it is now used much more generally, as indicated by our reference above to 'alternative states' that might be experienced. At the individual level the basic nature of welfare economics has been encapsulated as follows:

> People's tastes, the way they spend their money and arrange their lives, are matters economists have always regarded as something they should observe, but must not poke their noses into. They seem to feel that analysing people's tastes and their motivation would be an invasion of privacy and an abrogation of consumer sovereignty, and that it might expose them to the charge of pretending to know better than the consumer himself what is good for him. Instead, economists assume that the consumer is rational; in other words, they assume that whatever he does must be the best thing for him to do, given his tastes, market opportunities, and circumstances, since otherwise he would not have done it. The great advantage of such an approach is that it enables economists to look upon the consumers behaviour as a faithful reflection of his preferences and, conversely, to regard his preferences as revealed by his behaviour. That assumption, together with its implications, is known as the theory of revealed preference; on it are based many of the economists' arguments, conclusions, recommendations.[12]

Welfare economics is primarily concerned with social rather than individual welfare. However, the concept of **social welfare** that it employs follows from the way it treats individual welfare, and is neatly captured in the term 'consumer sovereignty'. In welfare economics, society is not an entity to which the concept of welfare is directly applicable. Society is a collection of individuals, and nothing more. Social welfare can, therefore, only be conceived of in terms of the welfares of the individuals comprising the society. If all individual welfares, utilities, increase/decrease, then social welfare increases/decreases. Of course, matters are rarely so simple. Much of the debate in welfare economic theory is about how individual gains and losses are to be balanced in arriving at an assessment of the direction of change in social welfare. Here, the important point is that for individual and, hence, social welfare assessment, the ultimate criterion is the extent to which individuals get what they want, where what they want is revealed in their individual behaviour. Hence the use of the term **consumer sovereignty** to describe the economists' approach to social welfare measurement. Welfare is improved/reduced to the extent that the wants of individuals are more/less satisfied.

The key points here are that welfare is to do with the satisfaction of individual wants, what determines wants is of no interest, and all wants are accorded equal status. This is not the way most non-economists see the question of human welfare. Even where the basic individualist position of economics is adhered to, most people would consider (a) that what an individual wants is not necessarily what is good for her, i.e. welfare improving, and (b) that, even leaving (a) aside, not all wants should be accorded equal status. The literature on all of this is very extensive.[13] Here we simply draw attention to a position on human welfare, that is in one sense the opposite to that taken by economists (while sharing its individualistic basis) and which is important in the sustainability debate. This is the position that approaches the question of welfare by way of human biology.

We briefly indicate the nature of this position by reference to the work of Boyden (1987), which is summarised in Boyden et al. (1990).[14] The basic idea is that humans are biological entities fitted by evolution for a particular lifestyle, and that welfare can be assessed by reference to the circumstances of that lifestyle. Thus, human health is first defined as:

> That physical and mental state that would have been likely to ensure survival and successful reproduction in the primeval habitat.

This is taken as equivalent to health as:

> a state of body and mind conducive to, and associated with, full enjoyment of life.

Health, so defined, is regarded as the same thing as well-being:

The word 'health' is used here in the broad sense to include not only physical
health, but also those aspects of well-being that are associated with enjoyment,
self-fulfilment and absence of distress.

Given this, a list of universal human health *needs* is derived from an
understanding of the hunter–gatherer life style. The emphasis here is to
highlight the essential difference of this approach from that of economics, where welfare is related to the satisfaction of *wants*. The list of
needs includes physical and mental stimulation, social interaction, the
absence of excess sensory stimulation, and biophysical requirements. It
is suggested that:

every item on the list, if satisfied, will make a positive contribution to health
and well-being in the great majority of humans.

and noted that:

too little or too much of a given condition may be detrimental to health.

Boyden does not explicitly discuss social, as opposed to individual,
welfare. However, it is clear that social states are to be judged according
to their implications for individual well-being, and by the environmental
impact generated. Industrial society is found, on both counts, not to be
healthy. Boyden also recognises the role of social, or cultural, evolution
in human history, and the way in which it has generated 'culturally
imposed health needs', which differ across cultures in a way that the
universal needs do not. Thus, for example:

in present-day society a motor vehicle is necessary for the satisfaction of
various universal health needs – such as the acquisition of food, social
interactions with friends or relatives, transportation to place of work ... the
experience of in-group approval and the avoidance of a sense of deprivation.

This aligns with our earlier discussion of culturally determined subsistence requirements. Also congruent with that discussion is the
observation that:

Throughout human history the culturally imposed needs have become
progressively more complex and demanding of resources and energy.

Boyden does not see affluence itself as promoting human welfare, since
it generates additional needs, actually creating scarcity rather than
reducing it.[15]

While few economists would take the view that there is no connection
between affluence and welfare, a number have questioned the closeness

of the connection. We can distinguish four main lines of criticism of the standard view coming from within economics:

1. The connection between welfare and affluence derives from the assumption that the economy does actually work so as to satisfy consumers' wants. The idea here is that firms prosper by supplying goods and services that individuals reveal demand for, and go out of business if they produce things not desired. Firms are supposed to respond to consumer demand. It has been argued that in the dominant areas of a modern industrial economy the causal sequence is, in fact, the reverse of this. Firms decide what to produce and then take steps to persuade consumers that what is produced is what they want. Firms are not, of course, always successful in this. However, the fact remains that the economy is not driven by consumer sovereignty, so that the link between affluence and welfare is broken.[16]

2. The connection between welfare and affluence is supposed to be enforced by the disciplines of the market which cause firms to serve consumer sovereignty. However, it is recognised by the great majority of economists that many of the things that contribute to welfare do not pass through markets. Some economists have argued that in affluent societies growth means that non-marketed disamenities increase more than the welfare-enhancing consequences of growth.[17]

3. The standard economics view treats all wants as of equal status. The physiological and psychological needs of the human being, and their relative intensities, are assumed to be fully reflected in revealed preferences. It has been argued that this is an assumption which is not supported by the evidence, and that individuals express wants the satisfaction of which is not welfare enhancing. To the extent that increasing affluence involves satisfying such wants, it is not welfare enhancing.[18]

4. The standard economics view ignores the implications of the fact that one individual's welfare is affected not only by her own consumption of goods and services, but also by the consumption of others. To the extent that individuals feel better by consuming more than others, or worse by consuming less, increasing the consumption of all individuals equally leaves the welfare of all individuals unchanged. Further, some particular items of consumption are what are called **positional goods**. These are such that the satisfaction involved in their consumption depends on the fact that it is confined to a small proportion of the population. Standard examples of positional goods are holiday homes with good views, good seats at the theatre, superior educational attainment. Increasing general affluence cannot increase the supply of positional goods.[19]

The view discussed above, that the economy is best seen as always delivering subsistence to the representative individual, can be seen as a generalisation of this last point.

Self-assessment of well-being

It is clear from introspection that one's personal sense of well-being at a point in time is strongly affected by two kinds of relativity. First, there is one's position relative to that of others. Second, there is one's position relative to one's past experience and the expectations and aspirations arising from that experience. Would the second kind not suggest that economic growth would be welfare enhancing for the representative individual? Over time in a growing economy, such a person consumes more, so that at any point in time the current level of consumption is high by the standards of past experience. This would surely make such a person feel better off. However, there are two considerations working in the opposite direction. First, what is relevant is not past experience *per se* but past experience as reflected in current aspirations. Individuals accustomed to increasing affluence are likely to aspire to its continuation, in which case the target is moving with the outcome. Second, to the extent that the cultural norm for the consumption of goods and services – the subsistence requirement as we have called it – increases with growth, increasing affluence will not mean increasing welfare for the representative individual.

Neither relativity effect would lead us to expect a positive relationship between national economic growth itself and increasing individual welfare. Some evidence bearing on this is shown in Table 4.3. It reports the percentages of individuals polled reporting various states of happiness. Over the 25-year period examined per capita income and consumption in the United States increased by more than 50 per cent. Yet, as Table 4.3 shows there is only a very slight upward trend in the proportion of people reporting themselves as 'very' or 'fairly' happy.

The study from which Table 4.3 is taken also considered self-assessed happiness variation by income at a point in time within the United States, and across 19 countries. It found that:

> Within countries there is a noticeable positive association between income and happiness – in every single survey, those in the highest status group were happier, on the average, than those in the lowest status group.

Cross-country income variations had less effect on happiness:

> ... the happiness differences between rich and poor countries that one might expect on the basis of the within-country differences by economic status are not borne out by the international data (Easterlin 1974).

Table 4.3 *Per cent distribution of population by happiness, United States, 1946-1970*

A. AIPO POLLS

Date	Very happy	Fairly happy	Not very happy	Other	Number polled
Apr. 1946	39	50	10	1	3151
Dec. 1947	42	47	10	1	1434
Aug. 1948	43	43	11	2	1596
Nov. 1952	47	43	9	1	3003
Sept. 1956	53	41	5	1	1979
Sept. 1956	52	42	5	1	2207
Mar. 1957	53	43	3	1	1627
July 1963	47	48	5 *	1	3668
Oct. 1966	49	46	4 *	2	3531
Dec. 1970	43	48	6 *	3	1517

B. NORC POLLS

Date	Very happy	Pretty happy	Not too happy	Number polled
Spring 1957	35	54	11	2460
Dec. 1963	32	51	16	1501
June 1965	30	53	17	1469

Note: * The question read 'not happy', rather than 'not very happy'.
Source: Easterlin (1974).

This study was published in 1974. Since that time social psychologists have done a great deal of survey work on the determinants of individual happiness in industrial nations. There appears to be a consensus that within a country at a given point in time, the income–happiness association is positive but weak:

> Objective circumstances have rather a small effect on satisfaction, especially such variables as income and education. Marriage, work and leisure have a greater effect (Argyle 1987).

The association between income and happiness appears to be strongest at low levels of income:

> Studies in advanced economies show, as one would expect that for every £1000 increase in income there is, indeed, an increased sense of well-being – but only for the poorest fifth of the population ... Beyond poverty or near poverty levels of income, if money buys happiness, it buys very little and often it buys none at all.[20]

The role of work in determining self-assessed happiness is always found to be very important. Satisfactory work is itself a major source of a sense of well-being. In economics it is assumed that individuals work only for the income arising, that work itself is a source of pain rather than pleasure. Surveys of individuals consistently find the opposite to be the case, above low levels of skill and discretion. They also find unemployment to be a major source of unhappiness:

> Unemployment makes most people very unhappy. There are serious effects on levels of mental ill-health, such as depression and suicide, and on health ... The effects are worst for people who are committed to the work ethic, for middle-aged men and for working-class people (Argyle 1987).

Finally in this section, we should make clear what is not being said here. First, in suggesting that for the representative individual in an affluent industrial nation the connection between further affluence and welfare enhancement is weak, we are not denying the existence of poverty in such nations. On the contrary, the point is that relatively poor individuals in such nations do experience real deprivation. Second, in suggesting that the historical experience of the development process has not involved a steady upward trend in welfare, we are not suggesting that the current situation of many people in the developing nations is not a matter for concern. Third, nor are we suggesting, by questioning the standard view of history to date as one of economic progress, that the historical development process should be reversed. This is simply impossible, even if desirable in some senses. The historical development process has been a process of cultural adaptation and evolution. Evolutionary processes are irreversible.

Measuring Economic Performance

The conventional indicator of economic performance is per capita national income. The use of per capita GNP, or GDP, as an economic performance indicator is widely criticised, from two standpoints. First, it is argued that national income is an inaccurate measure of the delivery of welfare to a nation's inhabitants. The second criticism is that GNP takes no account of the environmental impact of economic activity. From this standpoint, there is a call for 'green' national income accounting, to be discussed in Chapter 8. Here we look at an alternative, and much simpler, approach to constructing an indicator of economic performance which reflects environmental impact.

We considered the human development index (HDI) in Chapter 2. Recall that it uses data on GDP per capita measured in purchasing power parity dollars, and on life expectancy at birth. Here we use Y to indicate the former, and L to indicate the latter. *The human development report* (United Nations Development Programme 1992) reports HDI figures for 160 nations, for which its Table 1 also gives data on *Y* and *L*. The report also provides, in Tables 23 and 44, data for 132 countries on a greenhouse index. This is constructed by weighting the net emissions of carbon dioxide, methane and the chlorofluorocarbons according to their relative heat-trapping quality and summing to get an overall index of net greenhouse gas emissions. The result is expressed in equivalent metric tons of carbon per capita. Here we use *G* to refer to this index.

A simple environmentally adjusted economic performance indicator (EAEPI) across 132 countries is then given by $I = YL/G$, i.e. lifetime per capita GDP divided by per capita net greenhouse gas emissions. This index goes up with *Y* and/or *L*, and down as *G* increases. It is a measure of lifetime per capita income per unit of environmental impact. There are two main reasons for treating *G* as a measure of environmental impact. First, the enhanced greenhouse effect is widely seen as a major threat to sustainability: see Chapters 3 and 10. Second, *G* can be taken as a good proxy for the overall environmental impact of economic activity.[21] The major sources of carbon dioxide emissions are the combustion of fossil fuels and biomass, and land use changes, notably deforestation. Fossil fuels and biomass are now the major sources of extrasomatic energy use by humans. Their combustion releases many waste products into the atmosphere, in addition to carbon dioxide. Extrasomatic energy use is a good measure of the amount of matter moved and transformed by economic activity, and hence of extractions from and insertions into the environment. Fossil fuels are non-renewable resources which, when burned, cannot be recycled. Deforestation is a major source of biodiversity loss. The major methane emissions sources are in agriculture, which is a source of biodiversity loss. The chlorofluorocarbons are involved in the depletion of the stratospheric ozone layer, as well as being greenhouse gases.

The top dozen nations on the basis of *I* ranking are, with *Y* in parenthesis:

Mauritius ($5375)
Solomon Islands ($2626)
Cape Verde ($1717)
Morocco ($2298)
Fiji ($4192)
Malta ($8231)
Sweden ($14 817)
Switzerland ($18 590)
Chile ($4987)

Barbados ($83 351)
Cyprus ($9368)
Haiti ($962)

One reason for listing the top dozen nations is to get as far down the ranking as Haiti, so as to make it explicit that a high I rank does not carry the implication of a desirable place to live. Canada, which ranks first by HDI, with $Y = \$18\ 635$ ranks 48 by I; Australia ranks 7 by Y, 61 by I; the United Kingdom, ranks 10 by Y, 36 by I; the United States ranks are 6 and 43 respectively.

Does environmentally adjusted economic performance generally increase with per capita national income? In Figure 4.5 Y is measured along the horizontal axis, while a normalised version of I is measured up the vertical axis. The normalisation is with respect to the highest I score, so that Mauritius gets a score of 1 on the normalised index, and so on. In Figure 4.5 a data point is indicated by the HDI rank for the corresponding country. If Y and I were closely related and increased together, the data points would lie about the bottom left to top right diagonal. There are a large number of countries for which both Y and I are low, which is why the identifying numbers near the origin are indistinguishable. Outside of this bunching, as Y increases, with the exception of a few outliers e.g. 104, 105 and 48, I remains fairly constant. Clearly,

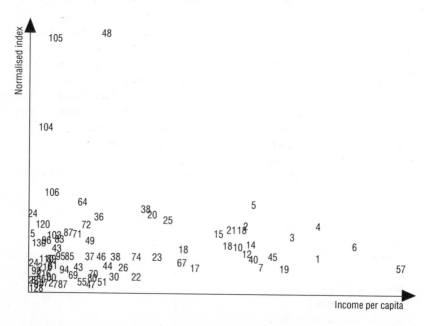

Figure 4.5 Environmentally adjusted economic performance.

Y and I are not very closely related and do not show much of a tendency to increase together: the rank correlation coefficient for Y and I is 0.57.

Many would argue that the numerator in I does not accurately reflect economic performance, in so far as welfare does not increase at the same rate as Y, over the whole range of variation in Y. Recall from Chapter 2 that the construction of the HDI actually uses adjusted income: above Y = \$4829, adjusted income increases with Y at a diminishing rate. If the EAEPI is constructed using adjusted income in place of Y, the general picture is much as in Figure 4.5.[22]

The index $I = YL/G$ is not to be seen as a definitive indicator for environmentally adjusted economic performance. No such thing exists, nor can it. Neither economic performance nor environmental impact can be properly measured by a single number. Both are multifaceted and there is no uniquely correct way of aggregating across these facets. However, I is easily calculated from published data and does provide some useful information. It confirms, for example, that some countries are better at transforming environmental impact, as measured by G, into lifetime per capita income, as measured by YL, than others. It also shows that 'better' in this respect does not correlate highly with the level of Y. The results shown in Figure 4.5, if nothing else, suggest some interesting lines for investigation. Among industrial nations, for example, why does Sweden do well compared with Canada? Among developing nations, for example, why does Mauritius do so well?

CHAPTER 5

Thinking about futures

Since the industrial revolution, the human population has grown rapidly, as has average per capita material throughput. However, there remain many poor human beings. To many commentators, it is obvious that addressing problems of poverty requires further economic growth. Others take the view that, in the light of economy–environment inter-connections, further growth is infeasible and so cannot solve the problem of poverty. This is the **limits to growth debate**, some contri-butions to which are considered in this chapter.

Limits to growth?

The limits to growth

In Chapter 1 we noted the 1972 publication of *The limits to growth* (Meadows et al. 1972). A sequel was published 20 years later – *Beyond the limits* (Meadows et al. 1992). This section is concerned with these two books and the reactions that they evinced, mainly from economists. They will be referred to as TLTG and BTL respectively.

TLTG reported the results of a study in which a computer model of the world system was used to simulate its future. The model comprised a representation of the world economy as a single economy, and some of the interconnections between that economy and its environment, in terms of limits. The model incorporated:

1. A limit to the amount of land available for agriculture.
2. A limit to the amount of agricultural output producible per unit of land in use.
3. A limit to the amount of non-renewable resources available for extraction.

4. A limit to the ability of the environment to assimilate wastes arising in production and consumption, which limit falls as the level of pollution increases.

The behaviour of the economic system was represented as a continuation of past trends in key variables, subject to those trends being influenced by the relationships between the variables represented in the model. These relationships were represented in terms of **positive** and **negative feedback effects**. Thus, for example, population growth is determined by birth and death rates, which are determined by fertility and mortality, which are, in turn, influenced by such variables as industrial output per capita, the extent of family planning and education – affecting fertility – and food availability per capita, industrial output per capita, pollution, and the availability of health care – affecting mortality. The evolution over time in the model of each of these variables, depends on and affects that of other variables. The model is complicated in detail, though not conceptually complex.

On the basis of a number of runs of the computer model, World3, the conclusions stated in TLTG were as follows:

1. If the present growth trends in world population, industrialisation, pollution, food production and resource depletion continue unchanged, the limits to growth on this planet will be reached sometime within the next 100 years. The most probable result will be a sudden and uncontrollable decline in both population and industrial capacity.

2. It is possible to alter these trends and to establish a condition of ecological and economic stability that is sustainable far into the future. The state of global equilibrium could be designed so that the basic material needs of each person on earth are satisfied and each person has an equal opportunity to realise his or her individual human potential.

3. If the world's people decide to strive for this second outcome rather than the first, the sooner they begin working to attain it, the greater will be their chances of success.[1]

The publication of TLTG created a furore. The reaction to it by economists was generally dismissive and/or hostile. According to one eminent economist it was 'a brazen, impudent piece of nonsense that nobody could possibly take seriously'.[2] What TLTG actually said was widely misrepresented. It was widely reported that it was an unconditional forecast of disaster sometime in the next century, consequent upon the world running out of non-renewable resources.

In fact, as the quotation above indicates, what was involved was conditional upon the continuation of some existing trends. Further, this conditional prediction was not based upon running out of resources. True, the first model run reported in TLTG did show disaster as the consequence of resource depletion (not exhaustion). But, the next reported run involved the model modified by an increase in the resource availability limit such that depletion did not give rise to problems for the economic system. In this run, the proximate source of disaster was the level of pollution consequent upon the exploitation of the increased amount of resources available, following from the materials balance principle. A number of variant model runs were reported, each relaxing some constraint. The conclusions reached were based on consideration of all of the variant model runs.

It was widely reported that TLTG said that there were limits to economic growth. In fact, what it said, as the quotation above indicates, is that there were limits to the growth of material throughput for the world economic system. As economic growth is measured it includes the consumption of the output of the services sector, as well as the agricultural and industrial sectors.

Beyond the limits

To date, the publication of the sequel BTL appears to have generated much less controversy than TLTG did. As far as economists are concerned, the situation has changed at least in so far as a Nobel laureate in the subject has said of BTL: 'We can all learn something from this book, especially we economists'.[3] The contrast in the reception accorded the two books might suggest some major change in analysis and conclusions between the original and the sequel. In fact, there is very little substantive difference in the conclusions, and apart from an updating of numerical values used, the model is essentially the original World3 with only minor modifications. The position taken in BTL is:

> As far as we can tell from the global data, from the World3 model, and from all we have learned in the past twenty years, the three conclusions we drew in *The limits to growth* are still valid, but they need to be strengthened. Now we would write them this way:
>
> 1. Human use of many essential resources and generation of many kinds of pollutants have already surpassed rates that are physically sustainable. Without significant reductions in material and energy flows, there will be in the coming decades an uncontrolled decline in per capita food output, energy use, and industrial production.
>
> 2. The decline is not inevitable. To avoid it two changes are necessary. The first is a comprehensive revision of policies and practices that perpetuate growth in material consumption and in population. The second is a rapid, drastic increase in the efficiency with which materials and energy are used.
>
> 3. A sustainable society is still technically and economically possible. It could be much more desirable than a society that tries to solve its problems by constant expansion. The transition to a sustainable society requires a careful balance between long-term and short-term goals and an emphasis on sufficiency, equity and quality of life rather than on quantity of output. It requires

more than productivity and more than technology; it also requires maturity, compassion, and wisdom (Meadows et al. 1992, p.xvi).

Two factors were likely to have been involved in the different receptions accorded to the original and the sequel. First, there has been a considerable change in the general climate of opinion, and an increase in the level of general awareness of environmental problems. Second, BTL involves substantial changes of tone and emphasis, and is clearer about the status of the analysis and conclusions. The conclusions in the sequel are, for example, explicitly stated to be 'a conditional warning, not a dire prediction' (Meadows et al. 1992, p.xvi). In TLTG the results from the various runs of the computer model were reported using graphs of the key variables against historical time, so that the onset of collapse of the system was dated at, say, 2050. This gave a spurious sense of precision, and was no doubt one of the reasons many readers thought that what was involved was a forecasting exercise. While the horizontal axes in the graphs reporting model run results are still dated in the sequel, there is greater effort devoted to dispelling the notion that this is an exercise in forecasting the date of disaster. The base case run of World3, i.e. the case incorporating preferred assumptions about the quantitative status of the four limits noted above and the relationships between variables, is Scenario 1. It is stated that: 'The strongest statement of certainty that we can make about Scenario 1 is that it portrays the most likely *general behaviour mode* of the system' (Meadows et al. 1992, p.134, italics in the original).

The graph for Scenario 1 shows industrial output growing until about 2025, and then declining steeply. Other variables, such as consumer goods per person, food per person, and life expectancy, behave similarly and switch from positive to negative growth at about the same time. Scenario 1 is not to be understood as a prediction, even a conditional prediction, that the onset of collapse will be some 30 years hence. Rather it is a statement that, given the conditions, the model indicates that collapse is inevitable at some time in the future, i.e. that the basic behaviour mode of the system is unsustainable. The question that arises is: if all that is really being made is a statement about the qualitative nature of the system, why present it in terms of numbers and dates in historical time?

There appear to be two answers to this question, one technical, the other presentational. The technical point is that the structure of World3 is so complicated, involving so many interrelated variables and relationships, that its properties cannot be analysed qualitatively. The model has to be numerically specified before even qualitative statements can be made about its behaviour. The point can be illustrated in a simpler context. Suppose we have a model in which one variable of interest, say,

x, is acted upon by two others, y and z. One of the determining variables, y, is related to x such that increases in it increase x. For z the relationship is in the opposite direction, increasing it means a decrease in the level of x. Suppose that both y and z are increasing at equal rates. We do not know whether x will be increasing or decreasing unless we know the relative sizes of the effects from the two other variables. In order, that is, to know the qualitative behaviour of this little system in terms of the net effect on x, we need to use quantitative information about the relationships involved, rather than just qualitative information.

World3 involves large numbers of variables and relationships. Analysis of its qualitative behaviour therefore requires that the relationships be stated not just in terms of directions of effect, but also in terms of strength of effect. In the jargon, the model needs to be 'parameterised' if its qualitative properties are to be understood. World3 is parameterised using historical data for 1900 to the present. All of the relationships are expressed in numerical terms, with the numbers used being selected for consistency with historical data. Hence, the output from the model is in numerical terms, and in the form of changes in the levels and rates of growth of variables, over future, historical time. While the object of the exercise is to assess the qualitative properties of system behaviour and key variables, the model output is in terms of quantitative statements, e.g. industrial output grows until 2025 then declines.

What is claimed in BTL is that the qualitative model properties are valid, conditional statements about the future of the actual world system. It is not claimed that the graphs for the various scenarios are conditional quantitative predictions about exactly when variables will peak, and at what levels they will peak. This is made more clear in BTL than in TLTG. The important point here is that the exercise is not about forecasting the date of collapse. It was no doubt a lack of clarity in this regard in TLTG that leads some commentators to suppose, incorrectly, that World3 has been totally discredited because TLTG predicted, they claim, that the world would run out of resources by date X, whereas in fact for many resources estimated reserves are now larger than they were in 1972.

So, one reason for having historical time on the axes of the graphs in TLTG and BTL is, no doubt, that this is the way the output came off the computer. One suspects that, at least in the case of TLTG, there was also a presentational reason. The authors were, and remain, convinced that they had an extremely important story to tell. Given this, it would be natural to want to attract attention to the story. Consider two ways of presenting the story. The first is that it has been ascertained, albeit using a numerical computer model, that the current general behaviour mode of the world economic system is such that it is unsustainable, i.e. it will experience collapse at some future date. To avoid this collapse, it is

necessary that policies be changed. The second is that a numerical computer model of the world economic system in its existing form indicates
that it will collapse around the middle of the next century, i.e. in some
75 years' time (from 1972). To avoid this it is necessary that policies be
changed immediately. Most likely the second version of the story would
attract more attention.

Criticism

We now turn to criticism directed, mainly by economists, at the analysis
using World3. This criticism, to date, relates to TLTG rather than BTL.[4]
The version of World3 used for BTL is stated to be little different from
that used for TLTG.

The major technical criticism has been that the quantitative settings
for limits used in the model are wrong. Thus, for example, there are
disagreements about how much land is potentially agricultural land.
The authors of TLTG and BTL claim that by considering many model
runs in which such constraints are varied across the range of plausibility,
they are satisfied that their conclusions are robust as regards the general
behaviour mode. Similarly, the methods by which the relationships
between variables are represented in the model, and the methods by
which the relationships are parameterised, have been criticised. Again,
the response is that the conclusions are not sensitive to such criticism.
World3 is now available in a form that can readily be run on desktop
computers, and the potential exists for many investigators to explore the
sensitivity of the general behaviour mode of the updated World3 to
variations in limit and relationship specification.

World3 treats the world economy as a single economy, so that all
variables are world totals or world averages and there are no international trade flows. While in reality there are very large differences
between industrial and developing economies, the model variables are
world totals or averages so that the relationship between food availability
and mortality in it is, for example, some kind of average between that in
the industrial economies and that in developing economies. Critics have
claimed that the actual relationships across countries are so different
that the average is meaningless, and hence the model output should be
disregarded. The force of this criticism depends in part upon what one
thinks the model is designed to achieve. The authors of TLTG and BTL
would claim that with respect to the general behaviour mode of the
system, treating the world economy as a single economy introduces no
significant error for conclusions about the system as a whole. Of course,
if one is interested in how different economies fare, one has to have a
model which distinguishes different economies. Several world modelling efforts were underway in the early 1970s. Some of these treated the

world economic system as comprising several distinct economies which trade with one another. Clark et al. (1975) give overviews of the various models, and discuss the research strategy involved in such modelling.

A more general type of criticism of World3 has been made by economists. These matters can be discussed using Figure 3.1 from Chapter 3, where we noted that there are possibilities for substituting for the services of the natural environment. First, recycling reduces demands upon assimilative capacities and upon stocks of natural resources. Second, the services of capital can substitute for the services provided by environmental assets. This involves both the accumulation of capital equipment, and the embodiment in that equipment of technological advances. In Figure 3.1, flows in the economy and between it and the natural environment are represented as single lines. This is a major over-simplification. Economic activity comprises many different production activities, and the consumption of many different kinds of goods and services. These vary widely in the demands that they make upon environmental services. Compare, for example, the production, and use by individuals, of motor vehicles with the production, and enjoyment by individuals, of theatrical performances.

A major element of the critique of TLTG by economists was that World3 overlooked these substitution possibilities and the implications of alternative patterns of production and consumption. The argument was that as growth proceeded, so environmental impact per unit of economic activity could be reduced by recycling, capital service substitution, and a changing composition of total economic activity. If these things occurred, then as growth proceeded, so environmental limits would recede. Growth need not actually hit any limits. The argument went further than noting the existence of these possibilities, and claimed that the problem of limits could, in fact, be ignored as these possibilities would indeed be realised as growth proceeded. This argument involves two, related, elements.

The first is historical. The standard historical pattern of growth and development has involved, first, a shift out of agriculture and into industry, and, second, out of industry and into services. Table 2.7 showed the percentages of the labour force employed in the three sectors for economies at different stages of development. Figure 2.1 showed, for an industrial economy, energy intensities when indirect as well as direct use is accounted for. Taking energy use as a proxy for environmental impact, Figure 2.1 shows that, per dollar of output, the services sector does have a smaller environmental impact than the industrial sector.

The second element of the argument, that limits will not be reached, is that there exists a cultural mechanism which will induce the required substitutions and structural shifts as growth occurs. This is the price mechanism. The argument is that to the extent that growth increases the scarcity of particular environmental services, i.e. approaches limits in respect of them, so their price will rise. As the price of an environmental service rises, so the demands made upon it will decrease, and substitutions for it will be induced. The operation of the price mechanism will be discussed in Chapters 6 and 7. Economists do not claim that economic growth will accommodate to, i.e. not run into, environmental limits by virtue of the invisible hand of market forces alone. They recognise the existence of market failure, see a role for public policy in correcting it, and have devoted much time and effort to studying these matters, as will be discussed in Chapter 7. At the time of the publication of TLTG, economists had published relatively little on these matters. By 1992, when BTL was published, the economic literature on policy for environmental protection was extensive. This literature is almost totally ignored in BTL, as is the general question of policies for environmental protection.

The market can only work properly where private property rights exist. And, it is clear that in regard to many environmental services they do not. Stocks of renewable resources frequently do not have owners: consider ocean fisheries. The environment as a waste receptacle is typically not owned: consider emissions into the atmosphere from fossil fuel combustion. The same is true of many amenity services: consider wilderness recreation, or the satisfaction gained from the knowledge that whales exist. For life support functions private property rights appear to be completely absent.

Some economists take the view that in many cases where private property rights do not exist, they can be created. Others see a limited role for this means of correcting market failure, and a larger role for ongoing governmental intervention in economic activity to control its environmental impact. Most take the view that as economic growth proceeds so the demand for environmental protection grows. It is argued that as individuals become more affluent, having their basic material needs satisfied enables them to turn their attention to environmental matters. This manifests itself in two ways. First, individuals as consumers demand more environmentally friendly products and services. This pushes the functioning of existing market forces toward environmental protection. Second, and assuming democratic institutions, individuals as citizens exert pressure on government to progressively introduce policies to protect the natural environment.

The upshot of all this is that most economists do not see environmental limits as requiring any fundamental reappraisal of growth as a major objective of policy. The next section considers further some of the arguments advanced by economists. Then the following section looks at some arguments advanced by biologists. The objective is not to answer the question 'are there limits to growth?'. This is not really the operative question, and can lead to discussion at cross purposes. For example, as noted above, whereas in TLTG and BTL the growth considered is in material production and consumption, for economists, growth refers to national income which includes material production and immaterial services in non-fixed proportions. The interesting questions concern threats to sustainability, where we are necessarily dealing with imprecision and uncertainty, whether policies to address supposed threats are desirable, and what forms they should take.

Economists on limits

Scarcity and growth

An important part of economists' case against the idea of limits in TLTG was as follows. If there were limits to the availability of natural resources this would mean that as growth proceeded so resources would become more scarce. If resources became more scarce, this would show up in economic data. Economists have studied the data and discovered that to date there is no evidence for increasing scarcity with growth. The evidence is that increasing demand has stimulated substitutions and technical change, rather than increased scarcity. This historical trend will continue. Therefore, there is no need to assume increasing future scarcities and there are no limits to growth.

The major study of the historical data usually cited here was Barnett and Morse (1963). This work analysed data for a number of resource extraction industries in the United States for the period 1870 to 1957. It found that, with the exception of forest products, the unit costs of production in these industries fell during this period. Barnett and Morse argued that any increasing physical scarcity of US resources had been offset by: economies of scale in production, technical change, substitutions between resources as inputs to manufacturing industry, discoveries of new deposits, and imports. Using these results against the arguments of TLTG involved several kinds of extrapolation. First, it extrapolated in space, effectively assuming the experience of one country to be applicable to the world. Clearly, importation of natural resource inputs to production is not a possibility for the world as a whole. Second, it extrapolated in time, assuming that what had happened in the past in resource extraction would happen in the future. Problems with this kind of extrapolation are discussed below. Third, it extrapolated from analysis of particular scarcities to the case of general scarcity. The TLTG argument is about material growth in a materially closed system, not about the non-availability of particular resource inputs.

More recent work by economists has noted that the unit cost of production in an extractive industry is not the only possible measure of scarcity.[5] Other possible measures are the prices of the products produced using the output from the extractive industry, and the *in situ* price of the resource itself.[6] To see the distinctions here, consider oil. The price paid for the right to extract oil is the price of oil *in situ*. Extracting the oil involves production costs, which are what were examined in the Barnett and Morse study. The result of the extraction activity is crude oil, which is an input to the oil refining activity, which produces outputs such as motor vehicle fuel. The price of motor vehicle fuel must cover the cost of acquiring extraction rights, the costs of extraction, and the costs of refining.

The idea that increasing scarcity would show up in increasing extraction costs is based on the idea that these increase as depletion proceeds. This reflects the assumption of extraction starting with the most accessible and highest quality deposits, and moving to less accessible and lower quality deposits as the better ones are exhausted. This need not be the case. New discoveries may turn out to be lower cost than existing known deposits. And, where extraction does track a decreasing quality gradient as depletion proceeds, technical progress may work to offset increasing costs. Non-increasing unit extraction costs do not necessarily imply that scarcity is not increasing.

Similar problems attend the use of product price as a measure of scarcity. Some commentators see an additional problem with this indicator. Price depends upon demand as well as the costs of supply. A resource may be being depleted, with no technical change working to reduce extraction and production costs, yet the price of the product need not be rising because the increasing use of substitutes for that product depresses demand for it. Economists typically do not see this as a problem. On the contrary they see it as a virtue of this indicator. If we consider oil again, the point that is made is that nobody is interested in oil in the ground *per se*. What is of interest is the services that extracted and refined oil can perform. To the extent that an increasing use of other means of performing the services of interest keeps the price of oil-based products down, it is argued, the relevant scarcity is not increasing.

In principle, economists see the proper measure of scarcity as the price of the resource *in situ*. The basis for this view is the assumption that there exist markets in which rights to extract now and at future dates are traded. Traders in such markets are assumed to be well informed. Then, if scarcity does increase, taking account of demand as well as supply, the price of rights to extract now and in the future will increase. In practice, problems with this measure are recognised. First, where markets for rights to extract in the future do exist, typically the futurity that they cover is not very great. For some resources there are no futures markets at all. Second, traders are often not well informed. Third, in many cases, markets in even current extraction rights do not exist, or are of limited coverage. Where private property rights in *in situ* stocks exist they are often owned by the firms in the extraction business so that there is no trade in them visible to external observers. The price of extraction rights is then only implicit in the behaviour of extracting firms. Fourth, in many cases the observable, or implicit, market in extraction rights is characterised by having relatively few participants, so that strategic behaviour can distort the market signals. Such distortions affect the price of products based on the resource. The most famous examples of this kind of problem are the oil price increases of 1973/74 and 1979.

For these reasons, economists find it difficult, in practice, to use the measure that they regard, in principle, as the correct one. A follow-up study to Barnett and Morse used both unit costs and product prices to test the hypothesis of increasing scarcity for some resources in the United States for the 1960s and 1970s. It concluded that:

> No single index of scarcity is without practical or theoretical flaws ... taken together, the two indexes of scarcity analysed here confirm the hypothesis that scarcity increased in the 1970s for nonrenewable energy resources and for some renewables (Hall and Hall 1984).

The question of increasing scarcity of the assimilative capacities for wastes is as relevant to the TLTG argument as increasing scarcities of resource inputs. Typically these assimilative capacities are not subject to private property rights and so do not have attached to them prices by which increasing scarcity could be signalled. The authors of this follow-up study note this. They also note, with approval, that during the 1970s in the United States environmental legislation was enacted to protect some assimilative capacities, with the effect of increasing costs in some extractive industries, which was 'a probable cause of increasing real prices in the extractive sector during the 1970s'.

Given all the difficulties and uncertainties attending indicators of scarcity, the main point is that the historical trends which might be extrapolated are ambiguous and open to differing interpretations. The reader interested in the details on particular resources, and alternative indicators, can consult the references cited.[7]

The ultimate resource

The ultimate resource by Julian Simon, was published in 1981. Simon's basic theme is that there are no limits to either the growth of human numbers or the material consumption levels of the average individual. There are three reasons for briefly considering Simon's position here. First, it is one of the most forthright attempts to rebut arguments for the existence of limits to growth.[8] Second, Simon is unusually explicit about the role of extrapolation in thinking about the future. Third, he is also

very explicit about the need for a value system as well as an understanding of the facts in reaching a view on policy questions. The first two
aspects of Simon's book are considered here, the third is examined in
the final section of this chapter, on science and policy. While in many
ways Simon is a representative, if outspoken, economist, there is one way
in which he is somewhat unrepresentative. This is in relation to the need
for active policy to promote environmental protection. Simon does not,
as do most economists who focus on the environment, pay much
attention to the need for, and design of, policies to correct market
failure.

Simon's basic position is that:

> there is no meaningful physical limit – even the commonly mentioned weight
> of the earth – to our capacity to keep growing forever (Simon 1981, p.346).

Much of the book is taken up with arguing the absence of limits in particular contexts. The essence of the argument in each particular case is
extrapolation of historical trends showing, according to Simon, decreasing scarcity. Most of the data used relates to the United States for 1800
to the 1970s, and the scarcity indicator used is price. In fact, for many of
the time series reported in the graphs, visual inspection suggests an
upward movement in price at the end of the period covered. However,
this is not necessarily a problem for Simon's position, since he is
concerned with extrapolation of long-term trends, and these could be
temporary departures from those trends. Indeed, consistency with his
core idea (see below) would require him to argue that this is what they
are.

Simon is explicit about the use of trend extrapolation in thinking
about the future:

> The economist's first approximation forecast is that these trends toward less
> scarcity should continue into the foreseeable future unless there is some
> reason to believe that conditions have changed, that is, unless there is some-
> thing wrong with the data as a basis for extrapolation (Simon 1981, p.21).

Far from finding any reason not to extrapolate decreasing scarcity,
Simon takes the view that the observed historical trend may well
understate future prospects for decreasing scarcity:

> You may object that extrapolating a future from past trends of greater and
> greater abundance is like extrapolating, just before you hit the ground, that a
> jump from the top of the Eiffel Tower is an exhilarating experience. But for
> the tower jump we have outside knowledge that there is a sudden discon-
> tinuity when you hit the ground. In the case of energy and natural resources,
> there is no persuasive evidence for a negative discontinuity; rather, the
> evidence points toward positive discontinuities – nuclear fusion, solar energy,

and so on. And historical evidence further teaches us that such worries about discontinuities have usually generated the very economic pressures that have opened up new frontiers. Hence there is no solid reason to think that we are about to hit the ground after an energy jump from the Eiffel Tower. More likely, we are in a rocket on the ground that has only been warming up until now and will take off sometime soon (Simon 1981, p.99).

This quotation indicates two important aspects of Simon's position. First, he takes the view that energy is the key natural resource, and that given enough of it, any desired material transformation is possible. Second, Simon sees human ingenuity manifested in technical innovation as the response to some problem as *the* historical trend to be extrapolated. As a particular example of this, consider his remarks on nuclear fusion as a power source. He notes an estimate that if fusion were a viable technology, the basic resource input exists in such quantities that, assuming a level of energy use 100 times greater than the present, it would last for one billion years. He also notes that it is not known with certainty whether fusion ever will be a practicable technology. He then quotes, successively, one view that the problem will be solved one day, another that the prospects for a solution have recently improved, and the statement that there is a scientific consensus that the commercial feasibility of fusion is likely to be established in the early 1990s.[9] Clearly, Simon believes, and wishes his readers to believe, that in thinking about the long-term future it makes more sense to assume the viability of fusion than to assume that it will never be available.

The historical trend that Simon heavily relies upon is technological adaptation to any problem arising from human demands upon the natural environment. Thus:

> Population growth spurs the adoption of existing technology as well as the invention of new technology. This has been well documented in agriculture, where people turn to successively more "advanced" but more laborious methods of getting food as population density increases – methods that were previously known but that were not used because they were not needed earlier. This scheme well describes the passage from hunting and gathering – which we now know requires extraordinarily few hours of work a week to provide a full diet – to migratory slash-and-burn agriculture, and thence to settled long-fallow agriculture, to short-fallow agriculture, and eventually to the use of fertilizer, irrigation and multiple cropping. Though each stage initially requires more labor than the previous one, the endpoint is a more efficient and productive system that requires much less labor (Simon 1981, p.199).

This understanding of the broad sweep of human history is in many respects the same as that discussed in Chapter 4 here. There are two main differences. First, Simon suggests, though does not explicitly state, that successful technological adaptation to a resource/environmental crisis is inevitable. Clearly, it is not. In human history many societies have failed to adapt. Second, Simon sees the long-run trend as necessarily welfare improving. Note particularly the statement that the endpoint is one which 'requires much less labor'. If the comparison is with the original starting point, the hunter–gatherer system (in reasonably favourable conditions), that this is simply wrong is indicated by his own earlier statement that in such conditions a full diet required 'extraordinarily few hours of work'. Simon would no doubt defend the general point of a long-run welfare-improving trend on the grounds that although we now work more, we also consume more. The connections between material consumption levels and welfare were also discussed in Chapter 4.

It is also important to note that Simon does not see the past, or the future, as a smooth unfolding of uninterrupted progress. On the contrary, crises and setbacks are required in order to call forth the technological innovations which are the basis for progress. The 'ultimate resource' is human beings, because they are the repositories of the ability to solve problems by means of innovation. Simon strongly objects to any policy intended to reduce the growth of human numbers, since this would limit the supply of this ultimate resource, and restrict the spread of the benefits arising from its exploitation. Simon does not claim that population growth never gives rise to problems. On the contrary, it is solving the problems thereby arising that has been, and will continue to be, the engine of progress in the long run.

The policy implications that Simon draws are discussed at the end of this chapter. Here we comment on his trend identification and extrapolation. Not all societies have solved their problems – some have simply ceased to exist. Many societies adapted not by, or at least not solely by, technical innovation. Rather, they adapted by geographical expansion. This is important because there is now nowhere for any society to take over except at the expense of some other society. The technological advances that have taken place mean that the potential for serious and long-term damage from economic activity to the natural environment is now much greater than has been the case previously. They have also increased the potential for such damage from conflict between human groups.

The point is that there is a discontinuity which suggests caution about extrapolation. Whereas for most of history the operative social unit was an extended family group, a tribe, or a nation state, existing in a relatively empty world, now it is the whole of humanity and there are no productive empty lands. Whereas for most of history humans could cause only local environmental damage, the potential for irreversible global damage is now seen to exist.

Growth as the solution?

Economists have advanced the argument that economic growth can itself do much to solve environmental problems. The basic idea is that for many environmental impacts, as per capita national income grows so impact per capita grows initially and then declines. This is illustrated in Figure 5.1, where the horizontal axis measures national income per capita and the vertical axis shows environmental impact per capita. An environmental impact here can be either waste discharge or resource extraction. The argument then is that for impacts where this sort of relationship holds, rather than economic growth being a threat to the environment, it is, in the long run, a means to environmental protection. It is recognised, however, that for some impacts, irreversible damage may occur before this relationship turns down, and that the relationship described above need not hold for all impacts.

The main arguments for relationships such as that shown in Figure 5.1 were covered earlier in this chapter. There is an additional point to be made regarding waste discharge impacts. Market failure is especially prevalent in relation to the environment's assimilative capacities, so that firms do not, in the absence of government regulation, pay for waste discharges into the environment. However, they do pay for resource inputs to production. Even where property rights are absent, so that *in situ* prices are zero, costs are incurred in extraction. The materials balance principle links material inputs to waste outputs. Since firms seek to minimise costs they will seek to economise on resource inputs, and to the extent that resource input levels are reduced per unit of output, so will waste discharges per unit of output be reduced. Also, it is argued,

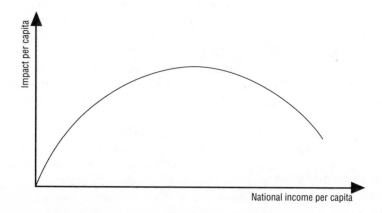

Figure 5.1 Per capita environmental impact and national income.

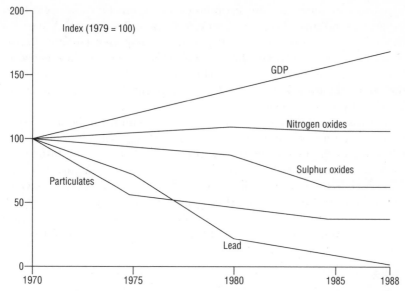

Figure 5.2 GDP and emissions in OECD countries.
Note: GDP and emissions of nitrogen oxides and sulphur oxides are OECD
averages. Emissions of particulates are the average for Germany, Italy,
Netherlands, United Kingdom and United States. Lead emissions are for
United States.
Source: World Bank (1992) Box 1.6.

firms will have incentives to minimise waste per unit of resource input
(Bernstam 1991).

The case for the inverted U relationship does not rest solely on
abstract argument. In recent years a number of studies have looked at
the relationship between per capita income and various kinds of environmental impact.[10] These have involved looking at both the histories of
economies over time and impact differences between economies with
different per capita income levels. Figure 5.2 shows trends over time for
averages across some industrial economies. For sulphur oxides, particulates and lead, these trends are consistent with the inverted U relationship hypothesis. In many industrial economies, energy use per unit of
economic activity has fallen in recent years. This is consistent with an
inverted U for energy.[11] If this type of relationship does hold for energy,
then this is important since, as we note elsewhere, energy use is a good
proxy for general environmental impact.

Let us take it that an inverted U relationship does hold between some
environmental impacts per unit of economic activity and the level of
economic activity, and consider the long-run implications of this.

Suppose that there are two economies. As shown in Figure 5.3, both experience no growth up until time 0. At time 0, economy A starts to experience economic growth at a constant exponential rate, i.e. its national income grows steadily at a constant percentage rate per year. Growth in economy B does not start until T years later, when it occurs at the same rate as in A. Think of A as the industrial economies, and B as the developing economies.

Now assume that for both economies the relationship between some impact per unit of national income and the level of national income takes one of the two forms shown in Figure 5.4. Then, one history for total world impact is shown in Figure 5.5, another in Figure 5.6. The difference between the two lies in what is assumed about the behaviour of the impact-income relationship as income gets very large. In Figure 5.5 the assumption is that the relationship is that shown as 'a' in Figure 5.4, so that impact reaches zero at some high enough income level. In

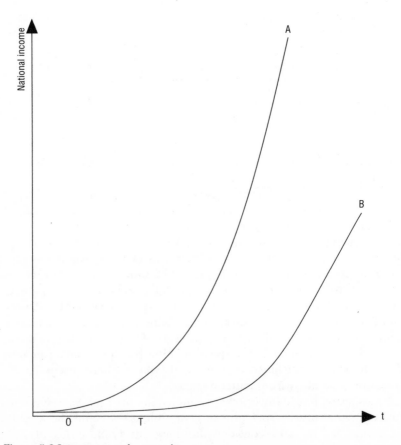

Figure 5.3 Income growth scenario.

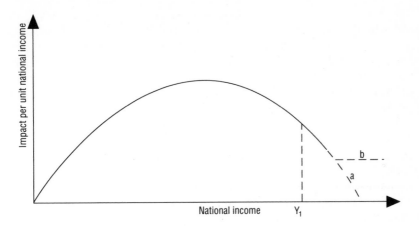

Figure 5.4 Impact per unit of national income.

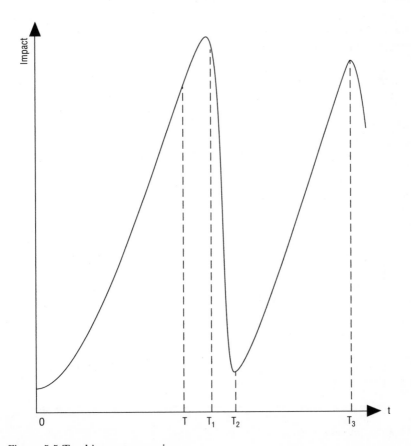

Figure 5.5 Total impact scenario one.

Figure 5.6 the assumption is that there is a lower bound to impact per unit of national income, as with b in Figure 5.4.[12]

The point here is about two kinds of extrapolation. Consider first Figure 5.5, and imagine an observer of the history of total world impact up to time T_1. At this time recent history shows total world impact declining. Extrapolation of this trend would clearly give rise to incorrect predictions for the future period T_2 to T_3. However, after T_3 the downward trend is resumed, and eventually world total impact goes to zero. The second kind of extrapolation is from historical data about the impact-income relationship, as in Figure 5.4. Suppose that the actual historical record is for income levels up to Y_1. Then simple extrapolation of that record gives the relationship shown by a, with impact eventually going to zero per unit of national income, and hence to zero in total. This is the basis for Figure 5.5. However, while it may be feasible for some impacts to go to zero in this way, it clearly cannot be the case for all impacts. However large a proportion of economic activity the service sector becomes, for example, it is going to require a material infrastructure and inputs of energy and materials. In which case, the laws of nature dictate some non-zero impacts on the environment from

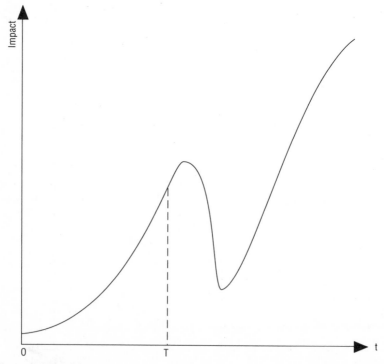

Figure 5.6 Total impact scenario two.

economic activity. If, for any impact, this extrapolation to zero is invalid, then for that impact the scenario with indefinitely continuing economic growth is as shown in Figure 5.6.

The scenarios in Figures 5.5 and 5.6 assume that both economies generate the same level of impact for the same level of income, although at a point in time the level of income in B is always lower than that in A. If it is technical progress that is driving the inverted U relationship, this means that there is no transfer of technology from A to B, so that B follows exactly the same trajectory as A, albeit lagging behind it always. This is, clearly, an extreme assumption. More reasonably one would assume some technological transfer from A to B so that, in effect, the inverted U for B would not have as high a turning point as that experienced by A. Allowing for such an effect would not alter the general nature of the trajectories shown in Figures 5.5 and 5.6 for total world impact. Particularly, in the case where there is a lower limit to impact per unit of income, Figure 5.6, it would still be true that eventually, given indefinitely continuing growth, impact would be growing without limit. This is going to be true for any impact for which such a lower limit exists, irrespective of the details of the scenarios considered.

The inverted U effect for waste emissions and resource use rates is undoubtedly important in thinking about the future. For some impacts of each type the evidence shows that it is operative. However, this does not mean that all impacts will eventually decline as growth proceeds. Even where the effect is operative, if it has a lower limit, continuing growth will eventually mean a rising impact. Whether this matters to human interests or not, and whether it constitutes a threat to sustainability or not, varies across impacts. In some cases it may not. In others, as noted above, a threat to sustainability may have been generated before the impact reaches its first peak in Figures 5.5 and 5.6. This is, in a very simplified form, the essential argument of BTL, where the position taken is that the threats so generated have not yet been irreversible.

Biologists on limits

Not all of the contributions and views to be briefly reviewed here are by biologists. However, they all come at the question of limits from a biological, or ecological, perspective. First we consider a perspective on the extent to which biospheric functioning is now dominated by a single species, humans. We then look at the related matter of biodiversity losses, and discuss why biologists see the current situation with regard to this as a major cause for concern about future prospects. Finally, we look at some biologists' views about what should be done about perceived threats to sustainability.

The appropriation of solar radiation

Figure 4.2 (p. 62) showed the structure of a trophic pyramid based on the capture of solar radiation by plants, or primary producers. **Net primary production** (NPP) is the amount of living tissue created by photosynthesis. NPP is the basis for the maintenance, growth and reproduction of all of the species that feed off plant life: it is the total food resource of the biosphere. Here we are concerned with estimates of the share of this food resource now appropriated by the human species.

Table 5.1 *Surface area and net primary production*

	percentages	
	Surface area	NPP
Terrestrial	29	59
Aquatic	71	41

Source: Vitousek et al. (1986).

Table 5.2 *Human appropriation of net primary production*

	percentages		
	Low	Intermediate	High
Terrestrial	4	31	39
Aquatic	2	2	2
Total	3	19	25

Source: Vitousek et al. (1986).

Table 5.1 shows that per unit area, the land surface of the earth produces more of this food than does the part of the surface covered by water. Although the aquatic zone accounts for 71 per cent of the total surface area, it accounts for only 41 per cent of total NPP. Table 5.2 shows three alternative estimates of the share of terrestrial, aquatic and total NPP appropriated by the human species. For the low estimate, what is counted is only the actual use by humans and their domesticated animals as food, fuel, fibre and timber. The intermediate estimate adds to this what 'is used in human-dominated ecosystems by communities of organisms different from those in corresponding natural ecosystems' (Vitousek et al. 1986, p.370). Thus, for example, whereas the low estimate uses the food actually eaten by humans, the intermediate estimate uses the NPP of the agricultural land on which the food is produced – the amount of wheat grown rather than of wheat-based products consumed. Finally, the high estimate also accounts for 'potential NPP lost as a consequence of human activities' (p.371). With regard to agriculture, for example, this estimate includes NPP lost as a result of turning forest into pasture for domestic animals. This estimate also allows for NPP losses on account of desertification and covering land with materials which prevent photosynthetic capture, such as roads and buildings. Note that the estimate for aquatic NPP appropriation is the same on the low, intermediate and high bases, reflecting the fact that human exploitation of marine ecosystems is still dominantly in the nature of hunting and gathering rather than farming, notwithstanding the use of technologically sophisticated methods. Note also that these estimates are necessarily somewhat imprecise. For this reason, they have been reported here as rounded numbers.

In relation to the high terrestrial estimate, the authors make the observation that:

> An equivalent concentration of resources into one species and its satellites has probably not occurred since land plants first diversified (Vitousek et al. 1986, p.372).

An alternative perspective on what is involved can be provided as follows. Take the low total estimate of 3 per cent. This is direct consumption by humans. The lower bound estimate of the total number of animal species cited by the authors of these NPP appropriation estimates is five million. Sharing NPP equally between species would give each 0.00002 per cent of the total. Thus the human species is now consuming 150 000 times an equal share. This calculation is simply intended to provide some perspective. It is not being argued that all species should have equal shares. Nor is it being suggested that ecosystem functioning requires equal shares. Clearly, it does not. However, the authors of these estimates believe that the share of NPP appropriation now achieved by humans does threaten the functioning of the biosphere:

> Observers who believe that limits to growth are so distant as to be of no consequence for today's decision makers ... appear unaware of these biological realities (Vitousek et al. 1986, p.373).

The particular, proximate threat to sustainability that the authors have in mind is biodiversity loss.

Biodiversity loss

Biodiversity loss is usually understood to occur when a species becomes extinct. The first problem in discussing biodiversity loss is that it is not known how many species exist. Some 1.6 million species have been identified (Myers 1979). There are a number of estimates of species numbers. The estimated number of species in existence appears generally to have been increasing over time. Myers (1979) estimates the total number of species at 10 million. Simon and Wildavsky (1993) cite a 1980 estimate of a range from 3 to 10 million. Ehrlich and Ehrlich (1992) give an estimate of 10 million, from a range of 2 to 50 million. Vitousek et al. (1986) give a range of 5 to 30 million for the number of animal species.

Given the uncertainty over the number of species in existence, estimates of rates of species loss are also clearly speculative in nature, and again a wide range can be found in the literature. Myers (1979) gives one per day for 1979, one per hour for the late 1980s, and a total of 1 million in the last quarter of the twentieth century. Simon and Wildavsky (1993) cite a 1980 estimate of 500 000 to 600 000 species losses for the last two decades of the century. Ehrlich and Ehrlich (1992) cite the following estimates. Their own, from Ehrlich and Ehrlich (1981), of 40 to 400 times the normal rate for birds and mammals. A 1989 estimate of an annual extinction rate of '4000 to 6000 species, some 10 000 times the background rate before *Homo sapiens* started practising agriculture'. Based on 1988 estimates, they note that it is 'conceivable that the rate is actually 60 000 to 90 000 species annually: 150 000 times background'.[13]

Many biologists take the view that there is now occurring an extinction 'crisis' or 'spasm' of the same order of magnitude as that which occurred some 65 million years ago, and involved the extinction of the dinosaurs. They also take the view that this is something which has significant, adverse implications for human interests, for the following reasons.[14] First, many known species of plants and animals are directly useful to human productive activity, providing inputs to the manufacture of drugs, and genetic material for crop-breeding, for example. Given that only a small proportion of the estimated total number of species in existence is now known to man, it must be assumed that many of the unknown species would also eventually turn out to be useful. If a species becomes extinct, its potential usefulness is irreversibly lost. Second, there is the idea that biodiversity is a form of amenity service, in the terminology of Chapter 3. That is, that humans would generally find an environment characterised by less biodiversity less enjoyable.

Third, plant and animal species play roles in the functioning of ecosystems, and of the biosphere as a whole. They are the basis for the life support functions of the natural environment. The exact role that most species play is unknown. For unidentified species this is necessarily true. But even for identified species that have been extensively studied, it is frequently unknown as to whether or not their extinction would adversely affect ecosystem function, from a human perspective.

Ehrlich and Ehrlich (1992) make this case for being concerned about species extinction in terms of the following analogy. Aircraft are constructed such that the component parts which constitute a viable flying machine are held together by large numbers of rivets. In fact, the number of rivets used in construction is in excess of the number estimated to be required. On walking across to board an aircraft you see a person removing rivets from it, who explains that they are to be sold to supplement her income. When questioned further, the person explains that the aircraft was constructed with surplus rivets, and she has been removing some before each take-off for some time, and that it clearly does not do any harm. Question: would you want to board the aircraft?

As a particular aspect of the system function question, there is the matter of the maintenance of the capacity for evolution. To the extent that the diversity of genetic material in existence is reduced, it must be assumed that evolutionary potential is reduced. The argument for maintaining evolutionary potential is that this is what will, through the emergence of new life forms, promote the ability of the biosphere to cope with stresses, including those originating in human activity. New life forms may also form the basis for directly useful inputs to production. In this connection, it needs to be noted that there is genetic diversity within species, as well as between species. A **population** is a group of individuals which actually interbreed. A **species** comprises those organisms capable of interbreeding, and generally comprises a number of distinct populations. Complete genetic identity is not necessary for interbreeding, and isolated populations of a species may come to exhibit substantial genetic difference. Thus, biodiversity, and evolutionary potential, is lost when populations are lost, even if the species remains in existence.[15] The rate of loss of populations is considered to be much greater than the loss of species.

In Simon and Wildavsky (1993), an economist and a political scientist argue that there is 'now no prima facie case for any expensive species-safeguarding policy without more extensive analysis'. They note the paucity of reliable historical data on species extinctions, and comment that:

> It is clear that without bringing into consideration some additional force, one could extrapolate almost any rate (of extinction) one chooses for the year 2000 ... many forecasters would be likely to project a rate much closer to the past ... on the basis of the common wisdom that in the absence of additional information, the best first approximation for a variable tomorrow is its value today ... (Simon and Wildavsky 1993, p.8, parenthesis added).

The 'additional force' that biologists would cite is the evidence on the human appropriation of NPP considered above, and the associated direct observations on the destruction of species habitats. Simon and Wildavsky note considerations of the latter particular kind in relation to tropical forests, but do not refer to any data on NPP appropriation. They deny the relevance of observed habitat loss on the grounds that there is a lack of 'systematic evidence relating an amount of tropical forest removed to a rate of species reduction' (p.8).

Simon and Wildavsky also take the extrapolation route to assessing the implications of biodiversity loss. They are sceptical about the benefits from species preservation. This is essentially on the view that past extinctions have not involved much cost to humans. Thus:

> Perhaps we should look back and wonder: Which species were extinguished when the settlers clear-cut the Middle West of the United States? Are we the poorer now for their loss? Obviously we do not know the answers. But can we even imagine that we would be enormously better off with the persistence of any hypothetical species? It does not seem likely. This casts some doubt on the economic value of species that might be lost elsewhere (Simon and Wildavsky 1993, p.13).

The relevance of the Ehrlich's rivet removal analogy here is obvious. Simon and Wildavsky appear to be unaware of the role of biodiversity in ecosystem function, seeing species as relevant to human interests only in so far as they are a source of direct inputs to production. Even on this basis, their extrapolation concerning the costs of species extinction is highly dubious if an accelerated rate of species extinction is accepted. It is standard economics that something becomes more valuable as the amount in existence declines. Of course, Simon and Wildavsky do not accept an accelerated rate of extinctions, so they are consistent. It is very difficult to see how the level of human appropriation of NPP reported above could do other than cause population and species extinctions at a rate faster than the normal or background rate. The Simon and Wildavsky position, i.e. no active policy to control the growth of human numbers and the continuing pursuit of material growth, would imply that the long-run trend of human NPP appropriation is upward.

Biologists' prescriptions

Basically, the prescriptions offered by many biologists mean the halting, or reversal, of this trend. Here we explicitly consider just two examples.

Following their analysis of the problem of biodiversity loss, Ehrlich and Dailey (1993) ask what it implies for policy. The answer is habitat preservation. The need for this has long been recognised, but the view has generally been that the required amount of the earth's surface could be a relatively small part of that of interest to humans. This view has underpinned the creation of national parks and reserves, with relatively little attention being paid to developments outside these areas. It followed, in large part, from the view that the objective should be the maintenance of species diversity. An increasing interest in intraspecies genetic diversity, and the switch to populations as the target of conservation, has been associated with an emerging view that biodiversity conservation requires habitat preservation on a larger scale, and that attention cannot be restricted to parks and reserves. The implication is:

> that *no* destruction, including fragmentation, of habitat should be taken lightly, even when there are no species known to be endangered in the area to be destroyed. Populations will inevitably be exterminated when any substantial habitat patch is lost ... (Ehrlich and Dailey 1993, p.67, italics in the original).

The adoption of the policies required to bring about such a state is seen as requiring 'a general change in human attitudes towards population and economic growth and related issues'.

Boyden et al. (1990) spell out their prescription in some detail. Their point of departure is the assessment that:

> something is clearly going seriously wrong with the relationships between human populations and the natural world.

The current relationships cannot persist over time without major damage to the functioning of the biosphere, with major adverse implications for human interests. Hence:

> The urgent task now facing humanity, then, is to design and implement societal changes that will ensure the protection of the ecosystems of the planet at the same time as satisfying the health needs of all sections of the human population.

They identify the essential characteristics of an ecologically sustainable society meeting such needs as three ecological imperatives:

> 1. The size of the human population on earth must be relatively stable (or decreasing).
> 2. The overall technometabolism of human society must be of a kind and intensity that can be indefinitely tolerated by the biosphere without interfering with its capacity to support humanity. This will necessarily mean drastically lower levels of use of fossil fuels as sources of energy than those today ...
> 3. The organisation of society and the economic system must be such that human health and enjoyment of life, and high rates of employment, are not dependent on high or increasing levels of consumption of the products of resource and energy-intensive industry, or on activities that decrease the productivity of ecosystems (Boyden et al. 1990, p.240).

Some of the implications of these ecological imperatives for a sustainable global society are spelled out in energetic terms, with particular reference to the role of fossil fuels in prospective climate change. First, it will be necessary to greatly reduce the human use of extrasomatic energy. Second, at that reduced level, it will be necessary to use a much smaller proportion of fossil fuels and a much larger proportion of the renewable fuels based on solar radiation and wind and wave power. The role of nuclear power is seen as very limited, and non-existent in the long-term, on the grounds of the hazards involved. Hence, an ecologically sustainable global society would need to use fossil fuels at a rate no greater than 40 per cent, and possibly as low as 20 per cent, of the current level of use. The sustainable global average level of per capita use of extrasomatic energy would be 20 Human Energy Equivalents:

> This is about one-fifth of the present North American figure, one-third that of Australia, half that of the UK, slightly more than that of Portugal, four times that of Africa as a whole and twenty times that of Nepal (Boyden et al. 1990, p.242).

Most of this extrasomatic energy would need to come from renewable sources.

Boyden et al. (1990) say a lot more about where we should want to be for ecological sustainability than about how to get there. They concentrate on policy targets, that is, rather than policy instruments. In this they are representative of most biologists. Economists, on the other hand, tend to concern themselves equally with target and instrument questions. The position taken in this book in relation to sustainability is that it cannot be translated at all precisely into statements about targets. Rather, the operationally useful way to proceed is to think about policy instruments to address threats to sustainability.

Science and policy

Well-informed individuals come to quite different positions on sustainability policy. Economists tend to favour the position that no radical departures from current practices are required. Biologists tend to believe that fundamental changes are urgently necessary. How is this difference to be understood? Which position is correct? Is it simply that economists do not properly understand the science, or that biologists do not understand how markets work? There is, no doubt, something in both of these answers, but they do not appear to be the whole explanation. We have previously considered the work of Simon, an economist, and Boyden, a biologist, and can use these to explore the origins of differences on policy. Neither is perfectly representative of their discipline. Perfectly representative economists and biologists do not make their positions on big questions like sustainability explicit.

To summarise, Boyden's position is that the current relationship between humans and the natural environment is not sustainable. If disaster is to be avoided, it is necessary to change human behaviour, particularly in regard to energy use. It is clearly desirable that disaster be avoided, if possible, and that policies be directed at this. The policies are not spelt out in any detail, but it is clear that they involve manipulating the preferences of individuals toward more sustainable lifestyles. While disaster is to be avoided if possible, it would not necessarily entail the end of the human race. The possibility of collapse followed by eventual recovery to a sustainable state is entertained. Collapse is to be avoided because of the human suffering that it would entail.

Simon does not rule out the possibility of future collapses. He sees them, however, as merely temporary interruptions to the long-term trend of human progress and improving individual welfare. While policies to improve the way that market systems manage economy–environment interconnections are not ruled out, policies to manipulate individuals' preferences clearly are. Both think history is important. Simon looks mainly at the economic history of the past couple of hundred years. Boyden looks at the long sweep of human history, from a biological perspective. For Simon, future prospects can be ascertained by the extrapolation of historical trends, unless there is some obvious and compelling reason not to so do. He finds no compelling reason with respect to the generally upward trend in human welfare that he has identified. Simon is not very interested in the material laws of nature. To the extent that they are considered, it is concluded that they can be effectively set aside by human ingenuity, as it is understood that they have been in the past. Boyden is very interested in an understanding of the laws of nature, and sees them as constraints on human activity which cannot be totally circumvented. Boyden does not ignore cultural adaptation. On the contrary, he explains the current situation in cultural terms, given the evolutionary background of the human species.[16]

While both think history is important, they draw rather different implications from it, mainly in relation to the extent to which cultural adaptation can circumvent the laws of nature. However, the differences here are not great in one important sense. Both Simon and Boyden see the prospect of future collapse and recovery. Neither sees the current situation as necessarily entailing the end of the human race. The radically different positions on what should now be done require more explanation than these different appreciations of history, the laws of nature, and their implications.

114 SUSTAINABILITY AND POLICY

The additional explanation is in terms of values, in the sense of views about how alternative states should be ranked, or preferences over those states. Simon is very clear about the role of values in arriving at policy positions. The final and one of the most important chapters in his book is entitled 'Ultimately what are your values?'. His point, that the facts alone cannot indicate what should be done, is developed in the context of policy on population. The following comment makes this general point, albeit in that specific context:

> But it is scientifically wrong – outrageously wrong – to say that 'science shows' that there is overpopulation (or underpopulation) in any given place at any given time. Science can only reveal the likely *effects* of various population levels and policies. Whether population is now too large or too small, or is growing too fast or too slowly, cannot be decided on scientific grounds alone. Such judgements depend on our values, a matter about which science is silent (Simon 1981, p.332, italics in the original).

To come to a view about what should be done, one needs both an appreciation of the possibilities, and a set of preferences for choosing between those possibilities. Boyden and Simon appear to use different values. While Simon is explicit about his value system, Boyden is not.

The value system which takes Simon to the position that there is no need for policies to induce radical changes involves two elements. First, it is utilitarian in that it holds that the more people there are in existence and the higher the average welfare of each such individual, the better. Second, that individuals are the best judges of their own welfare – what they want is what is good for them.

Boyden's implicit value system appears also to be essentially utilitarian. Otherwise it is difficult to see why policies should be advocated to prolong as much as possible the existence of the human species. However, Boyden rejects consumer sovereignty, taking the view that there are criteria according to which individual human welfare can be assessed, which are independent of the preferences of the individual concerned.

To summarise, the real difference between Simon and Boyden appears to come down to this. For Simon, it is entirely possible that at some point in the future there will be 20 billion humans living underground on a biologically dead planet, but all will be happy according to their own evaluations. This would represent another point in the ongoing story of human progress. According to Boyden, while unlikely, this is possible, but would represent disaster, and policies to avoid such an outcome are called for. There is no purely scientific basis on which to decide between these alternative positions on policy. They largely reflect different value systems. This is one of the reasons why thinking about sustainability issues is so difficult. The positions that individuals take involve an appreciation of future possibilities and a value system.

Debate on sustainability issues would be more productive if this were more generally recognised, and participants made their values explicit. Having said this, it is incumbent on me to do that. I reject consumer sovereignty as the ultimate test of alternative social states. This is not to say that what individuals want should be totally disregarded. It is clear that in modern circumstances any social system that tried to ignore individuals' preferences would not be viable. However, it is equally clear that individuals' preferences are, in large part, socially determined. In that case, those preferences cannot provide an independent criterion for ranking social arrangements. I do not have a simple alternative to offer. I do not think that there is one. Policies to address threats to sustainability have to be evaluated against many criteria.

CHAPTER 6

Economics

Economics can be defined as:

> the study of how people make their living, how they acquire the food, shelter, clothing, and other material necessities and comforts of this world. It is a study of the problems they encounter, and of the ways in which these problems can be reduced (Wonnacott and Wonnacott 1979).

Some aspects of this have been discussed in previous chapters. Here we are concerned with the way economics is taught in the English speaking world to university students. The objective is to briefly describe the framework in which economists operate. We focus on those issues which economists would see as most important in the debate about sustainability.

A brief history of economics[1]

The history of economics is often taken to begin in 1776, with the publication of *The wealth of nations* (Smith 1776). Adam Smith is now famous mainly for his enunciation of the doctrine of **the invisible hand**. Smith argued that in a system of competitive markets, selfish individual behaviour could serve the interests of society as a whole. This was a profound insight. However, Smith indicated clearly that the invisible hand could not cope with all economic problems, and wrote about many other topics in economics. Smith (1723–90) contributed to what is now known as **classical economics**, which was largely concerned with the prospects for long-run economic growth in the light of the necessarily limited amounts of good quality agricultural land. The conclusion was that economic growth had to be seen as an essentially transitory phenomenon. Because of this, economics became known as the dismal

science. In modern terminology, the classical economists saw environmental limits to growth.

The basis for this was acceptance of the **law of diminishing returns** in
agriculture, such that, beyond a certain point, as successively larger
amounts of labour are applied to a fixed amount of land, so output per
worker falls. Hence, beyond a certain point population growth implies
falling living standards. This, in turn, leads to the cessation of population growth. The long-run tendency must then be for the economy to
exist in a **stationary state**, i.e. a state of constant population size, with the
majority of the population enjoying only the material standard of living
consistent with subsistence. For the classical economists, the economy
was 'inevitably on its way to a rendezvous with poverty for most people'
(Samuelson and Nordhaus 1985).

As has been widely noted, for most of the economies of western
Europe in the nineteenth century, this prediction turned out to be incorrect. Population grew and material living standards improved. With
hindsight, the explanation for the classical error is simple: the classical
economists 'bet on the wrong horse of diminishing returns, just when
the technological advances of the industrial revolution were outpacing
that law' (Samuelson and Nordhaus 1985). Technology was effectively
augmenting the amount of land made available by nature. As a result of
migration and colonisation, the economies of western Europe experienced an expanding, as opposed to fixed, amount of available land. The
use of fossil fuels in transport made the new land overseas more
effectively available for agricultural and raw materials production for the
western European economies. Also, in those economies themselves, this
made available for agricultural production land which had formerly
been required to provide 'fuel', i.e. to grow feed, for the animals used in
transport and agricultural production.[2]

The role of technical progress was explicitly recognised by John Stuart
Mill (1806–73). Mill took the law of diminishing returns to be 'the most
important proposition in political economy', but noted explicitly that it
held 'for a given state of agricultural skill and knowledge'.[3] Mill took the
view that 'economic progress must be conceived as a race between technical change and diminishing returns in agriculture', noting that 'since
the 1820s, technical change has outstripped the forces making for rising
wheat prices' so that 'the standard of living has risen'. As compared with
the other classical economists, Mill was somewhat less dismal, for two
reasons. First, he envisaged that the cessation of growth could be much
delayed. The economy must eventually arrive at the stationary state, but
the date of arrival could be well into the future, and the level of material living standards involved could be higher than that applying (in
England) at the time that he wrote. Second, Mill considered that

economic growth involved costs as well as benefits. Indeed, he took the unrepresentative view that for the then advanced countries (such as England), economic growth had already reached a point such that further growth was less important than the better distribution of the existing level of output. This view was, in large part, based on an appreciation of the impact of economic growth on the amenity services provided by the natural environment.

The classical economists were not solely concerned with the question of environmental limits to growth. Another major, and closely related, concern was the distribution of income and wealth within society. Also, they sought to explain the determination of the relative prices of com- modities. Their explanation was in terms of the **labour theory of value**. This involved two parts. First, that prices were determined by the costs of supply. Second, that all production costs were ultimately labour costs. Marx (1818–83) adopted the labour theory of value, and in so far as he was an economist, he was a classical economist.

Marxist economics never abandoned the labour theory of value. Main- stream economics did, and in the process evolved from classical into **neoclassical economics**. This process of evolution began in the 1870s, and was substantially complete by the first decade of the twentieth century. By then it was generally accepted that prices were determined jointly by supply and demand. Whereas classical economics had focused exclusively on supply and costs of production, neoclassical economics introduced the study of the determinants of the demands for com- modities. This involved the analysis of consumers' preferences between commodities using the apparatus of utility theory. The question of price determination came to dominate the agenda of economics. While the question of economic growth did not entirely vanish from the agenda, it occupied a much less important place on it. The central question shifted from 'will economic progress continue?' to 'why do we observe the exist- ing pattern of economic activity?'. The role of the natural environment in relation to economic activity almost entirely disappeared from the agenda for economic inquiry.

The study of the determination of relative prices is variously known as the **theory of value**, **price theory**, or **microeconomics**. The last of these emerged to distinguish the subject matter from that of **macroeconomics**, generally taken to have been created by J. M. Keynes (1883–1946) in the 1930s. Prior to this, mainstream economics took it that there were no economic problems which were not appropriately analysed within the supply and demand framework developed for the explanation of relative prices. Keynes challenged this, arguing that some problems were appro- priately analysed using a framework that employed broad economic aggregates rather than focusing on individual markets. 'Micro' means small, 'macro' means large. Keynes argued that not all of the economic problems of concern could usefully be studied with the techniques developed for the 'small'. To this extent at least, the so-called Keynesian revolution was successful on a permanent basis. Standard economics programmes now involve courses in macro as well as microeconomics.

The problem with which Keynes was concerned was **economic stabilisation**. Economies which had experienced the industrial revolution showed a basic tendency to grow. However, they were also subject to variations about a long-run growth trend, known as **trade cycles** with periods of rapid expansion alternating with periods of slower, zero, or negative growth. In other words booms alternated with slumps. Some slumps were severe and prolonged, and involved persistent mass unemployment. In the period following World War I mass unemployment persisted in most industrial economies for over a decade. In *The general theory of employment, interest and money* (Keynes 1936), Keynes argued that the unemployment problem required new methods of analysis for its solution. Those methods were subsequently applied to the problem of inflation, and to the analysis of economic growth. **Growth theory** regained a prominent place on the economics agenda in the 1950s and 1960s. Inquiry then took a very different form from that which had characterised the classical period. There was no role for the natural environment, and the question of whether growth must eventually cease was not addressed.

By the 1970s a standard university economics degree programme would involve basic level courses in microeconomics and macroeconomics, together with some mathematics and statistics, followed by more specialised higher level courses within those areas. In the industrial economies after World War II the government, or public, sector typically grew in relative importance. As a result, courses in public sector economics came to be taught, drawing upon both microeconomics and macroeconomics.

As of 1970, very few economics degree programmes offered courses dealing specifically with the natural environment in relation to economic activity, although some aspects of the matter might have been dealt with somewhat incidentally in microeconomics and public sector economics courses. In the 1970s this situation began to change. Some economics degree programmes introduced courses on environmental and resource economics, as specialised higher level optional courses. Currently, the natural environment could largely escape the notice of most economics students, at least in so far as their formal economics education is concerned. It would be rare for the basic compulsory courses to consider the natural environment, other than as providing an example to illustrate some general issue.

Microeconomics

Microeconomics is concerned with the way that markets determine prices and quantities. Figure 6.1 shows the essentials of the standard demand and supply analysis of market functioning, where p, measured on the vertical axis, stands for the price of some commodity, and x, on the horizontal axis, for quantity. The **demand function** $D_m D_m$ slopes downwards from left to right, reflecting the assumption that, other things constant, individuals will wish to buy more of the commodity as its price falls. Given the crucial 'other things constant', this is a very plausible assumption, consistent with introspection, and confirmed, for most commodities, by everyday experience as well as systematic empirical research. The **supply function** $S_m S_m$ slopes upwards from left to right, reflecting the assumption that, other things constant, sellers will wish to

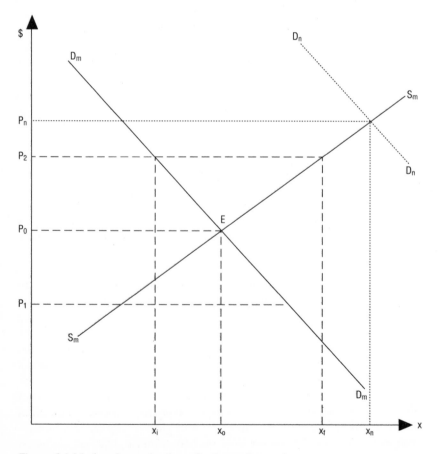

Figure 6.1 Market determination of price and quantity.

sell more the higher the price per unit. Again, given the condition 'other things constant', this is a very plausible assumption.

D_mD_m and S_mS_m intersect at E, determining the market clearing, or **market equilibrium**, price at p_0 and quantity at x_0. At the price p_0 sellers wish to sell the amount x_0, which is the amount that purchasers wish to purchase at that price. At x_0, the plans of buyers and sellers are mutually consistent, and it is in this sense that the market is in equilibrium. Consider, by contrast, the price p_2. At that price purchasers would wish to buy the amount x_i while sellers would wish to sell the amount x_f, and there would be a condition of excess supply. Conversely, at the price p_1 there would be a condition of excess demand.

The demand and supply functions are drawn to represent assumptions about the responses of buying and selling intentions as price, and nothing else, varies. If the level of some other relevant variable changes, then the function in question shifts. In the case of demand, one would generally expect that planned purchases would depend upon individuals' incomes, such that for a given price they would wish to buy more the higher their incomes. In Figure 6.1, D_nD_n is the new demand function consequent upon an increase in incomes. The shift from D_mD_m to D_nD_n means an increase in the market equilibrium price and quantity. One would expect the supply function to shift with changes in the structure of the costs of production. If the price of some input to production increased, increasing costs at all levels of production, then the supply function would shift upwards thereby increasing the equilibrium price and decreasing the equilibrium quantity.

Demand analysis

The demand for a commodity depends mainly on its price and the incomes of buyers. The **price elasticity of demand** for a commodity is the ratio of the proportional change in the quantity demanded to the proportional change in the price of the commodity. The **income elasticity of demand** is the ratio of the proportional change in demand to the proportional change in income. Given that the quantity of a commodity demanded falls with an increase in its price, the price elasticity is negative. Generally, we would expect quantity demanded to increase with income, giving a positive income elasticity. Commodities for which the income elasticity is greater than unity, so that as income grows demand increases more than proportionately, are called luxuries. Commodities for which the income elasticity is less than unity are known as necessities. In terms of price elasticity, a commodity for which this takes a value greater than unity – so that demand increases in greater proportion than price falls – is referred to as having an elastic demand, whereas demand is said to be inelastic if the price elasticity is less than unity.

The analysis of demand also covers the use of inputs to production by firms. One would expect the demand for an input to decrease/increase as its price increases/decreases. One would expect a firm's demand for an input to move in the same direction as the level of output produced by the firm. The concept of price elasticity can be used in connection with the demand for inputs to production. The concept of output elasticity for input demand corresponds to income elasticity in the case of consumer demand.

Figure 6.2 shows the history of the use of energy in the United Kingdom over the period 1968 to 1989.[4] It relates to both household demand and the demands of productive enterprises. This history can usefully be considered in terms of the influences on energy demand of its price, and of national income as an indicator of household incomes and the level of production. First, look at energy use per unit of national income. As shown in Figure 6.3, this declined over the period. Also shown in Figure 6.3 is the history of the price of energy in the United Kingdom. It increases from 1973 to 1985 and then declines somewhat.[5] If we use statistical techniques to estimate the price elasticity from this data, the result is − 0.24. Energy exhibits an inelastic demand.

The income elasticity of demand estimated from the same data is 0.22. This is positive in line with the economic presumption, and classifies energy as a necessity. The finding is that for this period in the United Kingdom, in terms of the influences of price and income, the demand for energy behaves as economics predicts. This finding would be replicated in the data for the same period for most industrial economies. Making energy more expensive does induce people to use less of

Figure 6.2 United Kingdom energy use.

it, other things being equal. The finding that energy has low price and income elasticities is also fairly standard across industrial economies. Price exerts less influence on energy demand than is the case with many other commodities.

To illustrate the role of price in the evolution of energy demand in the United Kingdom over this period, and to show the usefulness of the

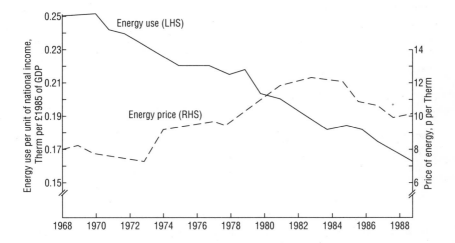

Figure 6.3 Energy price and use per unit of income.

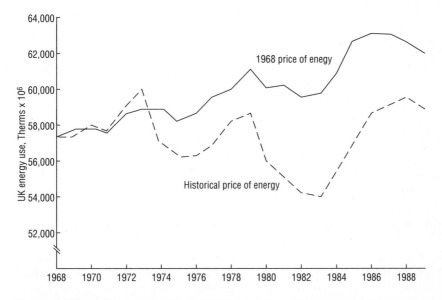

Figure 6.4 The effect of price on energy use.

empirical analysis of price and income elasticities, Figure 6.4 shows two histories. The dashed line, labelled 'Historical price of energy', shows how energy demand would have moved if it were driven by the estimated elasticities for price and income reported above, and actual price and income levels. The solid line, labelled '1968 price of energy', shows how it would have moved if driven by the estimated price and income elasticities and by the actual history of income, but with the price of energy constant at its 1968 level. The general upward trend of the price of energy over the period worked to reduce energy demand below what it would otherwise have been. This is representative of what many empirical demand analyses show – other things being equal – a higher price reduces demand.

Markets efficiency and equity

Supply and demand analysis is how modern microeconomics explains the determination of prices and quantities in a market economy. However, microeconomics is not just an explanation of how markets work, but also involves the idea that the outcomes produced are in some sense desirable. The core of neoclassical microeconomics is the modern version of Adam Smith's invisible hand story, stated as the **two fundamental theorems of welfare economics.**[6]

The two theorems are proofs that:

1. Given certain conditions, if a general competitive market equilibrium exists, it corresponds to an efficient allocation.
2. Given certain conditions, any efficient allocation can be realised as a general competitive market equilibrium with the appropriate set of lump sum taxes and transfers between individuals.

An **efficient allocation** is also known as a **Pareto efficient allocation**, and a **Pareto optimal allocation**: the state corresponding to an efficient allocation is sometimes referred to as **allocative efficiency**, or described as **allocatively efficient**. The meaning of the two theorems is as follows. A society faces the problem of allocating scarce means of production between competing ends. Given certain conditions, rational and selfish individual behaviour in markets will solve the problem in the sense that means will be allocated to ends – there will be a complete set of market equilibria determining the quantities produced, the prices at which trade takes place, and the distribution of output across individuals. Further, the outcome so determined will be socially desirable in the sense of being allocatively efficient. In such a state it is not possible to make one individual better off by her own assessment without making some other individual(s) worse off by her (their) own assessment(s). The market outcome will not necessarily be socially desirable in regard to justice or equity between individuals. However, to the extent that the outcome of market forces is judged to be inequitable, it can be made equitable by redistributing wealth between individuals, by lump sum taxes and transfers, prior to letting market forces determine the allocation conditional on the distribution of wealth.

Two important points should be noted. First, the theorems are exercises in deductive logic. Errors of logic aside, they are true in the sense that given the premises the conclusions hold. There are no errors of logic; the proofs of the theorems have been checked by numerous economists. The relevance of the theorems to the world that we live in depends on the extent to which the premises, the 'certain conditions' of 1 and 2, describe that world. Hence, the nature of the theorems as propositions about the way markets actually operate can be best understood by regarding them as statements about what it is necessary to believe in order to believe in the invisible hand. If one wishes to assert, that is, that everything can be left to markets and that outcomes will then be socially desirable, then the theorems spell out what one must believe about the conditions in which markets operate. They also give a precise definition of what 'socially desirable' means.

The second point is that according to the two theorems, two dimensions of the economic problem are separable. These are the problem of efficiency in allocation, and the problem of equity. The theorems say, in effect, that society can take a view on equity and achieve that view by redistributive taxes and transfers, then let markets achieve efficiency in allocation. Put the other way round, the theorems say that there is no case for interfering with markets on equity grounds: equity concerns can be separately and independently addressed by taxes and transfers. Now, what the proofs make clear is that this is true only given certain conditions, which include conditions on taxes and transfers to be discussed below. Most economists approach practical policy analysis on the basis of a presumption that the problems of allocation and equity can be dealt with independently.

Now consider the concept of efficiency in allocation, and its relationship to concepts of equity. To repeat, a state of allocative efficiency applies when it is not possible to make one individual better off except at the cost of making some other individual(s) worse off. This definition makes no reference to how well off the individuals involved are. Allocative efficiency is consistent with massive inequality.

To see what is involved here, consider a very simple hypothetical example. Two individuals, A and B, are shipwrecked and find themselves on an uninhabited island which has a supply of drinkable water, but on which there is absolutely no edible food. However, washed up with the two individuals is a supply of canned food together with a can opener. All initial allocations of the food supply are efficient, including the allocation in which A, or B, gets none. Given any initial allocation, there is no change to it which makes A/B better off except at the cost of making B/A worse off. Clearly, there is no necessary connection between efficiency and equity. This example also makes it clear that the efficiency criterion does not itself fix a unique allocation.

The two fundamental theorems say that, in the interests of justice and equity, lump sum taxes and transfers can be used to shift the economy from one allocatively efficient general market equilibrium to another. This can be illustrated using the market analysis used in Figure 6.1. Recall that the market demand and supply schedules are constructed for given production costs and given individual incomes. Suppose that there are two classes of individual, the rich and the poor, and that the commodity for which Figure 6.1 is drawn is bread, which the poor eat more of than the rich. Initially there is a distribution of income between the rich and the poor such as to give the demand function D_mD_m. This initial situation corresponds to efficiency in allocation. Now suppose that lump sum taxation of the rich is used to provide lump sum payments to the poor. Then the market demand schedule will shift up and to the right to a position such as that of D_nD_n. The market equilibrium price and quantity for bread increase to p_n and x_n respectively, and there will be adjustments in all other markets. The new economy-wide equilibrium is also an efficient allocation. The poor's bread consumption will now be higher and they are better off. If the new outcome is equitable, the initial situation was not equitable, notwithstanding being efficient.

An intuitive understanding of the idea of the efficiency property of competitive markets is as follows. What goes on in markets is voluntary exchange. Think of this in the case of two individuals who meet, each in the possession of different bundles of goods. They swap items from their bundles until there are no further exchanges that each sees as beneficial. Then, considering just these two individuals and the collection of items that they jointly hold, the allocation of that collection at the end of the swapping is efficient in the sense that if somebody came along and enforced a further swap, one individual would feel better off but the other worse off, whereas prior to the enforced swap both felt better off than they did with their initial bundles. The attainment of efficiency is the exhaustion of the possibilities for mutually beneficial voluntary exchange. Clearly, if one individual's initial bundle were much larger than the other's, we would not necessarily want to say that matters were equitable at the end of the voluntary trade process.

Conditions for efficiency: market failure

We now consider the 'certain conditions' referred to in stating the two fundamental theorems. These are the conditions under which a **competitive general equilibrium** (i.e. a situation where all markets clear at E

as in Figure 6.1) corresponds to efficiency in allocation. There are four basic conditions required for it to be the case that a competitive general equilibrium is allocatively efficient. Briefly, they are:
1. The rationality condition.
2. The price-taker condition.
3. The complete information condition.
4. The complete set of markets condition.

Before discussing these, two points should be noted. First, we assume here that the conditions for the existence of a competitive general equilibrium are satisfied. The question at issue is whether it can be taken that such an equilibrium has socially desirable properties. Second, the socially desirable property considered is that of allocative efficiency.

The **rationality condition** is satisfied when all **economic agents**, that is individuals in their roles as consumers of commodities, as workers and as the individuals responsible for the decisions taken by firms, do the best for themselves that they can in the circumstances that they face. Consumers maximise their utility, firms maximise their profits. The assumption that economic agents are rational is so deeply embedded in the way that economists think that this condition is frequently not explicitly mentioned in discussions of the relevance of the theory of welfare economics to policy analysis. Economics has been defined as the analysis of rational choice. When the assumption is discussed, it is typically defended on the basis that any alternative assumption would make analysis impossible. The **price-taker condition** is satisfied when all participants in market transactions act on the belief that they are unable to influence the terms on which transactions take place. Agents treat prices parametrically, that is, adjusting their behaviour to existing prices taken as given and fixed with respect to any possible action on their own part. In many introductory textbooks this condition is referred to as a large numbers condition, or the requirement that perfect, or sometimes pure, competition exists. **Pure competition** is where the numbers on both sides of the market are so large that no individual or firm can influence the market price. Some authors call this perfect competition, others take **perfect competition** to also involve the complete information condition discussed below.

In the case of **monopoly**, one firm supplies the whole of the market, and will realise that it can influence price by varying the quantity that it puts onto the market. Then the argument that makes the market equilibrium correspond with allocative efficiency breaks down because the supply function no longer properly reflects the costs to society of this commodity in terms of the alternatives foregone. The monopolist's supply function overstates those costs. This is essentially the case with any departure from price-taking behaviour on the part of sellers.

The **complete information condition** is satisfied when all agents know the prices ruling in all markets, and are fully aware of the implications for themselves of actually making any prospective market exchange. Recall that an allocation is efficient when it is not possible to make any individual better off except, given existing resources and technologies, by making some other individual(s) worse off, where 'better off' and 'worse off' are evaluated according to the preferences of the affected individuals. The efficiency criterion for judging alternative allocations is based on acceptance of consumer sovereignty. The job of the economy is seen as being to deliver what individuals want, to the extent that is possible given available resources and technologies. Clearly, the outcomes of market transactions can only be consistent with this if individuals know all of the opportunities open to them in terms of prices, and if they know what the consequences for themselves of taking up any of those opportunities will be.

Microeconomics takes individuals' preferences as given in two related senses. First, inquiry into the origin and determination of preferences is not part of the subject. Second, the given preferences are treated equally whatever their nature.[7] If people have a strong preference for commodities that might reasonably be regarded as frivolous luxuries, the market will provide lots of those commodities. This is what consumer sovereignty requires. As a criterion for economic performance, it looses much of its appeal unless one is prepared to believe that individuals know what is good for them. Similarly, market systems depend for their appeal on the assumption that they send accurate signals to individuals about relative social scarcities.

The **complete markets condition** requires that there exists a market in anything that is of interest to anybody. All of the inputs to production and all of the items over which consumers have preferences must be traded (by price-takers) in markets. This condition, in turn, implies another. Anything that it is of interest to anybody needs to be subject to enforceable individual private property rights. Such rights are a necessary precondition to market exchange – one can only sell (legally) what one owns. This is a very strong condition.

There are two cases of its breakdown usually distinguished in the literature. These are externalities and public goods. An **externality**, or **external effect**, exists when the activities of a firm or individual give rise to unintended effects on other firms or individuals and these effects do not figure in the costs and benefits associated with the activity of the firm or individual responsible for it. The reason the costs or benefits are not perceived by the responsible firm or individual is the absence of private property rights. A standard example of an externality is the release by a firm of wastes giving rise to atmospheric pollution. The release involves no costs to the firm since nobody owns the atmosphere, so that the firm cannot be charged for its use.

A **public good** is something that is non-rival and non-excludable in use. Things which are rival and excludable in use are called private goods. Many things are rival and excludable in use in the sense that if one individual or firm is to increase its use this involves denying that incremental use to some other potential user. Consider ice-creams or beer as examples of private goods. The market can handle these because exclusive use rights can be defined and traded. When I buy a beer, or an ice-cream, consumption of it is denied to anybody else (unless I make a gift of it, but this merely transfers the exclusive and rival use right). Such private goods are rival and excludable in use, and hence ownership in particular units can be defined and enforced. Standard examples of public goods are the services of defence forces, and the services of the judicial system. In neither case can individuals be excluded from enjoyment of the services provided. In neither case is one individual's enjoyment of those services rival to other individuals' enjoyment of those services. The services provided by many environmental assets have the characteristics of public goods.

Whereas the allocatively efficient provision of produced public goods such as defence and judicial systems is definitely not zero, the level of supply from profit maximising firms would be zero. This follows directly from their non-rival and non-excludable nature. If a public good is supplied at all, it is supplied in equal amounts to all. If individual A pays for the production for her of some public good, provision is also made to all other individuals without them paying the supplier anything. The other individuals can 'free ride' on A's payment. But A could free ride on some other individual's payment if that were forthcoming. Given non-rivalry and non-excludability in use, every potential user has an incentive to wait and let some other individual make the payment that will lead to the good being produced and supplied to all. No potential user will offer the payment to induce production and by virtue of the **free rider problem** the market provision of a public good will be zero. While the services that environmental assets provide do not need to be produced, where they are non-excludable and non-rival, problems arise in so far as they cannot be made subject to private property rights. This means that their use cannot be controlled by markets to give outcomes consistent with allocative efficiency.

No economist would claim that the conditions under which the results of the two fundamental theorems hold are completely satisfied in reality. By identifying the conditions under which the invisible hand works, they identify sources of **market failure**. Markets fail when they do not produce allocatively efficient outcomes. These are seen as desirable outcomes. To aim for a state which does not have the property of allocative efficiency would, it is argued, be foolish because in such a state it would be possible to rearrange affairs so as to make one individual better off without making anybody else worse off. Then, one role for government intervention in the operation of actual markets is to correct market failure so as to facilitate the attainment of allocative efficiency. Identification of the sources of market failure is a way of setting an agenda for policy.

Macroeconomics[8]

Whereas microeconomics is concerned mainly with the pattern of economic activity, macroeconomics is concerned mainly with the level of economic activity. The long-run trend of the level is the focus of inquiry into economic growth. Short-run variations about the trend give rise to an interest in stabilisation policy.

Economic stabilisation

Macroeconomics was invented as a response to the problem of mass unemployment in industrial economies in the period after World War I. At that time, inflation was not seen as a major problem. In the period after World War II the industrial economies did not, as some had anticipated, experience prolonged mass unemployment. For many of them, however, inflation was seen as a problem. In the 1970s many of these economies began to simultaneously experience persistent high unemployment and relatively high rates of inflation. This prompted some new thinking about the nature of macroeconomic problems, and some new policy directions.

Starting with unemployment, there are two questions. Why does it matter? Why does it occur? There are four reasons why large-scale unemployment is seen as a problem. First, it involves a waste of productive resources. Second, the unemployed suffer loss of income. Third, it causes suffering, additional to any material hardship due to income loss, to the unemployed by virtue of their feelings of alienation from mainstream society. This concern has a curious status in economics. While recognised in practice, in the core theory of economics it is a fundamental assumption that individuals require compensation for using their time to work rather than as leisure, getting no satisfaction from work *per se*. Fourth, to the extent that welfare payments prevent unemployment from causing serious material hardship, unemployment is costly in terms of public expenditure.

Prior to the **Keynesian revolution**, economists thought about unemployment in terms of an analysis which treated the labour market much as any other market. Unemployment was seen as being the consequence of a situation in which the supply of labour exceeded the demand for it. This arose because the wage rate was too high. According to the standard analysis of markets, a situation of excess supply should result in the price of the commodity in question moving down, so increasing demand, and reducing supply. The price would stabilise at the level which made demand and supply equal, so that the market cleared. In the case of the market for labour, the argument went, a persistent excess of supply over demand, unemployment, was due to the fact that the wage rate did not move down as required. Workers resisted wage cuts, and this caused unemployment. The generally advocated solution followed directly from this analysis. It was to get rid of the 'stickiness' in the wage rate and allow it to fall to its market clearing rate. Figure 6.1 (see p. 120) illustrates this idea if the horizontal axis refers to the quantity of labour and the vertical axis, the wage rate. At the wage rate p_2, labour offered is x_f and labour demanded is x_i, so that unemployment is $x_i x_f$. If the wage rate is reduced to p_o, the demand for and supply of labour are equal, and there is no unemployment.

Keynes challenged such prescriptions on the grounds that the labour market had characteristics which meant that standard market analysis did not apply. He argued that the wage reduction prescription overlooked a feedback connection between wages and the demand for labour. Wages comprise something of the order of 70 per cent of total incomes in an industrial economy. A reduction in wages therefore would have a significant effect on total incomes, and thus reduce total spending on consumption in the economy. Of the order of 90 per cent of wage income is typically spent on consumption. Since firms only hire labour in order to produce goods that can be sold, a reduction in the total amount of goods sold would reduce the demand for labour at every level of the wage rate. In individual commodity markets this kind of feedback is so weak that it can be ignored: cutting the price of widgets affects the incomes of widget firms and their employees, and this in turn has some effect on the demand for widgets, but the effect is very small. But, in the case of the market for labour for the whole economy, the equivalent feedback effect cannot be ignored. It means that a policy which seeks to cure unemployment by wage-cutting will not work, since the employment-enhancing effects of lower wage costs are offset by the effects of lower sales and production.

Macroeconomics looks at the economy as a whole in terms of broad aggregate components, and can thus allow for the sort of feedback effect described above. The invention of macroeconomics was Keynes' first major achievement. The second was to gain acceptance for the idea that governments in industrial nations could, and should, so manage the economy as to keep it, for most of the time, in a situation where the level of unemployment was low. Previously full employment was seen by economists simply as being the level of employment that went with a labour market where the wage rate moved so as to equate the supply and demand for labour. Full employment, on this view, did not correspond to any particular proportion of the potential labour force in work. In terms of Figure 6.1, on this view x_0 would represent full employment whether it corresponded to two or 10 per cent of potential workers unemployed.

The initial effect of the Keynesian revolution was to replace this with the idea that there was some proportion of the labour force unemployed that should be regarded as full employment. This proportion was not zero, on account of workers unemployed while moving between jobs. Further, the idea was that the economy could be so managed by the government that it would for most of the time achieve this full employment target without experiencing inflation. **Inflation** is a condition where prices and wages are generally rising. For Keynesian economists, unemployment in excess of that due to workers changing jobs was due to a deficiency of the total, or aggregate, demand for goods and services in the economy, while inflation was due to an excess of such demand. The job of the government was to manage the aggregate demand for goods and services so as to maintain full employment and avoid inflation. This came to be known as **fine-tuning** the economy. It was to be achieved by using monetary and fiscal policy to control the level of aggregate demand, and hence the demand for labour. From a situation of excessive unemployment, the economy would be stimulated by either, or both, of two policy instruments. **Monetary policy** would involve increasing the amount of money in circulation, to encourage spending by firms and individuals. **Fiscal policy** would involve altering the government's budgetary stance so as to inject spending into the economy, by increasing government expenditure and/or reducing taxes. With inflation occurring, the levers of monetary and fiscal policy would be moved in the opposite directions.

In many industrial nations, Keynesian macroeconomics and fine-tuning fell out of favour in the 1980s. There were a variety of causes involved. One was a perception that fine-tuning, in practice, resulted in a long-run tendency to persistent inflation. For most industrial economies, the period from about 1950 to the early 1970s was characterised by historically low levels of unemployment. But, it was also characterised by fairly steadily rising prices and wages.

Inflation is regarded as a problem for a variety of reasons. It makes those with income and/or wealth fixed in money terms worse off. If the general price level is rising at 5 per cent per year, the purchasing power of a currency unit is falling at 5 per cent per year. At this rate of inflation $100 in the bank looses half of its value within 14 years. This leads firms and individuals to engage in activities to protect their positions, diverting them from productive activities. It favours borrowers against lenders, since debts are usually denominated in fixed amounts of currency units. This tends to discourage saving, which then, as discussed below, raises interest rates and reduces economic growth. In practice not all prices and wages rise at the same rate, so that relative prices and wages change, sending firms and individuals distorted signals. This interferes with the ability of the market system to achieve efficiency in allocation.

Inflation adversely affects the nation's external trading situation, unless its trading partners are experiencing equal, or greater, rates of inflation. If the rates at which domestic currency exchanges for foreign currency are fixed, as they generally were until the mid-1970s, domestic inflation greater than that abroad reduces international competitiveness. The prices of exported goods rise in overseas markets, and in the domestic market domestically produced goods increase in price relative to imported goods. A deficit on the trade account is the result. In the mid-1970s many of the industrial economies abandoned **fixed exchange rates**, and let the values of their currencies be determined by market forces. In these circumstances the loss of competitiveness due to a high rate of inflation is avoided, as the domestic exchange rate falls to keep the relative prices of domestic and foreign goods constant. However, while **flexible exchange rates** can mitigate the balance of trade effects of a relatively high rate of inflation, they do so at the cost of transforming it into a terms of trade problem. A falling, or depreciating, exchange rate means that it is necessary to sell a larger volume of exports overseas in order to obtain a given quantity of imports, so that domestic consumption gets squeezed.

The view that more weight should be given to the objective of maintaining a low, ideally zero, inflation rate gained ground in many industrial economies. This was closely associated with the view that fine-tuning should be abandoned in favour of keeping monetary and fiscal policy constant over time. This it was argued, with low inflation, would produce a stable economic environment for firms and individuals, which would, in turn, mean efficiency in allocation, enhanced international competitiveness, and faster growth. In many industrial nations unemployment rose in the 1980s, reaching levels unprecedented in the period since World War II, and comparable to those of the 1930s. There was, and is, dispute over the exact causes of this. But there can be little doubt that one factor involved was the lower weight given to the objective of low unemployment as compared with the objective of low inflation.

Some commentators now take the view that unemployment should not be regarded as a problem for stabilisation policy, arguing that attempting to reduce unemployment by stimulating aggregate demand merely causes inflation. There are then two basic strategies for reducing unemployment. The first involves treating it as a microeconomic problem, and adopting policies to improve the functioning of the labour market. These would include: making unemployment a less attractive option for workers by reducing unemployment benefits; reducing the power of organised labour; and reducing the costs of employing workers. The second involves treating it as a long-term macroeconomic problem, to be addressed by achieving economic growth, which, by increasing total output, increases the demand for labour. These are not mutually exclusive strategies. On the contrary, they are generally seen as mutually reinforcing in so far as labour market reform is considered to be a prerequisite for faster growth.

Economic growth

In modern thinking about economic growth the central idea is that capital accumulation is productive, in the sense that foregoing a unit of consumption now in order to increase the size of the stock of capital equipment results in the availability of more than one extra unit of future consumption. The basic idea can be initially explained in terms of a story about Robinson Crusoe. Robinson is shipwrecked on the island with no tools. Suppose that he can work 12 hours per day. With no tools this is sufficient for him to gather an adequate but uninteresting diet of plant food. Robinson first works 12 hours a day entirely on food gathering. But, he becomes dissatisfied with his diet, and decides to spend one hour per day making a fishing line and hook. It takes seven hours of work to make the fishing equipment. So for one week Robinson eats a little less. But he is then able to go back to spending 12 hours per day on food acquisition, which now yields an improved diet. In fact, it then turns out that only 10 hours per day yields an adequate and varied diet. Robinson takes two hours leisure per day. But, then he realises that if he had an axe, he could build a shelter. So, for a few weeks he forgoes two hours leisure per day to make a stone axe. With the axe he finds that his plant-gathering productivity is improved. And so on and so on.

Robinson Crusoe experiences economic growth: he produces and consumes more and/or uses less effort, as the result of capital accumulation. However, note that the benefits arising do not come free. This sort of growth involves 'paying' now, by using some effort for investment rather than consumption, to benefit from extra consumption, including the consumption of leisure, in the future. Economists generally assume that individuals prefer consumption now to consumption in the future, other things equal. Thus, offered a choice between an apple today and the certain promise of an apple a year from now, an individual would opt for the apple today. There are, then, two opposing forces at work. On the one hand there is the productivity of investment in capital equipment, on the other there is impatience for consumption. The determination of the amount of investment, and hence the rate of growth, is the outcome of the interaction between these two opposing forces. Had Robinson Crusoe been very impatient, he might not have invested in fishing equipment. Had the fishing equipment not been very productive, he might not have been able to make an axe.

Economists see production as involving the use of inputs of capital and labour. The productivity of labour is seen as increasing with the amount of capital. However, the accumulation of capital requires that consumption is foregone. Foregone consumption is referred to both as **investment** and as **saving**. The former term is used for the increase in the size of the capital stock, the latter for the foregone consumption. Saving as foregone consumption involves sacrifice now. The consumption benefit from current investment occurs in the future.

Savings, investment and the interest rate

In discussing microeconomics we made the distinction between allocative efficiency and equity, or distributive justice. A similar distinction arises here. It is very important in relation to consideration of sustainability issues, and a lack of clarity about it frequently gives rise to confusion. This arises in, for example, debate over the practice of discounting in cost-benefit analysis, to be discussed in the next chapter, and in Chapter 10 in relation to consideration of what should be done about the enhanced greenhouse effect.

The following discussion is aimed at sorting out this confusion. It abstracts from many complexities and difficulties, in order to focus on the essentials of the economists' way of thinking about intertemporal issues.

Comparisons of current sacrifice and future gain must take account of impatience. In an industrial economy, unlike a Robinson Crusoe economy, saving and investment are acts undertaken by different agents. Firms invest, install capital equipment, and individuals save, forego possible consumption. It simplifies to assume that firms always borrow to get the funds to buy capital equipment, and individuals are the only lenders. Borrowing and lending behaviour are linked in the market for loanable funds, the price of which is the **rate of interest**. In Figure 6.5, S_aS_a is a savings function, showing total savings and lending increasing with the rate of interest. Individuals prefer current to future consumption, so that saving requires the inducement of interest paid on loaned funds. The amount saved increases as the rate of inducement, the rate of interest, increases. II is an investment function, showing total investment decreasing as the rate of interest increases. Interest is the cost of borrowing and investing, and as the cost rises so less of both is undertaken. Equilibrium in the market for loanable funds determines the level of saving (lending) and investment (borrowing),E_a, and the rate of interest, r_a. The position of the savings function reflects individuals' preferences between current and future consumption. If individuals were less impatient than as reflected in S_aS_a, there would be more savings and investment, and a lower rate of interest, as shown by S_bS_b, E_b and r_b in Figure 6.5.

Suppose a and b are two economies which are identical in all respects except that individuals differ in their preferences between current and future consumption, as shown in Figure 6.5. Then, economy b will have more savings and investment, and a lower interest rate. It will have less

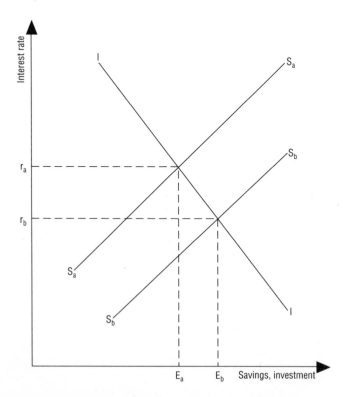

Figure 6.5 Savings, investment and the interest rate.

current, and more future, consumption. It is clear that for given individual preferences, the level of savings and investment, the interest rate, and the distribution of consumption over time, will vary with the slope and position of II. For both S_aS_a and S_bS_b, investment and savings, and the interest rate, would increase if II were shifted to the right.

What determines the slope and position of II? Answering this requires consideration of the behaviour of profit-maximising firms. A firm could borrow funds and re-lend them instead of using them to acquire an item of capital equipment. Leaving aside the costs of the transactions involved, if it did this it would just break even. It would pay interest at the rate r, and receive interest at the same rate. If a firm is to borrow to finance the acquisition of capital equipment, to undertake a particular investment, it must expect to do better than this. The **rate of return on investment** is the equivalent of an interest rate arising from investment. Suppose the sum P is lent at interest rate r for two years, with the first year's interest being re-lent. At the end of the two years the lender will get back an amount R, where $R=P(1+r)(1+r)=P(1+r)^2$. If investment in a piece of capital equipment is undertaken, where the cost of the equipment is P, and its use for two years means that the firm ends up with an amount R_1, then i_1 from $R_1=(1+i_1)^2$ is the rate of return on that investment. The firm will undertake the investment only if i_1 is greater than r: only, that is, if it can increase its profits by using the borrowed funds in this way.

Suppose now that the firm is considering two alternative pieces of capital equipment, 1 and 2, for which it has calculated rates of return of i_1 and i_2. It will prefer 1 to 2 if i_1 is greater than i_2, and vice versa. If i_1 and i_2 are both greater than r, both investments have the potential to increase the firm's profits. A firm can be thought of as listing all the investments it could undertake by their rates of return, in descending order. It will then maximise its profits by borrowing enough to undertake all the investments for which the rate of return is greater than the rate of interest. If the lists for all the firms in the economy are combined, we get the investment function for the economy, II. Profit-maximising firms will undertake all the investment projects for which the rate of return is greater than the rate of interest.

The position and slope of II are determined by the investment opportunities open to the economy. Comparing two economies, if one had an investment function to the right of the other, this would indicate that it had more investment projects that would be profitable at any given rate of interest. The levels of savings and investment, the rate of interest, and the actual distribution of consumption over time, depend upon the interaction of individuals' preferences for the distribution of consumption over time and the investment opportunities open to firms. It is this interaction that is relevant to consideration of **intertemporal equity**. To the extent that, for given investment opportunities, current individuals have a strong preference for current consumption over future consumption, individuals in the future will be less well-off.

Intertemporal efficiency is a state where it is impossible to increase consumption in any period except at the cost of reducing it in some other period. Intertemporal efficiency is clearly a more desirable state than its absence. If matters were arranged so that intertemporal efficiency did not exist, it would be possible to increase consumption in some period without decreasing it in any other. Future individuals could then be made better off without making current individuals worse off.

In thinking about economic growth as the outcome of the interplay between consumption impatience and the productivity of investment, economists assume that intertemporal efficiency applies. The question here is about the distribution of consumption over time, when there are no costless increases to be had in any period of time, cost being in terms of reduced consumption at another period(s) of time. The central idea in growth theory is that we can have higher future consumption at the price of lower consumption now. If intertemporal efficiency did not apply, the possibility would exist of higher future consumption without lower current consumption.

Intertemporal efficiency is about picking the right investment projects within a given total level of investment and for a given rate of interest. To see what is involved, consider two mutually exclusive investment projects, two alternative items of capital equipment, with rates of return i_1 and i_2, whose prices are the same, $P_1=P_2$. Suppose that both are profitable at the ruling rate of interest, r, and that there are no market failures so that the prices used in computing i_1 and i_2 properly signal the social values of the inputs to and outputs from these alternatives. Let i_2 be larger than i_1. This says that 2 is a better converter of current consumption sacrifice into future consumption gain than 1. Picking 1 rather than 2 would involve, for a given current level of consumption, a smaller future gain than is possible. It would involve inefficiency in intertemporal allocation. This would be due to violations of the conditions discussed above in the markets for loanable funds, often referred to collectively as **capital market imperfections**. That these exist is widely recognised. They mean not only that intertemporal efficiency is not attained, but also that the balance actually struck between current and future consumption cannot be assumed to properly reflect individuals' preferences. Not all commentators accept that this balance should reflect individuals' preferences. In **optimal growth theory** the implications of adopting alternative views about this balance are explored via the device of having a planner/dictator use a social time preference rate to distribute aggregate consumption over time, given knowledge of investment opportunities and returns. This device can also be used to explore the implications of an absence of capital market imperfections, by assuming that the **social time preference rate** used by the planner does reflect individuals' preferences. The main value of this sort of analysis is in demonstrating that the distribution of consumption over time, the optimal growth path, depends on both the ethical position embodied in the chosen social time preference rate and the assumptions made about the returns to investment. An ethical position, such as give present and future consumption equal weight, does not of itself determine the nature of the optimal growth path. The outcome depends also on the actual possibilities for shifting consumption over time by saving and investing. In this respect, the message from optimal growth theory is the same as that from analysis of the capital market using Figure 6.5 (p.136).[9]

Economists do not assume that capital accumulation is the only basis for economic growth. The role of **technical progress**, the adoption of new modes of production enhancing the productivity of labour and/or capital, is considered in both theoretical and historical inquiry. In the latter, the contribution of technical progress is taken to be that output growth that cannot be accounted for by increased inputs of labour or capital. In studies of industrial economies, it is typically found that this residual contribution is large relative to those explicitly accounted for.[10] Two points need to be made. First, many technical innovations require embodiment in new capital equipment, as in the Robinson Crusoe story above. To this extent, the rate of technical progress is constrained by the level of investment. An economy that produces brilliant ideas but does not invest will not experience growth. Second, in the history to date of the industrial economies, much technical progress has involved increased use of inputs of raw materials, energy, and the assimilative capacity of the natural environment.

Public sector economics

In industrial economies the government plays a large role in economic activity. The extent of government economic activity can be measured in a variety of ways. A basic distinction is between government expenditure on goods and services and total government expenditure. The difference between these is transfer payments, which are payments to individuals in respect of pensions and welfare benefits of various kinds. The situation varies between industrial economies, but for most total government spending would be of the order of 30 per cent, and expenditure on goods and services would be around 20 per cent. For some industrial economies these figures would be as high as 45 per cent and 30 per cent respectively.

Public sector economics is the study of government involvement in economic activity.[11] It is sometimes referred to as public finance. The government is seen as having four functions in an economy where the basic form of economic organisation is the market system:

1. To create and maintain the infrastructure required to support a market system, principally in the form of a legal system (broadly understood).
2. To correct market failure.
3. To stabilise the economy, and encourage economic growth.
4. To redistribute income and wealth so as to alleviate poverty and achieve the equity target that is determined by the political process.

The need for government to maintain social infrastructure, supply public goods, control the exercise of market power, and deal with poverty, has long been recognised. The stabilisation and growth roles were not fully acknowledged until the emergence of macroeconomics, though debate about the role of government in regulating the banking and monetary system has a long history. The significance of externalities, especially in relation to the natural environment, was not widely appreciated until the 1970s.

There are three central problems for public sector economics: first, the question of how much of which public goods to supply; second, the question of how best to raise the revenue that government needs to finance both the supply of public goods and transfer payments for the alleviation of poverty and the promotion of equity; and third, what forms of transfer payments to use in pursuit of these goals. Public sector economists consider these questions using the theory of welfare economics. The first question should be answered by reference to efficiency criteria, and thus, ultimately by reference to the criteria of consumer sovereignty.[12] The second and third questions are treated jointly. The two fundamental theorems of welfare economics tell us that if certain conditions hold, a market system can reach any efficient allocation after the operation of a system of lump sum taxes and transfers. **Lump sum taxes** and **transfers** are taxes and transfers that do not directly alter the incentives facing firms and individuals. In principle, government could figure out a set of lump sum taxes differing across individuals such that liability varied with ability to pay, but the information required, and the costs of administration, render this approach infeasible. Feasible lump sum taxes would be at a uniform rate per individual. It is recognised that such are politically infeasible, as they would be widely seen as unfair in that individual liability would not be related to individual ability to pay.

It can be shown that if several of the conditions necessary for markets to attain allocative efficiency are not satisfied, then correcting just one of these sources of market failure cannot be guaranteed to improve matters. It may make things worse, in the sense of moving the economy away from, rather than in the direction of, allocative efficiency. This is known as the **second best problem**. There are no general rules which can be applied to all cases to decide whether correcting some, but not all, sources of market failure will make things better or worse in terms of efficiency criteria. Each case has to be considered in all of its particular circumstances.

The tax/transfer problem is an especially difficult second best problem. If all of the conditions for markets to achieve efficiency in allocation were satisfied, equity and efficiency could be achieved by an appropriate set of individually differentiated lump sum taxes and transfers. This would be first best. But, the lump sum approach is ruled out in practice, and we are in the domain of the second best. Then the problem is designing a tax/transfer policy by searching for systems that are politically and administratively feasible, and which create the least possible distortions to the prices and incentives facing individuals and firms. The public sector economics literature contains many propositions about **optimal taxation**, which includes transfers, derived from such analyses. A difficulty with such propositions is that they vary according to precisely what is assumed about the feasibility of tax/transfer alternatives, and about the characteristics of firms and individuals. A further difficulty is that they assume that the conditions under which markets achieve efficiency are satisfied even though generally they are not. Some work has been done which incorporates this into the analysis, but general results are not forthcoming, because we are now in the realm of second best problems.

Nonetheless, economists do adhere to some general presumptions about taxes and transfers, deriving from the basic idea that tax/transfer-induced distortions to market signals should be minimised. Four beliefs widely held by economists are:

1. Income taxation distorts the choice between work and leisure such that, with reference to efficiency criteria, too much of the latter is taken.
2. The taxation of income from interest distorts the choice between consumption and saving, such that there is too little saving.
3. Commodity taxation as a revenue source should be at a uniform rate. However, differential rates may be justified by the need to correct market failure due, for example, to external effects.
4. Transfers for the alleviation of poverty and the promotion of equity should be in the form of money for recipients to spend as they wish,

rather than in the form of particular commodities, or money tied to expenditure on particular commodities.

Actual tax/transfer systems have been affected by these ideas to some extent, but many other ideas and motivations attend their design. One does not need to take on board the economists' entire way of thinking to arrive at conclusions pointing in similar directions to some of those above. Commodity taxation at a uniform rate, for example, has the virtue of administrative simplicity.

Growth and redistribution

An important element in the case for growth as a policy objective is as follows. In the absence of growth, policy to improve the lot of the poor means using the tax/transfer system to redistribute from the rich to the poor. The rich are likely to object to such redistribution. In any case, there are typically few rich from whom to take, and many candidates for the receipt of transfers. Spread over many poor, the sum available from the rich is likely to be insufficient to greatly improve the lot of the poor. This generates pressure to take not just from the rich, but also from the merely better off. If the economy is growing, the lot of the poor can be improved without the need to upset the better off. The imagery of cake-sharing is widely used. The absence of growth corresponds to a cake of fixed size. With growth the cake gets bigger, and with fixed shares everybody gets a bigger piece of cake.

The extent to which taxes and transfers need to be used for redistribution in the interests of poverty alleviation is reduced by economic growth. It is now the conventional wisdom, even for the mainstream political left, in most industrial nations that poverty alleviation is to be sought primarily through economic growth. Redistributive taxes and transfers are widely seen as playing a complementary, and essentially subsidiary role to growth.

However, growth itself may do nothing to reduce inequality. If the pattern of income and wealth shares is unchanging, inequality remains notwithstanding that over time growth lifts all above some poverty line defined in terms of an unchanging consumption standard. To reduce inequality, growth must be accompanied by redistributive taxes and transfers. In Chapter 4 we noted that for many commentators the historical experience of growth in many industrial nations has failed to deliver the promised gains. Arguably among the promised gains not delivered is poverty alleviation. While it is clear that in such economies the least well-off now have much higher material consumption levels than did the least well-off of, say, 50 years ago, it is also clear that poverty has not been eliminated. The point is not merely that inequality has not been significantly reduced. It is that poverty remains, since the normal consumption standard has increased along with economic growth. Individuals whose income is insufficient for the acquisition of subsistence needs as defined by cultural norms, as discussed in Chapter 4, are individuals in poverty. If this view of the nature of poverty is accepted, economic growth alone can do nothing to solve the problem. The solution requires the reduction of inequality.

Government failure

Economists do not see government intervention in economies basically organised on market lines as being necessarily benign. On the contrary, they are typically highly critical of much government activity. One obvious point is that government activity itself is typically free from competitive pressure for cost minimisation. Beyond this, criticism is directed both at the objectives that governments adopt, and at the means employed in pursuit of those objectives. Consider, for example, the problem of excessive pollution arising on account of market failure. Here, economists argue that the policy objective of governments should be the level of pollution consistent with efficiency in allocation. They then argue that the instrument of policy should be some form of price incentive, such as a pollution tax, for example. Often, what actually happens is that the target level of pollution is set on largely non-economic grounds, and that the means of achieving the target selected involves some kind of regulation of polluter activity. On both counts there is said to be **government failure**, government action which is inconsistent with the attainment of allocative efficiency. Another widespread, and widely noted, example of government failure is the practice of subsidising agricultural production.

Some economists, and others, have argued that the democratic political process can be understood by applying to it the assumption of self-interested behaviour used for the analysis of market processes.[13] Four types of participant in the political process can be distinguished here: voters, elected members of the legislature, workers in the bureaucracy, and pressure groups. Individual voters are assumed to cast their votes for the candidates they believe will best serve their individual interests. Elected members are assumed to act so as to maximise their prospects of re-election. Individual bureaucrats are assumed to seek to maximise the size of the bureaucracy, which improves their prospects for promotion and higher salaries. Pressure groups push special interests with elected politicians and the bureaucrats who advise them. The basic argument is that the outcome of the interplay between these participants is not going to be a set of policy objectives and instruments consistent with allocative efficiency, or with any particular notion of social justice. Rather, bureaucrats and pressure groups reduce the extent to which the electoral process causes the legislature to adopt policy targets and instruments that reflect the interests of the majority of individuals.

The role of information is crucial in this argument. Politicians lack accurate and detailed information about voters' preferences: voters suffer similarly in regard to candidates' intentions. Pressure groups exist to make politicians aware of the preferences of special interest groups. This is relatively easy precisely because they are special interests, focusing on particular concerns arising from strong views held by a relatively small number of individuals. Pressure groups access politicians directly and via the bureaucracy, members of which have an interest in expanding its size by increasing the range of government activity. They, therefore, amplify those pressure group signals which they see as requiring job-creating government activity. They also largely control the flow of technical information to politicians. The outcome is argued to be an excessively large government, with a mix of activities reflecting special interests rather than the preferences of the majority.

There are, of course, competing pressure groups. Outcomes then reflect the relative effectiveness of those competitors.[14] But, this does not affect the argument that outcomes do not properly reflect the preferences of the majority of individual voters – the 'silent majority'. Within limits, special interest groups control the behaviour of the political system, notwithstanding the formal apparatus of democracy. The limits are, in large part, set by the media. Here again the role of information is crucial. If the media devote enough attention to an issue over a long enough period, it becomes a matter of general interest and concern. Then, flows of information between voters and politicians are improved, with a consequent loss of influence by pressure groups and bureaucrats. However, in so far as media institutions are profit-maximising firms, the issues that they cover will be largely determined by an understanding of what is good for sales, rather than by assessments of the intrinsic importance to voters of alternative issues.

In this framework, economists can be seen as a pressure group.[15] In the main, they argue for policy objectives consistent with allocative efficiency, for policy instruments expected to minimise the costs of achieving targets, and for economic growth. Economists claim that the status of their arguments is different from that of other pressure groups, being based not on special group interest, but on disinterested analysis and special expertise. This claim should be judged against an appreciation of the nature of economics. This leads, especially where threats to sustainability are at issue, to more weight being given to their arguments about policy instruments than their arguments about policy objectives. This argument is developed further in subsequent chapters.

CHAPTER 7

Resource and environmental economics

This chapter considers the way that the analytical framework discussed in the previous chapter is applied to policy issues relating to the natural environment. The subject matter here is mainly standard resource and environmental economics.

Property rights

Chapter 6 discussed the conditions under which it could be claimed that the achievement of efficiency in allocation could be left to markets. One of the conditions was that there be a complete set of markets. Economists recognise the non-existence of private property rights as a source of market failure in relation to environmental services. A straightforward approach to this problem might be seen as the creation of **private property rights**. This is discussed after considering a widely quoted example of the problems arising where private property rights are absent.

The tragedy of the commons

Economists see incomplete private property rights as leading to the overuse of environmental inputs to economic activity. The problem is widely known as the **tragedy of the commons**. This terminology is actually misleading. We discuss the problem first in the context of renewable resource exploitation, where it is widely understood to involve harvesting to extinction. This is incorrect.[1]

The terminology is misleading because the problem arises not in the context of common property, but in the context of no clearly defined property rights. Common property rights exist when ownership is vested in some social group, as opposed to a private individual or firm. This is not the context in which the so-called tragedy of the commons arises. It arises where the resource is not owned at all, or is exploited as if it were not owned at all. The proper terminology is then **free access resources** rather than **common property resources.** The story often told under the rubric of the tragedy of the commons is actually a story about free access, not about common property. Free access can be shown to imply, quite generally, over-use. It cannot be shown to always imply over-use to the point of extinction, as is frequently claimed.

To clarify this, consider an ocean fishery outside of the jurisdiction of any nation state. Any firm with boats and gear can fish it at any time for no charge. The fish stock is exploited under a free access regime. Firms will exploit the fishery so long as they believe they can make profits by so doing. No firm will have any incentive to take less than its maximum feasible catch. For any firm to reduce catch size now in the interests of the future availability of fish would be irrational. It has no reason to suppose that its restraint would be matched by other firms exploiting the fishery. In the absence of restraint by all, restraint by one is not assured of being effective in ensuring the continued availability of the resource. Given the possibility that the resource will not be there to exploit in the future, any firm has an incentive to take as much of it as possible now. All firms face this incentive. There will be overfishing.

This does not necessarily lead to the fish stock being harvested to extinction. This may be the outcome in some circumstances. Whether or not it is depends largely on how the costs of catching fish behave as the stock gets smaller. Costs would be expected to rise as the stock size falls, if only on account of the increasing difficulty of finding fish. To the extent that this does happen, it will work to prevent extinction. For a given selling price for the fish, profits will decline as reducing stock size increases costs. When profits fall to zero, exploitation of the fishery will cease. Whether or not free access implies extinction depends upon whether or not profits are eliminated at a positive level of stock size. If the selling price for the fish can be increased as costs increase, this inbuilt conservation mechanism is less effective. Free access will be more likely to involve fishing to extinction: the higher is price in relation to cost; the more price increases with increasing catch cost; the lower the intrinsic population growth rate for the exploited stock; and the less sensitive are costs to declining stock size.

If free access exploitation does not necessarily mean extinction, the statement that it involves 'overfishing' implies some standard of reference for the 'proper' level of fishing. In economics, this standard is the catch that would correspond to intertemporal efficiency. It can be shown that if fish stocks were privately owned by competitive firms, the catch in every period would, in the absence of other sources of market failure, be that required for intertemporal efficiency. This is discussed later in the section on intergenerational equity and the environment.[2]

The Coase theorem

We now consider private property rights issues in the context of waste discharge and pollution. Suppose that there is a lake into which one firm discharges wastes from its production process, and which is also used as source by the utility which supplies a nearby town with its water. The lake is owned by neither the firm nor the utility, and its use is not socially regulated in any way. It is used as a resource input and waste sink under a free access regime. The costs incurred by the utility in supplying a fixed amount of drinkable water increase with the firm's level of waste discharge. This is an example of an externality phenomenon. Because it does not own the lake, the water supply utility cannot charge the firm for using it as a waste receptacle. The water treatment costs that the firm's waste discharge gives rise to do not show up in the firm's accounts, and therefore do not influence its behaviour.

Now, suppose that a property right to the lake were assigned to the water utility. It could then charge the firm for its use of the lake as a waste receptacle, extracting from the firm full compensation for the additional costs imposed on it by the firm's wastes. The Coase theorem shows that in this instance bargaining between the two parties will lead to the allocatively efficient level of waste discharge into the lake. The creation of the property right assigned to the utility corrects the market failure. The theorem shows that the market failure can also be corrected by assigning the property right to the firm, in which case the water utility compensates it for curtailing its level of waste discharge.[3]

In Figure 7.1 waste discharge is measured along the horizontal axis as d, and the vertical axis refers to dollars. MNB stands for **marginal net benefit**, net benefit being the firm's profit. The downward sloping MNB line shows how the firm's marginal profits vary with d. Marginal profit is the effect on total profit of a small variation in d. At d_2, a small reduction/increase in the waste discharge level would reduce/increase profit by $\$v_1$. Profit is reduced/increased because the costs of preventing waste discharge vary with the amount discharged. In the absence of any property rights, the firm's chosen output level would be d_1. To the left of d_1, MNB is positive so that increasing d would add to profits. To the right of d_1, MNB is negative, so that reducing d would increase profits.

MEC stands for **marginal external cost**. External costs are the costs imposed on the water utility by the firm. Marginal external cost is the effect on the total of such external costs for a small variation in d. At d_2

a small increase/decrease in d would increase/decrease the costs imposed on the utility by the firm by v_2. The upward sloping MEC line reflects the assumption that such incremental costs increase with the level of waste discharge. Given discharge at the level d_2, the impact on the utility's treatment costs of a small increase in d is greater than it would be at d_0.

Now, suppose that a property right to the lake were assigned to the water utility. Given that the firm had to so compensate the water utility, at what level of d would it operate? At d_0. The profits to the firm are now what it has left after paying compensation. Its choice of discharge level is dependent on how these residual profits vary with that level. These residual profits are maximised at d_0. As d increases from 0 the firm's marginal pre-compensation profits increase as shown by MNB. As d increases from 0 the firm's marginal liability for compensation increases as shown by MEC. Consider a d level to the left of d_0. From here, a small increase in d toward d_0 increases profit net of compensation, as MEC is less than MNB – the increase in compensation liability is less than the increase in profit. Similarly, to the right of d_0, decreasing d towards d_0 increases profit net of compensation liability, since MEC is greater than

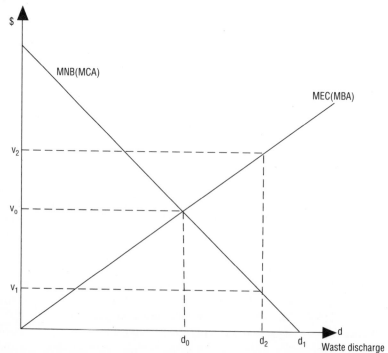

Figure 7.1 Costs and benefits of pollution damage and abatement.

MNB. Profits net of compensation are maximised at d_0. Given that it extracts full compensation, the utility is indifferent to variations in the level of discharge. Given that it must pay full compensation, the firm will want to be at d_0.

Now consider the alternative assignment of the property right, so that the firm owns the lake but allows the water utility to extract water from it. Now the water utility has an incentive to offer the firm payment to reduce its level of waste discharge. Consider an initial position d_1 and a small reduction in d. This would reduce the firm's profits according to MNB. It would also reduce the water utility's costs according to MEC. The maximum that the water utility could pay to secure a small reduction and be no worse off is given by the height of MEC. If it pays this maximum, for MEC greater than MNB, the firm will be better off in terms of profits plus payment from the water utility by making that small reduction than by declining the offer. Again, considering positions to the left and right of d_0, it can be seen that with this assignment of the property right, bargaining will lead to the d_0 outcome. From a point to the right it will be in the interests of the water utility to offer additional payment for further d reduction. The firm will be better off by reducing d and accepting the payment. However, it will not pay the utility to bribe the firm into reducing d below d_0, as then the bribe necessary to induce the firm to make a further small reduction in d would be greater than the cost saving to the utility.

The Coase theorem says that the bargaining outcome satisfies the requirements of allocative efficiency. In Figure 7.1 consider pollution reductions, or pollution abatement, from the level d_1. This involves costs and benefits to society, borne by the firm and accruing to the utility respectively, and shown by MNB and MEC. MNB is labelled MCA in parenthesis, for **marginal costs of abatement**. As d is reduced, so the cost to the firm and hence to society of a further small reduction increases. MEC is labelled in parenthesis MBA, for **marginal benefits of abatement.** As d gets smaller, so the benefit to the water utility and hence to society of a further small reduction decreases. The costs of abatement reflect increased production costs for commodities produced by the firm. The benefits of abatement reflect reduced costs in water supply.

To the right of d_0 MBA is greater than MCA, so that a reduction would reduce water supply costs by more than it would increase commodity production costs. At any level of d greater than d_0, society would gain from a further reduction in the level of pollution in the lake. At d_0 itself, MBA is equal to MCA and all such gains have been exhausted. Reducing d beyond d_0 would raise commodity production costs by more than the reduction in water supply costs. Hence, d_0 is the level of pollution in the lake that corresponds to allocative efficiency.

According to the Coase theorem, then, a pollution problem arising on account of undefined property rights can be solved by assigning property rights either to the victim of the pollution or to the generator of the pollution. In either case, bargaining in the new regime of clearly defined property rights will lead to the efficient outcome. That either assignment leads to the same outcome is a feature of the particular construction employed in this example. More generally, the Coase theorem says that under either assignment of property rights the outcome will be an efficient one. Recall from Chapter 6 that for given technological conditions there are many efficient allocations. Generally, the particular efficient outcome to which bargaining leads will depend on the property rights assignment: see for example, Hartwick and Oliwiler (1986). There is apparently quite a simple approach to the problem of environmental pollution. The problem arises because of the absence of clearly defined private property rights, so the solution is to create such.

While assignment of property rights to either party leads to the efficient outcome, it is not true that the two assignments are equivalent. They have quite different distributional implications. When the legislature assigns the property right to one or the other party it is conferring upon it a valuable asset. The party receiving the property right gains at the expense of the other. The question which then arises is: to whom should the legislature assign property rights, polluters or the victims of pollution. For many the answer to this question is, as a general matter, self-evident: equity demands that the property right always be assigned to victims of pollution. Unfortunately, this view does not survive close examination, except on a very peculiar notion of equity. It is entirely conceivable that in many contexts, the pollution generator(s) is poor and disadvantaged while the victim(s) is better off. In the example used here, suppose that the lake is located in a poor country where the firm produces fertiliser and the water supply is actually for a resort for tourists from affluent nations. This is not to say that distributional equity will always mean giving the property right to the polluter. On the contrary, the point is that there can be no general rule about how to assign the right. From an efficiency standpoint it does not matter who gets it. From an equity standpoint, each case needs to be judged on its merits.

Limits to private property rights solutions

The essential point of the Coase theorem is that a clear assignment of private property rights permits bargaining which leads to an outcome consistent with allocative efficiency. There are four reasons why this cannot be used as the basis for a general approach to solving pollution problems. These are distinct reasons, but in the majority of pollution problems that would generally be regarded as significant, all are operative.

First, the outcome of the bargaining will be as required for efficiency only if all of the conditions for the absence of market failure are satisfied once the private property rights have been established. It is necessary, for example, that neither party has the power to alter the other's bargaining position. Suppose, for example, that the firm could locate elsewhere, but the water supply utility could not. The ability of the latter, if granted the property right, to extract compensation from the firm could then be reduced by the firm's ability, at some cost, to relocate. More generally, the identification of the costs and benefits facing the potential bargainers with social costs and benefits relevant to efficiency requires that market failure is totally absent elsewhere in the economy. If this is not true, then as far as the pollution problem and bargaining are concerned we are in a second best world.

The second point is that bargaining requires identification of one party by another. It requires that a pathway from a source to a victim can be identified by both source and victim. The lake example was deliberately constructed to avoid this problem. Clearly, for most examples of pollution it is a problem. How do I identify the origins of the atmospheric pollution that I suffer when walking the city streets? If I cannot determine with whom to bargain, the fact that the legal situation empowers me to do so is irrelevant.

Third, there is the matter of the numbers involved on each side of the putative bargaining process. Again, the lake example was constructed so as to avoid the problems of large numbers, having just one pollution source and just one victim. If there are many sources or many victims, or both, then even if feasible, bargaining becomes very expensive. Suppose that urban atmospheric pollution affecting one million people is caused solely by one power plant for electricity generation, and think about victims with a property right in clean air bargaining to extract compensation. The costs of bargaining are known in the economics literature as **transactions costs**. The point is that transactions costs increase with the number of parties, and can become so large as to offset the pollution reduction gains from bargaining, and may simply prevent bargaining.

The fourth point is that most significant pollution problems involve non-rivalry in consumption. Typically, that is, pollution is a public 'bad' in that an increase in the suffering of one victim does not reduce the suffering of any other victim(s). While non-rivalry is, in practice, usually associated with large numbers of victims, as with the urban atmospheric pollution discussed immediately above, in principle it need not be, and it alone is sufficient to rule out the bargaining solution. Return to the lake example and suppose now that, apart from the firm discharging wastes, it has two users. As well as the water utility there is a food-processing firm extracting water from the lake. It also incurs costs which increase with wastes discharged into the lake. However, the way its costs vary with waste discharge levels is different from the case of the water utility. In terms of Figure 7.1 (p. 148) imagine a second MEC line for the food-processing firm, everywhere above the MEC shown and intersecting with MNB at the discharge level d_{00}. Clearly, d_0 and d_{00} cannot co-exist as actual discharge levels. There exist different mutually satisfactory outcomes for the waste-discharging firm and each of the other users treated separately. However, both necessarily experience the same level of water pollution. The problem thus arising for bargaining is most readily apparent in the case where the property rights are assigned to the polluting firm. In this case both the water utility and the food-processing firm have an incentive not to offer the waste-discharging firm payments to reduce its discharges, as they will hope to free-ride on the payments made by the other.

For these reasons the range of environmental pollution problems over which bargaining based on clearly defined individual property rights offers the prospect of a solution, in the sense of efficiency, is very limited. Why then consider the Coase theorem here? There are two reasons. First, some economists advocate private property rights solutions to a wide range of environmental problems. It is important to understand the nature of such solutions, and the reasons for the limited range of their applicability as the means to allocatively efficient solutions. As will be discussed below, property rights creation can be used as a policy instrument for the pursuit of social goals set according to other criteria. The second reason is that considering bargaining solutions helps to make clear the nature of an allocatively efficient solution to an environmental problem. Note that in the pollution example considered in Figure 7.1, the efficient level of pollution is not zero. In a particular case the efficient level of pollution depends on the slopes and positions of MNB/MCA and MEC/MBA. If MEC/MBA were very steep, the efficient level of pollution could be effectively zero.

Policy goals

Most environmental policy analysis done by economists is concerned not with sustainability as such, but with particular problems such as the control of pollution of various kinds, whether particular projects with environmental impacts should go ahead, or how particular resource stocks should be exploited. In thinking about such particular problems, market failure correction informs the analysis.

Consider a problem of environmental pollution. Suppose that an Environmental Protection Agency (EPA) is established and vested with all the necessary powers. The EPA has essentially two problems. First, to decide upon the target level of pollution abatement. Second, to decide upon the means by which that target is to be attained. The first problem is deciding upon the policy objective. The second is a problem in policy instrument choice. This section is concerned with the first of these problems. The second is dealt with in the next section.

Non-market valuation methods

According to standard economics the policy objective should be determined by allocative efficiency criteria. The EPA should aim for a level of abatement such that MCA is equal to MBA, as at d_0 in Figure 7.1. In order to determine the level of abatement corresponding to allocative efficiency, the EPA needs to know the parameters of the MCA and MBA functions, so that it can compute the level of d at which MCA = MBA. The problem is that the information from which these parameters could be estimated is not revealed in market data. If circumstances were such that the conditions for the applicability of the Coase theorem were satisfied, the EPA's task would be simple. Both the problem of goal setting and the means for goal attainment would be solved by the single act of property rights creation. But, typically the conditions are not satisfied, and the EPA needs information on how the costs and benefits of abatement vary with the level of abatement.

Economists have developed a number of **non-market valuation techniques** to deal with the problem that the EPA faces. In the case of firms, the basic strategy is to consider the effect on the costs of firms as the level of abatement varies. As illustrated above, this works both where firms are generators of and sufferers from pollution. Basically, the EPA would use technical data on production processes to construct models of the cost structures of affected firms, and use these models to compute estimates of the variation in total costs for affected firms with different abatement levels.

Individuals are typically treated as sufferers from pollution, in which case the MEC function taken to be required by the EPA should reflect their willingness to pay to have less pollution. The MEC/MBA function in Figure 7.1 would then give the variation of **marginal willingness to pay** for pollution abatement with the level of abatement. This would be assumed to be as shown in Figure 7.1, with willingness to pay for a small reduction in pollution decreasing as the level of pollution gets smaller. If a market in pollution abatement could be created, the marginal willingness to pay function would correspond to the demand function for pollution abatement. In figuring MEC/MBA in relation to individuals, the EPA's basic approach is that pollution abatement is to be treated just like an ordinary consumption commodity, and the demand function that would exist if there were a market in it has to be ascertained.

Given that such a market does not exist, there are two basic approaches to figuring marginal willingness to pay and its variation with the level of abatement. The first is a direct method, and involves simply asking people what they would hypothetically be willing to pay for a given increase in abatement. This is known as the **contingent valuation method** (CVM) as it involves presenting individuals with a hypothetical scenario and asking them what they would be willing to pay contingent on that scenario. The second method is indirect, and involves extracting willingness to pay information from observed behaviour. In the pollution context the application of this general approach is known as **hedonic pricing** (HP). The basic idea here is as follows. Suppose that there is an urban area where atmospheric pollution varies across districts in known ways. Then, one can attempt to infer willingness to pay to avoid pollution from variations in house prices across districts, after making allowance for house size, garden size, age of house, access to the city centre etc. Willingness to pay to avoid pollution in this way is then taken to be equivalent to willingness to pay for abatement.

Much of the economics literature on non-market valuation is concerned with environmental amenity services. To fix ideas here, suppose that the EPA is considering whether to allow the construction of a hydro-electric facility, which would involve flooding a remote valley currently used as a wilderness recreation area, and where there exists the only known population of a species of plant. The plant has no commercial uses. The valley is used by humans only for recreation. Assume that this is the only aspect of the project where external costs, or benefits, arise. All other consequences of the project are properly valued in actual markets. The problem then is to estimate individuals' willingness to pay (WTP) to avoid the environmental impacts that going ahead with the project would entail.

It is conventional in the literature to distinguish two sources of individual willingness to pay for the preservation of such an area. The first is referred to as **use value**, the second as **non-use value**, or **passive use value**.[4] The former concerns current and future planned on-site recreational use. The latter concerns willingness to pay for preservation over and above use value, which is independent of any actual or intended use by the individual concerned. One basis for non-use value would be an altruistic desire to preserve the area for use by others. In the case considered here individuals might also be willing to pay for preservation on the basis of the role of the plant in the provision of environmental life support type services, in so far as they consider the conservation of biodiversity and see the flooding of the valley as a threat to it.

In such contexts, standard economic methods for estimating willingness to pay, again, comprise the direct and the indirect. The direct method is CVM. Individuals are asked what their willingness to pay to avoid flooding would be. The **travel cost method** (TCM) seeks to extract willingness to pay from observations on actual behaviour. The basic idea is that the costs involved in visiting the area are a proxy for the value individuals place on these recreational services.[5] Economists have an inclination to prefer value estimates based, however indirectly, on actual behaviour, to estimates derived from answers to hypothetical questions. However, the relevance of TCM is clearly limited to use values, since travel expenditures relate to individual recreational use, not to recreational use by others or to life support service functions.

Assumptions and objections

All of these methods, HP, CVM and TCM, make the same fundamental assumption about how individuals relate to the natural environment. They assume that individuals regard features and uses of the natural environment as consumption commodities on an equal footing with ordinary commodities purchased in markets. They assume that individuals can and do make comparisons such that they are willing to pay for the environment by foregoing consumption of ordinary marketed commodities. Variations in the prospects for the survival of some species are, in a CVM study of passive value, for example, assumed to be regarded by individuals as variations in personal consumption of the same essential nature as variations in the number of meals eaten in restaurants or the number of visits made to the cinema. The common measuring rod is willingness to spend personal income on one rather than another. Because the environment is not marketed, this willingness to pay is not directly observable, but the assumption is that it is there to be discovered by one or more of HP, CVM or TCM.

These methods require that individuals regard ordinary commodities and environmental commodities as commensurable. Many non-economists find this **assumption of commensurability** implausible and objectionable, and reject it. Sagoff (1988), for example, attacks the approach to environmental decision making based on standard, neoclassical economics.[6] He argues that in regard to the making of 'hard' decisions, which include decisions about the environment, individuals act as 'citizens' rather than 'consumers'. The distinction is put as follows:

> As a citizen, I am concerned with the public interest, rather than my own interest; with the good of the community rather than simply the well-being of my family ... As a consumer ... I concern myself with personal or self-regarding wants and interests; I pursue the goals I have as an individual. I put aside the community-regarding values I take seriously as a citizen, and I look out for Number One instead (Sagoff 1988, p.8).

For Sagoff, in the citizen role the individual considers the benefits of a proposal, such as the hydro project, to the nation as a whole. This involves consideration of sentimental, historical, ideological, cultural, aesthetic and ethical values. Thus, the 'individual as a self-interested consumer opposes himself as a moral agent and concerned citizen' (p.67). Sagoff refers to this consumer/citizen dichotomy as 'the conflict within us'. Sagoff sees environmental decision-making problems as falling within the provenance of what he calls 'social regulation' and therefore matters for citizens rather than consumers. Social regulation is to be guided by 'ethical rationality' which emphasises the need for highly informed deliberation rather than choice on the basis of given, and likely poorly informed, consumer preferences. It is Sagoff's view that it is a 'category mistake' to treat the natural environment as coming within the domain of consumer choice. HP, TCM and CVM assume commensurability and are to provide inputs to social goal-setting according to the criteria of allocative efficiency and consumer sovereignty. Sagoff (1988) rejects this approach to social goal-setting in the area of environmental decision making.

At one level, what is at issue here is an empirical question. Do individuals treat ordinary commodities and states of the natural environment as commensurable? This is not a question on which economists have done any extensive empirical research. Indeed, the question is rarely mentioned in the economics literature.[7] Given the crucial role of the commensurability assumption to the valuation methods for environmental services that economics now uses extensively, this might be regarded as surprising. It might be argued that it is not necessary to address it directly. If the assumption produces reliable and useful results, it could then be argued, as some economists do, that this is itself a sufficient test of the assumption. There are two problems with this view. First, in regard to non-use values, there is no independent observational data against which to judge the reliability of the results that CVM produces. In this case, there is not, and cannot be, any market data with which to compare the results. Individuals simply cannot make discretionary payments out of personal post-tax income for species preservation, for example. It is sometimes suggested that expenditure on payments to funds which sponsor individual animals, or seek to raise the money to buy land to be set aside as nature reserves, can provide a benchmark against which to evaluate CVM results. An analogy should make clear the problem here. My annual contribution to charities to help the destitute would not necessarily have much to do with my views on the appropriate level of social support for the poor. My charitable donations will be constrained by my own income. I may be somewhat poor myself, but consider that society should spend more on the poor and less on weapons. On the other hand, when I make a charitable donation, there may be a satisfaction from so doing that has little to do with the particular objectives of the charity involved.

Second, the notion of 'useful' results begs part of the question that Sagoff and others are raising. The point being made is that consumer sovereignty is the wrong measuring device. Even if individuals do, in fact, find environmental states commensurable with ordinary consumption goods, the argument is that this is an ethically inappropriate way to decide the social questions arising.

Even if one believes that individuals do treat ordinary commodities and environmental services as commensurable, and one accepts consumer sovereignty as appropriate, in principle, for social decision making where the environment is concerned, there remains a problem for the standard economic approach. Consider, again, the notional hydro project, and recall that it involves the possibility of a plant species becoming extinct. Suppose that the species in question would be generally regarded as aesthetically unattractive, but is known to be a key species in the functioning of an ecosystem which includes the valley to be flooded. In conducting the CVM an attempt is made to transmit this knowledge to the individuals who are asked about their willingness to pay for preservation. Nonetheless, the survey reveals that total willingness to pay for preservation is insufficient to stop the project going ahead. It is not necessary to reject consumer sovereignty to have problems about accepting this outcome.

Can one be sure that the surveyed individuals have sufficient information about the consequences for them, taking account of their concerns for future individuals, of the threat to life support services arising from extinction of the species? Science, itself, cannot know with any exactitude what all the consequences would be. Even if it did, it would be difficult within the survey format to convey all of those consequences to individuals. Even if one regards consumer sovereignty as an acceptable criterion on ethical grounds, there remains the practical problem of giving individuals the information for proper choice in contexts where complex environmental issues are involved. From this point of view, questions about environmental functioning are simply not like questions about ordinary commodities. If I have to choose between consuming beer and whisky, I believe that I have enough information to make an informed choice. Matters are very different if the choice is between beer and species preservation.

The information problems raised here also arise where environmental decision making through market processes is feasible. It has been noted that individuals could, for example, actually buy land so as to prevent its use for anything but wildlife habitat. This does, in fact, happen.[8] There is, however, no reason to suppose that individual preferences and information would be such as to result in the amount of habitat preservation consistent with the requirements of sustainability. As will be discussed later in this chapter, a perfectly functioning market system does not guarantee that no species will be driven to extinction by human action. We do not know, from a sustainability perspective, which species are expendable. All methods for setting policy targets are subject to this kind of ignorance.

Policy instruments

The attempt to set social goals for environmental protection according to allocative efficiency criteria faces many difficulties of a conceptual and practical nature. Notwithstanding economists' advocacy of this way of setting environmental policy targets, it is, in fact, little used. This is undoubtedly due to public perceptions of the ethical and conceptual issues involved, as well as the difficulties involved in actually putting the principles into practice. Where environmental targets are set other than by reference to efficiency criteria, economists refer to **arbitrary standards**.

We now turn to the problem of the policy instrument choice, on the assumption that the policy goal has been determined. Given the ubiquity of arbitrary standards, we discuss the problem in that context, though basically the same considerations would arise in respect of a target derived from efficiency criteria. The discussion is developed in the context of an EPA and the control of pollution.

Instrument classification

Four categories of policy instrument for pollution control are usually distinguished in the economics literature:
1. **Command and control**, also referred to as regulation, or direct control, of waste discharger behaviour. This can take two main forms:
   –specification of allowable discharge quantities; and
   –specification of process and/or equipment.
2. Price incentive modification. Four principal options exist here:
   –**discharge taxation**;
   –**tradeable discharge permits**;
   –input taxation; and
   –payment for abatement.
3. Public provision of waste treatment facilities.

4. Manipulation of the social environment. Particular forms include:
   –publicity to generate social pressure on polluters;
   –education of actual and potential sufferers; and
   –education on environmental functioning.
Category 4 is often referred to by economists as **moral suasion**. The various categories are not mutually exclusive. Regulation of process/ equipment could, for example, be combined with payment in respect of costs arising, and adopted concurrently with a publicity campaign concerning the pollutant in question. Discharge taxation could be used to finance public provision of treatment facilities. Where the rate of taxation is set for EPA cost recovery, rather than to generate incentives for abatement, the tax is often referred to as a **user charge.**

Criteria for choice

There are a number of criteria which are relevant to the choice of policy instrument.[9] They include:
(a) Dependability. This concerns the degree to which the EPA can be sure that use of the instrument will result in the realisation of the target standard.
(b) Finance. Does the instrument generate revenues for the EPA, or does it give rise to spending by the EPA to be covered by payments to it from government?
(c) Cost. This refers to the real costs to society as a whole. Given existing technologies, does use of the instrument involve avoidable costs? This criteria is also referred to as efficiency. The least cost instrument is then described as the efficient instrument.
(d) Informational requirements. How much of what kinds of information must the EPA have in order to be able to use the instrument effectively?
(e) Monitoring and enforcement. Is the monitoring that the instrument requires the EPA to do feasible, and if so how costly is it? Monitoring is needed to judge compliance, and in some cases to assess payments. Enforcement problems arise in the event of non-compliance being detected.
(f) Permanence. Is the instrument's effectiveness dependent on circumstances subject to change, such as public interest?
(g) Flexibility. Does the instrument have the capability to keep doing its job in the face of changing economic circumstances? Or does it need frequent modification as circumstances change? In the latter case, the further question arises as to whether the modifications can be handled administratively, or need legislation.

(h) Equity. How are the costs generated by the instrument distributed across firms and individuals? One would expect such questions to be important to legislators in a democratic system.

(i) Dynamic incentives. Does an instrument encourage the adoption of new cleaner technologies, or does it encourage the retention of the existing technology?

(j) Continuing incentives. Does the instrument provide an incentive to reduce discharges by a fixed amount or does it provide an incentive to minimise discharges?

(k) Political considerations. These are likely to affect the actual choice of instrument at least as much as technical arguments about such matters as efficiency. Some who are active in the political process see an ethical dimension to the choice of instrument, in that those which appear to confer a right to pollute are immoral whereas those that stigmatise polluters are moral.

A given instrument will rank differently according to different criteria in different circumstances. Also, the weights to be given to the criteria are likely to vary with particular circumstances. In the case of a toxic discharge, for example, the dependability criteria would presumably be seen as very important. Where the discharge is considered a nuisance rather than a threat to human health, dependability is likely to get a smaller weight, and efficiency a larger weight. This is perhaps the most important point here. There is no uniquely correct choice of instrument for all circumstances.

Economic analysis of instrument choice

Economists have a strong presumption in favour of price incentive instruments. This derives from analysis of theoretical models of the behaviour of firms discharging wastes, as follows. Suppose (a) that there are a number of firms in an area discharging wastes of some kind, (b) that an EPA is established with all the necessary powers, and (c) that it, after due deliberation, adopts as its objective an arbitrary x per cent cut in total discharges. Now assume:

(i) that all of the firms are profit maximisers;

(ii) that all of the firms are price-takers;

(iii) that the environmental protection agency has complete information on the relationship for each firm between its profits and its level of waste discharge;

(iv) that the input and output prices facing all of the firms are determined in competitive markets; and

(v) that the EPA can costlessly monitor discharges to the extent required, and costlessly enforce compliance.

The fourth assumption means that profit reductions are real costs borne by society. Note, however, that there is an important distinction between profit reductions as perceived by society, and as perceived by the firms. Profits which disappear from a firm's accounts by virtue of tax payments or by virtue of payments to another firm are not real social losses. Profits which disappear from a firm's accounts by virtue of resource costs incurred to reduce discharges, abatement costs, are real social losses. Whereas only the latter count as costs to society, and are the resource costs with which the efficiency criterion (c) is concerned, an affected firm will regard transfers as real costs to it, additional to abatement costs.

Given these assumptions, the **least cost theorem** says that abatement costs are minimised where the EPA taxes emissions from all firms at a uniform rate per unit.[10] Actually, given these assumptions, this theorem does not, as it is widely understood establish a presumption in favour of emissions taxation over command and control of the form that specifies allowable discharges by firms. The EPA could achieve the same target at the same minimum cost by: paying the firms at a uniform rate per unit abatement; regulating the emissions level for each firm; creating emissions permits tradeable between firms with the total amount of emissions permitted equal to the arbitrary standard for total emissions. A preference for taxation over these alternative derives from considerations external to those captured in the assumptions specified above.

Payments for abatement, subsidising emissions reduction, involve the EPA paying the firms, and gives rise to an additional claim on government revenues. Such an instrument choice scores badly on the finance criterion, and would be seen by many as inequitable in most circumstances.

The real problem with the command and control option is in regard to assumption (iii). If regulation is to involve the same abatement cost total as uniform taxation, then the levels of abatement enforced by the EPA will have to differ across firms such that more is done by those firms where abatement costs are lower. For the EPA to be able to issue the individually tailored regulations involved, it would have to know the marginal abatement cost function for each firm. This is generally not feasible, and the operational version of command and control is seen as involving each firm cutting back emissions by the same x per cent so as to achieve an overall x per cent reduction. Because firms' abatement cost functions are assumed to differ, uniform percentage cutbacks would not be efficient.

The least cost property of uniform emissions taxation derives from the fact that it loads total abatement across firms such that those for which it costs less do more. Each firm would abate up to the level where its marginal abatement cost was equal to the tax rate, so as to maximise its post-tax profits. As a result, all firms would be operating with the same marginal abatement cost. Given this, there would be no reallocation of the total abatement between firms that could reduce the total cost of abatement. The EPA does not need to know each firm's abatement cost function to identify the differential abatement targets for each firm that minimise total cost. The reaction of the firms to the uniform tax identifies the least cost solution.

However, while it is dropping assumption (iii) that gives uniform taxation the cost advantage over command and control, doing this also reveals a problem for uniform taxation. This is that without this assumption, uniform taxation is not dependable, i.e. is not guaranteed to achieve the target level of total abatement. It will be dependable if the EPA sets the right uniform tax rate. But, in order to do this it needs to know the abatement cost function for every firm. In the absence of such information, it can set a tax rate which will achieve some overall abatement level at the lowest cost that is possible. But, the achieved level will not, except by chance, be the x per cent reduction in total emissions desired. The EPA could proceed by trial and error, setting a tax rate, observing the outcome, and adjusting the rate up or down as necessary. This would involve costs, and would obviously score badly against several of the other criteria listed above.

Tradeable permits have the attraction that where assumption (iii) is not applicable, they are both least cost and dependable. They are dependable because the total quantity of permits created by the EPA is equal to the emissions total that corresponds to the desired x per cent cutback. They are least cost because the market in permits allocates them to firms where it is cheaper to buy a permit than to abate. Firms where abatement is relatively cheap will abate rather than buy permits. The loading of total abatement across firms so as to minimise total cost is automatically generated by the profit-maximising behaviour of the firms. This outcome is crucially dependent on assumptions (ii) and (v). Where there are few firms, one may be able to exercise power in the permit market and distort its operation. Monitoring firms' compliance, ensuring that their actual emissions correspond to their permit holding, may involve the EPA in substantial costs. Note that such potential problems aside, the dependability and least cost properties of permits hold irrespective of how the permits are initially allocated by the EPA. It may, for example, give them to firms in equal amounts in the first instance, or sell them to the highest bidders. Choice between such alternatives does have implications against other criteria listed above, such as (b), (h) and (k).

Finally here two related points should be noted. The first concerns analysis. The arguments and conclusions reviewed above actually hold where firms base their decisions on a cost minimisation rather than a profit maximisation objective. Firms need to know less to minimise costs than to maximise profits. The second point is that, as noted in Chapter 6, there is a good deal of everyday experience and systematic empirical evidence that economic agents do respond to price signals in the way that economics predicts. Other things equal, it generally appears true that making things more expensive usually reduces their use. Essentially, the case for price incentive instruments for arbitrary standards rests on this empirical regularity.

Economists do not devote much attention to moral suasion type instruments. Environmental activists, on the other hand, often seem to prefer them to both command and control and price incentives. From an economist's perspective, one problem with such instruments is that they are hard to include in a rigorous analytical framework. Another is that they appear often to involve the deliberate manipulation of individuals' preferences, which is generally frowned upon by economists. To the extent that they are considered, they are usually dismissed as ineffective and unreliable.

Instrument choice in practice

The tendency of academic economists to disagree is often commented on. In the case of the choice of instrument for pollution control, there is a remarkable degree of unanimity. In the academic literature there is near consensus on the proposition that price incentive instruments are superior to command and control approaches. Analysis such as the least cost theorem can prove that, in certain conditions, taxation or tradeable permits offer cost advantages over command and control. But the size of that advantage, to be weighed against performance on other criteria, remains to be determined. To date, understanding of the quantitative trade-offs involved is based mainly on modelling studies rather than actual experience with alternative instruments. Pollution control practice has largely ignored the recommendations of economists in favour of price incentive systems, and has relied heavily on command and control, especially in the form of the regulation of process and/or equipment. A recent major survey of environmental economics asked the question: what has it contributed to the design and implementation of policy? The answer given was:

We have seen some actual programs of transferable emissions permits in the United States and some use of effluent charges (discharge taxes) in Europe. And with the enactment of the 1990 Amendments to the Clean Air Act, the U.S. has introduced a major program of tradable allowances to control sulfur emissions–moving this country squarely into the use of incentive-based approaches to regulation in at least one area of environmental policy. But, at the same time, effluent charge and marketable permit programs are few in number and often bear only a modest resemblance to the pure programs of economic incentives supported by economists (Cropper and Oates 1992, p.729, parenthesis added).

Interest in price incentives for pollution control appears to be growing. The authors of this survey state that:

> ... it is our sense that we are at a point in the evolution of environmental policy at which the economics profession is in a very favourable position to influence the course of policy. As we move into the 1990s, the general political and policy setting is one that is genuinely receptive to market approaches to solving our social problems. Not only in the United States but in other countries as well, the prevailing atmosphere is a conservative one with a strong disposition toward the use of market incentives, wherever possible, for the attainment of our social objectives (Cropper and Oates 1992, p.730).

Many non-economists would hope that this assessment is wrong, it would seem. As far as choice of instrument, as opposed to the selection of social objectives, is concerned, this is, as a general position, unfortunate. While the case remains to be made in any particular circumstances, a presumption in favour of price incentives, where feasible, as the means to agreed social ends has much to recommend it.

We have discussed the question of instrument choice in the context of pollution problems. It is in this context that matters have been most fully explored by economists. But, very similar issues arise in respect of the other environmental services to economic activity. In regard to renewable resource exploitation, amenity services and life support services, market failure is prevalent. In these areas the historical situation is very similar to that discussed above for pollution. The main form of social intervention adopted to date has been regulation, or command and control. Economists have argued for greater use of price incentive instruments. Latterly, policy advisers and legislators have shown more inclination to listen to what economists have been saying.[11]

Cost-benefit analysis and discounting

All policy-related economics is cost-benefit analysis: the merit of any policy is, ideally, to be determined by weighing the costs and benefits involved. However, here we follow an established terminology according to which **cost-benefit analysis** (CBA) refers specifically to the appraisal of investment projects from a social, as opposed to a commercial or financial standpoint, against intertemporal efficiency criteria. In saying this, an 'investment project' is to be understood as any activity involving current costs incurred so as to secure future benefits. It covers, for example, changes in government policy.[12]

Project appraisal

An investment project involves a flow of costs and benefits over time:

Period	Costs	Benefits
0	C_0	B_0
1	C_1	B_1
2	C_2	B_2
.	.	.
.	.	.
.	.	.
T	C_T	B_T

The **net present value**, *NPV*, of a project is given by

$$NPV = [B_0 - C_0] + [(B_1 - C_1)/(1+r)] + [(B_2 - C_2)/(1+r)^2] + \ldots\ldots$$
$$+ [(B_T - C_T)/(1+r)^T]$$

where *r* is the interest rate, the subscript *t* identifies periods, and where *T* is the lifetime of the project. The *NPV* criterion says that a project should go ahead if the *NPV* is positive or zero, but not otherwise. If firms select projects on this basis, they maximise their profits. If there is no market failure, they also act consistently with the requirements of intertemporal efficiency in allocation.

In regard to the first of these propositions, consider an illustrative project with the cost and benefit streams shown in Table 7.1. A firm could acquire a machine in period 0 costing $100. The machine's lifetime is three subsequent periods, during each of which operating costs are $10, and receipts from the sales of the output arising are $50, $50, $45.005. If the firm goes ahead with the project, its cash flow situation is given by *B–C* in each period.

Table 7.1 *Project cost and benefit streams*

Period	C	B	Cash flow
0	100	0	−100
1	10	50	+40
2	10	50	+40
3	10	45.005	+35.005

The logic of the NPV test applies however the project is to be financed, but is most readily explained in the case where the $100 to acquire the machine is to be borrowed. Then, for an interest rate of 5 per cent, the financial transactions involved are as follows:

Period 0: borrow $100.

Period 1: repay 1.05 times $100 (i.e. $105), using the net income of $40 from the machine plus a further borrowing of $65.

Period 2: repay 1.05 times $65 (i.e. $68.25), using the net income of $40 plus a further borrowing of $28.25.

Period 3: repay 1.05 times $28.25 (i.e. $29.6625), leaving a final surplus of $5.3425 from the net income of $35.005.

Applying the *NPV* formula above to the *B* and *C* figures in Table 7.1 gives an *NPV* of $4.6151, which indicates that the project should go ahead. The final surplus of $5.3425 is equal to $4.6151 x 1.05^3. That is, for $r = 0.05$, $5.3425 = $4.6151 \times (1+r)^3$, or $4.6151 = $5.3425/(1+r)^3$. The *NPV* is the sum that the firm would have to have lent at compound interest to end up with the same final surplus at the same time as that arising from undertaking the project. Equivalently, the *NPV* is the present value of the surplus that the project yields at the end of its life.

This illustrates the logic of the *NPV* criterion from the firm's point of view. If the interest rate had been 7.5 per cent, $r = 0.075$, repeating the steps above will give $NPV = 0$ and a surplus at period three of 0. If the interest rate had been 10 per cent, $r = 0.10$, the *NPV* and the eventual surplus are both negative. Firms that follow the *NPV* rule will select projects which increase their profitability.

In Chapter 6 we noted that firms investing up to the point where the rate of return is equal to the rate of interest satisfy the requirements for intertemporal efficiency. The non-negative *NPV* rule selects the same projects as does the rate of return rule. The rate of return for a project is the interest rate at which the project would just break even if the funds to finance it were borrowed. For the project in Table 7.1 the rate of return is 7.5 per cent. At higher interest rates the firm would decrease its profitability by borrowing to undertake the project, and the *NPV* on the project would be negative. At lower rates of interest the firm would increase its profitability by borrowing to undertake the project, and the *NPV* would be positive. In practice project appraisal typically uses the *NPV* variant as it is easier to apply and avoids some mathematical problems that can arise in calculating the rate of return. The important point is that, in the absence of market failure, both criteria maximise firms' profits and satisfy the condition of intertemporal efficiency in project selection.[13]

Correcting for market failure

The steps in conducting a CBA are:
1. Properly define the project.
2. Enumerate all of the consequences of going ahead with the project in each period of the project's lifetime.
3. Aggregate over consequences, using money prices, during each time period to get costs and benefits in each period, C_t and B_t.
4. Aggregate costs and benefits over time to get the project's *NPV*.
5. Conduct sensitivity analysis.

Step 1 involves identifying the unit of analysis. If two items of investment are so related that neither can fulfil its purpose without the other, then they are a single project. Thus, for example, a new coal-fired power station and the lines connecting it to the grid comprise a single project. Step 2 involves specifying the physical consequences of the project, and results, for the power station and lines, in a list of manhours of labour input, tons of cement and steel used, tons of coal burned, kilowatt-hours of electricity sent out, tons of carbon dioxide released into the atmosphere etc., for each period of the project lifetime. Note that this lifetime is defined by the longest lasting consequence. Thus, for example, the project lifetime to be used for appraising a nuclear power station is not given by the date at which it stops producing electricity, but by the date at which the nuclear wastes it produces cease to have the potential to do damage. This implies that if this date is to be affected by waste treatment, that treatment should be considered part of the project.

Step 3 uses prices to add across desired outputs in each period to get a benefit figure, B_t, and to add across inputs and deleterious outputs in each period to get a cost figure, C_t. In the absence of market failure, the prices used would appropriately be projected future market prices. Where there is taken to be market failure, adding across physically distinct factors to get B_t and C_t in money units uses **shadow prices**. The techniques that economists use to get shadow prices where project consequences are not priced at all in markets were discussed earlier in the section on policy goals. Shadow prices are also sometimes used instead of market prices where these exist, if it is believed that the market prices are not proper reflections of the social valuations that go with efficiency in allocation. Thus, for example, if import duties apply to some input, that input would be priced at its world price rather than at its domestic price. Again, if there were a high level of unemployment in the economy, it might be appropriate to charge labour inputs at less than the market wage rate.[14]

The result of step 3 is a series of numbers for the difference between benefits and costs in each period, $B_t–C_t$. Typically, this net benefit series will show negative numbers early on, and positive numbers later. Costs are incurred currently and in the near future so that benefits arise in the more distant future. For some projects, the time profile of B_t-C_t will, when the proper project lifetime is considered, have the further feature that the positive phase will be followed by a negative phase. This can arise when the project, although at the end of its useful life, continues to have adverse environmental impacts. Nuclear power plants fit this pattern. In any case, CBA requires that at step 4 money sums for net benefits at different dates be made commensurable with one another according to intertemporal efficiency criteria. This is the matter of discounting to be discussed below.

At each of steps 2 and 3 the analysis relates to the future, which cannot be known with certainty. Some of the issues arising are discussed in the next section. Step 5 involves reworking steps 2 to 4 for different numerical inputs, so as to examine the sensitivity of NPV to the various inputs to its calculation.

Discounting

The practice of dividing a sum arising at period t by $(1+r)^t$ to arrive at the equivalent **present value** is known as **discounting**. As t increases so $(1+r)^t$ gets bigger, so that costs and benefits are discounted more before entering into NPV determination. The further benefits and costs are into the future the less weight they carry in determining the project's NPV. Figure 7.2 shows how the weight per dollar, $W_t = 1/(1+r)^t$, of costs and benefits declines with t for selected values of r. In the project appraisal and CBA contexts, r is often referred to as a **discount rate**. For discount rates of 5 per cent or more, Figure 7.2 shows that $1, 50 years hence, has a present value of less than 10 cents.

Discounting involves normalising project net returns for their pattern over time. Consider the project described in Table 7.1 in comparison with one where:

Period	Cash flow
0	−100
1	0
2	0
3	0
4	0
5	0
6	115.005

For both of these projects there is an initial outlay of $100 and a total return of $115.005. With no discounting, these two projects are

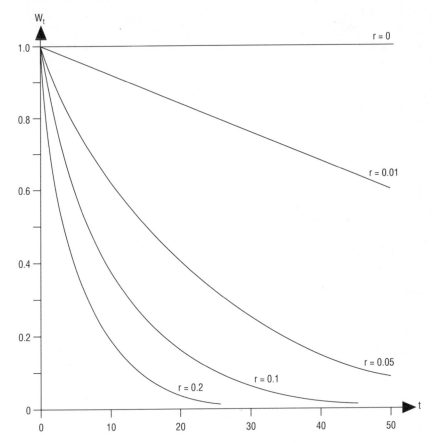

Figure 7.2 Discounting weights.

equivalent, equally attractive, ways of investing $100. However, it does not make much sense to regard these as equivalent projects. The second project involves the same initial sacrifice, but no return at all until period 6. Discounting and making the *NPV*/rate of return comparison adjusts for the differing time profiles of the returns. The project with less delayed returns is then preferred.

It is frequently said that discounting is unfair to future generations. In the CBA context, this criticism is simply misplaced, as CBA is about efficiency not equity. The objective of CBA is to select projects that are consistent with intertemporal efficiency, taking *r* as given. It is the given value of *r* that bears upon the question of the distribution of consumption over time, and hence upon the question of intertemporal fairness. Recall from Chapter 6 that *r*, together with the current level of savings and total investment, is understood as being determined by the inter-section of the savings and investment schedules: see Figure 6.5. The relationship of current to future consumption is determined by current total savings and total investment, not by decisions on which particular projects should now be part of total investment. This last statement assumes, of course, that particular projects are properly selected. If a project with a lower rate of return is adopted instead of one with a higher rate, then future consumption will be lower for a given level of current consumption.

The determination of r may itself involve market failure. If this is con-sidered to be the case, what is needed is policy to address that market failure. It is sometimes argued, for example, that the savings schedule in Figure 6.5 is shifted to the left on account of the taxation of income from interest, leading to a higher r and lower investment than would otherwise be the case. If this problem were removed, r would fall and investment increase, with a shift away from current toward future consumption. This problem is distinct from the issue of selecting projects so as to use efficiently whatever the current level of savings and investment is.

The idea that discounting in CBA is unfair to the future comes up frequently in discussions of the appraisal of projects involving long-delayed environmental impacts. On the basis of the effects of discount-ing as shown in Figure 7.2, the argument is that at typical interest rates, around say 5 per cent, environmental impacts, for good or ill, more than 50 years in the future have no effect on the decision about a project. As regards good impacts, tree-planting for example is often said to be discriminated against by discounting. On the other hand, it is argued that nuclear power plants for example pass CBA tests too easily, as any positive rate of interest means that the future costs of waste storage, or harm arising from storage failure, count for nothing in determining the size of *NPV.*

On the basis of such considerations it is sometimes argued that where a project involves long-delayed environmental impacts, its costs and benefits should be summed over time with no discounting, i.e. with r equal to zero. An alternative argument often encountered is that envi-ronmental impact costs and benefits should be discounted at a lower rate than other costs and benefits, which lower rate it is sometimes suggested should be zero. Both of these arguments serve only to confuse issues. If environmental impacts are regarded as commensurable with other inputs and outputs, there is no reason to discount them differently. If they are not regarded as commensurable, then CBA is simply an inap-propriate way to be considering projects with environmental impacts.

If it is accepted that environmental impacts are properly valued within the consumer sovereignty framework, then in CBA they should be treated as are other project inputs and outputs. The idea that environmental impact costs and benefits should not be discounted appears generally to stem from either a rejection of the commensurability assumption which underpins CBA, or from the idea that the shadow prices used to convert such impacts into costs or benefits represent systematic undervaluations within the consumer sovereignty framework. In the former case, rejecting commensurability means rejecting CBA: the problem of how to decide on which projects should be undertaken remains to be addressed within a different framework. In the latter case, CBA is not rejected and the problem is to value environmental impacts properly prior to discounting.

In this latter case it seems that what advocates of zero discounting of environmental costs and benefits often have in mind is that the relative scarcity of environmental services will be increasing in the future, and that discounting obscures this. If increasing future scarcity is an appropriate assumption, and discounting obscures it, then this is because, in calculating *NPV*, contemporaneous costs and benefits have not been properly represented. Suppose that a project involves the elimination of a wilderness recreation facility. Suppose further that a CBA has been done in which the relative price of wilderness recreation is treated as constant over future time, and that all costs and benefits are discounted using *r* equal to 5 per cent, giving a positive *NPV* for the project. Objectors claim that wilderness recreation costs should not be discounted. Then, assuming that their objection is not based on the non-commensurability argument, their claim must really be based on the idea that the proper assumption is that the value of wilderness recreation in comparison with other project inputs and outputs will be increasing over time. If the CBA is conducted on the assumption that the relative price of wilderness recreation is increasing at 5 per cent per annum, the effect on the computed *NPV* is exactly the same as discounting all costs and benefits except its loss at 5 per cent. Using a rate of increase for the relative price of wilderness recreation that is higher than the discount rate, means that it is effectively discounted at a negative rate.

Rejection of the assumption of commensurability is the basis for a general rejection of CBA where projects with environmental impacts are concerned. There is a different argument on which CBA may be rejected in particular cases. This argument does not require any departure from standard economics, as the rejection of commensurability does. Where a project is assumed to have effects on the distribution of total consumption over time it is not appropriately appraised by CBA. Thus, for example, if it is accepted that climate change will reduce the future capacity of the biosphere to support human life, then a 'project' to halt climate change is not properly considered by CBA. Such a 'large' project, say, the introduction of globally tradeable permits in green-house gas emissions, would have to be considered within a framework of analysis that explicitly looked at the distribution of total consumption over time, among other things. We shall consider this particular case in Chapter 10. The point is not that standard economics abandons the weighing of costs and benefits in such a context. It is that as far as comparing costs and benefits at different points in time is concerned, matters are treated differently in such a context, since what is involved is intertemporal equity rather than intertemporal efficiency.

CBA, as understood here, is for projects which are 'small' in the sense that they do not affect the distribution of total consumption over time. Such small projects do arise in the greenhouse context. Examples are: an investment in a hydro facility; an energy conservation investment; investment in research into solar voltaic systems; investment for switching between coal and natural gas for electricity generation. In such cases, the problem is to select projects consistently according to the efficiency objective, not according to whether it is appropriate to reduce total consumption now so as to increase future consumption above what it would otherwise have been.

Clearly, in practice the distinction between small and large projects is going to be somewhat fuzzy. It is, nonetheless, important to be clear about the nature of the distinction as made in economics. The distinction is, conceptually, a very useful one.

Finally, here, note that the matter of discounting in CBA as social project appraisal, is not, as the forgoing might have suggested, trivial in principle or in practice. We have proceeded on the assumption that there is just a single interest rate in the economy at a given point in time, determined as the market clearing rate at which total savings and investment are equal. This, in turn, implies that there is a single market where savers and investors, individuals and firms, interact, and also that there is no market failure here. None of this describes an actual economy, where there are many different markets in which lenders and borrowers interact, all of which have some degree of market failure. At any point in time in an actual economy, there will exist many rates of interest on different types of debt instrument. The question of which interest rate CBA should use has been, and still is, the subject of dispute among economists.[15]

Risk and uncertainty

Uncertainty is a major characteristic of the sustainability problem. In economics it is conventional to distinguish between risk and uncertainty. Situations involving **risk** are those where the possible consequences of a decision can be completely enumerated, and probabilities assigned to each possibility. Situations involving **uncertainty** are those where probabilities cannot be assigned to possible consequences. Situations where the possible consequences of a decision cannot be completely enumerated involve **radical uncertainty**. So, we have three types of situation involving what is commonly called uncertainty: risk, uncertainty, and radical uncertainty.[16]

Risk

Individuals generally appear to be risk averse, in the sense of being unwilling to accept a fair bet. Suppose that an individual is offered the choice between the gift of $2 and the gift of a ticket which is an entitlement to participate in a gamble on the toss of a fair coin. If the coin comes up heads the individual gets $4, if it comes up tails the individual gets $0. Actuarially the two gifts are equivalent, since the expected value of the ticket is $2–there is a 50 per cent chance of winning $4 and a 50 per cent chance of winning $0. An individual indifferent between the two gifts is **risk neutral**. Most individuals would prefer the gift of $2 to the gift of the gamble ticket, and are said to be **risk averse**.

Individuals differ in their degree of risk aversion. An individual's risk aversion can be measured as the difference between the actuarial value of a gamble and the sum of money that she would regard as of equal value to a ticket for the gamble. This is the cost of bearing risk for the individual, or her risk premium.

Now consider CBA which recognises risk. CBA adopts the criterion of consumer sovereignty, so that if individuals are risk averse, CBA should incorporate risk aversion. The *NPV* for a project should be calculated by adjusting each period's costs and benefits for the cost of risk-bearing, before discounting them in the usual way. Given that individuals differ in their risk aversion, and in ways largely unknown, this is difficult to do in practice. It is sometimes argued that risk should be handled by adjusting the discount rate so that 'riskier' projects have their *NPV* calculated using a higher discount rate. This practice has little to recommend it. It involves the assumption, in effect, that the cost of risk-bearing is increasing over time. Clearly, this need not be the case. Most economists would argue that it is preferable to use alternative guesstimates of the appropriate risk premium. There is an argument to the effect that this can be taken to be zero, on the grounds that society comprises many individuals who share the risk, so that the risk for any individual is trivial and can be ignored. However, where environmental impacts are concerned this argument typically does not apply, because they are in the nature of public goods/bads, i.e. non-rival and non-exclusive in consumption.

Uncertainty

However, in such cases these arguments are often of limited relevance, since the assignment of probabilities is impossible. Recall the hydro-electric power project example considered above in connection with the valuation of non-marketed environmental amenity services. One effect of going ahead with the project was the extinction of a plant population which may be the only one in existence. Suppose that the project is modified to include the attempt to re-establish the plant elsewhere. The attempt at relocation is an experiment of a unique nature, so that there can be no previous experience on the basis of which to assign proba-bilities for success and failure. In this case, CBA would be dealing with a situation of uncertainty rather than risk. Where uncertainty is involved there are no clear-cut decision rules. Indeed, the very notion of rational behaviour becomes somewhat questionable. Decision making can be considered using the ideas of **game theory**, where the outcome of a decision, or strategy, on the part of one player depends on the decisions of the other players, which decisions cannot be known in advance.[17] For many purposes it is assumed that there is just one other player, and that this player is 'nature'. Such constructs are known as **games against nature**.

Suppose that the *NPV* for the hydro project can be reliably calculated on two different assumptions. First, that the state of nature is favourable so that the attempt to relocate the plant species will be successful. This gives an *NPV* of $70 million. The alternative assumption is that nature is unfavourable so that relocation is unsuccessful, in which case the *NPV* is −$20 million Two decisions or strategies are available – go ahead with this project or undertake the next best alternative. Assume that this is a coal-fired electricity generation plant for which the *NPV* is $20 million whichever state of nature is assumed. The basic information is assembled in a **pay-off matrix**:

		State of nature	
		F	U
	P	+70	−20
Decision			
	A	+20	+20

Here F is for favourable, U for unfavourable, P indicates the decision to undertake the hydro project, and A the decision not to.

The decision turns on whether or not the relocation of the plant will be successful. The principle of insufficient reason says that if science is unable to say which of F and U is more likely, one may as well assign subjective probabilities of 0.5 to each and make the decision on that basis. Then the decision would be to go ahead with the project since 0.5 x 70 plus 0.5 x -20 gives 25 as the expected value for the decision P, while for A the expected value over the two states of nature is 20. This approach is generally regarded as having little to commend it.

According to the **maximax criterion**, one makes the decision which offers the largest best outcome. In the pay-off matrix one reads across rows and writes down an additional column showing for each possible decision the value of the best possible outcome. One then selects the decision for which the highest number appears in this new column. For the hydro project pay-off matrix, this selects P for which the best outcome is 70.

According to the **minimax criterion**, one makes the decision that gives rise to the least worst outcome. One reads across the rows of the pay-off matrix and creates a new column where the entries are the worst outcome for each decision row. One then selects the decision for which the entry in this column is least bad. In the example here this selects A.

The third criterion is **minimax regret**. The first step is to create a new pay-off matrix in which the entries are the difference between the pay-off shown in the original matrix and what the pay-off would have been had the correct decision been made. For the hydro example this regret matrix is:

	F	U
P	0	40
A	50	0

For F, the correct decision would have been P so that if P is made, there is zero regret and if A is made, regret is 50. For U, the correct decision would have been A so that if A is made, there is zero regret, while if P is made, regret is 40. One next creates a new column in which the entries are the largest regret in the corresponding row, i.e. 40 for P and 50 for A. The decision selected is then that with the smaller entry in this column, i.e. P.

We have considered four decision-making rules. Three, equal subjective probability assignment, maximax and minimax regret, say undertake the project; one, minimax, says do not. Maximax is basically an adventurous rule looking for large gains, minimax and minimax regret are cautious rules. There is no objective basis on which to choose between the rules. Further, it cannot be claimed that any one of them is rational, in the sense of doing the best that can be done in the circumstances, where the others are not. The choice of rule will depend on the decision maker's subjective feelings about the merits of the alternative rules.

Three points can usefully be made here. First, setting up the pay-off matrix and using it to consider alternative rules will itself be a useful exercise in improving understanding of the nature of the decision-making problem. Second, where the decision maker is acting on behalf of society, and where society's interests are understood to follow from the principle of consumer sovereignty, it might be argued that a decision maker should go for rules which are cautious in nature, in the light of the observed prevalence of risk aversion on the part of individuals. Third, it might be argued that this presumption in favour of caution is strengthened where consequences giving rise to losses involve irreversible impacts on the natural environment. This is essentially the basis for the **safe minimum standard** (SMS) approach to social decision making on projects with such consequences.[18]

Safe minimum standard

This approach was originally developed in the context of thinking about projects possibly entailing species extinction. It can best be discussed in the context of radical uncertainty, where the range of possible outcomes cannot be specified in advance. In the hydro example we can take this to mean that if the state of nature is unfavourable, and the plant species cannot be successfully located elsewhere, we simply do not know what the consequences will be and cannot come up with a number to put in the top right cell of the pay-off matrix. We indicate this by using a z of unknown size:

	F	U
P	+70	−z
A	+20	+20

SMS is based on the minimax regret criterion. The regret matrix is:

	F	U
P	0	z+20
A	50	0

so that the maximum regrets are z+20 for P and 50 for A. SMS says presume that z is large enough to make A the preferred decision on the minimax regret criterion. As made by Bishop (1978) the argument for this presumption is as follows. Species extinction involves an irreversible reduction in the stock of potentially useful resources which is the existing portfolio of species. In a state of radical uncertainty there is no way of knowing how large the value to humans any of the existing species might turn out to be in the future. Two kinds of ignorance are involved here. First, there is social ignorance about future preferences, needs and technologies. Second, there is scientific ignorance about the characteristics of existing species as they relate to future social possibilities and needs. The extinction of any species is, therefore, to be presumed to involve future costs which may be very large, even when discounted into present value terms. The argument here is essentially that the species that may become extinct may turn out to be one for which there is no substitute. Some might now argue that this argument has lost much of its force, given possibilities for storing genetic material. The counter-argument here would be that, first, it would be unwise to place reliance on as yet unproven technologies, and, second, that species need to be left in the natural environment to participate in the evolutionary process. What is lost is not just an existing species, but also the future evolutionary developments which will not occur because that species has been removed from the gene pool over which mutation and natural selection are to operate.

Applying the SMS criterion to projects which could entail species extinction would mean rejecting all such projects. It could be argued that the criterion should be applied where it is a particular population rather than the species as a whole that is at risk. Populations of a given species differ genetically, and the arguments for presuming a large value for a species could, in many cases, be extended to a population. In the hydro-electric example, the minimax regret criterion rejects the project threatening the plant, however small the excess regret associated with the project is, and however much better than the alternative it is, plant loss aside. SMS is a very conservative rule. It means forgoing current gains, however large, in order to avoid future losses of unknown, but presumed large size. In the example above, SMS means that A is selected, which means going ahead with a project with NPV equal to 20 rather than one with NPV 70 (ignoring the plant loss dimension).

A **modified SMS** has been proposed whereby the option which ensures the survival of the species should be adopted, unless it entails unacceptably large costs. This is less conservative, but leaves to be determined whether any given cost is 'unacceptably large'. An answer to this question would, presumably, be sought from the political process rather than economic analysis. In the example above, economic analysis is involved in establishing that the cost is a foregone NPV of \$50 million. But, if the logic of the SMS way of thinking is accepted, the acceptability of this cost is a matter of political judgement, not a matter for analysis. Indeed, the point is really more general. Once uncertainty, and especially radical uncertainty, is recognised decision making necessarily involves judgment and cannot be reduced to a purely technical exercise.

This is not to say that those responsible for making the judgment would not wish to be informed about costs and benefits, of course. It is to say that the matter inevitably involves subjective judgment.

Sensitivity analysis

The techniques of CBA and pay-off matrix construction can be used to facilitate the exercise of judgment. CBA can best be regarded as a way of organising and considering such data on a project as can be made available, rather than a mechanical procedure for arising at a decision. Given the computational power now routinely available, a sensible way to approach this is to do **sensitivity analysis**, calculating the project *NPV* for different sets of input data. The *NPV* can be calculated under different assumptions about the external costs arising from environmental damage, for example. For some projects a decision on the project is not sensitive to variations in such costs, while for others they will be critical. It may be that even on a zero valuation for environmental damage, *NPV* is negative. In this case, dispute about environmental valuation is unnecessary. If, on the zero environmental cost assumption, *NPV* is positive, its size shows what the present value of environmental costs would have to be in order to reject the project on the *NPV* criterion. This figure can then be used to inform debate and focus research on the project.

Sensitivity analysis may reveal that a project is robust, in the sense that *NPV* is positive over a wide range of plausible assumptions about the inputs to the *NPV* calculation. Or it may reveal sensitivity to variations in particular inputs. While this outcome does not produce an answer on the project, unless further research can eliminate those variations, it does identify those areas of the problem where judgment is required. Pay-off and regret matrices can similarly be used to identify critical and non-critical areas of the decision making problem. For the illustrative hydro project the decision depends on the particular decision criterion chosen. For some projects this may not be the case. One can use the pay-off matrix approach to consider how variations in the entry in one cell affect the preferred decision for a given criterion. Again, such sensitivity analysis will not eliminate the role of judgment, but can inform the exercise of it.

Of course, all this assumes that one is prepared to put numbers against environmental impacts which are commensurable with the other numbers. As we have noted, there are those who take the position that this is illicit. Whatever the intrinsic merits of this position, it does have the major drawback that it would appear to make discussion of the merits of any project impossible. A decision rule based on this position would presumably be the simple one that no project with an environmental impact should be undertaken. This would be an extended version of SMS. While simple this decision rule would not be very useful. It is very difficult to conceive of any project that has absolutely no environmental impact.

Intergenerational equity

Generally the use of environmental services in economic activity has a time dimension, in so far as current use has implications for future availability. The question of fairness between those alive at different points in time then arises. This is mainly seen as arising in relation to the use of natural resources, but also arises with respect to all of the other services that the environment provides. Here we discuss the issues arising in the resource exploitation context. The general nature of the arguments there carries over to the other contexts.

Renewable resources

It is convenient, again, to fix ideas by discussing ocean-fishing. Consider the exploitation of a species of fish, where there are many geographically distinct populations each of which is owned by a firm, which harvests the fish and sells the catch in a competitive market. Assume that each firm can costlessly exclude other firms from its fishing ground. This is the polar opposite to the free access situation considered in the first section of this chapter. It is known as the **sole ownership** case, and is an ideal construct used to bring out certain basic ideas. The key feature of the situation then facing a firm is that the fishery which it owns is a capital asset. The decision problem for the firm in each period is the size of the harvest to be taken. This decision implies a level of investment in the fish stock asset, it being the quantity of fish left in the water rather than harvested. It is assumed that the firm now decides all future harvests so as to maximise its profits over a long period.[19]

In economics it is usually assumed that fish stocks are subject to density-dependant growth, as illustrated in Figure 7.3. The size of the stock, S, is measured along the horizontal axis, the amount of growth, G, on the vertical axis. Growth is greatest at stock size S_{msy}, and at S_{max} growth ceases. The graph shown for the amount of growth is also a graph for **sustainable yields**, or **sustainable harvests**. Given, for example, the stock size S_0, taking the catch H_0 in a period will 'cream off' natural growth, leaving the stock size unchanged over time. Such a catch is then sustainable over time. For stock size S_0, a catch larger than H_0 would reduce the stock size, and if maintained over time eventually drive the stock size to zero. Note that given the density-dependant growth assumed, there is a largest sustainable harvest, H_{msy}, where msy stands for **maximum sustainable yield**. Of all the stock sizes that can be kept constant over time by taking a constant catch that creams off natural growth, S_{msy} offers the largest constant catch. For this reason, many take it as self-evident that a fishery should be managed so as to keep the stock size at S_{msy}.

This is not, generally, the outcome where fisheries are exploited under a sole ownership regime. Sole owners can be taken to restrict their attention to sustainable yield programmes of harvesting, consistent with the objective of long-term profit maximisation. Given this, their harvest size, and consequently their investment in the fish stock, will be constant over successive periods. The constant level of harvest/investment will be determined by equating the rate of return on this investment in fish with the interest rate, r. This is simply a particular application of the general rule for profit-maximising investment. The rate of return on investment

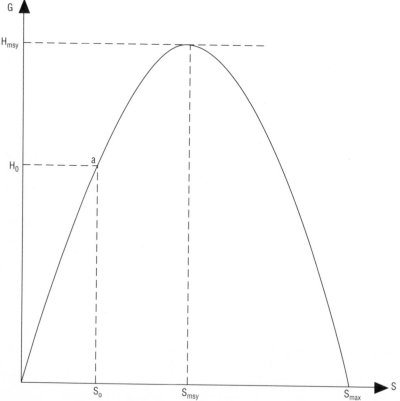

Figure 7.3 Density-dependant growth and sustainable harvests.

in fish varies with the size of the fish stock. It is the slope of the growth function shown in Figure 7.3, to be referred to as g.[20]

At the harvest level H_0, for example, a small reduction in harvest, an investment, would increase the rate of growth of the stock by the slope of the graph at a. The rate of natural growth gives the rate of return to leaving fish in the water now to reproduce and be available for harvesting in the future.

The rate of return on fish investment, g, varies with the size of the fish stock. At S_{msy}, g is zero, and for S greater than S_{msy}, g is negative. Given that r is positive, this means that the sole owner equating g with r will restrict his attention to stock sizes below S_{msy}.[21]

For the sole owner the profit-maximising sustainable harvest is not maximum sustainable yield. Further, note that as r increases so will the size of g which equates to it, and hence the corresponding sole ownership constant stock size will fall. For slow-growing species, a high interest rate implies low stock sizes. Thus sole ownership is consistent with some species being maintained at low population sizes, with the consequent risk of extinction due to environmental perturbations (either 'natural' or originating in economic activity, as with pollution). It is not true that harvesting to extinction can only occur under a free access regime.

Recall now that intertemporal efficiency requires the equalisation of rates of return across alternative types of investment. Profit-maximising firms invest up to the point where their rates of return equal the rate of interest, so that they are equalised. It follows that, in the absence of market failure, profit-maximising firms invest consistently with the requirements of intertemporal efficiency. We now see that this story applies to firms in the fishing business, operating under a sole ownership regime. This extends to the exploitation of renewable resources generally. Given sole ownership regimes, renewable resources are exploited as required for intertemporal efficiency. This may entail harvesting to extinction. This is not the general outcome. This is more likely, the slower growing the exploited resource stock is, the higher is the interest rate. This implies that low interest rates mean lower probabilities of harvesting to extinction.

Efficiency and environmental protection

Intertemporal efficiency in renewable resource exploitation is the standard against which economists consider the question of over-exploitation. Thus, when it is said that a free access fishery will be over-exploited, this means that more fish will be taken than is required for intertemporal efficiency. Sole ownership exploitation means, other sources of market failure absent, that intertemporal efficiency is obtained. For slow growing species this may entail a high probability of extinction. Some pollution problems involve cumulative effects over time. In such cases, efficiency may be consistent with the biological death of the receiving environmental media. This is more likely the higher is the rate of interest. An EPA optimally controlling discharges into a lake, for example, according to efficiency criteria may, that is, allow a discharge programme that eventually reduces its assimilative capacity to zero.[22]

Many non-economists find it shocking that economists generally accept as a performance target a criterion which may have these implications. How can anybody advocate environmental and resource policies which, if successful, do not afford complete protection to stocks of renewable resources and environmental waste receptacles? Is this not self-evidently unfair to future generations? The answer to these questions comes in three related parts. First, economists judge matters according to human interests only. Environmental damage matters only to the extent that it impacts on humans. Second, economists assume, in the absence of positive evidence to the contrary, the existence of substitutes for any given environmental base for a service or resource flow of interest to humans. Thus, if one waste receptacle becomes biologically dead and incapable of assimilating further wastes, it is assumed that another can be found. Or, if one renewable resource stock is exploited to extinction, another can be exploited. Further, there are assumed to be non-environmental substitutes available in many cases. Environmental assets are generally taken to be just like the assets that are items of man-made capital equipment, in that if one wears out it can be replaced. Given the assumed substitution possibilities, the matter of intergenerational equity is to be handled via the Hartwick rule. Third, economists generally ignore the interconnections between component systems in the biosphere, and between environmental functions in relation to human activity. The elimination of the assimilative capacity of a lake, for example, is assumed not to have any implications for other components of the biosphere of interest to humans.

In relation to the second of these reasons, some economists do recognise that there are some environmental assets for which it may be prudent to assume that there are no substitutes. The question of species extinctions was discussed in the previous section, and the idea of the SMS approach noted. It would be fair to say, however, that such arguments and proposals have had minimal impact on the way that the great majority of economists think.

Non-renewable resources

Now consider the intertemporally efficient depletion of non-renewable resource stocks. To introduce the basic ideas, consider oil and suppose that there are many oil deposits identical in terms of oil quality, extraction costs etc., and that each deposit is owned by a competitive price taker firm.[23] Assume away all market failure. Given this, oil will be depleted as required by intertemporal efficiency. Owners of oil deposits invest in oil in the ground, forgo extracting it, such that the rate of return on oil investment is equal to the rate of interest. This means that the rate of return on oil investment is equal to the rate of return on other investments, which is the condition for intertemporal efficiency.

There is one important difference between oil and fish in this context. The former does not reproduce itself and the stock does not grow in the absence of extraction. A barrel of oil left in the ground today is just a barrel of oil available tomorrow. Where then does the return to oil investment come from? It comes from the increasing scarcity of oil that necessarily goes with a positive rate of extraction. Oil left in the ground becomes more valuable per barrel over time. The value of a barrel of oil in the ground is the difference between the price of a barrel of extracted oil and the cost of extracting it. This is known as the **rent** on a barrel of oil in the ground, and will be referred to as R. As oil stocks are depleted so rent increases. The rate of return to leaving oil in the ground for a period is the proportionate change in rent over the period, R^* equal to $(R_t - R_{t-1})/R_{t-1}$ where $t-1$ and t refer to the beginning and end of the period. The condition for intertemporal efficiency in oil extraction/investment is that in every period R^* is equal to r, the rate of interest.

To see why sole ownership of oil deposits will, given no market failure anywhere, lead to the satisfaction of this condition, think of R as the price of the right to extract a barrel of oil. The firms owning the oil deposits sell these rights to firms in the oil extraction business. At any point in time the most that an extraction firm would pay for the right to extract a barrel of oil is R, the difference between the cost of extraction and the price for which the extracted oil can be sold. A competitive oil-owning firm has to decide how many unit extraction rights to sell in each period. Consider two periods, 0 and 1. Trade in extraction rights for both periods takes place at the start of period 0. If $R^* = r$, oil-owning firms will have no incentive to alter the balance of permits between the two periods, as this offers them exactly the same rate of return as does any other form of investment. If, however, the market in extraction permits is such that R^* is less than r, they will wish to alter the balance of extraction permits between periods 0 and 1. They will wish to sell more period 0 permits, and consequently less period 1 permits, as by so doing they will raise money which they can use to earn a rate of return r, which is better than the rate on oil investment currently on offer. But, a revised programme of permit sales between 0 and 1, with more 0 permits and less 1 permits, will reduce R_0, the price of period 0 permits, and increase R_1. This will increase R^* toward r. The situation is the converse where R^* is initially greater than r. Equilibrium in the market for permits to extract oil will only be reached when R^* is equal to r, as is required for intertemporal efficiency.

Recall from Chapter 3 that the Hartwick rule says that, for constant consumption given depleting oil reserves, the total rent arising from an efficient oil depletion programme should be invested in capital accumulation. This is exactly what is happening in the situation above. First, given no market failure, private property rights in oil deposits ensure that the depletion programme is efficient. Second, the rents arising are being invested. The owners of the oil deposits are equating the rate of return on oil investment with the rate of interest at the margin. The rule does not require that these owners themselves undertake capital investment projects. It does require that for the economy as a whole the rents are used for capital investment. The owners can be thought of as putting the funds arising as rents into the market where the rate of interest is determined along with total savings and investment. Given that the market is working properly, and that non-oil projects are being properly appraised, the oil depletion rents will be invested as required by the Hartwick rule.

Why then is the rule relevant to policy considerations, if market forces will ensure that it is realised. There are two reasons why the rule is, in fact, policy-relevant. First, in the real world, pervasive market failure means that fulfilment of the rule is not assured as the outcome of commercial behaviour by firms. Second, non-renewable resource rents are not typically left entirely with deposit-owning firms. Rather, they are subject to tax by government. The Hartwick rule is then relevant to the use that the government makes of the tax revenues arising.

There are two closely related reasons why the taxation of non-renewable resource rents is ubiquitous. First, resource rents are widely seen as being in the nature of unearned income, the taxation of which is required on the grounds of fairness. Rent is not a payment for effort. It is a payment arising from pure scarcity. Second, and following from this, rent could be heavily taxed without affecting the depletion decisions of resource deposit owners. Resource rent taxation at the rate of 99 per cent would not interfere with the attainment of intertemporal efficiency. This makes such rent a very attractive tax base, given that the taxation problem is seen as that of raising revenue while doing the least possible harm to the efficiency property of market outcomes.[24]

To the extent that resource rents are taxed, the Hartwick rule concerns the use by government of the revenues arising. It is concerned with possible government failure. It says that those revenues should be used to finance productive investment, rather than current consumption. Thus, resource rent revenues should be used to finance, for example, investment in infrastructure or education, rather than used to finance welfare benefits, arms expenditure, or reduced income taxation. Of course, in using this revenue for investment, government should select projects according to the positive *NPV* rule. In this form the Hartwick rule is, operationally, a general guiding principle rather than a precise rule. As such, it makes a great deal of intuitive sense. In relation to government, the operational version of the rule is that it requires that resource rent tax receipts are at least matched by expenditures on investment. Where this is not true, it can be said that government policy is not consistent with sustainability.

Recall from Chapter 3 that following the Hartwick rule is necessary but not sufficient for sustainability as constant consumption. Sufficiency depends on there being substitutes for the depleting non-renewable resources. It is sometimes suggested that where non-renewable energy resources are being depleted, sustainability requires that government ensure that some of the rents arising be invested in the development of renewable energy resource supplies.[25] Given all the conditions that mean that market failure is totally absent, this would be unnecessary. The price signals sent by markets would ensure that projects for renewable energy development would attract sufficient investment funds. Of course, market, and government, failure is actually pervasive so that this type of policy merits consideration.

Assumptions and policy

In this and the preceding chapter we have reviewed some of the basic ideas in economics and how they have been applied to issues arising from the interconnections between economic activity and the natural environment. In Chapter 6 we saw that on the basis of certain assumptions, the attainment of efficiency, but not equity, could be left to markets. The assumptions were of two types. There were **behavioural assumptions** about economic agents, and **circumstantial assumptions** about the conditions in which those agents operated. As regards behaviour, it is assumed that agents, firms and individuals, are rational. It is also assumed that rational behaviour takes place in an environment where there are complete markets, complete information and where all agents act as price-takers. Given all of these assumptions, the 'invisible hand' works and the market equilibrium is an efficient allocation. The main thrust of resource and environmental economics is to address the consequences of, and remedies for, violation of the complete markets assumption. The objective of remedial analysis is to prescribe corrections such that efficiency will be attained. Where information on individual preferences, and the technologies available to firms, is not revealed in markets, it is very difficult for a social agency to otherwise determine what constitutes efficiency. Hence, attention shifts to what economists call arbitrary standards, and the choice between alternative means by which to pursue them. In this analysis of policy instrument choice, the behavioural assumptions described above are retained, and the preferred instrument is that which does the job at least cost.

The behavioural assumptions used in these kinds of economic analysis are widely questioned. The consumer sovereignty criterion, which follows fairly naturally from these behavioural assumptions plus the circumstantial assumption of complete information, has also been widely criticised. The analysis of the means for achieving given goals is less sensitive to these questions and criticisms than is the analysis that uses the assumptions to define social goals. We can distinguish two claims for market systems and reliance on price incentives. One is that they are the best way to determine (subject to some caveats about equity) and realise (subject to some need to correct market failure) social goals. This is the claim made by most economists nowadays. The second is that for given social goals, price incentive systems are the best from among the range of alternative policy instruments available. The second claim is more robust to alternative behavioural assumptions.

Once multiple sources of market failure are recognised, which cannot be simultaneously dealt with, we are in the world of the second best where it is impossible to make confident statements about the welfare consequences of alternative social choices using the criteria of efficiency and consumer sovereignty. It is also impossible to make confident statements on any other criteria. Particularly, but not exclusively, where environmental impacts are involved we are dealing with uncertainty.

So where does all this leave us? The argument here is that standard economics has quite a lot to say that is useful about the problems associated with human use of the natural environment. What it has to say is most useful where it is concerned with the means to socially agreed ends. It is least useful where it seeks to prescribe those ends in terms of efficiency criteria. That leaves the ends to be otherwise determined, presumably by a democratic political process. This puts many of the problems that attend the economic approach into a different context, rather than solving them. To treat an individual as a voting citizen rather than a consumer in relation to environmental decision making, for example, does not improve the knowledge base on which she operates. Political decision making is as much attended by ignorance and uncertainty as are market transactions. The matter of government failure was discussed in Chapter 6.

On some views, the whole sustainability issue is so affected by uncertainty and indeterminacy that it is appropriate to focus on social decision-making processes rather than outcomes. This means a focus on information flows and institutions, and the neat distinction between policy objectives and instruments adopted here breaks down. It provides a rather different perspective on the activities listed against the moral suasion category in the section on policy instruments. These are then seen not as ineffective instruments for given ends, but as elements of the process from which imperfectly articulated ends emerge.

CHAPTER 8

Some new economics

The two previous chapters reviewed mainstream economics and its application to the analysis of policy in respect of the natural environment. Many commentators have suggested that a new economics is needed, and a variety of proposals in this direction have been made. In this chapter we review, and comment on, some of these proposals.

Green accounting

There has emerged a view that modifications to national income accounting procedures are crucial to the pursuit of sustainability. A representative statement claims that:

> A country could exhaust its mineral resources, cut down its forests, erode its soils, pollute its aquifers, and hunt its wildlife to extinction, but measured income would not be affected as these assets disappeared.

Here, 'measured income' is national income calculated on the basis of existing accounting conventions as gross domestic product (GDP). Further, it is claimed that:

> politicians, journalists and even sophisticated economists in official agencies continue to use GDP growth as the prime measure of economic performance

and that:

> only if the basic measures of economic performance ... are brought into conformity with a valid definition of income will economic policies be influenced toward sustainability.[1]

The call here is for a revision to national income accounting practices such that what is measured is sustainable income. In this context, sustainable income is the maximum consumption possible during a period, such that the society has the same wealth at the end of the period as at the start of it. Wealth is the total value of society's assets, including both assets produced by economic activity and environmental assets. We will call the measure of sustainable income **proper net domestic product (PNDP)**. The position exemplified by the above statements is that the availability of PNDP data is necessary for the attainment of sustainability. Green accounting, more properly **natural resource accounting** or **environmental accounting**, is the means by which PNDP data would be produced.

Current practices and problems

The most widely used national income measures are **gross national product (GNP)** and **gross domestic product (GDP)**. We will conduct the discussion initially in terms of GDP. The conventions now used for GDP measurement have their origin in the information requirements generated by the Keynesian revolution. The need was for a measure of the total demand for the outputs of produced commodities, so that the economy could be fine-tuned, to avoid unemployment and inflation. The accounting conventions reflect their origin in this need for information for demand management.

However, given that GDP measures total demand, it also measures the output produced to meet that demand. GDP came to be seen as a measure of economic performance. An increase in GDP meant that more was being produced. GDP came to be accorded status as a welfare indicator. Indeed, for many commentators it effectively became *the* welfare indicator, with the pursuit of GDP growth as the major objective for economic policy. However, the conventions by which the GDP measure is constructed are such that, even leaving aside environmental considerations, it is a seriously flawed welfare indicator. While economists have been writing about this for some time, this has had relatively little impact at the level of general public debate and perception. The majority of participants in the policy process do use GDP as a 'prime measure of economic performance'.

GDP actually measures three things. Or rather, GDP can be measured in three ways. Given the conventions for national income accounting, each way of measuring it yields, in principle, the same numerical result.[2]

First, GDP is the total output sold by firms measured by **value added**. GDP is not the total value of sales by firms. To see the distinction, consider a bakery which buys in mixed dough and sells bread. It spends

$x on the dough, and its sales amount to $y. This bakery's contribution to GDP is $y – $x, the value which it has added to the dough, not $y. The purchase of the dough is the purchase of an **intermediate good**, an input to its production produced elsewhere in the economy. In measuring GDP purchases of intermediate goods are netted out.

Second, GDP is the sum of the incomes earned by persons in the economy. This is the most obvious rationale for calling GDP 'national income'. The sum of incomes is equal to the value of total output produced by firms by virtue of the convention that output is measured in terms of value added. If we subtract from a firm's sales receipts the amount that it paid to other firms for intermediate goods, what is left is both the firm's value added and the amount that it necessarily pays to the people who work for it, and to its owners.

Third, GDP is total expenditure by individuals on consumption plus expenditure by firms on capital equipment, i.e. investment. Note that firms' expenditure on intermediate goods is not included here, only their expenditure on items of durable capital equipment. The distinction turns on whether or not the purchase by a firm is totally used up in current production. Thus, for the bakery the purchase of dough is not included in its expenditure for the purpose of measuring GDP. The dough is used up in current production. If, on the other hand, the bakery buys a new oven, this is an item of durable capital equipment not used up in current period production, and the expenditure involved is part of GDP.

Given these conventions, each way of measuring GDP should produce the same numerical result. The value added measure of firms' total output equals the incomes generated in firms which in turn, equals total expenditure on non-intermediate goods, known as **final expenditure**. In reality, the three ways of measuring GDP do not produce the same numbers due to errors arising in the collection of data from the very large number of firms and individuals in an actual economy. To preserve the principle, published national income accounts introduce a residual error term, and write the final output, expenditure and income numbers as the same after adding in that term. The expenditure measure of GDP is generally regarded as the most reliable.

Now, from the point of view of demand management for macroeconomic stabilisation, GDP is a reasonable measure. Changes in it reflect changes in the total demand for produced goods and services. As a measure of economic performance, GDP is, leaving aside environmental considerations, not satisfactory. It is not a measure of sustainable income. It does not measure the maximum consumption possible during a period which would leave the society with the same wealth at the end of the period as at the beginning of it. The society's wealth is its stock of capital, its productive assets. As it is used in production, so capital equipment wears out. The extent to which it wears out in a period is known as **depreciation**. A measure of sustainable income for a period would therfore be output less depreciation. It would measure not the total production of capital equipment during the period, but only the production of such over and above that required to compensate for depreciation.

Thus, GDP overstates sustainable income. It is universally agreed that the proper measure of national income for the purposes of monitoring national economic performance is **net domestic product (NDP)**. This is GDP less that part of it required to cover depreciation. However, GDP is much more widely used than NDP. The reason for this is that it is very difficult to measure depreciation accurately. National income statisticians prefer a number which is an accurate measure of an admittedly unsatisfactory concept to an inaccurate measure of a more satisfactory concept. Recall also that GDP is a satisfactory concept in relation to the requirements of macroeconomic stabilisation.

We now note some of the complications arising from trade between economies, and the role of government. We do this in the context of the measurement of GDP, but the considerations also apply to the net basis of measurement.

Taking international trade first, there are two points to note. The first concerns trade flows. For an economy which exports and imports, GDP is defined as indicated above plus the excess of exports over imports. There are two reasons for such a convention. First, production for export means incomes generated in the domestic economy, whereas importation corresponds to income generation overseas. Second, what is available for consumption or investment in the domestic economy is output from production in the domestic economy minus that part which is shipped overseas, i.e. exports, plus output produced overseas but shipped into the domestic economy, ie imports.

The next point relates to the distinction between GDP and GNP. **Factors of production** are primary inputs to production, i.e. inputs to production other than intermediate goods, and comprise labour services, capital services, entrepreneurship (organisation and risk-taking), and inputs of natural resources (including land). GNP measures the value of the output produced by domestically owned factors of production, irrespective of the physical location of production. The output produced overseas by a domestically owned and staffed factory is part of domestic GNP; the output produced in the domestic economy by a foreign-owned and staffed factory is not. GDP measures the value of the output produced by factors of production actually located in the domestic economy, irrespective of the national origin of the factors or their ownership. If the interest is in the level of economic activity in the domestic economy, as it is for macroeconomic stabilisation purposes, GDP is the more appropriate measure. If the interest is in the incomes earned by domestic factors of production, GNP is the more appropriate measure. For most economies, the difference between GDP and GNP is not very large.

Government economic activity complicates matters in several ways. First, the services provided by government are not typically sold in markets, and many are not subject to charges at the point of use. Such services do not fit with the conventions of national income accounting as described above, but are clearly part of national income. Their provision generates labour incomes, and provides services – such as education, policing, security from foreign aggression – for consumption by individuals. The practice adopted is to value these services at the costs of provision. Second, government makes **transfer payments** to individuals, such as retirement pensions, unemployment benefits, sickness benefits etc., which are grants rather than payments for factor services. This means that the total of the incomes actually received by individuals is not the same as the total of payments to factors of production. Third, government raises revenue to finance its own expenditure through taxation on personal incomes and wealth, and on expenditure. The former are known as **direct taxes**, the latter as **indirect taxes**. The existence of direct taxation contributes further to the divergence between total factor payments and total personal incomes received. The existence of indirect taxation complicates matters in so far as market transactions can be measured using prices which include or exclude the tax element.

As economic performance indicators, national income data are interesting when they are used to make comparisons. The comparisons can involve a single economy at different points in time, or a number of economies at a point in time, or the histories of different economies. In making welfare comparisons, adjustment should clearly be made for population size, and per capita national income used. For some purposes, GDP itself may be appropriate. Thus, for example, military capability and strategic influence would generally follow from total rather than per capita national income. Consider, for example, China and Australia. With regard to international comparisons, reference was made in Chapter 2 to the problems arising from the fact that domestic currencies differ, and that official exchange rates do not always reflect the relative domestic purchasing powers of those currencies. A related problem attends comparisons of GDP at points in time for a single economy. First, the data must be corrected for inflation. If the general price level doubles, the purchasing power of a currency unit halves. It is relatively straightforward, and standard practice, to adjust historical GDP figures for an economy so that they are expressed in terms of currency units of constant purchasing power. Such measures are referred to as **real GDP data**.

A more fundamental problem in making welfare comparisons over time for a single economy is that the relative prices of commodities change. In competitive markets, relative prices change when supply and/or demand functions shift. Supply functions shift with changing costs of production. Demand functions shift with changes in income and/or changes in preferences between different commodities. The problem for national income comparisons over time arises to the extent that it is changing preferences between commodities that drives changing relative prices. The idea that an x per cent increase in per capita national income means that the representative individual is x per cent better off depends crucially on the assumption that the preferences of the representative individual are the same at both points in time. This may be a reasonable assumption for periods just a few years apart, but is not reasonable for comparisons over 20 years or more. The validity of such a comparison also depends, of course, on the reasonableness of the assumption of a representative individual.

A number of other problems attending the interpretation of national income as a welfare indicator have been noted in the literature.[3] First, there is the problem of **defensive expenditure**, that is expenditure on goods and services which takes place in order to offset harm rather than to positively enhance individual well-being. An example is expenditure on policing. Suppose that criminal activity suddenly increases, that the government responds by increasing its expenditure on law enforcement, and that the effect is to restore criminal activity to its original level. No individual is better off. However, national income will have increased by the amount of the increase in public expenditure, less the amount by which private consumption expenditure falls due to increased taxation necessary to finance this public expenditure. While the basic nature of the defensive expenditure problem is clear, defining it for measurement purposes would be difficult. Standard national income accounting conventions do not attempt any correction. In fact, recognising defensive expenditure could be quite subversive. It can be argued that there is very little consumption that is not at least partially defensive in nature. We use medical services to avoid ill health, we eat to avoid hunger, we seek entertainment to avoid boredom, and so on. In modern industrial societies one might also take the view that much consumer expenditure is defensive with respect to feelings of deprivation engendered by advertising, and the expenditure of others.

Second, much of the activity that promotes well-being simply is not accounted for, since it involves neither market transactions in goods and services nor paid employment. A widely cited example of this type of problem is that of unpaid domestic work. This is contributory to individuals' well-being, albeit that much of it too can be seen as defensive, but it is not measured at all in national income. Suppose that a large number of individuals stopped eating at home, taking all of their meals in restaurants. For the same food consumption, national income would increase by virtue of, and in the amount of, the additional paid employment generated in the restaurants. The case would be similar with a switch from home to commercial laundering.

In both of these cases, it can be objected that there are corresponding improvements in well-being, in so far as the individuals no longer cooking or laundering in their homes would have more leisure, so that it is appropriate for national income to increase. There is some merit in this because of a third problem about national income as a measure of economic performance. This is the fact that national income does not increase with increasing leisure for constant output. If a sudden improvement in working practices meant that exactly the same quantities of every type of goods and services could be produced with, say, 10 per cent less labour input, national income would not change. Note, however, that if individuals bought more leisure goods for use with the additional leisure time, that would increase national income.

A fourth problem widely noted is that changes in per capita national income say nothing about concurrent differences in the distribution of personal incomes. Increasing national income is consistent with widening disparities between rich and poor.

Accounting for the environment

The emergence of the sustainability issue stimulated concern about problems with national income accounting conventions in relation to their treatment of the interconnections between economic activity and the natural environment. It is argued, as in the quotation at the beginning of this chapter, that, as measured, national income is not a measure of sustainable income in so far as it does not account for the effects of environmental degradation.

In this context, attention has focused on two matters. First, defensive expenditures to offset environmental degradation actually increase national income. Thus, for example, government expenditure to clean up a polluted river or lake would increase national income. Second, national income measures do not reflect the depletion and degradation of environmental assets caused by economic activity. The point here is that natural resources and the bases for waste assimilation, amenity and life support services are part of the stock of assets upon which economic activity is based, just as much as are items of capital equipment such as machines, buildings, roads etc. In order to measure sustainable income, it is necessary to include the value of environmental assets in the wealth which is to be held constant. Thus, it is argued, the depreciation to be subtracted from gross income to arrive at net, or sustainable, income should include natural asset depreciation as well as the depreciation of man-made assets. If this were done, it is argued, sustainable income, or PNDP, would be measured.

Modifications to national income accounting conventions are under active consideration by national and international statistical agencies, and some proposals for conventions for PNDP measurement have emerged from a series of conferences and workshops.[4] In essence, these proposals are as follows. First, defensive expenditures in respect of environmental damage would be identified, measured and subtracted from the conventional measure of GDP, to give a measure of 'environmentally adjusted GDP'. Next, 'environmental cost' would be subtracted to give a measure of 'sustainable GDP'. Environmental cost is the reduction over the period in the value of the total stock of environmental assets, to be measured by multiplying the physical change in the size of each environmental asset by a corresponding unit price and then summing the values arising across the different assets. Third, the depreciation of total man-made assets, the capital stock as currently defined, would be subtracted from sustainable GDP to give PNDP, the measure of sustainable income. These proposals do not address the problems of national income as a welfare indicator considered above.

There are three new tasks here for national income statisticians. First, the identification and measurement of defensive expenditure. Second, the physical measurement of all of the relevant environmental assets at the start and end of the period. Third, the valuation of each of the relevant measured physical changes in environmental asset size. None of these is trivial. However, we concentrate on the second and third, since it is the problems which arise there that reveal most sharply the fundamental difficulty in seeking to measure sustainable income. The complete enumeration of the environmental assets relevant to economic activity would itself be an impossible task. It is not known, for example, how many species exist. Many have not yet been observed and taxonomically identified and we cannot assume that the species that we do not know about are irrelevant to economic activity. Some of them may be very important, in, for example, the functioning of the systems that provide life support services. In fact, the PNDP measurement proposals do not envisage that all environmental assets would be accounted for. In principle, only those directly relevant to economic activity would be considered. In practice, it is envisaged that only those currently commercially exploited would be accounted for.

It is recognised that both the restricted principle and the envisaged practice mean that what would be measured would not be PNDP as such. The idea is that the result arising would be nearer to PNDP than national income measured on current conventions, and would promote economic management more in line with sustainability requirements. We return to this shortly. Suppose that all environmental asset stocks could be measured physically each year. For PNDP measurement there would remain the problem of the valuation of the annual changes. The basic idea in economics, discussed in Chapter 7, is that shadow prices should be attached to environmental assets which reflect individuals' willingness to pay for them. There are many problems in ascertaining individuals' willingness to pay. But, leaving these aside, there remains the deeper question of whether shadow prices so determined would be appropriate. As noted in the section on an energy theory of value below, on some views they would be ethically inappropriate, and there are problems about the information that individuals can have when coming to a view about their willingness to pay. There is no real reason to suppose that individual preferences align with sustainability requirements. If they do not, then using valuations reflecting those preferences will not measure the sustainability-relevant changes in the total stock of environmental assets.[5]

To illustrate, consider that, over a period, all environmental asset levels save two are constant. Suppose that what cannot really be known, is known. The numbers of a species of microbes decline dramatically, while the numbers of a species of charismatic mammal increase. The microbe species plays a key role in biosphere functioning in relation to human interests in life support services. The charismatic mammal is ecologically redundant; its extinction would have absolutely no effect on biospheric functioning of interest to humanity apart from some loss of amenity service. Willingness-to-pay surveys have revealed that individuals place no value on members of the microbe species, but a large positive value on the members of the mammal species. Then, according to these values, the total stock of environmental assets increases over the period, whereas a threat to sustainability has increased in magnitude.

The view is sometimes expressed that matters would be improved so long as environmental assets are given any positive value, where they are given zero value on current accounting practices. As the example here indicates, this is not the case. For zero values attached to microbes and mammals, there would be a recorded change of zero in the total value of the stock of environmental assets. A very small positive unit valuation of microbes and a very large unit valuation of mammals could produce an increase in total value, corresponding to an increased threat to sustainability, sending a more misleading signal than zero valuations for both microbe and mammal.

We conclude that, at the level of principle, the search for a measure of sustainable income (PNDP) is not going to be successful. This does not mean that there is no reason to collect and publish physical data on the state of environmental assets. On the contrary, it is only by means of the availability of such data that improved understanding of economy–environment interconnections will come about. The terms **natural resource, or environmental, accounting** are sometimes used to refer to the activity of providing data on the state of environmental assets in physical terms. Some countries have already instituted this kind of natural resource accounting.[6] **State of the environment reporting** also involves physical, as opposed to price and value, data, but here the organisation of, and interest in, the data is from an environmental perspective rather than an economic one.[7] Where relative prices are not used, it is impossible to describe the state of all environmental assets in a single number. One can say that oil stocks have decreased, fish stocks increased, and so on, but there is no way of expressing the overall effect as a single number – fewer barrels of oil in the ground cannot be subtracted from more fish in the water in the way that dollars worth of oil can be subtracted from dollars worth of fish.

The provision of public information on economic performance and associated environmental impact has a role in addressing threats to sustainability. The provision of such information can be regarded as a policy instrument, for the objective of addressing threats to sustainability, of the moral suasion class. One barrier to the adoption of policies to address such threats in the industrial economies would appear to be that many of the inhabitants have excessive faith in the ability of economic growth to improve human well-being, an incomplete appreciation of the connections between industrial expansion and the state of the environment, and of the likely implications of that for the future. The greater availability of understandable information on these matters is important. The point about PNDP in this regard is not so much that it is imperfect, but that its advocates raise false hopes about what it can do. More modest ambitions would be more appropriate. In Chapter 4 we considered a simple and inexpensive approach to the assessment of comparative economic performance adjusted for its environmental impact. The single number representation involved does not purport to capture all of the dimensions involved, as does PNDP. An alternative approach, not mutually exclusive, would be the systematic and regular reporting of movements in a small number of key environmental, economic and social indicators.[8] Debate over which indicators should be included would itself improve the level of awareness of the complex issues involved. The approach which seeks to wrap everything up in a single number for PNDP runs the risk of fostering the belief that matters are simpler, and better understood, than they are in fact.

One sustainability-relevant indicator follows from the Hartwick rule. In an operational form this says that the pursuit of sustainability requires that the rents actually arising in natural resource exploitation be invested in man-made capital. A sustainability-relevant indicator is then the ratio of net investment, i.e. total investment minus depreciation as reported in the existing national income accounts, to total natural resource rents. If the ratio is one or more, a necessary condition for sustainability is being satisfied. Otherwise it is not. It would be useful if national statistical agencies computed and published this ratio. They do not. Nor do any attempts to estimate it from published data appear to have been made. Pearce and Atkinson (1993) report the results of a closely related exercise. They compare total investment with a figure for the total of depreciation on man-made capital and the estimated depreciation of natural capital, which is the totality of environmental assets. If investment is greater than the sum of the two depreciations, we can say that a necessary condition for sustainability is being satisfied, subject to caveats about the accuracy of the estimated depreciation of natural capital. Of the 18 countries considered in Pearce and Atkinson, 10 have net investment equal to or greater than total depreciation. The eight for which a necessary condition for sustainability is not apparently being satisfied are all developing countries.

An energy theory of value?

Energy is clearly important in relation to an understanding of the sustainability problem. Some take the view that the most useful way to think about sustainability, and threats to it, is in terms of energy. It has been claimed, by economists, that energy analysts propose an energy theory of value, for which there is no need, and which would actually be unhelpful. Most energy analysts would deny that their purpose is an energy theory of value. The position taken here is that energy analysis is one useful way of thinking about sustainability issues.

Energy accounting

Energy accounting is the description of some actual production process, or processes, in terms of energy inputs.[9] To illustrate the insights that energy accounting can provide, consider the production of food. Table 8.1 shows the energy inputs to food production for a hunter–gatherer system, and for three agricultural systems. In the case of food, the output of the production process can also be measured in energy units. An adult human requires approximately 10 MJ of input food energy per day.[10] Table 8.1 shows the food outputs measured in energy units (MJ) and the ratios of output to total input and of output to labour input. The data refer to inputs and output per unit of land area (one hectare) per unit of time (one year). The four production processes shown in Table 8.1 have been selected in the light of the discussion in Chapter 4 here of the hunter–gatherer, agricultural and industrial phases of human history. The input accounting does not include the incident solar radiation, which would be approximately the same across all the cases.

Table 8.1 *Food provision energy accounts*

	1	2	3	4
Labour	0.37	5650	460	20
Animals		960	2180	
Machinery		230[a]	1010	18590
Fertiliser			450	11660
Pesticides			60	1090
Drying				4480
Irrigation				29620
Total Inputs	0.37	6840	4160	65460
Output	2.90	281100	22900	84120
Output/Input	7.8	41.1	5.5	1.3
Output/Labour Input	7.8	49.7	49.8	4206.0

Note: 1 – Hunting and gathering, Kung! Bushmen – Africa.
2 – Pre-industrial agriculture, Chinese peasant farming, 1935–37
3 – Semi-industrial agriculture, rice-growing – Philippines.
4 – Industrial agriculture, rice-growing – United States
Units are MJ per hectare per annum.
[a] Hand tools and ploughs
Source: Leach (1975).

The hunting and gathering food production process uses only human energy input. Hence the ratio of output to human energy input is the same as the ratio of output to total energy input. Pre-industrial agriculture uses animal, as well as human, muscle power, and some energy is used in making the tools used. As compared with hunting and gathering, there is a large increase in input and output. A hectare of suitable land both supports more individuals and requires more individuals to work it. The output to labour input ratio is much greater than for hunting and gathering. Semi-industrial agriculture uses limited amounts of inputs, fertiliser and pesticides, provided by an industrial sector. Industrial agriculture makes extensive use of industrial inputs and no use of animal

muscle power. The particular example shown is rice production in the
United States. Note, first, that output per hectare per year is vastly greater
than that for hunting and gathering, four times that for rice-growing in
the Philippines, but less than that for Chinese peasant farming. However, this form of rice production also uses much more extrasomatic
energy input than any of the others, and much less direct human energy
input as labour than the two other agricultural processes shown. The
ratio of output energy to input labour energy is much higher than for
any of the other cases. But, when we look at the ratio for total energy
input to total energy output, this particular version of industrial agriculture performs relatively poorly. Industrial agricultrue on this criterion,
is a much less efficient food production process than pre-industrial
agriculture, and less efficient than hunting and gathering.

Figure 8.1 shows the ratios of the energy content of output to the total
energy input for a large number of agricultural food production processes, calculated as in Table 8.1. ER stands for energy ratio. The broad
picture conveyed in Figure 8.1 and Table 8.1 is consistent with other
studies.[11] The accounts for Table 8.1 and Figure 8.1 do not include energy
used in processing, distribution, retailing and customer travel: input and
output accounting stops at 'the farm gate'. For full industrial agriculture
it is typically the case, as it is not for semi- and pre-industrial agriculture,
that substantial amounts of extrasomatic energy, and other inputs are
used in transforming the agricultural output into food actually available
to consumers (see Table 4.2, p.69).

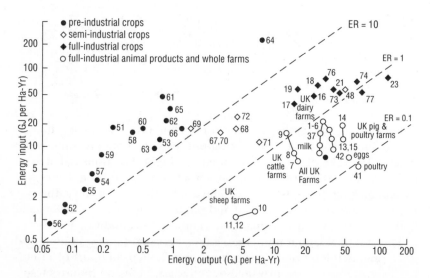

Figure 8.1 Food production: energy inputs and outputs.
Source: Leach (1975).

Basically the story of Table 8.1 and Figure 8.1 is that industrial agriculture, compared with pre-industrial agriculture and hunting and gathering, is characterised by high labour and land productivity and low energy productivity. Figure 8.1 shows that for some industrial crops and for most industrial animal products the ratio of energy output to input falls below 1. This is striking. If we consider the food-gathering strategies adopted by animals, clearly, for such strategies to be viable, the ratio of energy contained in food obtained to energy expended in food acquisition must be at least one.[12] This might suggest that an agricultural process with an ER less than one is to be regarded as non-viable. On the other hand, the processes for which ER is less than one in Figure 8.1 do actually operate, and contribute to the feeding of large populations.

The point is that in the case of animals, and pre-industrial food production processes, inputs and outputs are constrained to lie within the parameters set by the capture of solar radiation and the conversion efficiencies of plants and animals. Industrial agriculture is not so constrained, by virtue of the use of fossil fuels. This is most apparent in the case of artificial fertiliser application. Its production is highly energy, i.e. fossil fuel, intensive. Given available supplies of fossil fuel, industrial agriculture gives high labour and land use efficiencies. The main point revealed by the energy accounting is really the significance of the 'given' condition. Fossil fuels are non-renewable resources. Industrial agriculture, to date, has been dependent on the depletion of stocks of fossil fuel resources.

Consider now energy supply systems. Work, and hence energy, are required to make energy available. Suppose that a new oil field is discovered and its size measured in energy units is x MJ. This does not mean that energy availability has increased by x MJ. Getting the oil from under the ground and making it useful, itself requires work and energy, thus reducing the real increase in energy availability to something less than x MJ, say y MJ. Fossil fuels, and other energy sources, vary in the extent of the difference between x and y – coal differs from oil, and from nuclear power. Particular deposits of a given kind of fossil fuel also differ from one another in the relative sizes of x and y.

The analysis of these matters is known as **net energy analysis**. It involves the computation of the difference between x and y for various actual and potential sources of energy. An alternative way of doing this is the computation of the **energy return on investment (EROI)** as the energy content of the useable fuel obtained divided by the energy required to make the fuel available.[13] An energy source for which x – y is negative, or EROI is less than one, is a sink rather than a source. To illustrate the nature of the information yielded by these types of exercises, Table 8.2 gives some EROI figures for actual and potential energy supply systems.[14] Oil shale is a fossil fuel not yet exploited on any significant scale, so that the estimates for it are based primarily on engineering studies: at the lower end of the range of estimates, oil shale would be a sink rather than a source. This is also true for the two biomass sources shown in Table 8.2. Solar space heating is shown as a source, even when allowance is made for the production and use of a fossil fuel based backup system to provide heat when sunlight is not providing sufficient radiation.

Table 8.2 *Estimates of Energy Return on Investment*

Fossil Fuels	
Oil and Gas (Wellhead)	23.0
Coal (Mine head)	80.0
Oil Shale	0.7 – 13.3
Biomass and Solar	
Ethanol (Sugarcane)	0.8 – 1.7
Ethanol (Corn residues)	0.7 – 1.8
Solar Space Heating[a]	1.6 – 1.9

Note: [a] including fossil fuel backup.
Source: Cleveland *et al.* (1984).

Thermodynamics

Accounts tell us about what has happened. Thinking about future prospects requires either that we simply extrapolate the past relationships revealed in historical data, or that we use some additional information. In the case of industrial agriculture we could add to the accounting data the assessment that in the long run, fossil fuel depletion will increase energy prices, with the implication that food prices will also rise, and labour and land productivity will fall as less energy is used in food production. This assessment is based on the assumption that substitutes for fossil fuels will be more expensive than fossil fuels are currently. This assumption in turn derives from an appreciation of existing and foreseeable technologies.

Here we use the term **energy analysis** for the activity which is thinking about future human prospects, in the large and in detail, in terms of energy, using energy accounts and the scientific understanding of energy. The science of energy is **thermodynamics**, which we briefly discuss here.[15]

We first need to define some terms. Thus far in this book we have used the term 'energy' rather loosely. **Energy** is the potential to do work. It is a characteristic of things, rather than a thing itself. **Work** is involved when matter is changed in structure, in physical or chemical nature, or in location. **Power** is work per unit of time. Energy is actually measured in work units. One **joule** is the energy required to raise the temperature of one cubic centimetre of water by 0.239°C. Power is then measured in units such as joules per second. Consider an electricity generating plant. Such plants are referred to in terms of their size. A reasonably large plant would be around 1000 megawatts, or 1000 MW in size. This is the maximum amount of power that it can send out, i.e. 1000 x 10^6 watts, where one watt is one joule per second. The output of the plant over time is measured as power actually sent out. If a 1000 MW plant ran at maximum power for a day, it would produce 24 000 MW hours. It is output over time that determines the amount of input fuel used.

In thermodynamics it is necessary to be clear about the nature of the system under consideration. An **open system** is one which exchanges energy and matter with its environment. An individual organism is an open system. A **closed system** exchanges energy but not matter with its environment. An **isolated system** exchanges neither energy nor matter with its environment. Apart from the entire universe, an isolated system is an ideal, an abstraction.

The first law of thermodynamics says that energy can neither be created nor destroyed. It can only be converted from one form to another. This means that the energy of an isolated system is constant. Consider a fossil fuel power station, which is an open system. All of the chemical energy in the fuel input, say coal, is converted to other forms of energy. These are electrical energy, heat energy, and chemical energy in the residual matter which is discharged into the station's environment. Although all of the energy in the coal is conserved, from the human point of view some of the transformations are more useful than others. Seen strictly as a source of electricity, the power station has a thermal efficiency of less than one, in that not all of the energy content of the coal is converted to electrical energy. A modern power plant has a thermal efficiency of about 35 per cent. Combined heat and power plants use some of the 'waste' heat to warm buildings or run production processes. In this way more of the energy content of the fossil fuel input is captured for human purposes.

The second law of thermodynamics is also known as the **entropy law**. It says that heat flows spontaneously from a hotter to a colder body, and that heat cannot be transformed into work with 100 per cent efficiency. It follows that all conversions of energy from one form to another are less than 100 per cent efficient. This appears to contradict the first law, but does not. The point is that not all of the energy of some store, such as a fossil fuel, is available for conversion. Energy stores vary in the proportion of their energy that is available for conversion. **Entropy** is a measure of unavailable energy. All energy conversions increase the entropy of an isolated system. All energy conversions are irreversible, since the fact that the conversion is less than 100 per cent efficient, means that the work required to restore the original state is not available in the new state. Fossil fuel combustion is irreversible, and of itself implies an increase in the entropy of the system which is the biosphere. However, the biosphere is not an isolated system, but is continually receiving energy inputs from solar radiation. This is what makes life possible.

What has all this got to do with sustainability? Or with economics? From much of the literature, it might be supposed that the answers are 'not a lot'. Economics students are not required to become familiar with the laws of thermodynamics, and few economists mention them in their published work. Many of the contributions to the sustainability literature never mention thermodynamics, at least explicitly. The economist who did most to try to make his colleagues aware of the laws of thermo- dynamics and their implications (Georgescu-Roegen), referred to the second law as the 'taproot of economic scarcity'.[16] His point was that if energy conversion processes were 100 per cent efficient, one lump of coal would last forever. Material transformations involve work, and thus require energy. Given a fixed rate of receipt of solar energy, there is an upper limit to the amount of work that can be done on the basis of it. For most of human history, population and material consumption levels were subject to this constraint. The exploitation of fossil fuels removes this constraint. The fossil fuels are accumulated past solar energy receipts, initially transformed into living tissue, and stored by geological processes.[17] Given this origin, there is necessarily a finite amount of the fossil fuels in existence.

It follows that the use of fossil fuel energy must be an activity of finite duration.[18] In the absence of a substitute energy source with similar qualities to the fossil fuels, this implies a reversion to the energetic situa- tion of the pre-industrial phase of human history. Of course, the technology deployed in some new solar energy constrained human situation would be different from that available in the pre-industrial phase. It is now possible, for example, to use solar energy to generate electricity. However, while it is clear that a future without fossil fuel energy would be different from the past without it, it is also clear that it would be very different from a future with fossil fuel energy. It is difficult to envisage, for example, that a solar economy could build and operate a system for mass international air travel.

Conversely, the laws of thermodynamics have generally been taken to mean that given enough available energy, all transformations of matter are possible, at least in principle, and thus complete material recycling is possible. On this basis, given the energy, there is no necessity that shortage of minerals constrain economic activity. Past extractions could be recovered by recycling. It is in this sense that the second law of thermodynamics is the ultimate source of scarcity. It is this perception that both drives the interest in nuclear power, and the promise that it, particularly as fusion, is seen as offering. The economist who introduced the idea of the second law as the ultimate basis for economic scarcity subsequently attacked the view just sketched as 'the energetic dogma', and insisted that 'matter matters' as well (Georgescu-Roegen 1979). He argued that even given enough energy, the complete recycling of matter is, in principle, impossible. This has been dubbed 'the fourth law of thermodynamics' and its validity denied: 'complete recycling is physically possible if a sufficient amount of energy is available' (Biancardi et al. 1993). The basis for this denial is that the fourth law would be inconsistent with the second. The interesting point here is the disagreement over what is a very basic scientific issue. If qualified scientists can disagree over so fundamental a point, then it is again made clear that sustainability issues have to be regarded as involving uncertainty. It is also interesting that both sides to this dispute would agree that as a practical matter, complete recycling is impossible however much energy is available. Thus, the statement above rebutting the fourth law is immediately followed by: 'The problem is that such expenditure of energy would involve a tremendous increase in the entropy of the environment, which would not be sustainable for the biosphere'(Biancardi et al. 1993). Neither party to the dispute is suggesting that policy should be determined on the basis of an understanding that matter can actually be completely recycled. Thermodynamics is difficult for laypersons to understand. Even within physics it has a history involving controversy and, as noted above, disagreements persist.

Some popular myths exist about thermodynamics and its implications for the social sciences, and for economic activity.[19] It is, for example, often said that entropy always increases. This is true only for an isolated system. Classical thermodynamics involved the study of equilibrium systems, but the systems relevant to human interests are open and closed systems which are far from equilibrium. Such systems, which receive energy from their environment, have been characterised as involving the emergence of 'order out of chaos'.[20] A living organism is itself an open system far from equilibrium; the energy input is necessary for it to maintain its structure and not become disordered, i.e. dead. According to one commentator:

> The broad message of the far-from-equilibrium thermodynamics is to embrace time irreversibility as synonymous with phenomena of uncertainty, dynamic instability, discontinuities and emergence of novelty ... Purposeful action has to be understood not as the research of determinate control, but as exploratory adventure in the domains of somewhat indeterminate possibility (O'Connor 1993).

Notwithstanding this, thermodynamics does give rise to results that can be useful in thinking about future possibilities and informing current policy and social decision making. The point is not that nothing can be known or controlled, but that there are limits to knowledge and control.

Energy analysis

We illustrate the role of energy analysis by considering two examples of its application. First, we consider the question of the prospects for technical progress in the use of fossil fuels for electricity generation. The **thermal efficiency** of a power station is the ratio of the energy content of the electricity sent out to the energy content of the fuel burned. Over the last century the thermal efficiency of the best power stations has increased by a factor of 10, from around 4 per cent to around 40 per cent. This corresponds to an average annual improvement of 0.36 per cent per annum. If we extrapolate a continuation of this rate of change, in 167 years the thermal efficiency of the best plant will have reached 100 per cent. Should we believe that within the next two centuries the energy losses in burning a fossil fuel to generate electricity will have been eliminated?

The laws of thermodynamics give the answer 'no' to this question. They show that 100 per cent thermal efficiency is impossible. In fact, for an ideal power station, the upper limit to thermal efficiency is well below 100 per cent. It depends upon the difference between the temperature attained in the combustion process and the temperature of the power station's environment. The temperature attainable in combustion depends upon, among other things, the material from which the boiler is constructed. Given current understanding of feasible materials technology, this implies an upper limit to thermal efficiency of 68 per cent.[21] The calculation from which this figure is derived ignores three factors which would further reduce the limit. First, it ignores the fact that not all of the energy content of the fossil fuel can be converted to heat in the boiler. Second, it ignores losses as heat arising from friction associated with the moving parts of the power station. Third, the efficiency calculated this way is for an ideal system in which processes take place infinitely slowly. This cannot be a characteristic of any actual power station. So, the laws of thermodynamics indicate that there are limits to the prospects for technical progress in fossil fuel combustion for electricity generation. Similar considerations apply to all energy conversion processes.

Now consider the energy requirements in mining and processing mineral ore to produce metals.[22] This is relevant to extrapolation of past trends in metals prices. Figure 8.2 shows in (a) how the amount of energy required per ton of metal varies with the grade of ore, assuming no change in the technology employed. This relationship follows from the fact that as the ore grade goes down, so more material has to be moved and processed per ton of metal. Figure 8.2 shows in (b) the corresponding variation in the production costs for metal with ore grade. This follows from the relationship in (a), given that the energy input in metal production is an element of the cost of production. It assumes that the price paid for energy is constant, and that there is no technological change.

Figure 8.2 shows that as the grade of ore exploited decreases cost will increase at an increasing rate, other things being equal. Historically the exploitation of lower grade ore bodies has not always meant rising production costs for the corresponding metal. This is because other things were not equal. Cost constant or falling as ore grade declines could arise by virtue of improvements in the efficiency of energy use in mining and processing, and/or a falling price for energy. Both of these effects have been operative in the history of metals production to date. Extrapolation of the historical trend of a constant, or falling, production cost in the face of decreasing ore grade requires the assumption that either, or both, of these effects will continue to operate. Thermodynamics sets limits to the possible improvements in the efficiency with which energy can be used in mining and processing. Once such limits are reached, the metal cost will move upward as the ore grade declines, unless energy prices fall.

Note also that even if falling energy prices hold the cost of production constant, energy use per unit of metal is increasing. This implies increasing waste emissions in the energy supply industries. Also, with declining

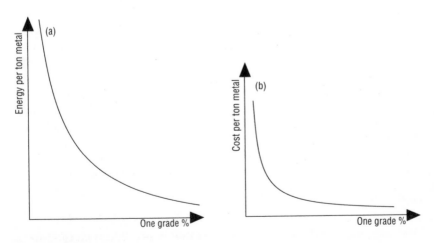

Figure 8.2 Ore grade, energy input and cost.

ore grade there is more waste generation per unit of metal in mining and processing. Using lower ore grades must involve increasing social costs per unit of metal. The simple extrapolation of historical trends in metals prices can be very misleading as to the prospects for costs.

The energy analyses discussed above measured all inputs and outputs in energy units, adding one joule of coal to one joule of oil, and so on. Clearly, one of the attractions of looking at things in terms of energy is precisely the possibility of this kind of aggregation. However, so doing ignores energy quality differences across fuels. This reduces the explanatory power of energy analysis, since it is clear that energy quality differences must play a major role in any understanding of energy in relation to human interests. A quantity of coal with energy content x joules is not a perfect substitute for a quantity of natural gas with energy content x joules. Energy quality has a number of dimensions. One is the quantities of wastes of various kinds arising per unit of useful energy made available. Coal, for example, is a 'dirty' fuel, compared with either oil or natural gas. Another dimension of quality is density, which is energy content per unit of mass. Oil is more dense than coal.

Solar radiation scores poorly on this dimension of quality. Its exploitation by humans requires its conversion to some other energy form. Photosynthesis is the basis for its use as food, and as biomass for combustion. The geological processes which converted the products of photosynthesis to fossil fuels increased density. It is this that makes fossil fuel use the key factor in the many individual technological innovations associated with the industrial revolution. One aspect of this was shown in our discussion above of agricultural energetics. Fossil fuel use greatly increases food output per unit of land input, supplementing solar energy receipts.

Solar power is widely advocated as an environmentally benign alternative energy source for industrial societies. A major problem here is the low density of solar energy as compared with the fossil fuels. For example, in terms of electricity supply it has been estimated that given present technology, to provide the same output as a 600 megawatt power station would require solar collectors covering an area of approximately 10 square miles.[23] The technology for the conversion of solar radiation to electrical energy can, no doubt, be improved, but it is subject to upper efficiency limits set by the laws of thermodynamics. Such improvements cannot change the inherent low density of solar radiation.

Energy and value

We now consider the idea of an **energy theory of value**. Two variants of an energy theory of value can be distinguished. The first is the claim that the actual prices of commodities and inputs to their production can be explained in terms of energy inputs and outputs. The second is the claim that prices should be determined in terms of energy inputs and outputs. In economics, a distinction is made between positive and normative statements. A **positive statement** concerns what is, a **normative statement** concerns what should be. We will call the first type of energy theory of value the positive theory, and the second the normative theory.

This distinction between 'is' and 'should' statements about prices is not solely applicable to an energy theory of value. The classical economists embraced a labour theory of value. Such a theory could be about the actual determination of prices, or about how prices should be determined. Some of the problems associated with the labour theory of value stemmed from a lack of clarity about this distinction. The neoclassical theory of value effectively conflates the questions of what determines prices and what should determine prices. According to it, prices are actually determined by supply and demand in markets. And, this is how it is considered that prices should be determined, given that markets satisfy certain conditions.

Supply functions reflect cost conditions, demand functions reflect individuals' preferences. The prices determined in competitive markets then signal relative scarcities according to the criteria of individuals' preferences. And, this is what they should do if the goal of consumer sovereignty is to be served. No input is, or should be, treated as prima facie more important, more valuable, than any other. Importance and value derives from individuals' preferences in relation to scarcities as reflected in costs of production, not from any *a priori* considerations, nor from the laws of nature alone.

The point of departure for an energy theory of value is the rejection of consumer sovereignty, plus the idea that energy is the ultimately important resource. An energy theory of value might also find motivation in that energy is a common unit of measurement. We noted above that although fuels can be measured in common energy units, they differ qualitatively. This suggests some problems for an energy theory of value. The labour theory of value faced a similar problem. While labour input can be measured everywhere in, say, units of hours, it is obvious that an hour of unskilled labour is not the same thing as an hour of skilled labour.

The positive energy theory of value is a claim about what is, and should, in principle, be empirically testable. The positive theory appears to have only once been explicitly tested against any data. The energy analyst who did the test published the results in the journal *Science*, and claimed that they were consistent with the theory. This claim has been rejected. in the literature, and appears not to have received any published support.[24]

The normative theory claims that prices are not in fact determined by energy but should be. This is not an empirically testable proposition. Actually, the normative theory has rarely been stated in exactly this way. Usually, the claim has been that energy analysis, rather than standard economic analysis, should inform policy, especially in relation to energy supply and use.[25] Many energy analysts have explicitly stated that their purpose is to provide additional information for decision making, not to advocate an energy theory of value. What seems to be the majority view among energy analysts is captured in the following:

> we do *not* subscribe to any 'energy theory of value'. Our approach ... aims to provide *description*, not *evaluation*. ... there is no way that descriptions of what is can be used to deduce what *ought* to be done. The decision about what to do involves a value judgement and, to be clear, this should be explicitly separated from the description of what is (Chapman and Roberts 1983, p.26, italics in the original).

An argument for a normative energy theory of value might proceed as follows. The laws of nature are such that energy is the ultimate scarce resource. It is the only thing of interest to humans for which there is no possible substitute. Therefore human affairs ought to be so conducted as to minimise the use of energy, as this will maximise the lifespan of the human race. To do this, commodities should be priced according to their energy intensities. Even if the value judgment, that the objective is to maximise the lifespan of the human race is accepted, there are problems here. The quantitatively dominant source of energy is solar radiation. Some round numbers expressed in very large units give the sense of what is involved. Annual solar receipts at the earth's surface are of the order of 2600×10^3 Quads. World annual extrasomatic energy use, almost entirely fossil fuels, is currently of the order of 0.3×10^3 Quads, i.e. annual terrestrial solar receipts are some 8000 times fossil fuel use. Photosynthesis has low efficiencies, but annual production is some 1.2×10^3 Quads, about four times fossil fuel use. The total remaining stock of fossil fuels is some 300×10^3 Quads, implying a lifetime of 1000 years at current use rates. Solar radiation looks like continuing at much the same rate for the next five billion years, irrespective of what humans do.[26]

Given this, the argument would seem rather to lead to a normative fossil fuel theory of value, as follows. It is the use of fossil fuels that has enabled humans to achieve a desirable way of life in at least some of the world. It is desirable that that way of life be extended, now and in the future, to as many people as possible. This requires that fossil fuel stocks are used so as to last as long as possible. This will be achieved if commodity prices are set to reflect the fossil fuel intensities of commodities, accounting for direct and indirect uses.

The problems here are that while the fossil fuels can be aggregated according to energy content, they differ from one another according to a number of dimensions of quality, and that in many uses there are substitutes, such as nuclear power. Some take the view that nuclear power is not an acceptable substitute, which itself involves a value judgment. It does not appear that there is a unique system for weighting the energy content of the different fossil fuels and their potential substitutes based solely on energetic considerations. It has been suggested that fuels be aggregated using quality weights derived from market prices (Cleveland 1992). A normative energy theory of value using such weights would hardly deserve the title, since they reflect the influence of individuals' preferences.

We conclude that the case for a normative energy theory of value cannot be made. As noted, for most energy analysts this is not a problem, as this is not their purpose. Their purpose is useful description. However, economists have also claimed that energy analysis does not provide useful description.[27] The claim is that energy analysis does not provide any information not already contained in economic data. The argument is that, for example, it is unnecessary to do a net energy analysis of a proposed new energy supply system, since if it fails the net energy test it will also fail on the basis of standard economic project appraisal methods, and vice versa.

This claim, in general, seems to be unwarranted for three reasons. First, energy analysis can more readily bring thermodynamic considerations to bear upon the assessment of future prospects. This is illustrated by the example of the implications of declining ore grades above. Second, in relation to the understanding of current and historical conditions, energy accounting makes plain what is implicit but not readily apparent in the economic data, and can suggest new perspectives. This is illustrated by the energy accounting of food production systems discussed above. One could regard the provision of information in energetic terms as a policy instrument of the moral suasion type. Voters, decision makers and their advisers, on this view, will gain relevant information more easily if it is presented in energetic, as well as economic, terms.

Third, actual economic data derives primarily from markets characterised by extensive market failure. The view that a net energy test will give the same result as a standard economic test is based on the fact that price must cover the costs of production, including the cost of energy inputs. Thus, in the absence of market failure, negative net energy would imply negative profit, and vice versa. This correspondence can break down if there is market failure. In appraising projects, economists would wish to see used prices which are not actual market prices, but the prices which would have applied in the absence of market, and government, failure. This is, in effect, cost-benefit analysis, which was discussed in Chapter 7. We noted there that correcting prices is difficult, often of unknown reliability, and contentious. In fact, most decisions on projects are taken on the basis of appraisal at market prices rather than on the basis of cost-benefit analysis. Further, we noted in Chapter 7 the difficulty in anticipating and enumerating all of the impacts associated with a project. We return to this in the following section.

Given that the use of extrasomatic energy is a good proxy for total environmental impact, since energy is what does work, the relative fossil fuel equivalent energy intensity of a commodity/process can be seen as a first approximation for its relative environmental impact. If this is accepted, it can be argued that energy analysis is a cost-effective way of generating relative environmental impact data.[28] Energy supply systems with a high energy return on investment (EROI) for example, will tend to be those for which environmental impact per unit of useable fuel output is relatively low, and conversely for low EROI. Energy intensity is not a perfect indicator of total environmental impact. Given the heterogeneity of environmental impacts, there is no perfect indicator. Unless that is, one fully embraces consumer sovereignty as the means of adding up heterogenous objects, and believes that individuals' preferences across types of environmental impact can be determined either through markets or surrogates for them. Otherwise, imperfect indicators are the best that can be looked for.

The conclusion here is that energy analysis can provide useful information, to be used with standard economic data. The information provided by energy analysis is not a perfect substitute for the results of a proper environmental impact assessment. But, an energy analysis will generally be much cheaper to perform than a full environmental impact assessment.

In neither the positive nor the normative sense does an energy theory of value work. We have argued that this is not a damning critique of energy analysis. The neoclassical theory of value has been similarly criticised. It has been claimed that it does not, in fact, explain relative prices satisfactorily, and that consumer sovereignty is an inappropriate basis from which to derive statements about what ought to be. In regard to the latter point, we note that the preferences of individuals change. This means that the standard of value changes. It would appear that one of the motivations for an energy theory of value has been, as it was with the labour theory, a desire for a constant standard of value. The search for an historically unchanging standard against which it can be judged what objects are 'really worth' is misconceived. The standard must change with human circumstances. Both as explanation and prescription, a theory for a hunter–gatherer society could not be the same as the theory for a modern industrial economy. Explanation and prescription need to be historically contingent. As such they will always be somewhat indeterminate.

Responding to uncertainty

We have stressed the uncertainties attending sustainability issues. In Chapter 7 we discussed some aspects of the way risk and uncertainty are handled in economics, and, particularly in cost-benefit analysis. In recent years the increasing prominence of sustainability on political agendas has given rise to the emergence of some new ideas about dealing with risk and uncertainty. These are now briefly reviewed.

The precautionary principle

The **precautionary principle** is gaining widespread acceptance, at the governmental and intergovernmental levels, as a concept which should inform environmental policy. Thus, Principle 15 of the June 1992 Rio Declaration is that:

> In order to protect the environment, the precautionary approach shall be widely applied by States according to their capabilities. Where there are threats of serious or irreversible damage, lack of full scientific certainty shall not be used as a reason for postponing cost-effective measures to prevent environmental degradation.

Article 130r, para. 2 of the Maastricht Treaty for the development of the European Community states that:

> Community policy on the environment shall ... be based on the Precautionary Principle and on the principles that precautionary action should be taken, that environmental damage should as a priority be rectified at source and that the polluter should pay.

In Australia, in 1992, the various levels of government (federal, state and local) signed the Intergovernmental Agreement on the Environment, which adopts the precautionary principle, and defines it as follows:

> Where there are threats of serious or irreversible damage, lack of full scientific certainty should not be used as a reason for postponing measures to prevent

environmental degradation. In the application of the precautionary principle, public and private decisions should be guided by:
(i) careful evaluation to avoid, wherever practicable, serious or irreversible damage to the environment; and
(ii) assessment of the risk weighted consequences of various options.[29]

The principle addresses a problem central to sustainability – inability to predict all of the future consequences for human interests of current actions with environmental impacts. However, it does not offer much in the way of guidance as to how the problem should be dealt with. To say that a lack of certainty should not inhibit measures to protect the environment from serious and irreversible damage, does not indicate what should be done and how much should be done. Nor does the principle suggest how one might set about answering such questions.

The nature of the precautionary principle is similar to that of the modified safe minimum standard. That says that a project with irreversible consequences which are unknown but could be serious should not be undertaken, unless the social costs of not undertaking the project are unacceptably high. It remains in any particular case to determine what 'unacceptably high' means. However, as compared with the standard cost-benefit analysis approach, the question to be answered has been changed. A wholehearted adoption of the precautionary principle would imply a similar reorientation, which can be considered in the project appraisal context. Currently, the situation is generally that there is a presumption in favour of going ahead with commercially viable projects. The presumption may be overturned in any particular case if it can be established that serious or irreversible environmental damage is entailed. According to a strong interpretation of the precautionary principle, the presumption is reversed. Since all projects have some environmental impact, it is necessary that any particular project be shown not to have serious or irreversible consequences before it can be approved. A loose analogy is a shift from the judicial assumption of the accused person's innocence unless guilt can be proved, to an assumption of guilt unless innocence can be proved.

Clearly, such a shift could have profound consequences for economic activity, given that many prospective projects involve genuine innovation and novelty, so that there is no previous experience upon which to base an assessment of their consequences. This is especially the case where long-term environmental impacts are involved. The question which arises is whether there are any policy instruments which are consistent with the precautionary principle, and which could constitute a feasible means for its implementation in such a way as to avoid an outcome which simply prohibits projects with uncertain environmental consequences.

Environmental performance bonds

Environmental performance bonds have recently been advocated as policy instruments consistent with the precautionary principle.[30] The basic ideas involved can be discussed by considering some firm which wishes to undertake a project involving technological innovation, so that there is no past experience according to which probabilities can be assigned to all possible outcomes. Indeed, in so far as genuine novelty is involved, there is radical uncertainty (see Chapter 7) in that not all of the possible outcomes can be anticipated. An example of such a project would have been the construction of the first nuclear power plant. In fact, many projects could involve radical uncertainty in so far as a technology for which there is historical experience in one environmental setting is to be employed in a different environmental setting. A large-scale example of this was the transfer to Australia of European agricultural practices.

Assume that there is in existence an Environmental Protection Agency (EPA) without permission from which the firm cannot go ahead with the project. The EPA takes independent expert advice on the project, and comes to a view about the worst conceivable environmental consequences of the project. Approval of the project is then conditional on the firm depositing with the EPA a bond of $x, where this is the EPA's estimate of the social cost of the worst conceivable outcome. The bond is fully or partially returned to the firm at the end of the project's lifetime, defined by the longest lasting conceived consequence of the project, according to the damage actually occurring over the lifetime. Thus, if there is no damage the firm gets back $x, plus some proportion of the interest. The withheld proportion of the interest is to cover EPA administration costs and to finance EPA research. If the damage actually occurring is $y, the firm gets back $x − $y, with appropriate interest adjustment. For $x equal to $y, the firm gets nothing back, forfeiting the full value of the bond. It is, of course, possible that $y will turn out to be greater than $x, in which case also the firm gets back $0.

The advantages claimed for such an instrument are in terms of the incentives it creates for the firm to undertake research to investigate environmental impact and means to reduce it, as well as in terms of stopping projects. Taking the latter point first, suppose that the EPA decides on $x as the size of the bond, and that the firm assesses lifetime project net returns to it as one dollar less than $x, and accepts that $x is the appropriate estimate of actual damage to arise. Then it will not wish to go ahead with the project. If, however, the firm took the view that actual damage would be less than $x, it would wish to go ahead with the project. The firm, itself, then has an incentive to assess the damage that the project could cause, and to research means to reduce that damage. Further, if it does undertake the project it has an ongoing incentive to seek damage-minimising methods of operation, so as to increase the eventual size of the sum returned to it, \$x – \$y. This incentive effect could be enhanced by having the size of the bond posted periodically adjustable. Thus, if on the basis of its research, the firm could at any point in time in the life of the project, convince the EPA that the worst conceivable lifetime damage was less than \$x, the original bond could be returned and a new one for an amount less than \$x be posted.[31]

Environmental performance bonds would entail the shift in the basic presumption about projects that the precautionary principle implies. At the end of the project lifetime, the burden of proof as to the magnitude of actual damage would rest with the firm, not the EPA. The presumption would be that the bond was not returnable. It would be up to the firm to convince the EPA that actual damage was less than \$x if it wished to get any of its money back. This would generate incentives for the firm to monitor damage in convincing ways, as well as to research means to minimise damage. In the event that damage up to the amount of the bond, \$x, occurred, society, as represented by the EPA, would have received compensation. If damage in excess of \$x had occurred, society would not receive full compensation. Recall that \$x is to be set at the largest amount of damage seen as conceivable by the EPA at the outset. A socially responsible EPA would have an incentive to take a cautious view of the available evidence, implying a high figure for \$x, so that society would not find itself undercompensated. This, it is argued, would coincide with the selfish motivations of EPA staff, since a higher \$x would mean more funding available for EPA administration and research.

Environmental performance bonds are clearly an interesting idea for an addition to the range of instruments for environmental protection, given the pervasiveness of uncertainty and the need for research addressed to reducing it. In the form discussed here, they do not appear to be in use anywhere.[32] The usefulness of these bonds would appear, as with other environmental policy instruments, to vary with particular circumstances, and clearly further consideration of the details of their possible implementation is warranted.[33] One limitation on the range of their applicability and acceptability would appear to lie in the matter of compensation. Many would take the view that there are classes of environmental damage for which the idea of compensation is simply inappropriate. On this view, there are environmental assets the services of which cannot be substituted for, and if no substitution is possible, then it is impossible to compensate for loss. On this view, the \$x to be set by the EPA should, in circumstances where damage to an irreplaceable environmental asset is conceivable, be indefinitely large, so as to stop the project going ahead. Further, there is major uncertainty about where substitution for environmental assets is, or is not, to be considered feasible. This leads to the view that policy for sustainability should be based on a presumption against any depletion of environmental assets.

Constraints for natural asset protection

This view has been put as follows: 'Sustainability requires at least a constant stock of natural capital, construed as the set of all natural assets'. This is proposed as a presumption, and a guide to the general stance that policy should adopt, rather than a strict rule. Thus, with K_N standing for the total stock of natural capital:

> Constancy of natural capital, or more strictly, the non-negativity of the rate of change in natural capital, relates probabilistically to sustainability because it is not inconceivable that societies can endure and progress with a declining K_N. We can only say that it is more likely that declining K_N will be correlated with declining sustainability (Pearce 1992).

Recall that in Chapters 3 and 7 we discussed the basic idea of the standard economic approach to sustainability, and saw that it required that the total value of the capital stock not decline. The same idea is involved in proposals for the measurement of sustainable income, as discussed above. The total value of the capital stock in these contexts is the value of all assets, the value of natural capital plus the value of man-made capital. The view being considered here is that sustainability requires that natural capital itself be not allowed to decline. This view reflects the presumption that services based on man-made capital can be substituted for those of environmental assets to only a limited extent. Pearce (1992) suggests several other reasons why natural capital should be accorded special status. Most of these appear to derive from the non-substitutability reason. It is noted, however, that the preservation of natural capital could be seen as respecting any rights accorded to non-human entities.

There is one major difficulty attending this approach as a guide to policy. This is the valuation problem again. Environmental assets are heterogenous, so that the measurement of total natural capital requires aggregation across different categories of things. It involves 'adding apples to pears'. This can only be done by assigning some kind of price to each asset, i.e. by finding some common denominator according to which the physical quantities of different assets can be added together. The problems of doing this have already been discussed here, and are recognised by advocates of the presumption that policy should avoid natural capital depletion. One possible response to the difficulty is to advocate that policy should aim to avoid the depletion, in physical terms, of any environmental asset. This would clearly give rise to problems where non-renewable resources are concerned, as it would imply zero usage rates. Recognising this, some advocates of the 'no natural capital depletion' position argue that non-renewable resource use should be allowed only to the extent that technology is shown to be producing substitutes based on renewable resources. An alternative position is to accept that environmental asset valuation is necessarily incomplete and imperfect, and to argue for avoiding the depletion of total natural capital imperfectly measured, as the best that can be done.

Ecological economics

The Greek word oikos is the root for 'eco' in both ecology and economics. Oikos means household, and we can say that ecology is the study of nature's housekeeping, while economics is the study of housekeeping in human societies. **Ecological economics** can be said to be the study of how these two sets of housekeeping are related to one another. It is anthropocentric, i.e. looks at matters from the perspective of human interests, and seeks to inform human housekeeping by an understanding of the implications for it of nature's housekeeping. In Chapter 6 we cited a definition of economics as:

> the study of how people make their living, how they acquire the food, shelter, clothing and other material necessities and comforts of this world.

Ecology has been defined as:

> the study of the total relations of the animal to both its organic and inorganic environment.[34]

The basic motivation for an ecological economics is the idea that the proper study of how 'people make their living' has to be located within an understanding of the relations of people to their 'organic and inorganic environment'.

The first issue of the journal *Ecological Economics* appeared in 1989. It contains several papers addressing the question: what is ecological economics to be about?[35] Here we will summarise the answers given by saying that it is about sustainability. The study of the natural environment suggests that there might be limits to the expansion of human economic activity. This has implications for dealing with human economic problems. Thus the introductory paper by the editor in the first issue of the journal says that:

Issues of sustainability are ultimately issues about limits. If economic growth is sustainable indefinitely by technology then all environmental problems can (in theory at least) be fixed technologically. Issues of equity and distribution (between subgroups and generations of our species and between our species and others) are also issues of limits. We do not have to worry so much about how an expanding pie is divided, but a constant or shrinking pie presents real problems. Finally, dealing with uncertainty about limits is the fundamental issue (Costanza 1989).

On the principles of division of labour and specialisation, it is tempting to say that the ecological economics pie is to be divided so that ecologists deal with the problem of whether limits exist, and what they are like if they do, while economists deal with the problems of what societies should do about the possibility that limits exist. As ecologists working in the new discipline learn more about the limits, the economists would refine ideas about policy. While tempting, and to some extent inevitable, such specialisation would be contrary to some of the basic ideas informing ecological economics. One of these is that addressing the sustainability problem requires not just greater information and expertise, but also an openness to new perspectives and ways of thinking. Dividing the problem up into ecological and economic components for specialists from each discipline will not promote this. Arguably, individuals working in ecological economics need to try to see the whole picture.

This is a problem which must be recognised, because the whole picture is very large 'Ecology' in the context of ecological economics is a shorthand for 'the natural science relevant to the question of limits', and 'economics' for the social sciences. To see what is involved here, note that we have, in this chapter, examined thermodynamics, which is a branch of physics. Several of the references cited in that connection either appeared in the journal *Ecological Economics*, and/or were written by individuals who could reasonably be described as ecological economists. Clearly, many of the natural sciences bear upon the question of the existence and nature of limits to human activity set by the environment in which it takes place.

On the other hand, the view of human nature taken by standard economics is a very narrow basis on which to think about human interests in relation to the environment. In Chapter 4, we tried to provide some historical perspective on the current human situation. Clearly, such a perspective must be an integral part of ecological economics. It naturally leads to a questioning of the standard assumptions made in economics about the relationship between welfare and the consumption of produced goods and services. Questions have been raised by philosophers and psychologists about the appropriateness of applying the model of human behaviour developed for the analysis of market behaviour to human interaction with the environment. This suggests that the following disciplines, at least, are also pertinent to an ecological economics: anthropology, history, psychology, philosophy.

Very few individuals have the capacity to be professionally familiar with even two disciplines. Ecological economics appears to require this plus some knowledge of a range of others. This is for all but the rarest individuals an impossible requirement. Certainly, it is impossible for this author. This would seem to imply that there cannot be an ecological economics understandable and useable by more than a few. There is something in this. At one level the goal of a genuinely comprehensive understanding of the sustainability problem in all of its dimensions is clearly unattainable. This does not mean that ecological economics should be abandoned. Some physicists now recognise, it seems, limits to the possible human understanding of the laws of nature. They do not, however, conclude that the study of physics is a waste of time. In the case of ecological economics, the operative point seems to be the need to recognise that any claim to have discovered the definitive solution to the sustainability problem is, almost certainly, false. It is not even clear that the problem can be definitively formulated. Given this, it would not be appropriate for an ecological economics to have a single agreed agenda, or a single methodology for addressing questions. An ecological economics will necessarily be eclectic, and somewhat inconclusive. Uncertainty is fundamental, and there is no uniquely correct way to proceed in the face of it.[36] This does not mean that nothing can be said about policy – the focus of the next two chapters. They draw upon the material discussed to this point and might be said to be one ecological economist's approach to addressing threats to sustainability.

CHAPTER 9

National policy

Sustainability is a global problem. This has three dimensions. First, there is the matter of inequality between nations. Second, many of the problems originating in economy–environment interconnections do not respect national boundaries. Third, action by one nation to protect the natural environment may have implications for its trade with other nations.

In this chapter policy is discussed in the context of a single industrial market economy. Transboundary environmental problems and international trade are largely ignored. They are considered in Chapter 10. The justification for proceeding thus is that the problem needs to be simplified in order to begin analysis of it. It is impossible to take all facets of the problem into account immediately.

This chapter is organised as follows. First, policy objectives are discussed in relation to threats to sustainability. Second, policy instruments for these objectives are considered. Then, the case for carbon taxation is examined. The final section looks at reform of the welfare system by means of the introduction of basic incomes. The argument is that, in industrial economies, carbon taxation and basic incomes could form the basis for a broad strategy to address threats to sustainability. Howwever, they do not comprise a blueprint for sustainability or render other instruments obsolete.

Policy objectives

The objective of sustainability faces two problems as the basis for a discussion of national policy. First, the problem is global in nature. However, national policy can be considered on the basis of its consistency, or otherwise, with the requirements of global sustainability. Second, sustainability is not a clearly defined policy objective. The sustainability problem is complex, multifaceted, and characterised by ignorance and uncertainty. To embrace sustainability as a policy objective leads neither to well-defined quantifiable policy targets, nor to unambiguous policy directions. Persons who agree on the desirability of sustainability may reasonably disagree about the implications arising for national policy.

This is not to suggest that sustainability is not a useful concept in relation to policy debate. Sustainability is a **contestable concept**, i.e. one that can be interpreted in a variety of particular ways, but which, at the same time, is widely agreed as representing a desirable state. The value of such a concept lies in expressing the essence of a generally agreeable goal, while leaving the particulars for ongoing debate. Contestable concepts as policy objectives are central features of the democratic political process. Consider, for examples: liberty, justice, democracy, freedom, and equality. It is rarely suggested that these are not useful concepts, or that they cannot, or should not, inform policy.[1]

While the general nature of threats to sustainability is reasonably clear, the particulars are unclear. At the level of detail, we are in a state of considerable ignorance about how the biosphere works in relation to current and future human interests, and about the possibilities for substituting for the services that it provides. However, we can make some progress by specifying policy objectives which relate to sustainability. We distinguish six objectives.

1. Environmental asset protection

The first objective is the protection, i.e. maintenance intact, of critical environmental assets. A critical environmental asset is one which performs an essential function and for which there are no substitutes. This objective and the associated definition raise two questions. Which are the environmental assets that perform essential functions? For which of these is substitution impossible? Firm answers are not generally available for either of these questions. The questions are not purely scientific, and answers necessarily involve judgment, tastes, and ethical views. Answers will differ across individuals, and vary over time. It is not possible to establish a definitive, generally agreed, and comprehensive list of critical environmental assets.

2. Improved understanding

Given this, there follow three further, closely related, objectives. First, 2a, improvements in scientific understanding of the way the biosphere functions, and of the technical possibilities for substitution for the services of the environment. Second, 2b, improvements in the level of general public awareness of current scientific understanding in these respects. Third, 2c, improvements to social institutions for debate about policy options.

3. Savings and investment levels

One of the few certain things in this area is that some environmental assets will be depleted. In the face of such depletion, sustainability requires the accumulation of capital. An adequate rate of capital accumulation, investment, is necessary but not sufficient for sustainability. No amount of capital accumulation can offset the depletion of critical environmental assets.

It follows that insufficient capital accumulation is a threat to sustainability. What amounts to sufficiency cannot be precisely defined or measured. Analysis of model economies suggests some rough guidelines. A lower bound for the required level of investment (over and above that necessary to cover the depreciation of man-made capital) would be set by the rents earned in natural resource exploitation.

The most that can be said is that avoiding threats to sustainability requires policies to encourage investment, which implies policies to encourage saving. It is difficult to see how the level of savings and investment could be too high in relation to the sustainability objective.

4. Project selection

Threats to sustainability arise not only in relation to the level of total investment, but also in relation to the way in which the total is allocated between alternative projects. If capital accumulation is to offset environmental asset depletion, it needs to take the appropriate forms, providing substitute services for depleted environmental assets – where this is possible. Also, projects which themselves generate threats to sustainability are to be avoided. Again, it should be noted that identifying such projects will, generally, be subject to considerable uncertainty.

5. Population size

Other things equal, threats to sustainability increase with the size of the human population. The population growth component of the sustainability problem is widely recognised. The **population problem** is often seen as a developing nations problem. Current and projected population growth rates are higher in the developing than in the industrial nations. However, it is not true that the industrial nations do not, from a global sustainability perspective, have a population problem. Resource extraction and waste insertion per capita are much higher in the industrial nations than in developing nations. Tables 2.1 and 2.14 show, for example, that per capita energy use is some 10 times greater in the industrial nations. They account for 23 per cent of world population, but 74 per cent of world energy use.

The category of industrial nations considered in Chapter 2 includes the former communist states of eastern Europe, and the USSR. If we focus more narrowly on the nations belonging to the OECD, they account for 15 per cent of world population and 63 per cent of world energy use (United Nations Development Programme 1992, Tables 43 and 45). For 1990 to 2000 the annual population growth rates projected are 2.0 per cent for the developing nations and 0.4 per cent for the OECD. For these growth rates, the population increases over 1900–2000 are 910 million for the developing nations and 40 million for the OECD. Given the current per capita use rates for energy, the OECD's increase in total energy use over this period would then be 46 per cent of that for the developing nations.

Clearly, from a global perspective on sustainability, the industrial nations do have a population problem. From such a perspective, it is clear that the objective of policy should, at least, be a rapid move to a zero growth rate for population. Many would take the view that the proper long-term objective should be a substantial reduction in population size. It is difficult to see how a reduced population level in any nation could represent a threat to sustainability. However, low rates of population growth in some industrial nations are already giving rise to concerns about long-term economic prospects. The perceived problem arises from a combination of low birth rates, in some cases below replacement level, with increasing longevity and low death rates, resulting in an ageing population. This implies a future with a smaller working population relative to the non-working population. Hence there are concerns about future living standards, and the prospect of intergenerational social conflict as each worker is required to support more aged non-workers. These concerns arise where it is taken that existing arrangements for individuals to automatically leave the workforce at a fixed age will continue. Increasing longevity and the changing nature of much work call into question the desirability of continuing with such arrangements.

6. Poverty and inequality

This has two related dimensions, the intergenerational and the intragenerational. The sustainability problem involves dealing with current inequality and poverty without creating future poverty, and inequality between generations. In this context, the intragenerational dimension is usually treated as applying as between nations (see Chapter 2). Confining our attention to an industrial nation, intergenerational equity can be taken to be covered by the objectives already listed. However, poverty and inequality currently exist in industrial nations. It makes little sense to worry about the future and foreign poor, while ignoring current poverty and inequality at home. Further, many would argue that greater equality within an industrial nation is necessary for general social acceptance of the consequences of the adoption of policies for sustainability. On this basis, equality is seen to involve more than levels of consumption, extending to cover full participation by all in economic and social activities, and political decision-making. Some environmentalists argue that wider and more effective participation in social decision-making is a necessary feature of sustainable development: see, for examples, Daly and Cobb (1989), or contributions to Ekins and Max-Neef (1992).

Were it not for inequality, it would be difficult to contend that poverty is now a serious problem in most OECD countries. For all but a few in countries such as the United Kingdom and Australia, there is no question that the material living standards of those with relatively low incomes are now considerably higher than they were for a majority of the population 100, or even 50, years ago. In the 1930s the children of the unemployed frequently went shoeless, for example. In the 1990s, with similar levels of unemployment, it is virtually unknown for children to go shoeless. The majority of the 'poor' in such countries now consume more than even the relatively affluent in the poorest developing nations. How then can it be said that poverty remains a serious problem in a rich industrial nation?

The answer lies in the conception of poverty as **relative deprivation** within a given society:

> Poverty can be defined objectively ... only in terms of the concept of relative deprivation ... Individuals, families and groups in the population can be said to be in poverty when they lack the resources to obtain the types of diet, participate in the activities and have the living conditions and amenities which are customary, or are at least widely encouraged or approved, in the societies to which they belong. Their resources are so seriously below those commanded by the average individual or family that they are, in effect, excluded from ordinary living patterns, customs and activities.[2]

What is customary in a society changes over time, and with economic growth. This was discussed in Chapter 4. On this view of poverty, economic growth, *per se*, has a limited role to play in reducing the incidence of poverty. The reduction of inequality has two roles to play in reducing the extent of poverty. First, redistribution from the better to the worse off is a means of making the latter somewhat better off in an absolute sense. Economic growth facilitates this by reducing the absolute sacrifice required from the better off for any given absolute improvement for the worse off. Here, the consequent reduction in inequality is largely incidental. In the second role inequality reduction is more central. The

consumption standard considered customary or normal will be determined in large part by the better off. The greater the degree of income
inequality, the greater the scope for the setting of a customary standard
which is beyond the means of those on low incomes. Economic growth
may merely aggravate this problem. The point is that it is not necessary
to be egalitarian to see a need for the reduction of inequality.

It should be noted that no reference has been made here to an objective
defined in terms of the growth of GNP per capita. Economic growth so
measured is of no direct relevance to sustainability. It is not necessary for
the pursuit of sustainability that there be a target growth rate of zero.
The successful pursuit of sustainability could result in a positive
measured growth rate over some periods. In principle, sustainability
would involve a constant, or increasing, stock of wealth defined to
include environmental assets. However, as noted earlier, the proper
measurement of wealth so defined is impossible. There is no single
indicator which can serve as a target for sustainability policy.

Policy instruments

The standard economics approach to the question of policy instruments
for environmental protection was discussed in Chapter 7. We now discuss how the instruments considered there align with the objectives set
out above.

Private property rights

Standard economics sees the question of environmental protection in
terms of the correction of market failure. Environmental problems are
seen as arising on account of the absence of private property rights in
environmental assets. Hence, the most obvious policy response might be
seen as the creation of private property rights in environmental assets.
This would be in pursuit of objective 1 from the list above. With the
creation of a complete set of private property rights, the market would
change the relative prices of all assets. The prices of environmental assets
which were being depleted would rise, so that their use would decline.
This would also encourage the development and use, where possible, of
substitutes. Given the changed relative prices of assets, production and
consumption patterns would become less environmentally damaging.
Changing relative prices would also work to promote objective 4, as
projects would be evaluated using relative prices reflecting environmental impacts.

There are two major problems with this approach. First, the range of applicability is limited since many environmental assets are inherently non-rival and/or non-exclusive in use. Second, where private property rights can be created, and other problems for the operation of markets are absent, the outcomes will be those that protect the environment as required by efficiency criteria. These outcomes are not necessarily consistent with sustainability requirements.

This is not to deny a role for the creation of private property rights. There are, no doubt, situations where it is feasible to create them where they do not currently exist, and where the outcomes arising would improve matters with regard to the protection of what are understood to be critical environmental assets. The point is that the usefulness of this type of policy instrument is to be judged on a case-by-case basis, in the light of a full consideration of all of the particular circumstances. For some, there is an ethical presumption that critical environmental assets should be collectively, rather than privately, owned. Collective, or social, ownership does not preclude leasing usage rights to private agents.[3] This is essentially what tradeable permits with limited lifetimes involve.

Moral suasion

Ignorance about economy–environment interconnections is the basis for the objectives indicated in 2 above. Moral suasion, i.e. manipulation of the cultural environment, aligns in general ways with these objectives. It is about changing the information bases of individuals and firms. Changing those would likely involve changes to preferences and behaviour. Some environmentalists seem to take the view that this is the most important class of instrument for sustainability promotion. There appears to be a widespread view that if enough people were properly informed about the sustainability problem, behaviour would change so as to meet threats to sustainability. Individuals for example, would modify their consumption habits, recycle their wastes, and generate the political pressure for other necessary reforms.[4]

Regulation, taxation and tradeable permits

Whereas moral suasion is a broad brush approach to threats to sustainability, regulation, taxation and tradeable permits are to be used to address specific threats on a case-by-case basis. Their relative merits vary with circumstances. They are instruments for the protection of particular environmental assets considered to be critical, objective 1. To the extent that use of such assets is affected, relative prices will change, and this will influence project selection, objective 4. Thus, for example, suppose that the harvest rate for some fish species is reduced by regulation, setting limits on allowable catches for existing fishery operators, and prohibiting new entrants to the fishery. The price to consumers of the fish species in question will rise. Projects for the farming of this species will become more attractive financially. Similar consequences would follow from control by taxation or tradeable permits. It is important to be clear that control of the use of environmental assets will raise the price of those assets, inducing substitutions in production and consumption, whatever the particular means for control. A preference for regulation over taxation appears sometimes to reflect the assumption that the latter will involve higher commodity prices whereas the former will not.

The case for the use of price incentive type instruments does not require the assumptions that all individuals are fully informed utility maximisers and that all firms are competitive profit maximisers. Price incentives move things in the required direction on weaker assumptions. And, experience shows that they do work, albeit imperfectly and with delays. Individuals and firms do actually alter their behaviour so as to use relatively less of things that become more expensive. The qualifier 'relatively' is important. Recall from Chapter 6 the discussion of price and income elasticities of demand. The response of the absolute level of use to a price increase depends upon the size of the price increase, the numerical values for the elasticities of the demand function, and other influences changing at the same time. If what is required is a reduction in use for sure, then quantity regulation or tradeable permits should be the chosen instruments.

Chapter 8 reviewed some suggestions for the development of a new economics. Some of these can be treated as proposals regarding policy instruments to address threats to sustainability. Proposals for the proper measurement of national income, in the light of economy–environment interconnections, could be regarded as a policy instrument from the moral suasion class, which would align with objective 2b. Energy accounting and analysis are intended to improve understanding of the way economic activity and energy use are related, and align with objective 2a primarily, but are also relevant to 2b. Performance bonds are a price-incentive type instrument primarily directed at objective 1. As well as having additional relevance to objective 4, performance bonds are also intended to address objectives 2a and 2b. They are, that is, designed to create incentives for the improvement of understanding about the implications of economy–environment interconnections, and the dissemination of that information so as to affect behaviour.

Mention also needs to be made of what might be regarded as institutional policy instruments. An example is the requirement that major development projects be subject to an Environmental Impact Assessment (an EIA). Such a requirement directly addresses objectives 1 and 4 above. This is also the case for a requirement that such projects be subject to proper cost-benefit analysis. To the extent that EIAs and CBAs generate and disseminate information, they also relate to objectives 2.

The instruments considered thus far here do not address objectives 3, 5 and 6. These objectives, and instruments for their pursuit, have received relatively little attention in the debates initiated by the 1987 publication of *Our common future*. It is to these matters that we now turn.

Savings, investment and taxation

Individuals' savings behaviour and investment by firms are linked via the rate of interest: see Chapter 6. The implications of government policy for savings behaviour are considered in public sector economics, where it is seen that matters are complex, and that firm general conclusions are not readily available. It is, however, widely believed that the taxation of income acts to reduce saving at any rate of interest, and that some shift from income to expenditure as the basis for personal tax liability would increase savings for a given interest rate. The basis for this is the fact that the taxation of income derived from interest earnings reduces the post-tax interest rate below the market interest rate. If the market rate of interest is 5 per cent and income is taxed at 25 per cent, then the rate of interest actually received on savings is 3.75 per cent. Hence, income taxation reduces the incentive to save. **Expenditure taxation** is the taxing of all commodities at a common rate. Liability arises only when commodities are purchased, and the amount of tax an individual pays depends on her total consumption expenditure. There is no disincentive effect on savings.

Many commentators urge some move from income to expenditure as the basis for personal tax liability. This is not only because of anticipated effects on savings and investment. It is also widely believed that income taxation adversely affects the supply of labour in a way that expenditure taxation does not. Income taxation reduces the gain from sacrificing leisure in order to earn, and so, it is argued, reduces the amount of leisure sacrificed. Expenditure taxation does not, it is argued, affect the incentives influencing the choice between work and leisure. Hence, switching from income to expenditure as the tax base would increase the supply of labour and effort.[5] Also, there are policing problems with income taxation which some argue are reduced with expenditure taxation. The status of many of these claims for expenditure taxation is disputed by some commentators and economists. It is pointed out, for example, that there are many influences on savings behaviour, or that income earned from interest on savings could simply be exempted from the income tax base (in some countries some forms of saving are tax-exempt). Nevertheless, expenditure, as opposed to income, taxation is widely advocated as a means of increasing saving, and the supply of labour. It is difficult to see how such a switch could adversely affect saving. On standard economic arguments, it would address the threat to sustainability arising from an insufficiency of saving and investment, i.e. serve objective 3. To the extent that saving is increased, the interest rate is lowered. This has implications for the distribution of consumption over time, and for project appraisal, such that greater weight is given to the future as compared with the present.

Population policy

We now turn to the question of instruments for influencing the rate of population growth, objective 6. This is a sensitive subject. While few industrial nations currently employ policies which have an impact on population growth as a stated objective, policies directed at other objectives may influence population growth, impacting on death rates and birth rates. Policy generally reflects the social consensus that the prolongation of life is highly desirable at any age, save in exceptional circumstances. Also, the structure of the tax/welfare system affects the costs to individuals of reproduction and child-care in a variety of ways. In some cases this impact is intended. Many tax/welfare systems, for example, intentionally subsidise child care. At the least, sustainability requires that the tax/welfare system does not generate incentives to reproductive behaviour such as to produce a positive population growth rate.

A specific policy instrument for population policy is the creation of **tradeable procreation permits**.[6] The first step would be the determination of the total quantity of permits to be issued, which would follow from the population growth objective. Population stabilisation would require a birth rate equal to the replacement rate. We will take stabilisation as the objective. Take it that in an industrial society the replacement rate is 2.1 births per female. Then, on attaining adult status, each individual would be given 105 permit units, with 100 units as a couple's requirement for the legal birth of one child. The permits would be freely tradeable. Individuals unable or unwilling to become parents would be sellers of permits. Couples wishing to reproduce in excess of replacement level would be potential buyers of permits. The price that permits would fetch would depend upon the demand in relation to the fixed supply. Note that the total quantity of permits to be issued could be varied over time, and set to achieve targets other than a growth rate of zero.

When informed of this proposal, people usually react with shock, and reject it out of hand on the grounds that human reproduction is too sacred to be associated with monetary transactions. If the need to control the growth of human numbers is accepted, this is somewhat premature. Given that objective, what are the alternative instruments? Presumably most people would give an answer which would fall under the heading of moral suasion. Here, as elsewhere, a major problem with moral suasion is that it may be ineffective. To be made effective it may have to become social coercion, so that it would be more nearly quantity regulation. The major problem with tradeable procreation permits would likely be the problem of enforcement – what would be done about parents giving birth in excess of their permit-holding? One approach would be to require them to purchase an additional 100 permit units from the government at a multiple of the going market price. The price could be recovered through the income tax system. Enforcement problems would be reduced to the extent that the climate of opinion favoured the objective of the policy. One imagines that the introduction of such a system would be impossible until after extensive public debate had moved opinion in the required direction. To the extent that the government took a lead in promoting such debate, it would be using moral suasion. As is generally the case, alternative policy instruments can be used in conjunction.

The tradeable procreation permit scheme has some attractive additional features. It is equitable: permit units would be issued equally to all adults. Second, with permits carrying a positive price, it could be assumed that children would be born to parents who desired them on the basis of a positive decision in favour of children, as against material consumption. This would, one imagines, do much good for child welfare.

Poverty policy

The major sources of poverty are relatively low incomes and/or relatively high expenditure requirements. The major recognised cause of relatively low income is the lack of paid employment, because of unemployment, or withdrawal from the workforce owing to age or ill health. On the expenditure side, society mainly recognises requirements on account of child-rearing, and ill health. Policy instruments for poverty alleviation come in three main categories. There are, first, policies aimed at reducing unemployment. These are discussed in the following section. Second, there are a range of policies which involve monetary payments, transfer payments, to designated categories of persons. The collectivity of such payments is known as the **social security system**, or the **welfare system**. Third, government provides a range of goods and services free of charge, either generally or to designated categories of persons. These are known as **benefits in kind**, or **indirect benefits**. The welfare system is generally extensive in industrial economies. In Australia in 1990/91, for example, transfer payments under the social security system accounted for approximately 30 per cent of all government expenditure. Of the total of these payments, 49.2 per cent was to retired persons, 15.1 per cent to persons suffering ill-health or disability, 16.7 per cent to unemployed persons, and 19.1 per cent was accounted for by payments to the parents of dependent children (ABS 1993a).

Government expenditure on social security transfer payments and benefits in kind is financed from tax revenue. The way in which that revenue is raised itself has implications for poverty and inequality. The next section considers the implications for poverty and inequality of carbon taxation, and the final section of this chapter looks at the operation of the tax/welfare system as a whole.

Government failure correction

Governments supply goods and services, operate the tax/welfare system, and have in place policies that directly and indirectly affect the behaviour of firms and individuals. Addressing threats to sustainability requires looking at the full range of government activity, against the objectives distinguished here. Aspects of the operation of the tax/welfare system that are relevant have already been noted. Against sustainability criteria, the removal of tax/welfare system incentives to child-bearing would be an example of government failure correction. The tax/welfare system is the main focus of the remainder of this chapter.

In the cause of protecting special interests, or of promoting equity and alleviating poverty, governments often employ policies that increase threats to sustainability. Fossil fuel production and/or use are sometimes actively encouraged, for example, by direct subsidies. In Europe, the operation of the Common Agricultural Policy has been argued to be environmentally damaging, and, particularly, to encourage energy-intensive production, for example. Where government is involved in the supply of goods and services, it is argued that the activity is not subject to the cost minimisation pressures on private sector firms, leading to waste in the use of all inputs, and the generation of avoidable environmental impacts. The state of the environment in the formerly centrally controlled economies of the Soviet bloc exemplifies, in extreme form, this type of effect.[7]

There are three main points here. First, government in relation to threats to sustainability is not necessarily benign. Its behaviour requires as much scrutiny as does private sector behaviour. Second, there are conflicting objectives for policy, and trade-offs have to be made. Third, government activity in a democratic society is itself affected by the operation of some of the policy instruments considered above. Moral suasion affects voter behaviour.

Carbon taxation

Here we look at the case for the introduction of **carbon taxation** as the basic strategy for addressing threats to sustainability. It is not put forward as the only policy instrument for so doing. It would be used together with other instruments, as they were appropriate in particular circumstances to meet particular problems. Carbon taxation would be implemented by taxing fossil fuel production according to carbon content. Imports of fossil fuel would be taxed at the same rates. The subsequent revenue would be used to reduce the taxation of income, so as to hold total government revenue constant.

Until recently, the literature on environmental taxes has ignored the revenue arising from their use. The use of taxes for environmental protection has not usually been seen as a means by which government can raise revenue needed to finance its expenditures. This, no doubt, has reflected the view that the total revenues arising from environmental taxes would be small. However, in recent years concerns about the enhanced greenhouse effect have put carbon taxation on the political agenda, carbon dioxide being the major greenhouse gas (see Chapter 10). Given that the major source of carbon dioxide emissions is fossil fuel combustion, and the extent of fossil fuel combustion in industrial economies, the revenue implications are too obvious to be ignored. Consequently, there has recently been some analysis and discussion of the comparative merits of carbon, or fossil fuel, and other tax bases such as income.[8]

The revenue-raising potential of carbon taxation can be illustrated using some broad-brush calculations based on the case of Australia. Using round figures, in 1988/89 fossil fuel combustion in Australia of 3550 PJ gave rise to the release of 300×10^6 tonnes of carbon dioxide. This is equivalent to 84 500 tonnes of carbon dioxide per PJ. Then a tax of $1 per tonne of carbon dioxide is equivalent to a tax of $84 500 per PJ fossil fuel. Assume that the price of fossil fuel in the absence of the carbon tax was $4 500 000 per PJ.[9] PJ stands for petajoule, where the prefix peta is for 10^{15}. Table 9.1 shows the effects of various rates of carbon dioxide taxation. The second column gives the consequent percentage increase in the price paid for fossil fuel. The third shows the total revenue arising for 300×10^6 tonnes of carbon dioxide emissions.

Then, in the fourth and fifth columns, this revenue is expressed as a percentage of the 1988/89 revenue collected by all levels of Australian government from all taxes, and from direct taxation.

Table 9.1. *Carbon dioxide tax rates and revenues*

Tax rate $ per tonne CO_2	Fuel price percentage increase	Tax revenue $billions	Per cent of total tax revenue	Per cent of direct tax revenue
5	9.4	1.5	1.4	2.5
10	18.8	3.0	2.8	5.0
20	37.6	6.0	5.7	9.9
40	75.1	12.0	11.3	19.8
60	112.7	18.0	17.0	29.7

Source: Total, i.e. federal plus state government revenue and total direct tax revenue are taken from ABS (1992), Tables 54 and 55.

The tax revenue figures in Table 9.1 arise by multiplying a fixed quantity of emissions, 300×10^6, by the carbon dioxide tax rate. They show what would happen if fossil fuel use and emissions were unaffected by the imposition of the tax. We would not expect emissions to remain constant after the imposition of the tax. Other things being equal, emissions and fossil fuel combustion would fall by an amount dependent on the price elasticity of demand for fossil fuel. A reduction in emissions would mean a reduction in the revenue from carbon taxation. Table 9.2 shows how fossil fuel use and carbon dioxide emissions, and the revenue from the tax, would respond to a tax rate of $20 per tonne of carbon dioxide, for various values for the price elasticity of demand for fossil fuel. The calculations involved here are simple. The percentage increase in the fuel price, 37.6 from Table 9.1, is multiplied by the price elasticity to give the percentage reduction in fuel use, and hence in emissions. The revenue from the tax is then found by multiplying the new level of fossil fuel use by the appropriate tax rate.

Table 9.2 shows that a given rate of tax is more effective in reducing emissions the higher is the price elasticity of demand for fossil fuel. To the extent that an objective is to reduce emissions and fossil fuel use, the higher the elasticity the better. On the other hand, a given rate of tax raises less revenue the higher is the price elasticity. To the extent that an objective is to raise revenue, the lower the elasticity the better.

What price elasticity value should be used for such a broad-brush appraisal of the revenue potential of carbon taxation? Should we assume a value of, say, 0.1 or a value of, say, 1.0? In part the answer to this

Table 9.2. *Price elasticity, emissions reduction and tax revenue.*

Price elasticity	Reduction of emissions and fuel use %	Revenue $billions
0	0	6.0
0.1	3.7	5.8
0.2	7.5	5.6
0.4	15.0	5.1
0.6	22.4	4.7
0.8	29.9	4.2
1.0	37.4	3.8
1.2	44.9	3.3
1.4	52.4	2.9

question depends on the time horizon adopted. The price elasticity reflects the costs associated with substituting other inputs for fossil fuel. In the short run, these would be expected to be high, so that the elasticity would be low. One year after the introduction of the tax, one would expect to observe little reduction in fossil fuel use and emissions, and the tax revenue close to that corresponding to a zero price elasticity of demand. It takes time to modify production processes and consumption habits. However, over time adjustments can be made and comparing the situation immediately following the introduction of the tax with that, say, five years later, one would expect to find the carbon tax revenue falling off somewhat, for a constant level of income. In the medium term one would not expect much in the way of technological innovation, adjustments would occur within the limits of given technology. However, over the longer term, one would expect technology to change in response to the changed price structure. Comparing the initial situation with that, say, 20 years after the introduction of the tax, one might expect revenue to have fallen quite substantially, for a constant level of income.

This is all somewhat imprecise. While the general nature of the responses to carbon taxation is reasonably clear, their magnitude cannot be forecast with any precision. Historical data can be used to measure what the price elasticity has been. While such exercises confirm that it is negative, the precision of the estimates arising is not great. Forecasting introduces further problems, such as what to assume about the future income level, and the error bands on any energy demand forecast will be wide.

We will shortly consider carbon taxation in relation to each of the six sustainability objectives noted at the start of the chapter. Before doing that, some more of the basic features of carbon taxation are reviewed.

Table 9.3 *Commodity price increases due to carbon dioxide taxation at $20 per tonne*

Commodity produced by	Price Increase %
1 Agriculture, forestry, fishing	1.77
2 Mining	1.69
3 Meat and milk products	1.77
4 Other food products	1.46
5 Beverages and tobacco	0.84
6 Textiles, clothing, footwear	0.95
7 Wood, wood products, furniture	1.31
8 Paper, printing, publishing	1.12
9 Chemicals	1.56
10 Petroleum and coal products	9.97
11 Non-metallic mineral products	1.89
12 Basic metal products	9.00
13 Fabricated metal products	2.76
14 Transport equipment	0.82
15 Other machinery and equipment	0.71
16 Miscellaneous manufacturing	0.89
17 Electricity	31.33
18 Gas	21.41
19 Water	1.34
20 Construction	1.60
21 Wholesale and retail	10.14
22 Transport and communications	2.28
23 Finance and business services	1.21
24 Residential property	0.42
25 Public administration	1.73
26 Community services	0.93
27 Recreational and personal services	1.62

Source: Common and Salma (1992b).

The first point is that such taxation would be simple to administer and collect. The costs involved in administering carbon taxation would be low. Unlike many environmental taxes, carbon taxation as proposed here would not involve major monitoring and enforcement problems. Fossil fuel producers/importers would simply pay a fixed amount of tax per unit of production/importation. Monitoring fossil fuel production/importation is straightforward, and the tax would be very difficult to avoid or evade.

For the purposes of Tables 9.1 and 9.2, we assumed a single fossil fuel. In fact, there are three currently in common usage: coal, oil, and natural gas. The amount of carbon dioxide released on combustion varies across the three fuels. The tax rate on each would be derived from the tax rate per unit of carbon dioxide emission according to the fuel's carbon content. The fossil fuel with the lowest carbon content is natural gas. If the carbon content of natural gas is set at 1, that of oil is approximately 1.3, and that of coal is approximately 1.9. Thus, the unit tax rates on the production/importation of these three fuels would be, approximately, in the ratios 1:1.3:1.9, with the rates in dollar terms then determined by the rate of carbon dioxide tax in dollar terms.[10]

The introduction of carbon taxation would affect the prices of all commodities. In Chapter 2 we discussed the pervasiveness of energy use in industrial economies, noting that use in production is indirect as well as direct. This was illustrated in Figures 2.1 and 2.2 (see pp.25 and 26), using data for Australia. The methods by which those data were derived can be used to calculate the carbon dioxide emissions arising both directly and indirectly, as a result of fossil fuel combustion, in the production of commodities.[11] Given the resulting data on **carbon dioxide intensities**, the impact on the prices of the commodities of any given rate of carbon dioxide tax can be computed. Table 9.3 shows the effects, on the prices of the commodities considered in Figures 2.1 and 2.2, of the introduction of a tax of $20 per tonne of carbon dioxide. The choice of this tax rate is not entirely arbitrary. It is approximately the rate calculated as necessary for Australia to cut its emissions in line with the so-called 'Toronto target' of a 20 per cent reduction on the 1988 level by the year 2005 (Industry Commission 1991). All commodity prices are increased by the introduction of carbon taxation: the relative increases across commodities depend upon the relative carbon dioxide intensities, which depend, in turn, on the amounts of the various fossil fuels used per unit of output. The calculations for the results in Table 9.3 assume that all fossil fuel producers/importers pass on to their customers the full impact of the tax, which is then fully passed on at every stage of the production process for all commodities. Given that all fossil fuels would be taxed, and that the demand for fossil fuels has a relatively low price elasticity, this would be a reasonable assumption. The calculations also assume that there are no substitution responses in production and consumption, whereby individuals and firms buy less of the items with relatively large price increases, and more of the items of which the price has increased relatively little. For these reasons, the results are to be regarded as generally indicative rather than as forecasts of the actual consequences of carbon taxation.

We now review the implications of carbon taxation in terms of the six policy objectives outlined at the beginning of the chapter.

Environmental asset protection

With the introduction of carbon taxation, the relative prices of commodities would change, discouraging the production and consumption of commodities with high carbon intensities, so reducing total carbon dioxide emissions. These emissions are a major source of the increasing atmospheric concentration of the greenhouse gases. Carbon taxation would directly address this threat to sustainability.

Fossil fuel combustion is the origin of several atmospheric pollutants. In addition to carbon dioxide, it involves emissions of: sulphur oxides, nitrous oxide, carbon monoxide, particulates, and hydrocarbons.[12] Generally, the problems associated with each of these are more localised than is the case with carbon dioxide. Sulphur oxide emissions are mainly from coal combustion, and cause respiratory illness, affect plant growth, and are involved in the corrosion of buildings and other structures. Sulphur dioxide is involved in the processes giving rise to acid rain. Nitrous oxides arise mainly in the use of petrol in motor vehicles, and are a cause of respiratory illnesses, as well as being greenhouse gases. Both sulphur and nitrous oxides are involved in the production of petrochemical smog. Carbon monoxide is toxic; it arises mainly from the use of petrol in motor vehicles. Some of the hydrocarbons released in fossil fuel combustion are considered to be carcinogenic. Particulates are a cause of respiratory illness in humans. They influence precipitation and also reduce incident solar radiation.

By reducing fossil fuel combustion, carbon taxation would reduce all of these atmospheric emissions. Its effects on environmental impacts would not be confined to these reductions. The higher prices for fossil fuels would have effects on all production activities. Agricultural production illustrates this. Figure 2.1 shows that agricultural commodities in Australia are relatively energy-intensive, when account is taken of indirect as well as direct energy use. This is reflected in Table 9.3, where the price increase for the agricultural sector is the seventh largest of the 27 shown. Australia is a typical industrial economy in this respect. Much of the use of energy by agriculture in an industrial economy is indirect, via the use of artificial fertilisers, the production of which uses large amounts of energy. Run-off from agricultural land is a major source of water pollution, largely due to high levels of fertiliser application. To the extent that carbon taxation made artificial fertiliser more expensive, it would discourage its use, and reduce this kind of environmental damage.

This is a particular example of an important general point. Extrasomatic energy use is required for the movement and transformation of matter on any significant scale. To a first approximation, it can be taken that reducing extrasomatic energy use per unit of economic activity reduces environmental impact per unit of economic activity. Carbon taxation would work to reduce the energy intensity of economic activity, and hence its generalised environmental impact. Of course, reducing the energy intensity of total economic activity would not mean that all resource extractions and all waste insertions decreased. Some particular individual levels of extraction and insertion would increase, and some of the increases involved might be environmentally damaging and threaten sustainability. There would be a need for policies and controls directed specifically at such particular problems. Although not a general panacea, carbon taxation would provide a useful basic approach, to be supplemented by an array of additional and specifically targeted policy instruments.

The fossil fuels are non-renewable resources, which have uses other than combustion. Two points arise. First, reducing fossil fuel combustion now would make more of this fuel available for use in the future, whether for combustion or other uses. As regards combustion, there is no necessary contradiction in wanting to reduce current use and increase future use. The future could be a very long time, so that increased total future use could be consistent with much lower future rates of use per period of time. Second, as regards the non-combustion uses of fossil fuels, they are the basis for the material inputs to a number of production processes, particularly in the chemicals industry. To the extent that carbon taxation reduced the use of fossil fuels for combustion, it would increase the quantities available for these other uses, now and in the future.

Increased fossil fuel prices would make other sources of extrasomatic energy more attractive. There would be incentives for the substitution of other energy sources for fossil fuels, as well as incentives for energy conservation and, in the longer term, it is possible that total energy use would increase. To the extent that total energy use is not reduced, some of the consequences claimed for carbon taxation here would not follow. However, so long as fossil fuel combustion is reduced, there would be less carbon dioxide emissions, and less of the other emissions discussed above. It is not true that the alternative energy sources are entirely benign with respect to environmental protection. Nuclear fission has a number of widely recognised problems associated with it. Hydro-electric facilities frequently impact on environmentally sensitive areas.

Biomass combustion does release carbon dioxide, but to the extent that this fuel is used on a sustainable basis, with new vegetation replacing that burned, there is in effect a closed carbon cycle, with the new vegetation absorbing atmospheric carbon dioxide. Biomass combustion does involve other atmospheric emissions. Harvesting biomass for combustion may involve other environmental damage, such as soil erosion. The remaining alternative energy sources – solar, wind, waves, tides, geothermal – are not generally seen as involving threats to sustainability, though local environmental impacts will generally be involved.

To the extent that carbon taxation induces substitution between energy sources, rather than reduced energy use, it may be appropriate to supplement it by taxation of, or other controls on, non-fossil fuel sources. In the case of solar energy this would likely be administratively difficult, but this source is currently regarded as involving little environmental impact. Biomass combustion could also be difficult to monitor and control. The use of nuclear fission and hydro-electric power would, however, be relatively easy to monitor, and taxation on the base of electricity sent out would be straightforward. The question of the desirability of supplementary control of non-fossil fuel energy use does not need resolution prior to the introduction of carbon taxation. It can be considered as experience of responses to carbon taxation develops.

Improved understanding

Carbon taxation would provide incentives for research and development work on alternatives to fossil fuel combustion as a source of extrasomatic energy, and on energy conservation. This would address objective 2a, improved scientific understanding, in relation to substitution possibilities in this area. It would also work to increase public awareness, objective 2b, of perceived threats to sustainability, using the price system as the means of signalling. Changing relative prices is a very effective way of transmitting information.

Savings and investment levels

The arguments for preferring expenditure to income taxation in relation to the level of savings and the supply of labour apply also to carbon taxation. Carbon taxation levied on the production/importation of fossil fuels would be passed forward through the chain of production processes, and finally impact on the prices charged to the buyers of all commodities. Hence, it would act like an expenditure tax, except that the rate would not be constant, but would vary across commodities according to carbon intensity. An individual's total carbon tax payment would vary with the carbon intensity of her consumption and would approximately reflect its general environmental impact.

Carbon taxation would differ from what is sometimes understood as an expenditure tax in one important respect. An expenditure tax is sometimes taken to mean a tax which impacts only on the expenditure of individuals as consumers, and does not impact on the expenditure of firms. This is usually to be achieved by allowing firms to reclaim any tax paid on their purchases of inputs to production. This is a feature, for example, of the system of value added taxation in place in the European Community. One reason for this rebate is to avoid adverse effects on international competitiveness arising from higher costs for inputs to production. Such rebates would not be allowed with carbon taxation.

They would negate one of the intended effects of the carbon taxation, that of generating incentives to producers, as well as consumers, to alter their patterns of purchases away from carbon intensive commodities.

Project selection

Carbon taxation would alter the relative prices used in project appraisals. It would make carbon intensive inputs to projects, both in construction and operation, more expensive. It would not, however, make carbon intensive outputs more valuable. These would rise in price to their purchasers, but the prices received by their producers would not increase. The extent of the market for carbon intensive outputs would decrease on account of the higher prices to be paid for them. The over-all effect would be to work against environmentally damaging projects, and projects to produce environmentally damaging outputs. Investment projects for energy conservation and the substitution of non-fossil for fossil fuel energy would become more attractive. Nuclear fission plants for electricity generation would, for example, become more attractive. To the extent that it increased savings, carbon taxation would reduce the rate of interest used in project appraisal and cost-benefit analysis.

Population size

Carbon taxation itself would presumably be neutral in its direct impacts on the incentives affecting reproductive behaviour. It is difficult to see that the pattern of change in relative prices illustrated in Table 9.3 would affect these incentives. We are assuming that the revenue arising from carbon taxation is to be used to reduce the revenue raised via income taxation. Precisely how the revenue from income taxation is reduced could affect the incentives influencing reproductive behaviour. Some nations now reduce an individual's income tax liability, for a given level of income, on account of responsibility for child rearing. If such allowances were increased as part of an income tax revenue reducing package, the costs of child-rearing would be effectively reduced. Whether this would affect reproductive behaviour would depend on the size of the changes involved, and on the way that other relevant influences were moving. The general point is that properly assessing the impact of carbon taxation requires considering in some detail the way the subsequent revenue is to be used. We return to this shortly.

Poverty and inequality

As illustrated in Table 9.3 (p.238), carbon taxation would differentially increase all of the prices facing consumers. Individuals differ in their patterns of commodity consumption according to their position in the income scale. It is widely believed that higher energy prices, which carbon taxation would cause, would hurt the poor most, since they spend larger proportions of their incomes on fuel. Carbon taxation would then increase inequality, i.e. be **regressive** in impact. The direct impact on prices would itself make all individuals worse off, but the effect would be greatest on the least well-off.

Table 9.4 presents evidence bearing upon this in the case of Australia. In Table 9.4, CPI stands for Consumer Price Index and the entries show by how much a carbon tax of $20 per tonne of carbon dioxide would increase the cost of living for households in each decile of the income distribution, and for all households taken together. A decile is one-tenth of the full range of income levels. Thus, households in the lowest decile are those with incomes lying in the bottom 10 per cent of the range of incomes, and so on.

Table 9.4 *Australian Consumer Price Index increases by decile for tax of $20 per tonne of CO_2*

	Accounting for all commodity price increases. %	Three fuel commodity price increases only %
Lowest	2.885	1.534
Second	2.995(h)	1.657(h)
Third	2.974	1.604
Fourth	2.850	1.444
Fifth	2.876	1.452
Sixth	2.774	1.353
Seventh	2.804	1.313
Eighth	2.774	1.278
Ninth	2.666	1.164
Highest	2.621(l)	1.097(l)
All households	2.785	1.311
h/l	1.14	1.51

Source: Common and Salma (1992b).

The results in the right-hand column of Table 9.4 are those arising when it is assumed that the only prices affected by carbon taxation are the prices of the fuels purchased by households: oil, gas, and electricity. These results are obtained by weighting the relevant price increases (those for commodities 10, 17 and 18) from Table 9.3 according to their shares of total expenditure for the relevant group. The largest cost of living increase is then for households in the second decile, and the smallest is for those in the highest. The h/l ratio of 1.51 means that the cost of living increase experienced by the worst affected is 51 per cent greater than that experienced by the least affected. This is a simple summary measure of the regressive impact.

Discussion of the regressive impact of carbon taxation, or of higher energy prices generally, usually deals with impacts measured as in the right-hand column of Table 9.4. But all commodity production uses energy, so that carbon taxation affects the prices of all commodities, as illustrated in Table 9.3. The left-hand column of Table 9.4 shows the cost of living increases when the increases in the prices of all commodities are accounted for. All of the increases from Table 9.3 are added using weights reflecting expenditure shares. Compared with the right-hand column, all entries are, naturally, higher. The impact across deciles is still regressive, but considerably less so than in the right-hand column. The poor spend more of their income on fuel than do the rich. However, non-fuel commodities also increase in price, and taking account of this reduces regressivity. These results are for a carbon dioxide tax rate of $20 per tonne. For higher/lower tax rates all of the entries in Table 9.4 would be higher/lower, but, the relativities would remain the same, and so the extent of regressivity would remain the same.

While these results are based on Australian data, their general nature would be expected to apply for any industrial nation.[13] The results in Table 9.4 are calculated on the assumption that household consumption patterns remain unchanged following the initial impact of the carbon tax on prices. This is unlikely to be a valid assumption except in the short term. We would expect that following the initial impact, consumption patterns would change over time so as to involve less use of the commodities whose prices had increased most. This would work to reduce the impact of the carbon tax on the cost of living. If those better off were more able to modify their consumption patterns than the poor, the degree of regressivity associated with carbon taxation would be increased. However, while such responses might well increase the regressive impact, it is very difficult to believe that they could increase the actual level of impact for households in any decile. In order for the longer-term adjustments to increase the cost of living impact, consumption patterns would have to shift so that more of the commodities whose prices had increased most were bought. It is not necessary to believe that all households are well informed utility maximisers to find this implausible.

The changed pattern of prices consequent upon the introduction of carbon taxation would also affect the behaviour of firms, given time for adjustment. Again, it is not necessary to believe that all firms are well-informed profit maximisers in order to believe that there would be some substitution of less for more expensive inputs. This would have two implications for the regressive impact of carbon taxation. First, it would tend to reduce at least some of the commodity price increases, as compared with the initial effects. The size of the reductions in price impacts due to substitutions between inputs would vary across commodities according to the substitution possibilities in the different lines of production.

The second implication concerns the demand for labour, and the prospects for employment. Carbon taxation would increase the price of energy as an input to production, and decrease the price of labour relative to the price of energy. To the extent that labour and energy are substitutable as inputs to production, carbon taxation would increase the demand for labour, other things being equal, at a constant wage rate. Thus carbon taxation would address the problem of unemployment, and hence of poverty.

Are energy and labour substitutable inputs in production? The first point to note is that a major feature of the history of the development of the industrial economies has been the progressive substitution of extrasomatic energy for human, and animal, muscle power. Clearly, as a technological matter, this process is reversible. It is hardly feasible, however, that industrial society would contemplate the wholesale abandonment of machines in favour of muscles. What is at issue is not the total disavowal of the use of extrasomatic energy, but substitution at the margin between it and human inputs. Clearly there are possibilities for such marginal substitutions in many production lines. Think of the use of machinery and power tools, for example, in the building industry. In my youth, I worked, with many others, carrying bricks up ladders on building sites. Nowadays, one only sees 'hod-carriers' working on very small building jobs, and most bricks are lifted on hoists. Given some increase in the cost of the energy to run the hoists, the scale of building job on which it would be cheaper to use muscle power rather than a hoist would increase.

In the period following the so-called 'energy crisis' of 1973/74, economists conducted many empirical studies into the substitution possibilities between energy and other inputs, mainly in manufacturing industry. The inputs considered were capital equipment, labour, and energy (and sometimes raw materials). The results obtained were mixed, and there was some disagreement as to their implications. However, that disagreement was almost entirely over whether capital and energy were substitutable. It was widely agreed that the results were generally consistent with energy and labour as substitutes in production. This is consistent with intuition. The substitution of energy for labour generally involves the use of machinery, capital equipment, driven by the energy, as with the hoists on a building site. Further, over the period studied, the cost of energy had generally been falling in relation to the cost of labour, and energy and capital had been substituted for labour. While there was general agreement that energy and labour were substitutable in production, estimates of the degree of substitutability differed widely. The literature on these matters is highly technical and makes extensive use of econometric techniques. Berndt and Field (1981) review this literature, and include a comprehensive bibliography.

Analysis of these matters is complicated by the fact that over time, as opposed to economists' assumption of other things being equal, many things are happening simultaneously. As well as the relative costs of energy and labour changing, the relative costs of capital and energy are also changing, for example. And driven by such changing relative prices, and other events, effort is directed at changing the technical possibilities for substitution, by creating new types of machine and process, as well as making substitutions possible within the existing technology. Some of these efforts are successful, others are not. The successful efforts are introduced into actual use over time, so that the existing technology is changing over time, simultaneously with substitutions within the bounds of existing technology. One would expect that the direction of efforts to change technology would itself be influenced by changing relative costs. If it is expected that, relative to labour, energy is going to keep on getting more expensive, effort will be devoted to looking for technologies that economise on energy rather than labour, and vice versa.

Abstracting from such complications, to the extent that energy and labour are substitutes in production, carbon taxation would tend to work to increase employment. This will not be true for all occupations and in all industries. Carbon taxation would reduce the demand for some commodities. The employment outcome in an industry would depend on the balance between the inducement to substitute labour for energy and any negative impact on the industry's output level. In the coal industry, for example, one would expect employment to fall. In the industry producing solar water heaters, one would expect employment to rise, with both effects working in the same direction. Associated with an increase in the demand for labour, there could also be an increase in the wage rate. However, the cost of living would, as we have seen, increase for all workers. The effect on the standard of living is given by the change in the **real wage rate**. This is the money wage rate change divided by the change in the average price level, the Consumer Price Index (CPI). If the money wage rate increases by x per cent and the CPI by y per cent, the real wage rate changes by (x-y) per cent. Economists would generally assume that carbon taxation would reduce the average real wage rate, i.e. would assume that x is smaller than y taking the economy as a whole. In fact, they generally assume that carbon taxation would reduce the average material standard of living in an economy. We return to this shortly.

While at the aggregate level the expectation is of increased employment and reduced real wages, this would be consistent with quite different outcomes for different groups of workers. [The presumption for increased employment is conditional on our assuming away international trade effects in this chapter.] Hence, the impact on poverty and inequality is very difficult to predict. However, in considering the impact of carbon taxation on real wages, we have ignored the effects of the income tax reductions that we are assuming to go with it. The impact on poverty and inequality of a switch from income to carbon taxation depends not only on the labour market impact, but also on the way that income tax revenue is reduced. The reduction could be achieved, for example, by increasing the income level at which individuals start to pay tax. This would, in terms of the proportional increase in post income tax income, mainly benefit those at the lower end of the income distribution, and tend to reduce post-tax inequality. Alternatively, the reduction could be achieved by reducing the income tax rate. This would be more beneficial to the better off, and tend to increase post-tax inequality.

Also, it should be remembered that not all adults are employed. One effect of the income/carbon tax switch would be to increase employment and reduce unemployment. It cannot be assumed that it would eliminate unemployment. Some adults, such as the old and the disabled, are not in the labour force at all, i.e. are neither actual nor potential workers. Unemployment, old age, and ill health are major correlates of poverty. Typically, poor individuals in these categories do not pay income tax, but are recipients of transfer payments from government. A proper assessment of the effects of carbon taxation on poverty and inequality must take account of individuals in these groups. If the levels of transfer payments are held constant with the introduction of carbon taxation, the recipients will become worse off, since they face the commodity price increases arising. It is not, of course, necessary that the levels of welfare payments be held constant. But, to the extent that these payments are raised and the introduction of carbon taxation is revenue-neutral, i.e. does not change the government's budget deficit, there will be less of the carbon tax revenue available for reducing the revenue from income taxation.

The question which arises is whether it is possible to design a total package around carbon taxation which is revenue-neutral and which does not exacerbate problems of poverty and inequality. This is a very complicated question. Table 9.5 reproduces some of the results from a study which addressed this question for the United Kingdom. The impact of carbon taxation on commodity prices was determined in the

Table 9.5. *Household welfare changes by decile for
alternative tax/transfer packages – United Kingdom*

	Option 1 %	Option 2 %
Lowest	+39	+38
Second	+13	+14
Third	−2	0
Fourth	−5	−3
Fifth	−7	−7
Sixth	−7	−7
Seventh	−7	−7
Eighth	−7	−7
Ninth	−7	−7
Highest	−5	−6
% CO2 reduction	−16.6	−17.8
% Revenue change	−0.7	−1.4

Notes: Option 1 – CO2 tax at 11p per kg used to cut VAT and Petroleum
Excise and to increase welfare benefits.
Option 2 – CO2 tax at 12p per kg and smaller Petroleum Excise
cut with larger increase in welfare benefits.
Source: Symons et al. (1991).

same way as described above for Table 9.4. The operation of the United
Kingdom's tax/welfare system was modelled together with a simulation
of how consumption patterns would change with the changed commodity prices. Various options for the use of the carbon tax revenue were
considered. Table 9.5 shows the results for two options which made the
worst off better off, where welfare is measured as household
expenditure.[14] Note that the Unied Kingdom already operates a system
of indirect taxation, value added tax or VAT, which is regressive in
impact. So, the main tax reduction offset considered was in respect of
VAT rather than income taxation. In the United Kingdom one of the
fossil fuels, oil as petroleum for use in motor vehicles, is already subject
to taxation. This needs to be reduced if the tax introduced is to achieve
the proper carbon relativities across the fossil fuels.

For both of the alternatives reported in Table 9.5, the simulations show
households in the two lowest deciles experiencing substantial gains,
while all other households experience relatively small losses. These
results show that it is possible to design revenue-neutral packages which
offset the regressive impact of carbon taxation. This is an important area
for further investigation and debate.

Neither of the simulations considered in Table 9.5 produces exact
revenue-neutrality. Given all of the approximations involved in constructing the models, it would be wrong to look for precision. The outcomes

should be regarded as effectively revenue-neutral. Analysing the introduction of carbon taxation subject to the revenue-neutrality requirement
is a useful way of focusing on some aspects of the issues involved.
However, it should not be taken that changes to the tax/welfare system
need always be revenue-neutral. It may be desirable to increase revenue
so as to reduce a deficit in the government's budget. In many industrial
nations the question of measures for the reduction of budget deficits is
currently under active consideration. One option which could be
looked at is carbon taxation as an additional source of revenue. Compared with such alternative sources of increased revenue as income
taxation, this would have a number of advantages, as set out above.
Deficit reduction would imply a lower interest rate, by reducing government demand for loanable funds. The implications of a lower interest
rate for sustainability have already been noted.

Alternatives for reducing unemployment

One of the advantages claimed for carbon taxation is that it would alter
the incentives facing firms in such a way as to encourage them to shift
the mix of inputs to production away from energy in favour of labour. A
brief discussion of alternative approaches to the problem of unemployment is appropriate here.

Economic growth has long been seen as the solution to the problem
of unemployment. The idea behind this is simply that expanding the
total output of goods and services would increase the demand for
labour. The experience of most industrial economies in the past decade
has called this view into question. Generally, notwithstanding economic
growth, the unemployment problem has got worse, rather than better.
In many industrial economies there has emerged a particular problem
of increasing long-term unemployment among males, especially the
unskilled. Why has economic growth not solved the unemployment
problem? Some would argue that the problem is only that growth has
not been fast enough, and that the appropriate response is simply to
increase growth rates. However, it is increasingly recognised that feasible
rates of economic growth are unlikely to do much to solve the problem
in the foreseeable future, especially the problem of long-term unskilled
male unemployment.

The problem is that the impact of economic growth on the demand
for labour depends on the pattern of growth – which sectors of the
economy are expanding and which declining – and on the behaviour of
labour productivity. If output is growing at x per cent and output per
person at y per cent, the demand for labour grows at (x-y) per cent. If
output growth is largely concentrated in sectors where unskilled labour

requirements per unit of output are low, then the growth of demand for unskilled labour will not match the growth of total output. This is compounded to the extent that there is rapid growth in labour productivity in sectors employing lots of unskilled labour. This has been the recent pattern in many industrial economies and it is expected to continue. An exception to this generalisation is the growth of some parts of the personal services sector, such as the tourism industry. Here there is a relatively large requirement for unskilled labour per unit of output, and output growth has been relatively fast. In many industrial economies, employment prospects are seen as strongly linked to the prospects for such sectors, in which labour productivity grows relatively slowly. Labour productivity growth depends largely upon the substitution of capital and energy for labour inputs to production. Such substitution has been greater in manufacturing than in personal services, and this is expected to remain the case into the future. It is technically easier to use power-driven machinery to replace, say, an assembly worker in a car plant than to replace, say, a waiter.

Few commentators are now prepared to argue that economic growth alone, and of itself, can be seen as the solution to a widely acknowledged long-term unemployment problem. Additional responses are increasingly canvassed. A sampling of the ideas that have been put forward is as follows:

(a) Reductions in the welfare benefits available to the unemployed, making the alternative to employment less attractive.
(b) The abolition of minimum wage legislation, which is argued to keep the wage rate for low skilled labour too high for it to be profitable to employ much of it.
(c) The provision of retraining, job-search and relocation assistance for unemployed workers. Such measures, would be intended to improve the operation of the labour market, better matching workers' skills to those in demand, and making it easier for unemployed workers to find and take up job vacancies.
(d) The subsidisation of employment. Money formerly spent on unemployment benefits would instead be used to make payments to firms taking on additional workers.
(e) The abolition or reduction of forms of taxation, such as payroll taxes or compulsory employer insurance contributions, which add to the cost of employing labour.
(f) The repeal of employment protection legislation, which, it is argued, effectively increases the costs of using labour.

This list is taken from an editorial article, 'Jobless Europe', in *The Economist*, 26 June 1993. It gives a figure of 17 millions for unemployment in the EC, and includes a graph giving the forecast level for 1994 as, approximately, 20 million. The ideas listed here are those described in the article as 'good'. The article rejects the stimulation of aggregate demand – a 'dash for growth' – as an appropriate response. It does not do this on environmental grounds. The basis for rejection of this option is the view that the problem is 'structural' and therefore not amenable to solution by expanding the level of output.

Suggestions (d), (e) and (f) are directed at increasing the demand for labour, by operating on the incentives facing firms when selecting the mix of inputs to production. This is also what carbon taxation would be expected to do. It would also raise government revenue, whereas (d), (e) and (f) would not. Suggestion (e) would actually mean a reduction in revenue, and (d) would reallocate expenditure. The point is not that proposals for the reduction of unemployment such as those listed above lack merit. It is that all are based on a recognition that economic growth itself cannot deal with the problem, and that, given this, carbon taxation should be added to the list of proposals to be considered.

The cost of carbon taxation

We noted above that economists would presume that carbon taxation would reduce the average material standard of living. The basis for this is as follows. Assume that technology cannot be changed and that the total level of output is fixed. In this context, carbon taxation raises the price of energy relative to labour, increasing the demand for labour, and reducing the demand for energy, as inputs to production. If output is constant and more individuals are employed in producing it, output per employee, the average material standard of living, falls. To the extent that input combinations are fixed, so that labour cannot be substituted for energy, using less energy implies less output.

This presumption that reduced energy use in production implies a reduction in material living standards is frequently disputed by non-economists. It is claimed that economies can reduce their use of energy without suffering lower material living standards. Economists frequently characterise such as claims that **free lunches** are on offer. They do not believe in the availability of free lunches. This is because they assume that all production is carried out in a technically efficient manner, such that no unnecessary inputs are used. For any given level of output the minimum feasible amounts of each input are used. Then, reducing the use of any input must require the use of more of some other input(s) for a fixed level of output, or a reduction in output. In either case, output per unit of the other inputs falls. Essentially, the claim that there are free lunches available in the energy conservation context is the claim that as far as energy is concerned, the assumption of technical efficiency in production is incorrect. In such circumstances, an increase in the price of energy can lead to the elimination of waste in its use, with no implications for the output level.

Do economies operate in a technically efficient manner? Economists assume that they do on the grounds that firms that waste inputs would be incurring avoidable costs. Competition is assumed to eliminate firms that do not minimise costs. Hence, the assumption of competition is, it is argued, equivalent to the assumption of technical efficiency in production. On this basis economists routinely construct their models on the assumption that there are no free lunches to be had. However, the matter is clearly an empirical one. The question is whether firms typically operate in technically inefficient ways. This question is not easy to resolve from historical data. A major problem is disentangling the question of technical inefficiency from technological change. Where energy conservation, meaning less energy input for the same level of output, has taken place, usually the technology in use can be argued to have changed. The dispute over the availability of free lunches concerns the case where the technology, as embodied in the existing stock of capital equipment, is unchanging.[15]

Economists would expect permanent changes in the relative prices of inputs to influence the direction of technological change. At a given point in time the state of knowledge will permit items of capital equipment to be designed to use, within limits, alternative combinations of energy and labour. The designs actually produced will reflect, among other things, the expected future relative prices of energy and labour. The point about 'among other things' is that different designs will generally involve different costs for the capital equipment embodying them. In this case, the choice of design will be influenced by the cost of capital, the interest rate, as well the costs of energy and labour. The lower the rate of interest, the faster will the stock of capital equipment be changed to incorporate designs reflecting the new relative prices of labour and energy. It is possible that technological change induced by carbon taxation can, over time, work to offset any lowering of material living standards consequent on its initial introduction. Realisation of this possibility requires investment. We have already noted an insufficiency of investment as a threat to sustainability, and that a switch from income to carbon taxation could be expected to encourage saving, thus lowering the interest rate and increasing investment.

Weighing the pros and cons

To summarise, in favour of carbon taxation we have enumerated the following:

1. Environmental protection.
2. Increased saving and investment.

3. Increased employment.

4. Longer lifetimes for fossil fuel reserves.

Here points 1 and 4 are directly and obviously relevant to addressing threats to sustainability. Point 2 makes more investment possible in projects to substitute for environmental services, and means that projects will be appraised at lower interest rates. Point 3 addresses an important economic and social problem in industrial economies.

Against carbon taxation we have noted:

5. A lower material standard of living.

6. An increase in inequality.

7. Some induced environmental damage due to the switch to non-carbon energy sources.

We have noted that the outcome at point 5 depends on current technical efficiency in energy use and on the prospects for technological change, and that the problem at point 6 could be addressed via concurrent changes to the tax/welfare system.

What is the balance between the pros and cons? Is carbon taxation a good thing? The answer to this question is largely a matter of judgment. It cannot be answered purely in terms of economics and/or science.

Economists have done a good deal of work attempting to measure the costs of carbon taxation in terms of material living standards. This involves constructing a model of the economy, and then using it to simulate the effects of carbon taxation. The type of model usually involved is what is known as an **applied general equilibrium model**. The applied part of the terminology arises from the fact that such models are supposed to mimic, at least approximately, the behaviour of some actual national economy, rather than being purely abstract constructs. The general equilibrium part arises from the fact that such models are general in the sense of covering the whole economy, and that they work by solving for market clearing equilibria, given some specification of the determinants of supply and demand functions. The models differ in the degree of detail that they involve in terms of the number of different commodities distinguished, the different sorts of tax modelled, etc. The basic purpose of these models is to ascertain what happens to the economy given some shock to it, such as the introduction of carbon taxation.

While models of this type differ in detail, they share certain common features. In terms of the foregoing discussion, the important ones are as follows:

a. They allow firms and individuals to respond to changed relative prices by making substitutions in production and consumption.

b. The numerical output from the models is generally very sensitive to variations in what is assumed about substitution possibilities, or equivalently to price elasticities. The assumptions made are generally recognised as being crude approximations.

c. They do not include any representation of economy–environment interconnections. It follows that the environmental impacts of variations in the level and composition of economic activity are not modelled. Hence, any environmental protection benefits from carbon taxation are not accounted for.[16]

d. They involve the assumption that there is no technical inefficiency anywhere in the economy. Free lunches are excluded by assumption.

e. They represent the economy at a single point in time. No dynamic processes are involved. Hence, the technology is fixed and changed relative prices are not allowed to induce technological change. Similarly, effects arising via an impact on the level of saving and its subsequent implications for the evolution of the capital stock are not incorporated.[17]

f. They do not distinguish households according to their position in the income distribution. The household side of the economy is basically treated as a single entity. Hence they cannot address the questions of inequity generated by carbon taxation and of accompanying measures to offset it.[18]

Comparing these model features with points 1 to 7, it will be apparent that these models simply cannot produce results for several of the pertinent questions attending carbon taxation. The sort of question that they answer is : 'if carbon taxation is introduced at the rate $x per tonne, what will be the short-run effect on the average material standard of living?' The general nature of the answer forthcoming follows from the assumptions. The particular numerical answer is conditional on the numerical specification of a particular model, and especially on the numbers used to represent substitution possibilities. These models should be regarded as means for investigating some aspects of the problem, and hopefully providing some broad qualitative insights, rather than the source of definitive, or even approximate, numerical predictions.

Applied general equilibrium models are continuously evolving to address new problems. Efforts are being made to extend them to include representations of some of the features noted above as currently absent. However, the work involved is conceptually and technically diffi-cult, and for many of the issues the historical data which would be required to properly calibrate the extended models are not available. While the models will no doubt be improved in many respects, there is no real prospect of models providing definitive answers to questions such as 'on balance, is carbon taxation a good thing?'. The answer to this question will remain in the domain of decision making in the face of uncertainty.

We conclude this section with some observations concerning the size of the impact that carbon taxation might have on material living standards in an industrial economy. This discussion is only about the costs so measured. It takes no account of any of the environmental benefits arising. The possible benefits from slowing carbon dioxide accumulation in the atmosphere are considered in the next chapter.

To fix ideas, suppose that a model has produced the result that the introduction of carbon taxation at the rate $x per tonne would lead to a fall of 5 per cent in national income per capita. This is not an entirely arbitrary number. It is at the upper end of a range of figures for the cost of carbon taxation produced by a variety of models.[19]

It is not envisaged that economic growth will cease with the introduction of carbon taxation. At a growth rate of 2.5 per cent per annum, national income would double in 28 years. If this year it fell by 5 per cent but thereafter continued to grow at 2.5 per cent, then in 28 years it would be up by 95 per cent rather than 100 per cent. It is possible that carbon taxation could also reduce the growth rate. Suppose that it meant a 5 per cent reduction in the current level and a reduction in the growth rate to 2 per cent. In this case, 28 years from now, national income would have increased by 65 per cent rather than 100 per cent. Many would doubt that the connection between individual welfare and national income is so close that this difference should be regarded as reason for rejecting carbon taxation. Others, of course, would take a different view. One's view would presumably depend, in part, on what is assumed about the distribution of the costs involved.

Consider now some illustrative calculations, intended to give some sense of what a 5 per cent reduction in national income might imply. In 1991/92 Australian national income by major expenditure components was as follows (ABS 1993b Table 2.2).

		$Ax10^6
	1. Private Consumption	154850
+	2. Government Consumption	49957
+	3. Investment	51768
+	4. Exports	57539
−	5. Imports	55964
−	6. Statistical Error	1208
=	7. Gross Domestic Product	256942

Taking 5 per cent of the GDP figure gives $12847x10^6$. Given the importance of saving and investment for sustainability, and to put the cost where it would be most obviously hurtful to individuals assume that it is consumption that is to bear the full cost. Further, assume that the entire cost falls on private consumption, it being desirable to protect government expenditure on education, health care, etc. In this case,

$12 847x10^6$ represents an 8.3 per cent reduction in private consumption.

Table 9.6 shows how weekly expenditure on goods and services per
person differs across household income quintiles. The lowest quintile
comprises those households where income is in the bottom 20 per cent
of the range of household incomes, and so on. Persons in the middle
quintile spent $165 per week. If every Australian in 1988/89 had a
weekly expenditure of $165, total Australian private consumption
expenditure would have been 12 per cent lower than it actually was. If
all individuals consumed at the middle quintile's average level, the
8.3 per cent reduction in consumption would be overachieved by some
50 per cent. Recall that the 5 per cent GDP cost is taken from the upper
end of a range of estimates.

Table 9.6 Australian weekly expenditures by quintile: 1988/89

	Household expenditure $	Persons per household	Expenditure per person $
Lowest	243	1.65	147
Second	363	2.5	145
Third	489	2.97	165
Fourth	620	3.26	190
Highest	896	3.52	255
All	523	2.78	188

Source: Table 1, ABS (1990).

While instructive, calculations of this kind do not account for the costs
that adjustment to carbon taxation would impose on particular individuals. It would, for example, cause many workers in the coal industry to
loose their jobs. While it would be expected to create jobs in other
sectors, this would take time, and the displaced coal workers would not
necessarily be able to fill the new jobs. We now consider the operation
of the tax/welfare system, and a proposal for its reform that, among
other sustainability relevant features, could ease the human suffering
involved in adjusting to the shock of carbon taxation.

Basic incomes

In this section we describe the outline of a major reform to the tax/
welfare system that has been proposed for industrial economies. Before
doing that, it will be useful to discuss existing tax/welfare systems. This

provides a background to discussion of the proposal, and amplifies some of the points raised earlier in this chapter.

Existing tax/welfare systems

Table 9.7 gives data describing the operation of the tax/welfare system in Australia in 1988/89. The details of such systems vary across industrial nations, but most involve the four elements shown in Table 9.7. These are:

a. Transfer payments, shown at 2, are money payments from government to individuals, on the basis of their characteristics, or of some demonstrated need. In many nations some or all of these transfer payments are means tested, in that while the potential for receipt exists on the basis of some characteristic such as parenthood, the actual level of payment depends upon income, and may be zero at some income level. In some cases transfer payments are not means tested, but the income arising is taxed.

b. Benefits in kind, shown at 5, are goods and services provided by government, where the full cost of provision is not charged at the point of use. Examples are the provision of medical treatment, education, and housing.

c. Revenue to cover transfer payments and benefits in kind is raised by taxation. Direct taxation, shown at 3, is where the taxpayer directly transfers money to the government, as with income taxes, wealth taxes, capital gains taxes, estate duties, etc.

d. Indirect taxation, shown at 6, passes from taxpayer to government via some intermediary, as with sales or commodity taxes. Expenditure taxation is an indirect tax, as are carbon and energy taxation.

The first row of Table 9.7 shows how income from non-governmental sources varies across quintiles.[20] The second row shows transfer payments decreasing as private income increases. Transfer payments are typically intended to have just this incidence, being intended to alleviate poverty generated by the market system of income determination. The third row shows direct tax payments increasing with private income. This is entirely intentional, with direct taxation generally seen as the main means for promoting equality in post-tax incomes. As shown at 4, the net effect of transfer payments and direct taxation is to produce a narrower range of disposable than private incomes.

Analysis of the impact of the tax/welfare system frequently stops at disposable income. However, this does not give the full story of the impact of government activity on poverty and inequality. The imputed value of the benefits in kind varies across the income distribution. Row 5 shows that the value of benefits received in kind declines as income rises as far as the fourth quintile, then rises. Indirect tax payments arise when taxed goods and services are purchased. Comparing 6 with 4, it can be seen that the ratio of indirect tax payments to disposable income falls as income rises. Looking at expenditures which include the payment of indirect taxation does not properly reveal how the level of consumption of goods and services varies. Hence, in Table 9.7 the bottom line, 7, shows disposable income plus the value of benefits in kind minus the indirect tax payment component of expenditure. This is labelled **effective income**, to indicate that it gives a true picture of variation in the ability to consume goods and services in total.

Comparing 7 with 1 in Table 9.7 shows that the total effect of the tax/welfare system is to substantially reduce inequality. Table 9.8 shows this, and the contribution to the overall effect of each element of the total system, by expressing, for each of the first seven rows of Table 9.7, each entry in terms of its ratio to the entry for the third quintile. For private income, the highest/lowest ratio is 2.3/0.09 = 25.6. For disposable income the highest/lowest ratio is 1.93/0.57 = 3.4. For effective income, the highest/lowest ratio is 1.78/0.78 = 2.3.

The extent to which the tax/welfare system increases equality varies considerably across industrial nations. The data for Australia illustrate the way in which industrial nation tax/welfare systems are generally understood to function, in that the main role in reducing inequality is performed by the direct tax system and transfer payments.

Table 9.7 *Australian weekly income per person by quintile, 1988/89: ($)*

	Lowest	Second	Third	Fourth	Highest
1. Private income	14.56	85.82	168.05	236.19	386.92
2. Transfer payments	72.69	44.24	14.83	8.26	5.46
3. Direct tax	1.41	10.89	31.93	51.97	101.00
4. Disposable income = (1+2)-3	85.83	119.79	150.95	192.49	291.39
5. Benefits in kind	58.31	45.89	36.21	33.94	35.12
6. Indirect tax	15.37	17.32	21.13	24.80	31.70
7. Effective income = (4+5)-6	128.78	147.74	166.03	201.62	294.80
Persons per household	1.69	2.51	2.96	3.25	3.50
Number of dependant children per household	0.32	0.76	1.05	1.05	0.95
Retired persons per household	0.92	0.69	0.3	0.2	0.2
Proportion of households – single parent with children	10.84%	8.31%	3.72%	0.84%	0.00%
Proportion of households – principal income from transfer payments	79.73%	38.31%	2.60%	0.00%	0.00%

Source: ABS (1993a).

Table 9.8 *Operation of the Australian tax/welfare system: 1988/89*

	Lowest	Second	Third	Fourth	Highest
1. Private income	0.09	0.51	1.00	1.41	2.30
2. Transfer payments	4.90	2.98	1.00	0.56	0.37
3. Direct tax	0.04	0.34	1.00	1.63	3.16
4. Disposable income	0.57	0.79	1.00	1.28	1.93
5. Benefits in kind	1.61	1.27	1.00	0.94	0.97
6. Indirect tax	0.73	0.82	1.00	1.17	1.50
7. Effective income	0.78	0.89	1.00	1.21	1.78

A proposal for reform consistent with sustainability

In most industrial nations there is vigorous debate over reform of the tax/welfare system, and many have recently introduced, or are actively considering, major reforms. Participants in these debates are driven by two quite different motivations. On the one side there is a perception that reform is necessary primarily in order to contain, or reduce, the costs of existing welfare systems. This perception arises largely from observing increasing unemployment, an ageing population, and reduced prospects for economic growth, together with a belief that taxation, and especially direct taxation, should not be increased. On the other side there is a perception that reform is necessary primarily to improve the performance of the tax/welfare system in reducing inequality and alleviating poverty. On this side there is a greater willingness to contemplate increase in the cost of the system.

The **basic incomes** proposal, derives from the second perceived need for reform.[21] While originally seen as simply a tax/welfare reform, the proposal has implications for the functioning of the labour market, and has been discussed in relation to the environment and sustainability. In the last two respects the relevance of the proposal would be enhanced by complementary changes, noted below, not usually discussed in the literature on basic incomes.

Proposals for basic incomes start with an examination of the existing system of transfer payments. The problems usually identified are:

a. Existing systems are complex and involve high running costs. They are difficult to understand by intended beneficiaries, system administrators, and those who pay for them, i.e. taxpayers.

b. Existing systems involve, to varying degrees, the means testing of potential recipients. This contributes to complexity, and is degrading to those tested.

c. The actual operation of means testing very often gives rise to a variety of **poverty traps**, whereby it is not worth a recipient's while to take employment as this will involve a loss of benefits which largely, in some cases almost entirely, offsets the employment income gain. This works to increase unemployment, and increases the cost of the welfare system.

d. Existing systems are not actually very effective in alleviating poverty. Many of those entitled to benefits do not apply for them because they do not realise that they have entitlements, and/or because they are deterred by the existence of means testing.

e. It is morally wrong to make the alleviation of an individual's poverty conditional on satisfying a set of criteria which are necessarily going to be somewhat arbitrary in nature. Conditional poverty alleviation gives rise to alienation, and fosters the emergence of an underclass. Poverty traps effectively keep many individuals more or less permanently in the welfare recipient underclass.

The essential feature of the basic incomes proposal is the abolition of all existing transfer payments, to be accompanied by the introduction of a basic income unconditionally payable to everybody. This basic income would be paid at frequent intervals, weekly or fortnightly, in order to avoid cash-flow problems, and would be tax-exempt. Clearly, such a system addresses all of the problems identified above. Its efficacy in alleviating poverty would, however, depend crucially on the level at which the basic income is set. This, together with a definition of 'everybody', would also determine the cost of the proposal.

Proponents of basic incomes believe that the payment to each individual should be at a level such that the individual would not be in poverty if this were her only source of income. Precisely what this means differs among proponents. As will be clear from much of the foregoing discussion there is no generally agreed procedure for determining the amount of money necessary to an individual for the avoidance of poverty. Some proponents take the monetary value for a basic income from existing governmental standards for welfare payments, such as the level at which the state retirement pension is set. Others argue that such standards are inadequate. The level of payment matters not just for the direct effect in the alleviation of poverty, and for the cost of the system, but also for the implications of the scheme in the labour market.

It is generally envisaged that 'everybody' means literally everybody. That is to say that most basic income proponents see a basic income being paid to every individual in the population, from birth. Some see the level of payment to children as being somewhat below the adult rate. The need for payment to, or on account of, children follows from the costs of child-rearing, and consequent child-related poverty for those on low incomes. However, looking at basic incomes in the context of sustainability policy suggests that payment should be restricted to adults. If population stability, or decline, is an objective, it makes little sense to subsidise procreation. There is a serious dilemma here.[22] The sufferers from child-related poverty include the children involved, as well as the parents. It is one thing to take the view that parents who ignore the signals sent by society – no subsidisation for procreation – have to bear the consequences, but quite another to argue that the children should. The children took no part in the procreation decision, and could not be influenced by any incentives in the matter of their birth. Further, child poverty is widely accepted as being largely self-perpetuating.

There are two broad strategies for dealing with this dilemma in a manner consistent with sustainability. Neither is entirely satisfactory. There is a fundamental conflict of objectives. First, basic incomes could be restricted to adults, and poverty relief then necessitated by child-rearing costs could be dealt with on a means-tested basis, and/or by the provision of benefits in kind. Second, basic incomes could be paid to all individuals, with a tradeable procreation permit system in place. The latter would prevent the incentives possibly generated by the former affecting actual behaviour.

With basic incomes in place, unemployment as currently measured in official statistics would go to zero, since nobody would be in receipt of a transfer payment on account of not being employed. Similarly, the concept of retirement would alter. Currently, this concept is largely determined by social security arrangements which make the transfer payment of a retirement pension conditional on reaching a specific age. With basic incomes in place, there would be no age-related transfer payments. Individuals could, in effect, take state-funded retirement periods at any age. It would make a great deal of sense to complement this by legislation banning employer termination of a person's employment solely on the grounds of age. This would address the problem envisaged as arising from an ageing population.

Generally, basic incomes would do a great deal to free up the supply side of the labour market. Since there would be no means testing, poverty traps inhibiting the taking of employment would no longer exist. This would be particularly important in respect to part-time and low-paid work. Individuals would be more able to move into and out of employment. Some see in basic incomes the prospect of a reduction in the supply of labour, particularly for low-paid and uncongenial jobs (Vogt 1967). The extent of this problem would depend upon the size of the basic income in relation to wage rates in those jobs. It should be noted that to the extent that the introduction of basic incomes had this effect, wage rates in those jobs would be expected to increase. Many would regard this as desirable, on the grounds that work that the majority regard as uncongenial – for example, refuse collection and disposal, and dishwashing – should be better paid.

It would make a great deal of sense to complement the introduction of basic incomes by taking steps to reduce the non-wage costs of hiring labour. This would work to increase the demand for labour. Any taxes on the use of labour should be abolished, and legislation for statutory job protection repealed. The latter is usually of little benefit to the poor in any case. Minimum wage legislation could reasonably be repealed, given a basic incomes system in place. The way in which the financing of basic incomes could be tailored to increase labour demand is discussed below.

In what way are basic incomes relevant to sustainability? First, it is argued that they would do much to reduce alienation and promote social cohesion, which in turn would foster individual attitudes consistent with sustainability.[23] A related argument is that basic incomes would increase individuals' opportunities for public service and community action. Second, it is argued that basic incomes would create opportunities for individuals to explore new forms of livelihood.[24] Given greater opportunities for part-time work, or the removal of the need for any paid employment, individuals could, for example, grow more of their own food. This pre-supposes that individuals have access to some land. Some proponents of basic incomes see them as encouraging decentralisation and reversing the movement of population to cities and suburbs, with more labour-intensive commercial agriculture as well as more non-commercial food production (Vogt 1967).

Costing the proposal

We have argued that one threat to sustainability could arise through an insufficiency of savings and investment. The allocation of total investment between alternative projects is also important. It would appear that the major implication of basic incomes for the level of savings would arise through the method of finance, while the implications for project selection would come mainly through any effects on the relative prices of inputs to production, which, in turn, would depend on the method of finance and on labour market reactions. We now turn to the cost and financing of basic incomes. Table 9.9 presents some calculations, intended to illustrate these matters in broad terms. Again, the choice of Australian data is dictated only by convenience, and the calculations should not be understood as a proper costing for Australia. This would involve the use of an applied general equilibrium model, though it is doubtful whether one currently exists that captures all of the considerations that should properly be taken into account.

The level of basic income is fixed at $6700 because this is approximatly the level of the transfer payment to retired persons in 1990/91, the year to which all of the data refer. The justification for using this standard for setting the level of basic income is basically convenience in establishing a reference point. Some would argue that this level for the basic income would mean that an individual dependent solely on it would experience poverty. The interested reader can change this number and then carry through the steps shown in Table 9.9 to get an alternative bottom line. The cost of basic incomes is determined (a) on the basis that they are paid at this rate to adults and children, and (b) that they are paid only to adults. An adult is an individual aged 15 or more. Again, alternative assumptions, such as part-payment to children, can be made and carried through.

Table 9.9 *Illustrative calculations for a basic income system*

Basic income payment per person per year		$6700
Adult population		13 494 000
Child population		3 798 000
Basic income cost		
(a) Paid to total population		$115 856 x 10^6
(b) Paid to adult population		$90 410 x 10^6
Existing personal benefits		$37 180 x 10^6
	(a)	(b)	
1.	115 856	90 410	Basic income cost
2.	49 892	49 892	+ Direct tax revenue
3.	165 748	140 302	= Cost
4.	37 180	37 180	− Offset
5.	128 568	103 122	= Revenue requirement
6.	257 331	257 331	Direct tax base
7.	50.0%	40.1%	Direct tax rate − 5 ÷ 6
8.	47.6%	37.7%	With carbon tax at $20 per tonne
9.	43.0%	33.1%	With carbon tax at $60 per tonne

Sources: ABS (1993a), ABS (1993b).

The calculations at steps 1 through 9 are as follows. The gross cost of basic incomes is given by the cost of making the payments plus the revenue from direct taxation. As will be seen, direct taxation is not to be abolished. This is simply a convenient way of doing the calculation. The offset to this gross cost is the existing expenditure on personal benefits, i.e. all transfer payments. These are to be abolished. This gives a revenue requirement at 5. Initially we assume that this is to be met solely from direct taxation. The base on which direct tax was levied is shown at 6, and the tax rates arising as required to finance basic incomes and restore the direct tax revenue to be used to meet other demands upon it is then shown at 7. If we divide the figure at 2 by that at 6, we find that for 1990/91 the actual rate equivalent to those shown at 7 was 19.4 per cent. Clearly, even if restricted to adults, basic incomes would imply a substantial increase in the average rate of direct taxation.

We have noted that income taxation, the dominant component of direct taxation, is generally understood to have adverse implications for the supply of labour and savings. Reduced savings would be a threat to sustainability. We discussed, in the previous section, the substitution of carbon for income as a tax base, and noted that this would be expected to increase the supply of labour and savings. So, it would make sense, given a concern to promote sustainability, to consider reducing the direct tax costs of basic incomes by raising some revenue by carbon taxation. In Table 9.1 we related carbon tax rates to revenues arising, and noted some caveats – see also Table 9.2. At 8 and 9 in Table 9.9 we show the average direct tax rates arising when carbon dioxide is taxed at $20 and $60 per tonne. We noted in the previous section that carbon taxation would address threats to sustainability arising from the environmental impact of economic activity in an industrial nation. Carbon taxation would affect relative prices so as to influence project selection in the direction of reduced environmental impact, and would encourage the use of labour rather than energy in production.

The use of carbon taxation for the partial financing of basic incomes would appear to have a good deal to recommend it. This is not to say that other means of finance should not be considered as well. In Australia, for example, there is no taxation of wealth. The transmission of wealth from one generation to the next is an important basis for the perpetuation of inequality.

CHAPTER 10

The international dimension

In the previous chapter we discussed domestic policy in relation to threats to sustainability, from the perspective on an industrial nation. This chapter considers the international dimensions of the sustainability problem. There are two. First, sustainability is a global problem, both in terms of equity and environmental asset protection. Second, nations trade with one another, and domestic policies have to be considered for their trade implications.

First we review the basis for international trade, and arguments about its desirability. Then the nature of international environmental problems is discussed in relation to the question of whether there is a case for restricting trade on sustainability grounds. Then we focus on the problem of prospective global change, obviously a major threat to sustainability, and a complex policy problem which exemplifies the key role of uncertainty in dealing with sustainability problems.

International trade and sustainability

The case for trade

The dominant idea concerning international trade in economics is the **theory of comparative advantage**.[1] The theory is used both to explain why trade occurs and to show that free trade is beneficial to all participants. In both respects, the core of the theory is the role of specialisation. In the absence of international trade, national specialisation is impossible. Parties to trade exploit the benefits of specialisation in production, which exist because of comparative advantage, reflecting differences in endowments of factors of production. A standard example considers agricultural and manufactured commodities. A nation with good soils and a favourable climate will have a comparative advantage in the former over nations with poor soils and poor climate. Even if this nation is more productive in both agricultural and manufacturing production, it will gain by specialising in the former where its productivity advantage is greatest, where it has comparative advantage, exporting agricultural products and importing manufactures. It can then convert agricultural output into manufactured goods on more favourable terms than in a state of **autarky**, i.e. economic independence or self-sufficiency.

Given differing comparative advantages, all nations can gain from a move from autarky to free trade. This is true even where one can produce all commodities more cheaply, i.e. it has absolute advantage. The theory shows that all participants can gain from trade but it cannot be shown that the distribution of gains accords with any particular concept of justice.

The development of the theory of comparative advantage usually makes three assumptions about the conditions of production in all countries. First, that it occurs under **constant return to scale**, so that if all input levels are increased by x per cent, output increases by x per cent. Second, that it always involves technical efficiency, so that no inputs are wasted. Third, that it takes place under competitive conditions, so that all firms in all nations act as price-takers and cannot exercise market power, as would be the case with a monopolistic producer. Most economists take the view that dropping these assumptions strengthens, rather than weakens, the case for free trade.

First, to the extent that there are potential **economies of scale**, such that for an x per cent increase in output, input requirements go up by less than x per cent so that unit costs fall, free trade will promote the realisation of such, by increasing the size of the market served by specialised producers. The second and third matters both relate to market size as well. The argument in favour of free trade in both cases is that opening the domestic economy to imports increases the competition faced by domestic firms. This reduces the market power of domestic firms, and encourages them to minimise their costs by eliminating technical inefficiency.

The theory of comparative advantage is usually developed in a timeless context, in that techniques of production are taken to be fixed, as are the endowments of factors of production. Most economists see relaxing these assumptions as strengthening, rather than weakening, the case for free trade. First, it is argued that the greater competition involved in free trade will drive technological innovation. And, to the extent that nations trade with one another, a technological innovation in one will be more readily adopted elsewhere. As regards economic growth, it is argued that with international trade, growth in individual nations is mutually reinforcing. If A grows and trades with B this increases the demands for B's exports, inducing growth in B. This, in turn, increases the demand for A's exports, enhancing growth there. And so on. A particular version of this relates to trade between rich and poor nations. The **trickle down hypothesis** is that growth in rich countries is good for poor countries because it expands the markets for their exports, so that greater affluence in the rich nations trickles down to the poor.

The theory of comparative advantage is developed for situations where all countries can produce all commodities. This is not generally the case. If A has no oil deposits, it cannot produce oil. Less limiting cases arise where production is technically feasible, but would be prohibitively expensive so that it would not be possible to sell the output – Iceland could grow oranges in hot houses, but a domestic market for the output at a price to cover the costs would be non-existent. In such circumstances the argument for trade is that it extends the range of choice open to a country's consumers. Icelanders can consume oranges grown overseas by exporting fish: inhabitants of countries without oil deposits can drive cars by exporting some cars in exchange for oil.

Finally, mention should be made of the view that international trade is desirable because, as compared with a situation of autarky, it promotes peace and harmony between nations. If A has no oil but B has and will not trade, then A may be motivated to invade B to gain access to oil. Trade reduces the potential for international conflict, on this view.

There are arguments to the effect that restrictions on trade may be justified in some circumstances. There are three basic ways in which a nation can restrict its external trade. It can place physical restrictions on flows of commodities across its borders. These usually take the form of **import/export quotas**, where a government-issued permit or quota is required to engage in trade; such permits may be tradeable. It can levy charges on commodity flows across its borders, such as **tariffs** on imports, or, less commonly, levies on exports. These charges are a source of government revenue, and tariffs particularly have been important in this role in some countries at some points in history. Finally, it can subsidise domestic producers.

The theory of comparative advantage focuses on the gains from specialisation, but it is recognised that it can also involve some costs. A country that gives up producing some commodity faces the prospect that it will become unavailable if foreigners refuse to supply it. This may happen in times of international conflict. Hence, economists see a role for restricting trade and specialisation on strategic grounds. Certain commodities may be identified as of special strategic importance, and a decision made to maintain domestic production despite some cost penalty.

The **infant industry** argument is that temporary protection of a domestic industry may be justifiable so that it can make a potential comparative advantage actual. Essentially this argument derives from recognition that whereas the theory takes comparative advantage patterns as given and fixed, they are partly the product of historical experience. Thus, for example, at a point in time, A may have an existing timber products industry which can produce more cheaply than the same industry in B, notwithstanding the fact that B is better endowed with forests. This arises because prior to trade, A developed timber-processing capacity, whereas B did not. Then, the infant industry argument would allow B to restrict the import of timber products from A so that its domestic firms could put in place the processing capacity to realise their underlying comparative advantage.

The comparative advantage story assumes that opening up to trade allows only produced commodities to cross national frontiers. The basic inputs to production – labour, capital, natural resources – are assumed to be immobile after opening up to trade. In the case of many types of natural resources, immobility follows from purely physical considerations – oil deposits are necessarily fixed in location, for example. In the case of capital and labour immobility arises from institutional arrangements adopted by sovereign states. Suppose that such arrangements did not exist, so that labour and capital could move freely across national frontiers. Then, there would be a tendency to equality across nations in the earnings of these factors. Just as free trade in a commodity leads to a single international price, transport costs aside, so free movement of factors of production would tend to produce **factor price equalisation**. Without factor mobility, free trade in commodities can act as a surrogate means to factor price equalising tendencies. A low-wage country moving into the export of labour-intensive products would see domestic the demand for labour increase, tending to increase wage rates, for example.

Views on the desirability of factor price equalisation differ. The argument that it can involve increased wage rates in low-income countries is matched by arguments that it can also involve reduced wage rates in high-income countries. The latter problem is made more pressing by the fact that in the world today capital is highly mobile across national boundaries, whereas labour is generally relatively immobile. The international mobility of capital means that there is a tendency toward the equalisation of rates of return on it in different countries. To the extent that a country has high labour costs, on account of high wages and/or low labour productivity, the rate of return on capital employed in it will be low. Capital will flow from such a country to others where labour costs are lower, implying a higher rate of return on capital. For a country

suffering a capital drain on this basis, there will be unemployment, unless
labour costs are reduced.[2]

Trade, poverty and inequality

The role of international trade in relation to the prospects for poor
nations is a matter of some dispute. The standard view in economics is
that developing economies should benefit from trade. First, this is what
the theory of comparative advantage predicts. Second, there is the
trickle down effect. Third, there is the matter of technological transfer
from industrial nations. We noted above that whereas standard trade
theory assumes factor immobility, the modern reality is that capital is
highly mobile. This would generally be taken to be advantageous to
developing nations. To the extent that they can attract capital inflows
from overseas, this supplements domestic savings, the inadequacy of
which is often seen as a brake on development, as well as introducing
new technologies. Developing countries could be expected to attract
capital inflows on account of low labour costs, and where they have
natural resources for exploitation.

There are a number of arguments to the effect that developing nations
do no get the full benefits from, or actually suffer from, participation in
international trade. First, there is the **terms of trade argument** for pro-
tectionism in developing countries. This sees the developing countries
as exporters of primary products and importers of manufactures (see
Chapter 2), with the terms on which primary products exchange for
manufactures showing a long-run tendency to weaken. Because the
world price of primary products tends to fall relative to that of manufactures, developing countries have to export more primary products
per unit of manufactures imported. On this argument, the benefit to
developing countries from trade falls over time unless they move into
manufacturing. This is to be done by trade restrictions imposed to
promote the growth of infant industries in the manufacturing sector.

A related matter is the relative instability of world prices for primary
products. The instability of primary product prices is due to a number
of factors. The level of demand varies with the trade cycle in industrial
economies. On the supply side there are the effects of natural events
such as climatic variation affecting agricultural yields. The adjustment of
supply to demand variations is often only possible with a substantial
delay, so that, for example, a new ore facility planned when demand was
rising may just be coming on stream as demand growth levels off or goes
into reverse. Price, and quantity, instability feeds through into instability
in export earnings.

Instability in export earnings is connected to another trade-related
problem facing many developing nations, that of international indebt-

edness. If a nation's import bill exceeds its export earnings, there are a number of options open to it. It can allow its currency to depreciate against foreign currencies, so that one unit of domestic currency exchanges for less units of foreign currency than formerly. This makes its exports cheaper in foreign currency terms, and tends to increase their volume. It makes imports more expensive in domestic currency terms, and tends to reduce their volume. However, it also worsens the terms of trade, since a given volume of domestic production now exchanges for a smaller volume of imports. For a given level of domestic production, this implies lower domestic living standards. The demand for imports also depends directly upon the level of domestic consumption, so an alternative, or additional, response to a deficit on the balance of trade is to reduce domestic consumption so reducing imports, while also freeing domestic production for export. Neither of these options is attractive to any country, and they are especially unattractive to poor countries. Hence, the third option, borrowing from overseas, is attractive, if it is possible. Countries which persistently borrow to meet deficits on the balance of trade run up international debts.

Balance of payments deficits are not the only reason why developing countries incur foreign debt. The other reason is overseas borrowing to finance domestic investment. For whatever reason it is incurred, foreign debt needs to be serviced, i.e. interest has to be paid on it. The payment of interest on foreign debt is itself a call on the country's export earnings. For a given level of export earnings, less can be spent on imports the greater is the foreign debt servicing requirement. For some developing countries the problems associated with foreign debt servicing have become very serious, and are impeding development by reducing the availability of funds for domestic investment, and/or reducing the, already low, consumption standards of much of the population.[3]

One manifestation of the international mobility of capital is overseas borrowing to finance domestic investment. Capital mobility also takes the form known as **direct foreign investment**. In the former case, residents in the domestic economy borrow from overseas residents to finance domestic projects to be owned and operated locally. In the latter case, overseas residents directly finance projects in the domestic economy, which they will own and operate. In this case there is no debt servicing requirement arising for the domestic economy. There will be a flow of profits repatriated to the overseas owners in so far as the projects are successful (in the sense of generating profits). Direct foreign investment has the advantage over foreign borrowing that whereas the latter gives rise to a debt-servicing requirement irrespective of the success of the project, with direct investment the flow overseas is conditional on profitability. Direct overseas investment is also often argued to be a more effective means for technology transfer. However, foreign ownership generally means foreign management and control, and it is frequently argued that this does little to promote development. Profits sent overseas are not available for reinvestment in the domestic economy, and local management capabilities are not developed.

The theory of comparative advantage treats nations as the entities which trade. This is not the way international trade generally works. Trade tends to take place between firms and individuals located in different nations, on the basis of gains accruing to firms and individuals. The total of the gains to the inhabitants of a nation are not necessarily distributed equally within the nation. They may well be distributed very unequally. The theory of comparative advantage itself indicated that an opening to trade will directly benefit firms and workers in some sectors and harm others. To some extent, this is supposed to even itself out over time as capital and labour move from contracting to expanding sectors. But there will remain an unequal domestic distribution of the net benefits from trade.

Some argue that in many cases trade actually worsens, at least in the short run, the lot of the poor. An example would be where an opening to trade means an expansion of agricultural production for export by methods not feasible on small land holdings. Profits earned in production for export enable large land owners to expand their holdings at the expense of subsistence farmers, who are forced into the wage economy where jobs are scarce. Advocates of trade for developing countries tend to argue that such effects are transitory, as the growth induced by the profits in the export sector will eventually create employment opportunities for the displaced subsistence farmers.

Arguments can, then, be advanced both ways in regard to the questions of whether free international trade works to reduce inequalities in average incomes between industrial and developing economies, and to improve the lot of the world's poor. What does the historical record, since say 1960, show about the net effect of the conflicting considerations? This is not a simple question to answer, for four reasons. First, the historical record differs greatly across developing economies. Second, and relatedly, increasing involvement in international trade has not been the only factor determining the historical experience of developing countries over this period. Different countries have faced different circumstances and adopted different policies. Third, international trade has not been, and is not, free of restrictions. The extent to which developing countries have been affected by trade restrictions varies. Fourth, the historical record consists of data on various indicators for many individual countries, and different commentators give different weights to different indicators.

According to the United Nations Development Programme (UNDP):

In 1960, the richest 20% of the world's population had incomes 30 times greater than the poorest 20%. By 1990, the richest 20% were getting 60 times more. And this comparison is based on the distribution between rich and poor *countries*. Adding the maldistribution within countries, the richest 20% of the world's *people* get at least 150 times more than the poorest 20%.

The UNDP estimates that the extent of international maldistribution as between people, as opposed to nations, doubled over the period 1960 to 1990. It identifies two main reasons for the persistence, and widening, of such disparities:

> First, where world trade is completely free and open – as in financial markets – it generally works to the benefit of the strongest. Developing countries enter the market as unequal partners – and leave with unequal rewards.
> Second, in precisely those areas where developing countries may have a competitive edge – as in labour-intensive manufacture and the export of unskilled labour – the market rules are often changed to prevent free and open competition (United Nations Development Programme 1992).

Consequently, the UNDP calls for more, rather than less, free trade, together with a number of other changes at the international and national levels. This is essentially the position taken in the Brundtland Report (World Commission on Environment and Development 1987). Both of these reports stress the need for protection of the environment to accompany greater foreign trade. Free trade and environmental protection are seen as necessary components of sustainable development.

Trade and the environment

The standard economics position is that environmental considerations do not undermine the case for free trade:

> Trade *per se* is not a direct cause of environmental problems. Some distortion must be present – most obviously, the absence of an appropriate environmental policy – in order for there to be a possibility that international trade will create or worsen environmental problems (Anderson and Blackhurst 1992.)

There is, that is, no environmental case for policies to restrict trade, provided that policies are employed to address environmental problems directly. This condition limits the immediate relevance of the conclusion. Appropriate environmental policies are not generally in place. In the case of many threats to environmental assets, introducing these policies would require international agreement and cooperation.

This position on trade and the environment is based on acceptance of consumer sovereignty/allocative efficiency as the appropriate basis for the weighing of gains and losses. To see what is involved consider transport and a particular trade example. Trade on the basis of comparative advantage will involve more transport than autarky. According to the standard theory, the costs involved in the additional transport are compensated for by the benefit from specialisation in production. Transport is largely based on fossil fuel combustion and therefore gives rise to environmental damage.[4] The standard response to questions about the role of international transport is to advocate internalising the externalities involved. If this is done, it is argued, then we can be sure that the environmental damage arising at the resulting level of transport is indeed compensated for by the gains from specialisation.

Now, supposing that externalities have indeed been internalised, there might remain trade in wine between France and Australia. Some people have very discriminating palates. Some rich Australians are willing to pay a lot to drink some French rather than some Australian wine, and perhaps vice versa. Even with externalities internalised, the transport of wines between Australia and France will involve some damage to environmental assets. Reasonable persons might well take the view that given that damage to critical environmental assets should be minimised, there are other sources of it that should take precedence over this kind of trade, notwithstanding that it passes the willingness-to-pay test. The externalities arising in transport are not now, generally, internalised.[5]

The economics literature distinguishes three different types of situation in regard to trade and the environment. The essentials can be explained by considering that there are just two countries, A and B. In all three cases trade flows both ways. In Type I situations, any environmental damage arising from a country's economic activity is confined within its own frontiers. In Type II situations, economic activity in one of the countries causes damage in the other. Such situations are known as **unidirectional international externalities**, or **unidirectional environmental spillovers**. In Type III situations there are **reciprocal international externalities**, or **reciprocal environmental spillovers**. A flow of damage across a national frontier does not necessarily involve a material flow. In the case of **transboundary pollution** it does involve such a flow. Country A, for a Type II example, discharges residuals into a river which flows through it, and then on through B. A Type II example where no material transboundary flow is involved is as follows. A is clearing native forest for agriculture and thus depleting its wildlife, making species extinct. The inhabitants of B care about wildlife and species diversity in A, and suffer on account of what is happening in A.

This example reveals an important distinction between standard economic analysis and consideration of threats to sustainability. If the inhabitants of B were totally unconcerned about the environmental damage occurring in A, and were not willing to pay anything at all to stop it, then standard economics would see the matter as an example of a Type I situation. There is no transboundary damage flow. The matter is different from a sustainability perspective. The reduction in global biodiversity is a threat to sustainability relevant to the citizens of A and B. This exemplifies the point made in previous chapters – the criteria of consumer sovereignty are not the same as the criteria for sustainability.

A situation is of Type I from the perspective of both standard economics and sustainability where: it is physically confined within national boundaries, does not affect persons overseas, and does not involve damage to any critical environmental asset. Many environmental problems have these characteristics. This does not mean that such problems do not have an international dimension to them. Suppose that in the absence of trade both A and B produce widgets, and that in both countries this causes pollution. There are no pollution spillovers – domestic production causes only domestic pollution. Suppose then that trade in widgets occurs. If we adopt the consumer sovereignty/allocative efficiency criteria, and make some simplifying assumptions, the implications are clear.[6] For a given country, they depend upon whether it becomes an importer or an exporter of widgets. Suppose A becomes an importer. Then it gains whether or not is has an emissions control policy in place, as it benefits both from cheaper widgets and reduced pollution. For B, a widget exporter, trade means increased widget production and hence more pollution. If B has a policy of emissions control through, for example, taxation, that secures the allocatively efficient level of emissions, the gain due to increased production will be larger than the loss as a result of increased pollution. Without such control, the loss may exceed the gain. If it is impossible to control emissions in B, some restriction of exports to reduce pollution may be justified. However, export restriction can never produce as good an outcome as free trade together with proper control of emissions, and this type of approach to the pollution problem is known as a 'second best policy'.

This analysis says that country B as a whole is better off with trade and optimal emissions control. It does not say that all of the inhabitants of B are better off. The owners of widget-producing firms in B are likely to favour unrestricted trade and oppose emissions control. Suppose now that B is just one of a number of countries exporting widgets. If emissions controls are being considered in B but not in other countries, the argument will be advanced that B's competitiveness in widget production will be damaged. B's widget producers will argue that they, and B, will loose business to **pollution havens** in countries with lower environmental standards. The potential loss of competitiveness in international trade frequently figures in debates over domestic environmental policy (Cairncross 1992).

An example of a Type II situation is the so-called **acid rain problem**. While there is disagreement about some of the dimensions of this problem, it appears to be agreed that a major element is the long-distance transport in the atmosphere of some of the emissions arising in fossil fuel combustion.[7] Often this transport crosses national frontiers so that some of the damaging depositions take place in a country different from that where the fossil fuel combustion occurs. The damage is mainly in the form of the corrosion of buildings and other man-made structures, the loss of biotic populations in rivers and lakes, and harm to forests which reduces timber productivity and the amenity services provided. In relation to the damage to environmental assets, its extent for a given level of deposition varies with geological and soil conditions in the deposition area. The problem of acid rain is seen as serious in Europe and North America.

Where some activity in A is causing damage in B, but not in A, the situation between the nations is analogous to that of the two firms considered in Chapter 7 in connection with the Coase theorem. If a supra-national Environmental Protection Agency existed, it could assign a property right to either A or B, who could then bargain an improvement over the situation of no property rights On one assignment A would offer B compensation, on the other B would offer A inducements to curtail the level of its damaging activity. In the latter case, the **victim pays principle** applies. It also applies in the absence of any supra-national agency with property rights granting powers. Given no damage arising in A, or that the government and citizens of A do not care about any domestic damage, A has no incentive to introduce policies to curtail the activity generating damage in B. The prospect of conditional payment from B would create such as incentive. Many would regard such payment as bribery.

An alternative approach involves direct restrictions on trade. Suppose A exports to B the commodity X, the production of which gives rise to the damage experienced in B. Then prohibition by B of imports of X from A is sometimes argued as the way to deal with the unidirectional spillover arising. Environmentalists in a number of industrial countries have called for bans on the importation of tropical timber in order to reduce the rate of forest clearance in tropical countries, with a view to halting biodiversity losses there. The effectiveness of such an approach is generally questionable. First, import bans would be a second best policy in that they would involve foregoing some of the gains from trade. Bribery, on the other hand, could in principle be tailored so as to retain the gains from trade while limiting the damage. Thus, in the logging case, B's payment to A could be conditional on the observance of logging practices that minimise environmental damage. Second, it will not generally be the case that B is the only destination to which A exports X. If there are many nations importing X from A, an import ban by B alone will be ineffective, and securing general agreement to ban imports may be difficult.

Where, as in the case of acid rain, the damage arising in B is not due to a single identifiable production activity in A, the possibility of this kind of import ban does not exist. A problem which arises with bribery is that of monitoring compliance. In the case of payment for following less damaging logging practices, for example, B would need to prescribe the nature of those practices and to be assured that the prescriptions were being followed. It could be argued in favour of import bans that, where feasible and effective, they avoid monitoring problems in that, for example, there is a direct reduction in the quantity of timber felled.

Import bans proposed by environmentalists receive a good deal of media attention, though they are not much used by governments. An exception is trade in endangered species. Barbier et al. (1990) discuss many of the issues arising in the context of the trade in ivory and efforts to reduce the rate of decline of elephant numbers in Africa. Equally, it is difficult to find examples of explicit bribery. However, the principle involved is important in understanding the interests of various parties with regard to international agreements for environmental protection.

The prime example of a Type III situation is the so-called greenhouse effect. This will be discussed at length below. Here we simply note the main features of the problem, to exemplify Type III characteristics. All countries burn fossil fuels releasing carbon dioxide into the atmosphere, where all emissions mix globally. The climate-relevant parameter is the global atmospheric concentration of carbon dioxide in the upper atmosphere. The origin of any particular molecule of carbon dioxide is irrelevant to its role in the world climate system. Driven by increasing rates of fossil fuel combustion, global carbon dioxide concentrations are increasing. According to the basic physics of the world climate system, increasing carbon dioxide concentrations imply, other things equal, a warmer world. All nations are involved in driving up atmospheric carbon dioxide concentrations: all nations experience the climate change and its consequences.

Overview

The main points to emerge here are as follows. First, it makes little sense to be for or against international trade *per se* on sustainability grounds.

Arguments can be made in some cases that free trade promotes sustainability objectives, while in others contrary arguments can be made. The empirical evidence is not, at the general level, decisive either way. The case for free trade in relation to sustainability has to be considered on a case-by-case basis, in relation to particular country circumstances, particular sustainability objectives and problems, and particular commodities.

Second, where it can be agreed that trade is creating or exacerbating environmental problems with sustainability implications, the appropriate policy response is not always to restrict that trade. One does not have to accept all of the standard economics terms of reference to see the force of argument that trade restrictions are, in some circumstances, an avoidable second best way of addressing the environmental problem of concern. Equally, one does not have to accept the doctrine that restriction on trade should never be considered.

Third, the current world situation is not one of general free trade. Restrictions on trade are ubiquitous. In some cases the evidence would suggest that removal of restrictions should promote sustainability objectives, both those relating to poverty and inequality and those concerned with the natural environment.[8]

In any case, opting out of international trade is no longer an option for any nation. Given modern communications, and assuming democracy, it is difficult to see any government being able to run an economic policy based on autarky. If a government were considering opting out of international trade, voters would likely see the prospect of retrogression in their living standards. This is not to say that it may not be both feasible and desirable from a sustainability perspective for some countries to restrict trade in some products.

The basic claim for free trade is that it increases consumption in all participating nations. Many take the view that the global level of economic activity is already close to, or beyond, the limit that the biosphere can cope with. On this view, international trade is a direct major threat to sustainability precisely because of its perceived benefit. If this view is accepted, and if it is agreed that trade does improve the lot of the world's poor, then a fundamental conflict of objectives arises. Improving the lot of the poor requires more free trade, but more free trade threatens sustainability.

There are essentially two types of response to this dilemma. The first is to argue for trade and growth together with policies to protect critical environmental assets. This is the response that asserts that sustainable development is feasible. The second is to argue for the cessation of growth in the world economy as the means to ensure that biospheric limits be respected. If this position is taken, then either, the world's poor are to be effectively abandoned, or there will have to be a programme of international redistribution of income and consumption analogous to a national tax/welfare system.[9]

These two positions are not mutually exclusive. In the light of the uncertainties attending our understanding of the nature and role of environmental assets, and an acceptance of the need to deal with inequality and poverty, the appropriate strategy involves both policies intended to protect critical environmental assets and, in the industrial nations, a willingness to accept some international redistribution of consumption. Since effective policies to protect critical environmental assets will require a high level of international cooperation, some international redistribution will be necessary to create the incentive structure compatible with such cooperation. Just as in a national economy the pattern of production and consumption cannot be left to market forces to determine, so the pattern of international trade needs to be socially managed. The major problem with this prescription is that there currently exists no world analogue to the government of a nation state to which the task of social management could be assigned. To the extent that the world economy is socially managed it is on the basis of agreements between sovereign nations, and by international institutions established by such agreements. The effectiveness of national sovereignty is itself limited by the existence of transnational corporations (TNCs). In 1985, 600 TNCs in mining and manufacturing with annual sales of more than US$ one billion were identified. These 600 TNCs 'created more than one-fifth of total industrial and agricultural production in the world's market economies'.[10] Many of these TNCs are global in scope, owning and controlling assets in many countries. In size, some larger than many national economies. Their interests do not necessarily coincide with those of any of the nation states where they own and control assets.

The global climate change problem

The global climate change problem is often referred to as the **greenhouse effect**. This usage is in some ways unfortunate. The climate change problem is a matter of uncertainty, and some controversy. The greenhouse effect is neither uncertain nor controversial. Nobody disputes that the earth is warmer than would otherwise be the case by virtue of the presence in its atmosphere of greenhouse gases. Nor is there any dispute over the proposition that in recent history, human activity has been a cause of increasing concentrations of greenhouse gases in the atmosphere. The proposition that these concentrations will continue to increase in the foreseeable future is also relatively uncontroversial. It is when we consider the implications of, and appropriate responses to, an **enhanced greenhouse effect** that matters become controversial. On one view this is the major global threat to sustainability, and warrants immediate policy action. At the other extreme, the view is that there is really nothing much to worry about, and no need to do anything now.

This is a large and complex matter, with every facet attended by major uncertainty. In this respect, it is the example par excellence of the nature of sustainability problems. What follows is an overview of the main issues. The climate change/greenhouse literature has grown rapidly in the past five years, and is now very large. A comprehensive bibliography, covering all aspects, would itself be a longish book.[11]

Scientific background

Figure 10.1 shows the basic physics of the greenhouse effect.[12] Most of the solar energy reaching the earth is absorbed at its surface, warming

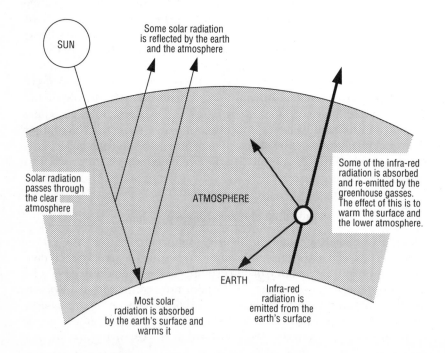

Figure 10.1 The greenhouse effect.
Source: Houghton et al. (1990).

it. The earth's surface emits infra-red radiation, some of which is then absorbed and re-emitted by the greenhouse gases in the atmosphere. This re-radiation is in all directions. Some is downwards back to the earth's surface, where it causes further warming. The presence in the atmosphere of greenhouse gases means that less heat is lost to space than would otherwise be the case. The greenhouse gases act rather like a blanket around the earth's surface. It is generally accepted that the mean surface temperature of the earth is 33°C higher than it would otherwise be, due to the greenhouse gases in the atmosphere.

The greenhouse gases in the atmosphere are not the only influence on global temperature and climate. The solar flux itself varies over time. Changes in the earth's orbit around the sun alter the impact of any given flux rate. Particulate matter, **aerosols**, in the atmosphere also absorb and reflect radiation, and affect cloud formation. An increase in the atmospheric concentration of aerosols would generally be understood to have a cooling effect. Aerosols are released into the atmosphere by natural processes such as volcanic eruptions, and by human activities such as fossil fuel combustion. For aerosols and greenhouse gases, the term **anthropogenic** is used to describe emissions due to human activity.

The principal greenhouse gases are: water vapour, carbon dioxide, methane, nitrous oxide, and the chloroflourocarbons (CFCs, discussed in Chapter 3 in relation to their role in depletion of stratospheric ozone). Water vapour is by far the most important greenhouse gas by volume: its atmospheric concentration is 3000 ppmv (parts per million by volume), to be compared with the figures for the others given in Table 10.1. The atmospheric lifetime of water vapour is short, of the order of one week. Water vapour as cloud cover has a dual role in the global climate system, in that as well as acting as a greenhouse gas, it can also have a cooling effect by reducing the solar radiation reaching the surface. The effect of clouds varies diurnally: in the day they cool, at night they warm. The net role of cloud cover in the enhanced greenhouse effect is disputed. The upper part of Table 10.1 shows how several greenhouse gases vary in terms of atmospheric lifetime (the average residence in the atmosphere of a molecule), atmospheric concentration (all the greenhouse gases taken together comprise less than 0.1 per cent of the atmosphere), and current anthropogenic emissions rates.

Greenhouse gases differ in the warming effect per molecule of gas. In comparing the warming effects of the gases, account needs to be taken of the quantities in the atmosphere. The relative contributions to **global warming potential**, shown in the lower part of Table 10.1, also depend on atmospheric lifetimes, and hence on the time horizon being considered. This last point is sometimes overlooked. To emphasise it, in Table 10.1 contributions are shown for three different time horizons.

Whatever the time horizon adopted, carbon dioxide is by far the most important of the gases in terms of warming potential. This is one of the reasons that discussion of the enhanced greenhouse effect is often conducted only in terms of carbon dioxide. Another would appear to be that it was the first greenhouse gas to be recognised as such. The results given in the lower part of Table 10.1 are based on a number of estimates and assumptions, attended by varying degrees of uncertainty. It is generally understood that the dominant role of carbon dioxide is not sensitive to these uncertainties.

Table 10.1 *Greenhouse gas comparisons*

	Atmospheric lifetime[a]	Concentration 1989 ppmv[b]	Current emissions anthropogenic[c]
Carbon dioxide	120	350	26000
Methane	10	1.7	300
Nitrous oxide	150	0.31	6
CFC-11	75	0.000025	0.3
CFC-12	110	0.000045	0.4

Proportional contributions to global warming potential		
% 20 years	% 100 years	% 500 years

	% 20 years	% 100 years	% 500 years
Carbon dioxide	51	68	81
Methane	37	17	8
Nitrous oxide	3	5	4
CFC-11	3	3	1
CFC-12	6	7	6
	100	100	100

Notes: [a] – units are years.
　　　　[b] – ppmv – parts per million by volume.
　　　　[c] – units are megatonnes per annum.
Source: Houghton et al. (1990).

Table 10.2 gives the major sources and sinks for three greenhouse gases. Sinks can either involve physical removal from the atmosphere or chemical transformation into a non-radiative gas. Biomass combustion is not a net source for carbon dioxide if the biomass is harvested on a sustainable yield basis, as the growing vegetation then fixes carbon equal in amount to that released by combustion. However, sustainable yield harvesting is not general, and deforestation contributes to increasing carbon dioxide concentrations. While the global carbon cycle is better understood in quantitative terms than are the sources and sinks for methane and nitrous oxide, major gaps in knowledge of it still remain.

It is generally agreed that the atmospheric concentrations of the greenhouse gases have been increasing in the recent past. In the case of carbon dioxide, whereas at the start of the industrial revolution the concentration was 275 ppmv, it is now around 350 ppmv, an increase of 27 per cent. For methane, the concentration is understood to have doubled from the mid-nineteenth century to the present. It is widely agreed that these increases are anthropogenic in origin. It is also widely agreed that on current trends in human activity rates these concentrations will continue to increase into the future. Majority scientific opinion is that, if nothing is done to alter current trends, the consequence will be global climate change.

Table 10.2 *Sources and sinks for greenhouse gases*

	Sources	Sinks
Carbon dioxide	fossil fuel combustion* biomass combustion* soil tillage* volcanoes oceans	oceans soil vegetation**
Methane	rice paddies* ruminant animals* fossil fuel production* landfills* wetlands	oxidation in atmosphere and soil
Nitrous oxide	fossil fuel combustion* biomass combustion* agriculture* oceans bacteria in soil	conversion to molecular nitrogen

Notes: * – A source wholly or partially anthropogenic.
    ** – Human behaviour affects this sink, especially forestry.
Source: Houghton et al. (1990).

Future prospects

Figure 10.2 presents three scenarios for global mean temperature, prepared by a group of experts in 1987. The vertical axis measures differences from the current global mean set at 0°C. Since 1987 there has been an enormous amount of scientific effort devoted to the study of the prospects for climate change. The Intergovernmental Panel on Climate Change (IPCC) was established in 1988 to provide authoritative assessments. The first IPCC reports were published in 1990, based on work by 170 scientists and peer review of that work by another 200 scientists (Houghton et al. 1990). A further report updating the 1990 assessment was published in 1992. It was based on the work of some 500 scientists, and was adopted by IPCC at a conference attended by 130 delegates from 47 countries. IPCC assessments represent the position of the majority of the scientific community. According to the 1992 IPCC report, the best available estimate of the rate of change of global mean surface temperature over the next century is '0.3°C/decade (range 0.2 to 0.5°C/decade)' (Houghton et al. 1992, p.17). This estimate is the same as the middle scenario shown in Figure 10.2. The lower limit of the IPCC range is higher than the low scenario in Figure 10.2: the upper IPCC limit is lower than the upper scenario.

By the standards of the past one million years, the earth currently appears to be in a relatively warm phase. A rate of change of 0.3°C per decade would be higher than the earth has experienced in the past 10 000 years, and high by longer historical standards.[13] It is this rate of change that most concerns many scientists. Systems in the biosphere can adapt to change, but it takes time. The fear is that many systems would be unable to adapt fast enough to cope with 0.3°C per decade, so that the prospect is one of collapsing natural systems, and of an enhanced rate of species extinction, threatening the life support services of the natural environment.

The complex nature of the enhanced greenhouse effect is outlined in Figure 10.3. Economic activity gives rise to emissions of greenhouse

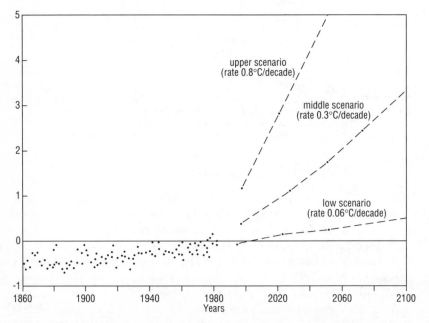

Figure 10.2 1987 Climate change scenarios.
Source: Jaeger (1988).

gases. The effect on atmospheric concentrations also involves the sinks for the gases, which are themselves affected by economic activity, for example when forest clearing reduces carbon-fixing potential. The evolution of atmospheric concentrations drives climate change. This is not just a matter of the global average temperature. It is the general understanding that a warmer world would also be one where other climatic parameters would be different. Warming would increase with latitude,

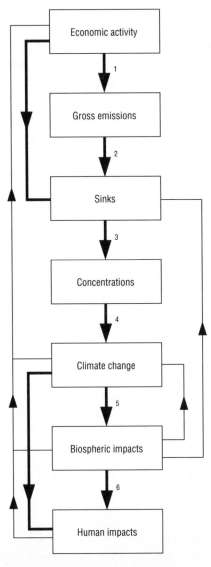

Figure 10.3 The enhanced greenhouse effect problem.

so that the latitudinal temperature gradient would become less steep. This would affect air movements and precipitation. It is expected that with higher temperatures there would be more precipitation, more frequent extreme events such as storms, and more variability over time in precipitation. The area of the globe where tropical storms occur would expand.

All of these climatic changes would impact on the functioning of the biosphere, which would, in turn, produce impacts on humans additional to those direct from climate change. Figure 10.3 is drawn to reflect the view that the human impacts arising via biospheric impacts would likely be at least as important as those impacting directly. Thus, for example, the physiological and psychological effects on humans might well cause lesser problems than changed agricultural productivities and biodiversity losses in natural systems.

As shown in Figure 10.3 by the lighter lines, the enhanced greenhouse effect involves potential feedback effects. The chain of causation is not just in one direction. First, the impact of climate change on the biosphere may itself influence the link between concentrations and climate change. Thus, for example, the absorption of incident radiation, and hence warming, at the earth's surface is affected by the extent and nature of the vegetation. Second, biospheric impacts may alter the functioning of the sink processes for greenhouse gases, so modifying the link between emissions and concentrations. Plant growth rates are affected by temperature, available moisture and carbon dioxide concentrations. Third, climate change, its biospheric impacts, and its human impacts are all likely to affect economic activity, with implications for greenhouse gas emissions. Examples of the sorts of things that could be involved here are as follows. In relation to the human impact of climate change, higher temperatures and increased moisture could lead to an increase in the use of air conditioning, increasing fossil fuel combustion for electricity generation. With regard to the biospheric impact, changed spatial patterns of agricultural productivity could markedly affect international trade, creating demands for the creation of new transport infrastructure, thus increasing economic activity levels in at least some parts of the world, implying increased emissions levels. In terms of climate change itself, this could affect tourism activity and thus economic activity: it has been suggested, for example, that higher summer temperatures in northern Europe would reduce the annual temporary migration south.

Over a 100-year time horizon, the sea level increase generally envisaged is primarily due to thermal expansion of the water in the ocean, and some melting of glacial ice. Significant melting of the polar ice sheets is not generally foreseen within such a time horizon. As of 1990, the IPCC's best estimate of the rate of sea level rise was 6 millimetres per annum, so that by the end of the next century the level would have risen 65 centimetres (Houghton et al. 1990). In 1992, the IPCC put the rate of sea level change due solely to thermal expansion in the range of 2 to 4 millimetres per annum (Houghton et al. 1992). The effects of sea level rise are: recession of shorelines, inundation of existing coastal areas, loss of wetlands, increased salt water intrusion in estuaries, and increased salt-water intrusion of coastal freshwater aquifers.

Ideally, the assessment of future prospects in relation to the enhanced greenhouse effect would be by use of a single quantified model of the full system depicted in Figure 10.3. No such model exists. Rather, assessments are made using models of various parts of the total system, together with informed judgment. The feedback effects depicted in Figure 10.3 are generally ignored, and attention is focused on modelling the stages along the heavy line flowing from economic activity to human impacts. The feedback effects are generally poorly understood, even in qualitative terms. This is not to say that the processes along the heavy line are well understood. Some are, in broad terms, but none are understood in the detailed quantitative terms that accurate prediction would require.

Predicting future carbon dioxide emissions

This involves the relationship between economic activity and gross anthropogenic emissions, at 1 in Figure 10.3. Typically this is dealt with by using a model which produces output in terms of emissions levels over time, from inputs which are assumptions about activity levels and other key parameters. These models usually only deal with carbon dioxide emissions, and focus on the energy sector of the economy. Many of the models used were first developed in the 1970s in response to the 1973/74 oil price shock and the perceived problem of future fossil fuel scarcity.

Reilly et al. (1987) report results for future carbon dioxide emissions from such a model: see also Edmonds and Reilly (1983). In this model the world is divided into nine regional economies, which trade with one another. Six fuels are distinguished. In each regional economy the demand for each fuel depends upon population size, the level of output, labour productivity, the state of technology, and the relative prices of the fuels. Energy supplies increase with energy prices, given such constraints as are imposed by the size of fossil fuel reserves. The model works by finding the prices which make supply equal to demand in each market. This model has 79 numerical parameters. Noting the uncertainties about the appropriate values to use for these parameters, Reilly et al.

(1987) report the results of an analysis of the sensitivity of the model predictions to variations in the parameter values input. The principal conclusions are that:

a. The median predicted growth rate for carbon dioxide emissions is positive but lower than the historical rate post World War II.

b. The range of variation around the median outcome is very great – across a random sample of 400 numerical specifications of the model, the range of growth rates which includes 90 per cent of outcomes is from +3.0 per cent to −1.4 per cent per annum.

c. The three most important sources of uncertainty about future emissions are uncertainty about future labour productivity, uncertainty about future efficiencies in energy use, and uncertainty about the income elasticity of energy demand in the developing nations.

Table 10.3 Sensitivity of carbon dioxide emissions forecasts, IEA model

Year	Lower bound	Base case	Upper bound
1975	1	1	1
2000	1.25	1.49	1.85
2025	1.33	2.28	4.56
2050	1.48	3.24	8.82
2075	1.64	4.27	8.29
South energy demand income elasticity	0.5	1.4	2.2

Table 10.3 here gives some results on the sensitivity of emissions projections to variations in the number used in the model for this income elasticity. The model is available in a smaller version which can be run on a desktop computer (PC). This version distinguishes fewer regional economies. In it the region which is the 'south' corresponds reasonably closely to the region which is the 'developing nations' in the full version of the model. The PC version is supplied with parameters set at what are considered the most likely values, base case values, but upper and lower bound estimates are also supplied, and the model settings can be switched between the three values for each parameter. For the income elasticity of demand in the south, the possible values are: base case, 1.4; upper bound, 2.2; lower bound, 0.5. Table 10.3 shows, in index number form, the results obtained running the PC version of the model for each of the three settings for the income elasticity of demand in the south – all of the other model parameters take the same value across the three runs. Clearly, emissions projections are very sensitive to variations in this parameter. Looking just 25 years out from the base date, the

range of increase is from 25 per cent to 85 per cent. Looking 100 years out it is from 64 per cent to 729 per cent.

Climate modelling

The next stages in the heavy line sequence in Figure 10.3 at which modelling is employed are 2 and 3, where gross anthropogenic emissions levels are mapped into atmospheric concentrations. We shall not discuss this modelling here. It is complex, specialised, and difficult to describe without the use of special scientific terminology. Houghton et al. (1990, 1992) provide discussion and further references.

Stage 4 is where models are used to translate input data on atmospheric concentration into output on climate change. We consider this in two stages. First, the modelling which considers the implications of a once and for all change in atmospheric concentration. Second, that which produces output for rates of change over time.

General circulation models (GCMs) are large computer models of the physics of the earth's atmosphere.[14] The entire atmosphere is represented as a set of vertical columns based on surface grid squares, typically of size 3°x3°. The models incorporate the physics sketched at the beginning of this section, and are used to solve for the consequences of an imposed increase in the concentration of carbon dioxide, used as a surrogate for greenhouse gases generally. Usually the imposed increase is a doubling, from 300 (approximately the pre-industrial carbon dioxide concentration) to 600 ppmv. The resulting global mean temperature increase is known as the **climate sensitivity**. There are a number of GCMs in existence. The 1990 IPCC report (Houghton et al. 1990) gave a range of model climate sensitivities of 1.5 to 4.5°C. The models all find that the temperature increase will be greater in higher latitudes. Beyond this, there are wide differences across the models in the regional pattern of temperature increase. The uncertainty about regional climate change is much greater than about global averages.

The results from these GCMs refer to the consequences of a carbon dioxide doubling, once the climate system has settled down to a new equilibrium. But what people want to know is how the climate will evolve over time. For its 1990 report the IPCC used a **box-diffusion model** for the purpose. Such a model is much simpler than a GCM, and focuses particularly on the thermal coupling between the ocean and the atmosphere, which is the main influence on the rate at which warming occurs for a given climate sensitivity. The GCMs referred to above contained no representation of this coupling. The inputs to a box-diffusion model are a scenario for emissions, and a climate sensitivity. The 1990 IPCC report used a climate sensitivity of 2.5°C, which is in the middle of the range reported. This was combined with four different emissions scenarios to

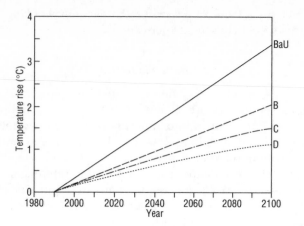

Figure 10.4 1990 IPCC climate change scenarios.
Source: Houghton et al. (1990).

produce the global average temperature change scenarios shown in
Figure 10.4 here. The details of the assumptions driving the emissions
scenarios are in Houghton et al. (1990).

The results shown in Figure 10.4 can be compared with those in
Figure 10.2, from 1987, which were produced in essentially the same way.
The main difference is that whereas the IPCC results use single climate
sensitivity and emissions scenarios which are either a straight extrapolation of trends, Bau for business-as-usual, or reductions of these, the
results in Figure 10.2 are derived from combining different climate sensitivities with a wider range of emissions scenarios. Thus, for Figure 10.2:

> Each of the scenarios includes the time lags in the climatic response as a result
> of the ocean's heat capacity. The middle curve ... reflects a scenario of
> continued present trend of emissions (except for CFCs ...) and a moderate
> climate sensitivity ... The upper curve ... reflects a scenario of accelerated
> greenhouse gas emissions and a relatively high climate sensitivity as predicted
> by some models. The lower curve ... reflects a scenario of radically curtailed
> GHG emissions and a relatively low climate sensitivity ... The ceiling of 5
> degrees on the temperature graph has been imposed because of the dubious
> relevance of present climate models in simulating the response to a global
> warming higher than around 5 degrees (Jaeger 1988).

In the light of this, the approach taken by the IPCC in 1990 to putting
an upper limit on the rate of change for global mean temperature can
be seen as somewhat conservative. It came from a business-as-usual emissions scenario, combined with a medium climate sensitivity.

Since the 1990 IPCC report, results from a new generation of GCMs
have started to become available. These do include representation of the

thermal coupling of ocean and atmosphere, and can be used for **transient simulations**, i.e. to produce directly rates of change over time. It is these models together with some modified emissions scenarios that are the basis of the results given in the 1992 IPCC report cited above. The new emissions scenarios are of the same nature as those used for the 1990 report.

The range of scenarios for future climate change arises from uncertainty about future emissions levels, uncertainty about sinks, and uncertainty about the response of the climate system to changing concentrations of greenhouse gases. The IPCC does not attempt to apportion climatic uncertainty across these factors. The experts responsible for the results in Figure 10.2 offer the judgment that uncertainties about emissions and uncertainties about climatic response contribute about equally to the overall uncertainty. It was their judgment that 'there is a 9:10 chance that the actual future pattern of GHG-induced climate change will lie within the bounds set by the upper and lower curves' (Jaeger 1988). This implies a 10 per cent chance that it will lie outside those bounds. It is fairly widely accepted that the possibility exists that future prospects could be worse than the IPCC upper limit of 0.5°C per decade increase for global mean temperature.

Not all climate scientists endorse the IPCC position. A minority take the view that the IPCC is overstating the prospects for climate change, because of the fact that the GCMs do not properly account for features of the climate system which would work to reduce temperature change, i.e. negative feedbacks (Balling 1992). The IPCC acknowledges problems with the models, particularly in respect of the effects of aerosols and cloud formation. The possibility of positive feedbacks, which would work to speed up climate change, in the actual global system also exists. There are, for example, at current temperatures very large quantities of methane trapped beneath the surface in tundra regions. Sufficient warming would release this methane into the atmosphere, accelerating global warming. This is generally regarded as extremely unlikely within the next 100 years.[15]

Is there any actual evidence of climatic change due to anthropogenic releases of greenhouse gases? The trend in concentrations has been upward for some 200 years, so that some take the view that if the GCMs do properly represent the global climate system, we should already be seeing climate change. According to the 1992 IPCC report: 'global mean surface air temperature has increased by 0.3° to 0.6°C over the last 100 years'. Not everybody accepts this, arguing that the observations on which it is based are biased upwards. However, leaving this aside there remain problems in accepting this record as positive evidence for the operation of an enhanced greenhouse effect. The IPCC 1992 report notes that:

... the size of this warming is broadly consistent with predictions of climate models, but it is also of the same magnitude as natural climate variability. Thus the observed increase could be largely due to this natural variability; alternatively this variability and other human factors could have offset a still larger human-induced greenhouse warming.

... the unequivocal detection of the enhanced greenhouse effect from observations is not likely for a decade or more (Houghton et al. 1992).

Climate change impact

The analysis of climate change impacts involves studying stages 5 and 6 in Figure 10.3. The first point to be made is the obvious one that the extent of impacts will depend upon the extent of climate change. Though obvious, this is important, since it follows that impact assessment is necessarily subject to the uncertainty attending the assessment of climate change itself. Impact obviously has to be assessed at a local level. The extent of uncertainty about regional climate change is much greater than it is about the global average. However, even if the climate change to occur in a given region were known with certainty, the extent of consequent impacts would remain uncertain. We simply do not know enough about the way natural and human systems function in relation to climate variation, and variability, to forecast impacts for given climate change with any confidence.

There is large literature on impact assessment. The IPCC climate change studies referred to above were carried out by its Working Group I. The IPCC Working Group II conducted a parallel study of impacts, published as Teggart et al. (1990).[16] We shall return to impact assessment when we discuss the setting of policy targets for emissions abatement.

Having emphasised what is unknown and uncertain, we repeat the point that there are some things that are known, or at least universally agreed upon. First, that there is a greenhouse effect, such that the earth is warmer than it would be if there were no greenhouse gases in its atmosphere. Second, that greenhouse gas concentrations have been increasing on account of human activity, and are most likely to continue to increase as a result of human activity. In considering policy, it is necessary to keep in mind what is known, as well as what is uncertain.

Policy options

It is useful to distinguish three types of policy response:
1. **Prevention policies**, intended to slow or halt the rate of increase in atmospheric concentrations of greenhouse gases.
2. **Mitigation policies**, intended to offset or ameliorate the climatic effects of increased concentrations of greenhouse gases.

3. **Adaptation policies**, intended to facilitate human adjustment to the impacts of climatic change consequent upon increased greenhouse gas concentrations.

These are not mutually exclusive classes of policy response. Policies intended to slow the rate of increase in concentrations could, for example, be combined with policies to adapt to some climate change. Examples of each type of response, in relation to carbon dioxide, are:[17]

1. Reductions in the use of fossil fuels. Switching between fossil fuels with different carbon contents. Removal of carbon dioxide from power plant smokestacks, its sequestration as carbon, and disposal in such manner that there is no leakage to the atmosphere. Switching from fossil fuel combustion to biomass combustion, with the biomass harvested on a sustainable basis. Reforestation, with the timber eventually harvested to be used so as to prevent carbon dioxide release to the atmosphere, such as by encasement in plastic.
2. Release particulates into the atmosphere. Release into the atmosphere gases that offset the effects of the greenhouse gases. Promote cloud formation. Steer tropical storms away from populated areas.
3. Facilitate outward migration from adversely affected areas. Compensate those who are adversely affected. Build defences against rising sea levels. Stop new development in low-lying coastal areas. Change agricultural practices, use different plant and animal varieties. Research new plant and animal varieties.

Most attention focuses on prevention policies, and particularly on reducing carbon dioxide emissions arising in energy supply and use. This is, no doubt, because it is the most obvious response, and is the best understood. As discussed in Chapter 9, it would involve other sustainability-relevant advantages.[18]

A key characteristic of preventative policies is that their effectiveness depends upon international agreement and cooperation. Whatever one nation does to reduce emissions (or enhance sinks) will have little effect on global atmospheric concentrations, and therefore on climate change prospects, unless at least a majority of other nations takes similar action. The enhanced greenhouse problem is an example of a reciprocal externality.

To appreciate the ineffectiveness of unilateral policy action on carbon dioxide emissions, consider the data of Table 10.4 for five nations plus the European Community (EC). The emissions data refer to those arising in fossil fuel combustion. These six economies account for over 70 per cent of the total of world emissions.

The United States is the largest national contributor to carbon dioxide emissions. Its per capita emissions are more than 20 times as large as India's, and more than twice those for the EC. It accounts for approximately a quarter of total world emissions. While this is a very large share, it is clear that even the United States acting alone to cut emissions would have a limited impact on total emissions. This is even more the case than Table 10.4 suggests, since over the next 50 years it is reasonably certain that the United States' share of the total will substantially decline, as the developing economies grow and increase their use of fossil fuels. Current per capita fossil fuel use in countries such as India and China is low by the standards of the industrial countries. If, as they plan to do, they follow the development path previously experienced in the industrial world, these per capita levels will grow substantially. Countries such as India and China currently do not see their national interest as requiring the abandonment of economic growth in the interest of slowing prospective global warming.

Table 10.4 *Emissions, income and population: selected nations, 1988*

	Carbon dioxide per capita[a]	Carbon dioxide per unit of GDP[b]	GDP per capita[c]	Population[d]	Carbon dioxide total[e]	Share of world total[f]
US	21.39	1.09	19.59	248.2	5310	23.7
USSR	13.01	1.50	8.66	288.7	3756	16.7
EC	8.47	0.61	13.89	325	2753	12.3
Japan	8.68	0.58	14.96	123.2	1069	4.8
China	2.37	7.54	3.12	1112.3	2638	11.8
India	0.84	3.03	0.28	833.4	699	3.1

Notes: [a] – Tonnes.
    [b] – Tonnes per thousand US$.
    [c] – Thousands US$.
    [d] – Millions.
    [e] – Tonnes x 10^6 (megatonnes).
    [f] – %.
Source: Based on Grubb (1990b).

Table 10.4 shows that nations differ in the efficiency with which they turn fossil fuel combustion, and hence carbon dioxide emissions, into national income. The USSR emitted more than twice as much carbon dioxide per dollar of national income as the EC and Japan, and the United States 40 per cent more. This suggests considerable scope for greater efficiency in energy use, and reduced emissions per unit income in such places. In India and China, emissions per unit income are much higher than in the industrial nations. However, given the low income levels and the technologies employed, the scope for increased efficiency in energy use is such countries is seen as relatively limited for the foreseeable future. At the stage of development at which they are, significant reductions in energy, i.e. fossil fuel, use would be seen as prohibitively costly in terms of material living standard improvements foregone.

In terms of the incentives for participation in collective action, the situation is broadly as follows. The bulk of future growth in emissions is expected to occur in developing countries. They see curtailing that growth as impairing their prospects for improving the material living standards of their citizens. Problems associated with global warming are in the future, and anyway uncertain. The industrial countries could be more inclined to act, they are better able to afford the costs involved, but they see that if they act alone the impact on the enhanced greenhouse effect could be limited, as the developing countries to some extent replace their foregone emissions. This refers to the industrial nations collectively. If they are considered separately, then any one considering action to reduce emissions faces the prospect of reduced competitiveness in international trade. Whatever the true extent of this problem in any particular case, industrial interests will argue that it is a serious problem.

Targets for prevention policy

Here we shall assume that there is a world government which has the powers of the government of a nation state. This enables us to focus on the question of what would be an appropriate prevention policy target, leaving the related questions of instrument choice and securing international agreement for later consideration.

The first question is: what would be required to stabilise atmospheric concentrations of the greenhouse gases? Figure 10.5 shows the IPCC scenarios for carbon dioxide emissions and concentrations that go with the temperature change scenarios shown in Figure 10.4. Stabilising emissions would not stabilise concentrations within the time horizon shown. This is because of the lags in the system arising from the long atmospheric lifetime for the gas. It is the concentrations, not the emissions rate, that are relevant to climate change.

Figuring out what needs to be done about emissions to stabilise concentrations is complex, as there are several greenhouse gases. Also, results are uncertain due to ignorance about the relevant biospheric processes, especially with regard to the operation of sinks. To give some sense of the magnitude of the changes to current trends that would be required for the stabilisation of the concentration of greenhouse gases, we report the results of one calculation.[19] For the stabilisation of the concentration at current levels by the middle of the next century, it involves:

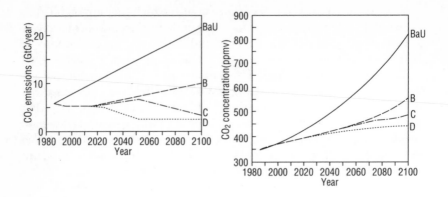

Figure 10.5 Scenarios for emissions and concentrations.
Source: Houghton et al. (1990).

1. The complete phase-out of CFCs, by 1995.
2. The halting of deforestation by the year 2000, and reforestation by
   2020 such as to absorb 6000 million tonnes of carbon. Translating this
   absorption capacity into forest area depends upon a number of
   assumptions. The upper limit on the estimated increase in the world
   forest area required for 2000 to 2020 is 5 per cent.
3. The reduction, by 2020, of carbon dioxide emissions from fossil fuel
   combustion to 30 per cent of the current level.
4. The reduction, by 2020, of the annual rate of increase in methane and
   nitrous oxide concentrations to 25 per cent of the current rate.

It should be noted that the claim is not that this scenario would prevent
climate change. It is that it would stabilise greenhouse gas concentrations at their current level. The modelling work reviewed above
implies that achieving this could still result in some climate change.

Weighing costs and benefits

Application of the standard economics approach to target-setting to the
enhanced greenhouse effect, requires that emissions be abated to the
level where the marginal benefits of abatement are equal to the
marginal costs involved. Benefits are the damages from climate change
that are avoided by the reduction of greenhouse gas emissions. Using
this approach to determine the optimal level of global greenhouse gas
abatement faces a number of difficulties. The two most obvious are the
assessment of the damage avoided by emissions reduction, and the fact
that whereas costs would be incurred now, the benefits thereby secured
lie in the future.

The first of these problems is partly a question for scientific inquiry: if emissions are reduced by x per cent now, by how much will future climate change impacts be reduced. Figure 10.3 indicates that this is a very complex problem, involving massive uncertainties. Given estimates of physical damage reductions of various kinds, it remains to put them in terms that are comparable with the cost estimates. This involves valuation and aggregation, the problems associated with which were discussed in Chapter 7. The second problem is all about valuation. How do we compare current costs with future benefits? Scientific inquiry can contribute nothing to the resolution of this question. It raises the contentious matter of discounting, also discussed in Chapter 7.

Attempts to determine the optimal abatement target for greenhouse gases are rare. The reasons for this emerge from consideration of one such study, Nordhaus (1991). The principal conclusion there is that:

> the appropriate level of control depends critically upon three central parameters of the climate–economic system: the cost of control of GHGs, the damage from greenhouse warming, and the time dynamics as reflected in the rate of discount of future goods and services along with the time lags in the reaction of the climate to emissions.

The model used is recognised as a gross simplification of the climate–economic system, and it is noted that:

> estimates of both costs and damages are highly uncertain and incomplete, and our estimates are therefore highly tentative.

The uncertainty is highlighted by presenting the results for the optimal target arising under three different sets of assumptions:

1. Using 'identified' damages from climate change, and a 'middle' assumption about the discount rate, the target is a 2 per cent abatement of total greenhouse gas emissions from current levels. This would involve 'very little' reduction in carbon dioxide emissions, and come mostly from the CFC phase-out to which the industrial nations are already committed.
2. Using 'medium' damages and a 'middle' assumption about the discount rate produces an overall abatement target of 11 per cent. This would involve a 2 per cent reduction in carbon dioxide emissions from fossil fuel combustion, with the rest of the abatement coming from CFC phase-out.
3. Using a 'high' damages estimate and a zero rate of discount gives a target of 33 per cent abatement for greenhouse gas emissions. This would involve a substantial reduction in carbon dioxide emissions from fossil fuel combustion.[20]

While 'medium' and 'middle' might be suggestive of capturing the best estimates/assumptions about the crucial parameters, Nordhaus does not commit himself to any one of these targets as a best estimate of what is optimal.

Table 10.5 *Nordhaus estimates of 'identified' climate damage costs for the United States*

Sector	Impact estimate
Farms – impact of greenhouse warming and carbon dioxide fertilisation	−10.6 + 9.7
Forestry, fisheries	small + or −
Construction	positive
Water transportation	?
Energy and utilities –	
electricity demand	−1.65
non-electric space heating	+1.16
water and sanitary	negative ?
Real estate (land rent component of sea level rise) –	
loss of land	−1.55
protection of coast	−3.74
Hotels, lodging, recreation	?
Total (central estimate)	−6.23

Notes: Units are US$ billions, at 1981 prices.
A minus sign indicates a cost, a plus sign indicates a gain.
Source: Nordhaus (1991).

The damages from climate change give the benefits of abatement. Table 10.5 shows the estimates used by Nordhaus of the damage arising in the United States consequent upon a doubling of the greenhouse gas concentration in the earth's atmosphere. These are the basis for the 'identified' damages used in case 1 from the list above. The assumption made is that the estimated United States loss of one-quarter of 1 per cent of national income (GNP) is the appropriate estimate for the world as a whole. Nordhaus recognises that some economies may be more vulnerable to climate change impacts than the United States, so that the 'medium' damage estimate, case 2, is double this – one-half of 1 per cent of world income. Finally, the 'high' damage estimate, case 3, arises by multiplying identified United States damage by a factor of four, to get 1 per cent of world income. This is intended to take some account of the impacts omitted from the accounting in Table 10.5.

The first point to note about the estimates in Table 10.5 concerns the derivation of the total from the components. The items for which no number appears are treated as giving rise to zero $ cost. The total is then calculated taking as the damage cost for the impact on farms the midpoint of the range shown for it, which is US$ –0.45 billion. The range is from a cost of US$ 10.6 billion to gain of US$ 9.7 billion. If these endpoints are used, the total is either US$ –16.38 or US$ +3.92 billion, which correspond to –0.68 per cent and +0.16 of the United States national income. The total damages could, that is, be almost three times as large as the estimate used, or they could be gains rather than damages. This ignores the items for which no number appears.

The second point is that these 'identified' items are all costs based on impacts which affect economic activities with outputs sold in markets. Nordhaus explicitly notes emissions in respect of 'non-marketed goods and services' such as 'human health, biological diversity, amenity values of everyday life and leisure, and environmental quality'. There are a number of other omissions which may have been determined as inoperative in the case of the United States, but which cannot be ruled out globally, such as storm damage and salt-water intrusion into coastal freshwater aquifers. It is clear that the total for impact damage derived from the summing of these identified costs should be regarded as a lower bound.

So, the Nordhaus study puts a lower bound (which could be as high as 0.68 per cent of national income) to an unknown range for the effects of a carbon dioxide doubling on the United States. We have already noted that for many commentators, it is the rate of change of climate that is seen as the problem. The Nordhaus calculations ignore the rate of change and its implications. We can also note that the significance of United States based estimates for other countries, even after multiplication by a factor of four (which for 0.68 per cent in the United States would make the high world damage estimate 2.72 per cent of world income), is questionable. However, the main point to be drawn is that any quantification of the benefits of greenhouse gas build-up abatement, or preventative policy, is characterised by massive ignorance and uncertainty.[21] Further research is unlikely to greatly reduce this uncertainty. It involves valuation as well as assessment of physical and biological impacts.

Although Nordhaus' approach to determining the greenhouse gas emissions abatement target involves weighing costs and benefits, it would be wrong to call it a cost-benefit analysis, as that term was used in Chapter 7, to refer to the activity of project appraisal from a social perspective. The greenhouse gas abatement target determination case is quite different. Nordhaus is not dealing with a problem in allocative efficiency. He is dealing with a problem about the distribution over time of human welfare, assumed to depend solely on total consumption. It is not a question of allocating inputs to this project rather than that one. It is a question of the costs, in terms of consumption, to be incurred now

in order to raise future consumption levels above what they would otherwise be. This does involve discounting future benefits, which are the
higher future consumption levels, but the issues involved are different
from those which arise in the context of cost-benefit analysis as project
appraisal.

The discount rate Nordhaus uses for making future consumption
benefits commensurable with current consumption costs is known as the
consumption discount rate. It depends upon the relationship between
society's rate of time preference for current over future consumption,
and the growth rate assumed for the economy.[22] The discount rate used
will be higher the higher the time preference rate is, and lower the
higher the rate of growth assumed. This makes a good deal of sense. For
any given rate of time preference, future benefits will now count for less
the better off we assume the future to be. If a positive growth rate is
assumed and a zero rate of time preference used, the consumption
discount rate will be negative. If zero growth is assumed, then the
consumption discount rate is the rate of time preference, and is zero if
that is zero. This is the case for target 3 above. For 1 and 2 the 'middle'
discount rate used is 1 per cent, corresponding to a positive rate of time
preference and a positive assumed growth rate, with the former
exceeding the latter.

Arbitrary standards

The value of the Nordhaus study is in identifying the things that we
would need to know, but do not, to determine an optimal target for
greenhouse preventative policy. Some of those things, such as current
market costs and future physical and biological impacts, we could, to
varying degrees, learn more about by further research. The question of
the appropriate rate of time preference, on the other hand, is not
amenable to resolution by further research.

Operationally, the problem of thinking about a target for preventative
policy is a problem of decision making in the face of uncertainty. This
too involves ethical questions, and the exercise of judgment. Scientific
and economic research are not, of course, irrelevant. Rather, the limits
to their ability to resolve the problem are to be explicitly recognised
from the outset. A framework for considering decision making in the
face of uncertainty was laid out in Chapter 7. In using it for the enhanced
greenhouse problem we continue to assume the existence of a world
government. The problems are compounded when this assumption is
dropped, as will be seen below.

Table 10.6 is a pay-off matrix for a game against nature in the climate
change context. The question at issue is whether the notional world gov-

ernment should adopt as a target for preventative policy the abatement of greenhouse gas emissions by x per cent. The possible responses are 'yes' and 'no'. 'EGE' stands for enhanced greenhouse effect, 'Bau' for the decision to continue with business as usual, i.e. not to adopt the x per cent cut standard, and 'Abate' indicates that the x per cent standard is adopted. The entries are normalised on business as usual giving rise to zero cost in the event that there is no enhanced greenhouse effect. 'No EGE' means that the state of nature is favourable in that increasing greenhouse gas concentrations will not lead to climate change. If the decision is not to abate and nature is unfavourable, there is an enhanced greenhouse effect, and damage costs arise in amount a. If the decision is to cut emissions by x per cent and there is no enhanced greenhouse effect, nature is favourable, the costs of unnecessary abatement are b.

Table 10.6 *A pay-off matrix for a greenhouse emissions abatement target*

		State of Nature	
		No EGE	EGE
Decision	Bau	0	−a
	Abate	−b	±z

The bottom right-hand cell refers to the outcome where there is an enhanced greenhouse effect and abatement action is taken. If it were known that a cut of x per cent would completely avoid climate change, the entry here would be equal to a − b, where benefits a are obtained at the cost of b. This could be a positive or negative number. Generally for a cut of x per cent, it is not known what the impact on climate change will be. Hence, this entry is shown as z, which may be positive or negative.

Supposing that numerical values for a, b and z were known, what should the decision be? There is no technical answer to this question. It is a matter of judgment for the decision maker. A variety of rules have been suggested. The minimax rule would indicate selecting the decision for which the worst outcome is the smallest of the worst outcomes that might arise. It is a cautious rule.

However, in the case of the climate change problem, it is unrealistic to assume that the numerical values for a, b and z could be known. So, the minimax rule does not help very much. The safe minimum standard approach says that in the face of all the uncertainties, and given that the no abatement outcome when there is an enhanced greenhouse effect could be catastrophic, it should be assumed that a is the largest negative entry in the matrix. Then minimax says go for the abatement decision. The modified safe minimum standard approach says do this if the costs are not unacceptably large. This is an interesting way of reformulating the decision-making problem, rather than a solution to it, since it remains to determine what is unacceptably large.

So, the notional world government would have to exercise its judgment, rather than look for a simple technical rule for dealing with the uncertainties confronting it. Its situation would actually be considerably more complex than Table 10.6 might suggest. First, it assumes that there are just two possible states of nature to consider: business as usual either gives rise to climate change or does not. Any actual deliberation using the pay-off matrix approach would involve multiple state of nature assumptions, used with each decision. Second, Table 10.6 assumes that future benefits have been made commensurable with current costs. The problems involved here were discussed above. Third, it is not the case that the only options are do nothing or cut emissions. Currently, for example, prospective climate change is being used as the basis for calls for more funding for research into climate change, and into energy conservation technology, as alternatives, or complements, to emissions abatement. The former research is intended to reduce uncertainty at some future date, the latter to provide less costly means of emissions abatement.

There is in fact no world government to deal with the decision-making problem. Some of the implications then arising, notably the question of incentives for international agreement and cooperation are now to be considered, together with the question of the instrument(s) to be used for the attainment of any agreed global emissions reduction target.

Instrument choice for prevention policy

Chapter 7 discussed the economic analysis of pollution control, distinguishing between the question of setting the target and that of the choice of instrument. With respect to the first question, the usefulness of economics is limited. The operationally useful part of the economic analysis of pollution is that which deals with the second question, instrument choice for the attainment of arbitrary standards. The enhanced greenhouse effect can be regarded as a pollution problem, and the analysis of this second question used to consider the choice of instrument to address this threat to sustainability. To simplify and bring out the main issues, we restrict explicit attention to carbon dioxide emissions arising in fossil fuel combustion.

This pollution problem has the following characteristics:
(i) It involves a stock pollutant. What matters is the accumulated stock of carbon dioxide existing in the atmosphere, not the current flow of emissions. The current flow adds to the stock, which also naturally declines due to the operation of sinks. However, the rate

of decay is slow. Current emissions have implications reaching far into the future.

(ii) It is very complex in its physical and biological dimensions.

(iii) It is also complex in its socioeconomic dimensions, originating in the energy system of the world economy. This underpins the current functioning of the world economy. The impacts of climate change on socioeconomic systems would be multifaceted and interconnected, involving adaptations of various kinds, such as movements of people and changed patterns of trade.

(iv) The problem involves ignorance and massive uncertainties at each of the physical, biological and socioeconomic levels. The short-term prospects for significant reductions in these uncertainties are questionable.

(v)   There is a non-zero probability of catastrophic outcomes. This is most obviously true at the local level and in regard to sea level rises, but is also true at the global level given that the climate system may involve thresholds for positive feedback effects.

(vi) Carbon dioxide emissions arising in fossil fuel combustion are a case where monitoring can be indirect, and accurate, at low cost. This is because knowledge of combustion technology and of the fuel involved fixes emissions.

(vii) To a first approximation carbon dioxide emissions into the atmosphere mix perfectly and are equally dispersed throughout the entire atmosphere. No nation acting alone can significantly influence the future evolution of atmospheric concentrations.

The fact that there are other greenhouse gases increases the complexity of the problem, and enhances uncertainty.

The following observations arise. First, characteristic (i) means that intergenerational equity problems are central. This is enhanced by characteristics (iv) and (v). Prevention requires what is seen as costly action now, to avoid costs anticipated in the future. Second, complexity and uncertainty, characteristics (ii), (iii) and (iv), mean that setting control targets according to optimality criteria is infeasible. Analysis can illuminate the issues, but the quantitative information to use it to set targets is either unavailable or disputable. Targeting policy is a problem of decision making in the face of uncertainty. This together with the non-zero probability of catastrophe, characteristic (v), suggests placing considerable weight on the dependability criterion when comparing alternative instruments. It would seem desirable to select instruments that give some assurance what whatever the emissions reduction target adopted, it will be realised (or bettered). Characteristic (vi) implies that in this case, as distinct from many pollution problems, monitoring is not a major problem.

Characteristic (vii) gives rise to a number of observations and considerations. There arises a reciprocal externalities problem, implying the need for international consensus and coordination. This is unlikely to be easily achieved. International action may be seen as implying some loss of national sovereignty. Equity outcomes across nation states will vary according to the policy instrument adopted. This has implications for the incentives to participate in international action. Instruments should be compared according to the incentives for participation that they generate. Before looking at the alternative instrument types, the problems facing the achievement of an international consensus on action to reduce emissions need to be considered.

The free-rider problem

The relevant actors here are nation states. The question of whether they will act to reduce emissions can be treated in two parts. First, will they act individually? Second, will they act collectively? An analytical construct widely known as the **prisoners' dilemma game** gives the answers 'almost certainly not' and 'it all depends' respectively. The prisoners' dilemma gets its name because the basic structure involved was originally developed for a context where two individuals are arrested for a crime. If both confess, both receive somewhat reduced sentences. If neither confesses, both receive the standard sentence, as they are guilty and can be proved so at some trouble to the police. If only A confesses the guilt of both, she gets a much-reduced sentence, and correspondingly for B.

Table 10.7 *The incentive structure with reciprocal externalities*

		B	
		SQ	EPA
	SQ	1/1	2/0.8
A			
	EPA	0.8/2	1.5/1.5

Table 10.7 uses illustrative numbers for a two-country reciprocal externality case. SQ stands for 'status quo', and EPA for Environmental Protection Agency. Each country can be in one of two states, following recognition of the existence of the problem. It can do nothing, making no attempt to do anything about the control of its domestic emissions. It can set up an EPA mandated to control domestic emissions to some arbitrary standard. In Table 10.7 it is assumed the the arbitrary standard would be the same in each country, that the two economies are of the same size, and have the same costs of emissions abatement. These assumptions are not essential to the argument, but do simplify it.

Given two states for each nation, there are four possible outcomes, each represented by a cell in Table 10.7. In each cell, the number to the left of / refers to country A, that to the right to country B. The numbers are for the welfare of the representative individual in each nation. They can be thought of as being per capita income adjusted for pollution damage. The numbers are normalised so that when both countries do nothing to control emissions, welfare in each is unity. This serves to emphasise that these are purely imaginary numbers. The numbers in the other cells arise as follows.

In the top right cell, A does nothing while B sets up an EPA. As compared with the full status quo, A gains while B loses. B incurs the domestic costs involved in emissions abatement, and suffers a loss of competitiveness in international trade, while gaining some benefit from the reduced pollution due to its own emissions, but not those of A, being reduced. A gains exactly the same pollution reduction benefit, benefits from B's loss of competitiveness, and incurs no abatement costs. The bottom left cell shows the numbers reversed, as it refers to the reciprocal situation. Comparing the cell for the full status quo with these two cells, it is clear that for neither country is there an incentive to act alone. To do so would confer gains on the other country, and involve domestic losses.

The bottom right cell is for a situation where both counties set up EPAs. In this situation, the reduction in the level of emissions is twice that occurring when either acts unilaterally. Both incur domestic abatement costs, but neither suffers from any loss of competitiveness. Both countries are better off than in the full status quo. But neither is as well-off as if it did not act and the other did. Each country has an incentive to **free-ride** on the emissions abatement of the other, if it can. Given that each has this incentive not to act on domestic emissions, in the absence of some kind of agreement between the nation states, there will be no emissions abatement anywhere. However, if each could be assured that the other would act if it did, there would be incentives to act as both would be better off than in the full status quo. This is the nub of the matter in reciprocal externality situations. All parties are better off as participants in an effective international agreement that each acts to reduce emissions, but none has an incentive to act unilaterally. Indeed, each has an incentive to try to free-ride on the efforts of the other. The operative problem is the negotiation of international agreements on emissions abatement.

The actual problem in the enhanced greenhouse effect case is much more difficult than Table 10.7 suggests, for a number of reasons. First, negotiation of credible agreements is more difficult where there are many countries involved. An agreement is credible only if all potential participants believe that its terms will be adhered to by all. This raises questions of compliance, monitoring and enforcement. Second, given that countries actually differ in size, income level, abatement costs etc., all would not gain equally from participation. Nations, and individuals, often feel strongly about equity, and may be prepared to forego available gains on the basis that others would make larger gains. Third, in the enhanced greenhouse context there is massive uncertainty about the potential global costs and benefits associated with any particular proposed global target for emissions reduction, and about the gains to particular nations that would ensue.

Based on the discussion in Chapter 7, three broad classes of instrument for pursuit of a global emissions reduction target can now be considered – quantity regulation (also known as command and control), taxation, and tradeable permits.

Quantity regulation

This would involve each nation being required to cut back on emissions by a given proportional amount from some base-year level, or to emit only up to a certain absolute amount. Use of this class of instrument would not lead to standard attainment at least cost. It would be a choice implying inefficiency for the world economy. However, leaving aside enforcement problems, this choice would have the property of dependability – the global target would be realised.

If national targets were internationally agreed, there remains the question of the means by which a nation would seek to realise its own particular target. This question could itself be decided as part of the international agreement, or left to the individual nations. The latter would involve a smaller perceived sacrifice of national sovereignty than the former. This could be expected to make it the more likely outcome. Under this outcome each nation could adopt quantity regulation or price incentive systems as domestic instruments for the attainment of its agreed emissions reduction target. The former would imply domestic inefficiency in target attainment. Carbon taxation at a uniform rate would imply that some domestic reduction would be attained at least cost, but the reduction would not necessarily be that agreed to. Tradeable permits would mean target attainment, dependability, together with domestic efficiency.

The central question in negotiating this type of international consensus would be the determination of the national targets. It seems likely that perceptions of equity between nations would dominate consideration of this question. The simple approach of equal proportional cutbacks across all nations would penalise nations already fossil fuel efficient and the less developed nations. An alternative suggestion is that the agreed global emissions total would be shared equally on a per capita basis. This could be seen as favouring developing as opposed to industrial nations. Obviously, many variants on these simple allocation rules are conceivable.

For carbon dioxide emissions from fossil fuel combustion, monitoring compliance would be relatively simple and inexpensive. Emissions could be derived from fossil fuels combustion data.[23] Enforcement of compliance raises more difficult problems. A system of fines for non-compliance would be the obvious approach. They would have to be administered by an international agency, so that some loss of national sovereignty would be involved. The proceeds could, it has been suggested, be used to finance greenhouse research and/or technology transfer. Alternatively, it has been suggested that trade sanctions could be used against non-complying nations.

Taxation

This would involve an international agreement to tax carbon dioxide emissions at a uniform rate across all sources in all nations. It could take two forms. The first would involve the tax being levied by an international agency, the second would involve it being levied by nation states. In both cases taxation would be globally efficient, i.e. least cost, but not dependable. The common global tax rate would realise some emissions reduction at the least possible cost as measured in terms of pre-tax prices, but it would not guarantee the attainment of the global target for emissions reduction.

Taxation by an international agency would mean revenues accruing to it, and if the tax were set at rates intended to realise significant global emissions reductions these revenues would be substantial. In 1990 global carbon dioxide emissions were approximately 20 000 megatonnes. Taxation at the rate of US$20 per tonne would then yield of the order of US$400 billions per annum. Some perspective on the revenue potential is as follows. From Table 2.3 and 2.5 (see pp.10 and 12), the GNP in US dollars can be calculated for the countries shown. The results are, as round numbers in billions of US dollars: Canada, 500; Australia, 240; Mexico, 178; Mauritius, 2; Algeria, 56; El Salvador, 6; Bangaldesh, 21; and Guinea, 2. The global carbon tax revenue potential is larger than the size of all but the largest national economies.

This gives rise to problems and possibilities. The problems concern the perceived loss of sovereignty by nation states which would be involved in the creation of an international body with significant spending power. The possibilities concern the related questions of equity and participation incentives. Rules can be devised according to which the international agency would disburse its revenues, and which would promote equity and create incentives for participation. A rule could involve, for example, countries receiving a share of total revenue dependent on population size, or on per capita national income, or on both. This would favour large developing nations, such as India and China, and might be expected to encourage their participation which would otherwise not be seen by them as consistent with their national interest. Of course, such rules would work against the narrowly perceived interests of industrial nations and, to that extent, discourage their participation.

The tax base would actually be fossil fuel combustion, with the rate varying across the fuels according to carbon content, so that tax liabilities would be relatively easily assessed. Compliance enforcement problems would arise where nations refused to pay their tax assessments. This would be tantamount to openly leaving the international consensus, and would presumably be dealt with through trade and/or political sanctions.

The problems of perceived national sovereignty loss and revenue disbursement could be avoided by a form of agreement which had the common tax rate across nations levied by nation states themselves, the revenue arising remaining with the nation collecting it. This would involve the loss of the possibility of promoting equity and encouraging participation by some key players.

The discussion here has assumed that what is at issue is taxation intended to provide incentives to reduce carbon dioxide emissions. In other contexts, taxation of emissions is frequently in the form of user charges intended to raise finance for administration costs for other control methods, and/or to finance waste treatment facilities, rather than to create incentives for abatement. In the carbon dioxide context international taxation at a low rate to provide revenue for a fund to finance research and/or technology transfer to developing nations has been suggested. It can be argued that this would reduce the problems of securing international consensus, and would be the first step in a learning process leading to incentive-motivated international agreements on taxation, as well as perhaps having some small immediate incentive effects.

Tradeable permits

Tradeable emissions permits are generally considered to be both efficient and dependable. They score over quantity regulation on the first count, and over taxation on the second. If these properties carry over to the particular context of the control of global carbon dioxide emissions, tradeable permits look very attractive there.

The first point to note is that the carryover requires that permits are freely tradeable across national frontiers between emissions soures. The carryover does not hold if permits are tradeable only between nation states, since a nation state could then choose to attain the target emissions level for which it holds permits by quantity regulation of the sources within its borders. In this case, dependability at the global level holds, but efficiency does not. It seems intuitive that permits tradeable between nation states would offer efficiency advantages over international quantity controls whatever form of control nation states adopted within their borders, although this does not appear to have been demonstrated analytically. In principle, an international consensus could involve a two-stage commitment to tradeable permits – tradeable national permits to be subdivided and allocated within nations by tradeable individual source permits. A nation that sought to meet the target corresponding to its permit-holding by the use of the tax instrument would face the problem that this instrument is not a dependable means of realising a target.

Permits tradeable between nations would perhaps be seen to involve less sacrifice of national sovereignty than would internationally administered taxation. The intragenerational equity implications would depend primarily on the initial allocation of permits. It is difficult to see how this could be negotiated by nation states except on the basis that permits be attached to nation states rather than to individual emissions sources. As with internationally administered taxation, there are problems and possibilities here. The initial allocation would be contentious, but would offer opportunities for addressing existing inequities between states and for creating incentives for some to particpate. It has been suggested that initial national allocations based on equal per capita shares of total allowable emissions would serve the cause of international equity, and generate incentives for participation by developing nations (Grubb 1990a).

It was noted that quantity regulation and taxation regimes for the control of carbon dioxide emissions could actually be run on the basis of the control of fossil fuels combustion. It is not clear that this advantage readily attaches to tradeable permits. The use of permits relating to fossil fuels use rather than emissions would require that permits be defined in carbon dioxide equivalent fuel units, with one coal unit exchanging for 1.78 natural gas units, for example. With regard to compliance enforcement, the situation here would be essentially the same as with quantity regulation.

Economic modelling

The discussion of alternative policy instruments for a global carbon dioxide emissions reduction target against criteria such as feasibility, efficiency, dependability, equity and participation incentives does not reveal any one of them as clearly superior. While such a qualitative review is useful, it is clear that quantification is desirable for judging the trade-offs across the instruments. One needs some idea of the relative sizes of the various effects involved, so that pluses and minuses can be compared. Because this cannot be derived simply from experience with the alternative instruments, it must therefore be determined from quantitative modelling. This is now an active research area in economics. To date, the models have addressed a limited subset of the issues canvassed above. Given this and the speculative nature of the parameter estimates involved, the numerical results available have to be taken as illustrative of the magnitudes which might be involved, rather than as firm estimates. Most of the modelling work in the international context is with applied general equilibrium models, and the remarks on these in Chapter 9 apply here.

A recent survey finds that:

> estimates centre on a global loss of GDP of around 2 to 4 per cent in order to reduce emissions by about 40 to 60 per cent relative to what they would otherwise be (Winter in Anderson and Blackhurst 1992).

The survey notes that costs 'depend on various parameters of economic behaviour' and that in the modelling studies 'there are wide variances in the assumptions used concerning some of these parameters'. Here we consider a model which produces estimates of the global costs of carbon dioxide emission reductions which lie at the higher end of the range revealed in this survey.[24] The world is divided into six regional economies, as shown in Table 10.8. Two types of energy source are distinguished: fossil fuel and other. These are substitutable for one another in production, and energy and other inputs are also substitutes in production. International trade involves fossil fuels, but not non-fossil energy, and products produced using both energy sources. The costs of reducing carbon dioxide emissions are measured as percentage reductions in GDP. No account is taken of any environmental benefits arising from the reduced use of energy invovled in securing the emissions reductions.

The results shown in Table 10.8 refer to three alternative routes to the achievement of a global 50 per cent reduction in emissions. In options 1 and 2 each economy acts to cut its emissions by 50 per cent. In 1 this is done by the imposition of the required rate of tax on the production of fossil fuels. In 2 it is the consumption of fossil fuels that is taxed. It should noted that in terms of the discussion of instruments above, both of these are, from the global perspective, in the nature of quantity regulation. Each economy is required to cut emissions by 50 per cent. It does this using the tax instrument. There is no loading of abatement between economies where it is least costly – all cut equally. Hence, neither of these options would be an efficient way to achieve a global 50 per cent cut in emissions.

Table 10.8 *Costs associated with alternative instruments for emissions reduction*

Region	1	Option 2	3
EC	–4.0	–1.0	–3.8
North America	–4.3	–3.6	–9.8
Japan	–3.7	0.5	–0.9
Other OECD	–2.3	–2.1	–4.4
Oil exports	+4.5	–18.7	–13.0
Rest of world	–7.1	–6.8	1.8
World	–4.4	–4.4	–4.2

Notes: Results are for a global 50 per cent reduction achieved by:
  – Option 1 is national fossil fuel production taxation.
  – Option 2 is national fossil fuel consumption taxation.
  – Option 3 is uniform global taxation.
Source: Whalley and Wigle (1991).

This is shown in Table 10.8, where world costs are higher with both 1 and 2 than with option 3, which does involve the use of the global tax instrument. A uniform global tax is levied and collected by an international agency. This is a least cost means of achieving the global target. With this option, individual economies cut emissions by different percentages, but the global outcome is a 50 per cent reduction. The cost saving in adopting the least cost instrument, as compared with equal percentage reductions, in not great – 0.2 per cent of world GDP. This suggests that if an international agreement were reached which chose to ignore the theoretical cost minimisation case for uniform global taxation, the costs thereby incurred for the world as a whole would not be very great.

The results for the separate economies show how the distribution of costs varies with instrument choice. In options 1 and 2 tax revenues accrue to the individual economies, and are spent there. Option 1 then benefits carbon energy exporters (called oil exporters in Table 10.8) at the expense of importers, especially the Rest of World which includes the developing nations together with the formerly centrally planned economies. The developing nations do slightly less badly where 50 per cent reductions in each economy are achieved by a fossil fuel consumption tax. In this case, the oil exporters suffer heavily. The costs to the fossil fuel importers are reduced because the before-tax world price of fossil fuel falls, and the tax revenues are recycled within those economies. Except in the case of Japan, there remain costs, for the reasons discussed in Chapter 9. The result for Japan here appears anomalous.

Option 3 involves a uniform global tax levied and collected by an international agency. This is what gives rise to the minimised world cost. The agency disposes of the revenues by grants to each economy based on their population size. The per capita grant is the same throughout the world. In this case not only do we have minimised cost to the global economy, but we also have a distributional impact that works to reduce inequity by, generally, transferring funds to the developing economies. As noted, this is important for the incentives for participation that arise. The distributional impact of the use of tax revenue accruing to an international agency could be made even stronger by, for example, adjusting the per capita payments such that they increase as per capita income decreases. Of course, to the extent that the industrial countries are not convinced that they can afford to have income redistributed in this way, the incentives for them to participate would be reduced by this kind of modification.

These results are interesting, but it should be kept in mind that they are attended by numerous qualifications and uncertainties. They should not be regarded as predictions. It should also be remembered that they refer only to costs, no environmental benefits of any kind being accounted for. The model assumes that the initial state is one where technical efficiency holds everywhere, and does not allow the changed relative input prices following the introduction of the taxes to drive the direction of technological change.

Unilateral action

The general view is that unilateral action, say by introducing carbon taxation, would involve costs but no benefits. For most countries, the share of total world emissions is small, so that even a substantial reduction by it would have a negligible effect on total emissions. However, there are considerations pointing in the opposite direction:

a. It has been argued that nations acting unilaterally will gain moral authority and thereby exert more influence in international negotiations.

b. It has been argued that energy markets are characterised by numerous market and government failures, the correction of which would reduce the costs of providing energy-based services, in the process reducing carbon dioxide emissions.

c. We also noted in Chapter 9 that fossil fuel combustion is associated with many forms of pollution in addition to carbon dioxide emissions. To the extent that unilateral action on carbon dioxide emissions produced reductions in these other environmental impacts, they would be domestic benefits.

Whether or not it makes sense for any country to act unilaterally on carbon dioxide emissions therefore involves, like so much else in the sustainability area, a balance of conflicting considerations. In an ideal world, we would turn to experts and models to tell us which way the balance of advantage lies. Unfortunately, the necessary models do not exist, and the experts do not know. Here, as elsewhere, we have to live with ignorance and uncertainty, and to exercise judgment. While we, and the politicians we elect, must not ignore model results and expert opinion, neither should the responsibility for judgment be passed entirely to them.

CHAPTER 11

Postscript

Chapter 1 noted how the 1987 publication of the Brundtland Report, by the World Commission on Environment and Development (WCED) put economy–environment interactions on political agendas under the rubric of 'sustainable development'. WCED believed that an active follow-up to its report was imperative if the policy changes necessary for the attainment of sustainable development were to occur. It called for the transformation of its report into a UN Programme of Action on Sustainable Development, and recommended that:

> Within an appropriate period after the presentation of the report to the General Assembly, an international Conference could be convened to review progress made and promote follow-up arrangements that will be needed over time to set benchmarks and to maintain human progress within the guidelines of human needs and natural laws (World Commission on Environment and Development 1987, p.343).

As a result, the United Nations Conference on Environment and Development (UNCED) took place in Rio de Janeiro in June 1992. This was the 20th anniversary of the Stockholm Conference: this timing was intentional. UNCED was preceded by over two years of preparatory international negotiations. One hundred and seventy-eight nations sent delegations, and the meeting was attended by 107 heads of government (or state). During UNCED several parallel and related conferences took place in Rio de Janeiro; the meeting for NGOs involved more participants than UNCED itself. It has been estimated that more than 30 000 people were there in total (Rogers 1993).

The preparatory negotiations dealt with four main areas: draft conventions on biodiversity conservation, global climate change, forest management, and the preparation of two documents for adoption at

UNCED. The main outcomes were as follows. There was complete agreement on the, non-binding, adoption of the *Rio Declaration* and *Agenda 21*
(United Nations 1993). The first of these comprises 27 short statements
of principle in regard to global sustainable development. The second is
a long document covering over 100 specific programmes for the attainment of global sustainable development: many of these programmes
involve resource transfers from the industrial to the developing nations.
Agenda 21 called for the creation of a new United Nations Commission
for Sustainable Development, to monitor and promote the implementation of its recommendations. It also called for the creation of a support
structure for this commission within the United Nations Secretariat.
Agreement was also reached on the, non-binding, adoption of a set of
principles for forest management. The industrial nations reaffirmed
their previous, non-binding, commitments to a target for development
aid of 0.7 per cent of their GNP.

Two conventions were adopted, by some 150 nations in each case,
which would be binding on signatories when ratified by them. These
covered global climate change and biodiversity conservation: the latter
was not signed by the United States at the Rio meeting, but it did sign in
1993 after a change of administration. While binding, these conventions
do not commit individual nations to many specific actions. In the case of
the climate convention, for example, it was agreed that the objective was
the stabilisation of greenhouse gas concentrations in the atmosphere at
a level that would avoid danger, within a time-frame that would allow
adaptation. Neither the level nor the time-frame was quantified. The
industrial nations agreed to take steps to limit emissions of greenhouse
gases with the aim of returning to 1990 levels by the year 2000.[1]

Many environmental activists, as well as many concerned to promote
economic development in poor nations, regarded the actual achieve-
ments at UNCED as disappointing, in so far as there was a lack of
binding commitments. Suzuki in Rogers (1993), complained that Rio
endorsed the idea of sustainable development rather than calling for
sustainability as the objective. According to Suzuki 'Rio failed to meet
even the most pessimistic of expectations' and 'was more than a failure:
it is dangerous because it is being touted as a great success'. However, it
did confirm that economy–environment interconnections, albeit under
the sustainable development rubric, were, and would remain, firmly on
the world political agenda.[2] Despite the lack of specific commitments,
there were agreements with the potential to lead to further developments. The recommendations concerning the structure of the United
Nations have been acted upon and are clearly an important institutional
innovation. In the case of climate change it was agreed that there would
be two international meetings during the following decade to review

progress toward the aim adopted by industrial nations, and the possibility was left open that the aim could be amended in the light of new information. Also, all signatories agreed to regularly provide information on their greenhouse gas emissions and on their efforts to mitigate climate change.

The convening of, and the outcomes at, UNCED suggests that while the need to address global problems arising from economy–environment interconnections is widely accepted, detailed agreement on the nature of the appropriate policy responses is limited. Further, there is clearly reluctance on the part of national governments to incur costs associated with policy responses. Either the widely shared perception that there is a sustainability problem will cease to exist, or debate over policy responses will continue. The first of these possibilities appears unlikely.

This book has argued that the debate concerns social decision making in the face of uncertainty. The problem is especially difficult because the society in question is the whole of humanity. At this global level, social institutions are weak in comparison with those at the national level (Mendez 1992). Policy will evolve largely through interactions between nation states, based on perceptions of national interest. It has also been argued that economics has a limited role to play in the debate about what the objectives of policy should be. These objectives should be set in an attempt to reduce poverty and address environmental threats to sustainability, rather than according to the criteria of consumer sovereignty. The point here is not that nothing can be left to the market. It is that the parameters within which markets operate to allocate production and consumption need to be set, as with carbon taxation for example, by reference to criteria other than consumer sovereignty.

It has also been argued that there is a strong prima facie case for using economic, or price, incentives as the means for the pursuit of social goals. The argument is not that these are always and everywhere the appropriate instruments. It is that they merit careful consideration where it is decided that there are threats to sustainability that need to be addressed. It appears that many who are concerned to protect the environment reject the economic test for the determination of the appropriate level of protection, and take it that this means also rejecting economic arguments about instrument choice. This is unfortunate and unnecessary. It is unnecessary because the economics of instrument choice is separable from the economics of target setting. It is unfortunate because socially determined prices and the private incentives they generate have a great deal to recommend them as means to address threats to sustainability.

Notes

Chapter 1

1 McCormick (1989) provides a modern history of environmental concerns and their interaction with political processes: see also Worster (1985).

2 The quotation is from the caption to Figure 46 (p.165) of Meadows et al. (1972). TLTG refers to a configuration of the model system that is sustainable as an 'equilibrium state', and notes that: 'A number of philosophers, economists and biologists have discussed such a state and called it by many different names, with as many different meanings.' (p.170). Among economists, the most widely used alternative names have been 'steady state' and 'stationary state': see Daly (1973). Actually, economists are (largely) consistent in the meaning they give to the concept referred to by these names: it involves constancy over time in the size of the human population, in the size of the capital stock, and in the level of per capita income.

3 A good, if somewhat intemperate, example of the reaction of most economists is Beckerman (1972) which also dealt with another claim, published almost simultaneously with TLTG, Goldsmith et al. (1973) that economic growth is subject to environmental limits. Beckerman (1974) further develops the critique of the limits to growth school and provides a good account of the case for economic growth as seen by economists.

4 See Arndt (1978) for an historical account of the post World War II climate of opinion in regard to the desirability of growth as a policy objective, as well as for reaction to TLTG.

5 See World Commission on Environment and Development (1987, p.40). There are now many definitions of sustainable development in the literature. For a review see the Appendix to Pearce et al. (1989). The term predates the Brundtland report: see McCormick (1989).

Chapter 2

1 The *Human development report* comes out annually, and each edition updates the statistical material and provides commentary on selected topics. Each year the World Bank produces a *World development report* which covers similar ground and provides related statistical material. The 1992 edition, is particularly concerned with the relationships between economic development and the environment.

2 The HDR provides a very brief account of PPP adjustment. For a full technical description of the procedures involved see Kravis et al (1975).
3 See, for example, Figure 2.1 in Dicken (1992).
4 From Tables 2.1 and 2.13 in Dicken (1992).
5 The figures are taken from Table 7.2 in Mendez (1992).
6 For further discussion of this see World Commission on Environment and Development (1987) and United Nations Development Programme (1992).
7 Data from Table 2.5 in Dicken (1992).
8 The institutional circumstances of ODF and ODA, and of international capital flows generally, are complex. Mendez (1992) gives a useful introduction to the complexities, and emphasises the limited extent of transfers from the rich to the poor at the international level as compared with what happens within industrial countries in particular.
9 Actually, not all of the conversion uses of coal shown in Table 2.15 are for electricity production. However, the other conversion uses are small, and can be ignored for purposes of illustrating the point being made here. For details on the other conversion uses of coal, see ABARE (1991).
10 The methods for this type of energy accounting are discussed in Thomas (1977). The methods can also be used to perform a similar accounting for carbon dioxide emissions. Some results arising are reported in Chapter 9 here.
11 Actually, the figures are properly per unit delivery to final demand, which comprises use for investment, use by government and use for export, as well as consumption by households. However, since the fuels use implications are the same across these components of final demand, the statement in the text is true.
12 See Note 11.
13 The rank correlation coefficient is discussed in introductory statistics texts. To see how it works consider three items ranking as follows against four different criteria

	I	II	III	IV
A	1	1	3	2
B	2	2	2	3
C	3	3	1	1

Then the rank correlation coefficients are: for I and II, 1; for I and III, −1; for I and IV, 0.75.

Chapter 3

1 Holister and Porteous (1966).
2 The literature now contains a number of such schematic representations. They should be regarded as variations on a theme, rather than as competitive. See, for example: Barbier (1989), Jacobs (1991), Pearce and Turner (1990), and Pezzey (1992). Perrings (1987) provides a mathematical model of the relationship of economic activity to the natural environment.
3 Readers seeking a rigorous account should consult an environmental science text such as Watt (1973) and/or an ecology text such as Krebs (1972). Bowler (1992) is a history of the environmental sciences.
4 For a good non-specialist account of matters nuclear see Patterson (1983).
5 See, for example, Lovins (1979). Ramage (1983) and Hall et al. (1992) provide detailed information on the characteristics of energy sources.

6 It did not always. A useful point of entry to the history of the biosphere is the work associated with the Gaia hypothesis: see Lovelock (1979) and Lovelock (1988). Wallace and Norton (1992) distinguish between the scientific and metaphysical aspects of this work, and consider the policy implications arising.

7 For further discussion of ozone depletion see Chapter 5 Meadows et al. (1992).

8 See Chapter 8 for further discussion.

9 Elton (1993) is an ecological comedy thriller about the commercial marketing of life support systems in an environmentally degraded world.

10 Hartwick (1997) first spelled out the rule which is necessary for constant consumption given that production involves the use of a non-renewable resource, which is now known as the Hartwick Rule. Solow (1974) had previously considered the question of the feasibility of constant consumption in the same circumstances, and the model might more properly be called the Solow-Hartwick model.

11 This is proved in Hartwick (1977). Common (1988), in Chapter 7, provides a numerical illustration, and discusses the nature of the substitution possibilities.

12 The idea of efficiency in resource exploitation is discussed in Chapter 7.

13 See Solow (1974) for further discussion on this.

14 For a recent non-technical exposition, by a Nobel Laureate, which links the Hartwick rule to the national income accounting considerations, see Solow (1992). See also Chapter 8 here.

15 The distinction made here follows Holling (1973, 1986).

16 See also Conway (1987).

17 Conway (1987) p.102 notes several – inertia, elasticity, amplitude, hysteresis, and malleability – and provides references discussing them. See also Holling (1986).

18 Common and Perrings (1992) provide a formal synthesis in terms of a mathematical optimisation model. They find that if constraints to protect the ecosystem function are imposed, it may be necessary to abandon consumer sovereignty as the sole criterion of economic performance.

19 This attribute list is based on an unpublished 1992 paper, The framing of policy problems in sustainability, by Stephen Dovers of the Centre for Resource and Environmental Studies, at the Australian National University.

Chapter 4

1 See, for examples, Krebs (1972), Watt (1973), or Kormondy (1969) for discussion of ecosystems as concepts and actualities, and their role in ecological analysis.

2 This is a very simplified description of what agriculture involves. For a fuller, but still brief, account see Chapter 4 ('The First Great Transition') of Ponting (1992). See also, for example, Bayliss-Smith (1982).

3 See Ponting (1992), Sahlins (1974), Lee and De Vore (1968). Boyden et al. (1990) state that: 'In general hunter–gatherers are less likely to be sick than modern city dwellers, but when sick they are more likely to die'.

4 Chapter 3 of Ponting (1992) gives more information and cites examples in regard to environmental impacts and cultural practices. On Australian Aboriginals, whose burning practices have been called 'firestick farming' and are now believed to have played an important role in creating current

Australian landscape features, see Blainey (1975) and Dingle (1988). Wilkinson (1973) discusses cultural practices which had the effect of controlling population size.

5 Wilkinson (1973) proposes an ecological model of the historical experience of economic development, in which technological innovation and the exploitation of new resources are the successful adaptations to ruptures to ecological equilibria for human societies. See also Common (1988b).

6 See Sahlins (1974), Lee and De Vore (1968), Dingle (1988) for descriptions of hunter–gatherer economies.

7 See also Lee and De Vore (1968).

8 The source for Figure 4.4, Schor (1991), is entitled *The Overworked American: the unexpected decline of leisure.* Schor argues that in the United States working hours are now higher than they were 40 years ago, despite large increases in labour productivity. This is explained in terms of a number of economic and social factors operating in the United States – the same trend did not occur in western Europe – especially a weak labour union movement operating in an economy heavily orientated toward the consumption of goods and services supplied in the market. Scitovsky (1976) notes related phenomena and stresses the Puritan influence on American social attitudes.

9 The essay, 'Economic possibilities for our grandchildren' appeared in Keynes (1931). In this essay Keynes distinguished between absolute and relative needs. He recognised that the demand for relative needs could not be sated by economic growth. However, he appears to have regarded this as a relatively minor problem, and did not see it as preventing attainment of a state where individuals would face no serious economic problem.

10 Figures taken from 'Economists (should) rule, OK', *The Economist,* 14 August 1993. According to this article, whereas economists 'used to be safely locked inside their ivory towers, nobody can now escape them. Their views fill newspaper columns and airwaves: a single word from one of the elect can send markets into a spin'. The article advocated more economists in government, as ministers rather than advisers. It may have been slightly tongue-in-cheek, as it concluded: 'The economists are still waiting for their chance to put the world to rights. They need only one (quarter-century) turn in the sun, and then they will go away. Honest'. The 'quarter-century' is based on a reference to an article by Keynes said to have been written in 1932 in which he is said to have predicted that economists would be the most important group of scientists in the world for 25 years, after which, having worked their magic, he hoped they would never be important again.

11 From a journal that generally adheres to the tenets of standard economics, the point being made by *The Economist* here is, however valid, rather curious. According to standard economics, any voluntary exchange is welfare enhancing to both of the parties involved. Given conditions in the United States, this would cover the exchange of money for the services of a lawyer, doctor or real estate agent. The state does not compel middle-class people to use any of these services. *The Economist,* no doubt realising its difficulty, has middle-class people purchasing these services 'readily – though not always voluntarily'. The significance of, and basis for, this distinction is not explained.

12 Scitovsky (1976, p.vi). The next sentence describes this approach as 'unscientific', and much of the book is an elaboration of the basis for this description. On any reasonable understanding of 'scientific' Scitovsky's position is justified.

13 See, for example, Scitovsky (1976) for discussion and further references. The economics position on welfare is actually a special version of the philosophical position known as utilitarianism. See, for example, Penz (1986).

14 The quotes which follow are from Boyden et al. (1990, pp.42–6).

15 In Xenos (1989) it is argued that general scarcity is a purely modern phenomenon in human history, and depends upon the existence of an extensive market system: 'What results from this development is a social environment in which the realm of choice is constantly expanding, thus expanding the experience of scarcity' (p.79). See also Durning (1992) for a critique of the 'consumer society'.

16 The best-known exposition of this critique is Galbraith (1967).

17 Mishan (1967) is an early exposition of this view.

18 Scitovsky (1976) argues this case.

19 The term positional goods was made popular by Hirsch (1977). The idea that an individual's welfare depends in part upon her consumption, in total and pattern, relative to that of others has a long history in economics. Adam Smith wrote about it in the eighteenth century. Keynes (1931) distinguished between absolute and relative needs: 'Needs of the second class, those which satisfy the desire for superiority, may indeed be insatiable'. Notwithstanding this long history, the point involved has had little impact on the thinking of most economists.

20 From an article by Robert Lane, 'Why wealth doesn't always buy happiness', in *The Guardian Weekly*, 26 August 1993, summarising some themes from Lane (1991).

21 A third reason is the availability of the data. The 1993 HDR does not give data for G. Measuring greenhouse gas emissions is difficult and expensive. However, at the 1992 UN Conference on Environment and Development signatories to the climate convention committed themselves to preparing greenhouse gas inventories. It should in due course, then, be possible to update the EAEPI considered here.

22 The rank correlation coefficient for the index and income when adjusted income is considered is 0.86. Common (1993) gives the full set of data for Y and I, and some variant indices.

Chapter 5

1 As quoted in the preface to the sequel, Meadows et al. (1992), p.xiii.

2 This judgment was delivered by Wilfred Beckerman in a public lecture to mark his accession to a chair of economics at the University of London. An abridged version of the lecture appeared as a main feature article in *The Times*, which is not what usually happens to inaugural lectures. It was subsequently published in full in an academic journal – Beckerman (1972).

3 Jan Tinbergen in a Foreword to Meadows et al. (1992).

4 Cole et al. (1973) is a critique of TLTG from a modelling perspective. Maddox (1972) approaches TLTG from a natural science perspective.

5 In the following paragraphs we draw on Hall and Hall (1984). Deadman and Turner (1988) discuss similar issues and explicitly discuss recycling. See also Brown and Field (1978) and Cleveland and Stern (1993) for discussion of alternative measures of scarcity and their appropriateness for differing circumstances and questions.

6 The unit price of a resource *in situ* is referred to in the economics literature as its rent. Rent was discussed in Chapter 3 in connection with the Hartwick

rule, and will be discussed again in Chapter 7. Energy use in production as a scarcity indicator is discussed in Chapter 8.

7 Ozdemiroglu (1993) reviews some of the literature and provides further evidence on trends using the price indicator. See also Cleveland and Stern (1993) for references to the literature.

8 Simon (1981) does not explicitly address TLTG. The explicit targets of his attack are the movement for population control in its various manifestations.

9 Simon (1981) p.121. In December 1993 a 'breakthrough' in fusion research was widely reported. The headline in the UK newspaper *The Guardian* was 'Fusion test heralds clean fuel', and the opening sentence was: 'Cheap, safe and plentiful energy moved a step closer yesterday after a US breakthrough in which scientists mimicked the power of the sun to produce energy from hydrogen fusion'. An input of 24 million watts is reported as producing an output of 3 million watts! The next day the science correspondent of *The Observer* concluded an article on the same event as follows: 'All we can say is that the promise of fusion power is awesome. To date, however, progress has been poor, and the immediate prognosis looks bleak. So treat all the hype and headlines with caution'.

10 See, for example, Bernstam (1991), Panayotou (1993), and World Bank (1992), and additional references provided in those sources. Also, for a number of natural resource inputs, over periods of varying length in the twentieth century, Ozdemiroglu (1993) finds evidence for an inverted U type relationship between price and time. This is consistent with a relationship as illustrated in Figure 5.1.

11 Bernstam (1991) analyses data on energy consumption and income per capita for a number of countries at different income levels, and finds consistency with the inverted U hypothesis.

12 For Figure 5.6 the lower bound is set at 10 per cent of the maximum level of per capita emissions. The numerical level set for this lower bound does not affect the nature of the history shown in Figure 5.6. Figures 5.5 and 5.6 were generated from a very simple computer simulation, where it is easy to alter the values taken by various parameters, such as the lower bound on impact.

13 The International Union for the Conservation of Nature periodically publishes lists of threatened animal species throughout the world: IUCN (1990). Common and Norton (1992) consider the situation in Australia, which is the only industrial/high human development nation generally classified as a 'megadiversity' nation.

14 For a fuller discussion of these matters, and of policy to preserve biodiversity, see, for example, Ehrlich and Ehrlich (1981), Myers (1979), Wilson and Peter (1988), and articles in two special issues of the journal *Ambio* in 1992 (vol. XXI, no. 3) and 1993 (vol. XXII, no. 2-3). See also Barbier et al. (1994).

15 The case for thinking about biodiversity in terms of populations rather than species is made in Ehrlich and Dailey (1993), where it is noted that there are different definitions of these terms in use.

16 See also Diamond (1992).

Chapter 6

1 Blaug (1985) is a good standard textbook on the history of economic thought. Heilbronner (1991) is more suited to non-specialists.

2 On colonisation and migration see Ponting (1992), and Cipolla (1962). On the use of fossil fuels in agriculture, see Leach (1975).

3 The quotations in this paragraph are from Blaug (1985).

4 The data for Figure 6.2 are taken from Department of Trade and Industry (1993), Table A5, Annexe A.

5 The data for Figure 6.3 come from the following sources. Energy use per unit of national income is energy use divided by gross domestic product at factor cost measured in constant 1985 prices from CSO (1993). The relative price of energy is derived by first dividing expenditure on energy, taken from the source cited in Note 4, by energy use. This gives a much larger increase in the price of energy than that shown in Figure 6.3, since it makes no allowance for inflation. Over the 1968–89 period in the United Kingdom, all prices and wages rose considerably. What matters for energy demand is the price of energy relative to that of other commodities, so the price series derived as the ratio of expenditure to quantity must be corrected by dividing it by a general price index. The general price index used was that implicit in the series for GDP at current and constant 1985 prices from CSO (1993).

6 Comprehensive and rigorous treatments of these matters are exercises in abstract mathematics. What follows here is only a brief overview. See, e.g., Layard and Walters (1978) for a more complete, and somewhat mathematical, treatment. Chapters 2, 3 and 4 of Common (1988a) cover the essentials, presuming no background in economics, and using only diagrams and very simple algebra.

7 But see Note 12.

8 Introductory texts such as Wonnacott and Wonnacott (1979) and Samuelson and Nordhaus (1985) deal with macroeconomics together with microeconomics. Dornbusch and Fisher (1994) is an intermediate macroeconomics text.

9 The optimal growth literature is difficult, using relatively advanced mathematics. See, for example, Chapter 16 in Intriligator (1971) for a brief but rigorous treatment of the standard neoclassical model. Chapter 7 in Common (1988a) covers the basic ideas without advanced mathematics, and relates optimal growth to resource depletion. See also Common (1985).

10 Dornbusch and Fisher (1994) give an introduction to growth theory and accounting in Chapter 17. Maddison (1991) uses growth accounting techniques to look at the historical situation in several industrial economies.

11 The first widely used undergraduate textbook in public sector economics was published in 1959: Musgrave (1959). A good modern text at an introductory level is Stiglitz (1986). Atkinson and Stiglitz (1980) is a standard graduate text.

12 Some public sector economists recognise 'merit goods', where decisions about the level of provision are to be taken outside of a strict application of the consumer sovereignty principle. Merit goods may be bads, and need not be public in nature. Education is not non-rival in consumption, but is often treated as a merit good. This is now less frequent than was once the case, as many of the reasons for so treating it can be captured within the externality framework. Tobacco and alcohol consumption are sometimes treated as merit bads. Again, the perceived need to treat these as merit bads has lessened with the realisation that the externality framework can capture many of the objections to these forms of consumption.

13 See, for example, Downs (1957), Buchanan and Tullock (1962), and Buchanan and Tullock (1980).

14 The chapter by Everret in Dietz et al. (1993) analyses the history of environmental legislation in the United States over the period from 1970 to 1990 in terms of the relative effectiveness of environmentalists and industrial interests.

15 Nelson (1987) looks at the role of economists as a pressure group in influencing choice of environmental policy instruments in the United States. McCloskey (1985) argues that economics should be regarded as rhetoric.

Chapter 7

1 The terminology and understanding originate with Hardin (1968).

2 Clark (1976), Dasgupta (1982) and Conrad and Clark (1987) consider renewable resource exploitation, making use of relatively advanced mathematics. Fisher (1981) and Hartwick and Oliwiler (1986) are graduate texts, which use some mathematics. Tietenberg (1992) and Common (1988a) provide introductory, non-mathematical treatments. Anderson (1985) uses the theory to explore Canadian policy issues.

3 For fuller accounts of the Coase theorem see for example, Common (1988a) Hartwick and Oliwiler (1986), Tietenberg (1992).

4 Non-use or passive use value is frequently regarded as comprising three distinct types of value: existence value, option value and quasi-option value. See, for example, Pearce et al. (1989), Cummings et al. (1986), Mitchell and Carson (1989), Randall (1986). However, in applications of CVM, these are rarely estimated separately. Typically, what is estimated is 'total non-use value'.

5 For an explanation of the travel cost method, see Common (1988a).

6 See Common et al. (1993) for a review of some of the related literature, and further discussion. Sagoff is a philosopher. Goodin (1991) and Norton (1986) are other contributions from philosophers in this area.

7 But see Common et al. (1993), or Blamey and Common (1994) where a small experiment is reported, which found that some 65 per cent of respondents considered that a preservation issue should be decided politically rather than by a market test.

8 See Anderson in Bennett and Block (1991) and Anderson and Leal (1991), Chapter 6 especially, for examples of such activity.

9 See Baumol and Oates (1979) and Bohm and Russell (1985).

10 See Common (1988a) for an introductory treatment of this theorem. See also Common (1989) and Cropper and Oates (1992) for further discussion and references to the literature.

11 Cropper and Oates (1992) discuss the use of economic instruments mainly in relation to pollution control: see also Tietenberg (1992) and Opschor and Vos (1989). James (1993) surveys the situation in Australia in relation to the use of economic instruments for environmental objectives, noting their use for pollution control, for irrigation water allocation, and for some fisheries. On the latter see also Part 5 of Wallace (1992). James notes that with respect to amenity services from publicly owned environmental assets, what is involved is user charges for cost recovery rather than charges intended to ration use. Chapter 8 in Moran et al. (1991) describes the use of tradeable permits in the control of a New Zealand fishery.

12 The foundations of cost-benefit analysis are discussed in Mishan (1975), and see also Pearce and Nash (1981).

13 In the interest of getting at the basic ideas, the treatment here of the NPV and rate of return criteria ignores a number of complexities and difficulties. For further discussion see Mishan (1975), Pearce and Nash (1981).

14 See Mishan (1975), and Sugden and Williams (1978).

15 See Chapter 8 of Common (1988a) for a brief introduction to the basic issues involved. Taking matters much beyond this gets quite technical. Pearce and Nash (1981) review some alternative approaches in Chapter 9. Lind (1982) contains an excellent and comprehensive overview as well as several interesting contributions, but is heavy-going for the uninitiated. See also Lind (1990).

16 See Pearce and Nash (1981) for discussion in the CBA context.

17 A concise overview of game theory and its applications in economics is Weintraub (1975). Binmore (1992) is more up-to-date and comprehensive, but more difficult. Game theory has also been used in biology: Maynard Smith (1982).

18 Originally proposed by Ciriacy-Wantrup (1968) and developed by Bishop (1978). See also Randall (1986).

19 See the references from Note 2 for a fuller treatment of the issues discussed here.

20 Actually this is a major oversimplification. The rate of return also depends on the price that caught fish sell for, and the cost of catching fish.

21 This is not strictly true where it is recognised that the rate of return to fish investment depends on things other than g. In the more general case where the rate of return depends on costs and price, equating it to r can lead to S above, at, or below S_{msy}. However, the effects in the more general case of increasing r are as described in the text for the special case.

22 This was demonstrated in Forster (1975).

23 For a fuller discussion at an introductory level see Chapters 6 and 7 of Common (1988a). Hartwick and Oliwiler (1986) is a standard intermediate level text: see also Fisher (1981). Hartwick (1989) is a concise mathematical treatment: see also Conrad and Clark (1987), Chapter 3, and Dasgupta (1982).

24 This is at the level of principle. In practice, it is very difficult to identify the rent element in the accounts of firms operating oil deposits, so that the tax base is actually defined in some other way. We are also ignoring such matters as risk and exploration incentives: see Garnaut and Clunies-Ross (1975). For discussion of resource rent taxation in practice see Anderson (1985), Chapter 5 especially.

25 See Baines and Peet in Dietz et al. (1993), Peet (1992) and Jacobs (1991).

Chapter 8

1 The quotation is from Repetto et al. (1989), where revised national income estimates for Indonesia are reported. For similar critiques of current national income accounting conventions see, for examples, Daly and Cobb (1989), Jacobs (1991), Pearce et al. (1989), and Anderson (1991).

2 The description of standard national income accounting conventions given here is necessarily brief and incomplete. Macroeconomics texts, such as Dornbusch and Fisher (1994) for example, go into more detail on principles and practice. Beckerman (1980) is a thorough exposition of the principles and practice of national income accounting. Usher (1980) examines the

basis for placing a welfare interpretation on national income measures, and considers some issues relating to resource depletion.

3 See, for example, Mishan (1967), Zolotas (1981), and Daly and Cobb (1989).

4 The description of such proposals given here is based on Bartelmus et al. (1992): see also Lutz (1993) and Ahmad et al. (1989). While these proposals indicate how it is envisaged that PNDP could be measured, there is a view among many national income accounting experts that actually following them would be impracticable, and would interfere with the effectiveness of the published data for its original purpose. There is, on this view, much to be said for collecting and publishing data on stocks of environmental assets, but this data should be kept separate from the main national income data and published as satellite accounts. Economists have considered the requirements for PNDP measurement from a theoretical perspective: see, for example, Mäler (1991). This work is discussed in Common et al. (1993), where it is noted that the results arising depend upon the specification of the model used, and that there is no uniquely correct model.

5 Common and Perrings (1992) show formally that honouring consumer sovereignty does not generally imply meeting sustainability requirements.

6 See Pearce et al. (1989) and Peskin with Lutz (1990).

7 See Parker and Hope (1992) for a survey of the state of the environmental reporting around the world. Friend and Rapport (1991) discuss information requirements, and availability, for sustainability. Common and Norton (1993) discuss information requirements for biodiversity conservation.

8 See for example, Anderson (1991) and Young (1990, 1992).

9 Figures 2.1 and 2.2 gave the results of an energy accounting for the production of commodities in Australia, such that direct and indirect energy inputs are accounted for. Results from similar exercises for the United States and Germany are reported in Thomas (1977).

10 MJ stands for megajoule, where the joule is a basic unit of energy measurement, and mega means 10^6 so that one megajoule is one million joules. For a discussion of energy units and conversion factors, see for example, Hall et al. (1992), Ramage (1983), or Slesser (1978).

11 See Bayliss-Smith (1982), Gifford (1976), and Hall et al. (1992).

12 See Lawton (1973), where a discussion of animal food acquisition is explicitly linked to the energy accounting of agriculture in the United Kingdom.

13 Net energy analysis is discussed and used in Chapters 9, 10 and 14 in Thomas (1977). EROI is discussed in Hall et al. (1992).

14 It is a problem in considering energy analysis results that different studies use different conventions as to what is included, and as to the setting of the boundaries for the system under consideration. Consequently it is possible to find in the literature apparently contradictory results for the same system.

15 For fuller, but non-technical, treatments of aspects of thermodynamics, see, for example, Hall et al. (1992), Peet (1992), Ramage (1983), and Slesser (1978).

16 Nicholas Georgescu-Roegen trained originally as a physicist. The quotation here is from Georgescu-Roegen (1979). The view that it encapsulates is set out more fully in Georgescu-Roegen (1971), and see also Georgescu-Roegen (1976) where the entropy law provides the basis for a critical appraisal of the reaction of most economists to Meadows et al. (1972).

17 Apparently there is now a view that the origin of natural gas is geological rather than biological, with the implication that it may exist in much larger quantities than currently understood. This is not, apparently, generally accepted.

18 In economics it is sometimes envisaged, in abstract models, that positive use of a finite stock of a resource can last indefinitely. This arises by having the usage rate go to zero 'asymptotically', that is it approaches zero but never actually becomes zero in finite time. In such a case, for most of the future, the usage rate is infinitesimally small. While this may make for mathematical elegance and tractability, it clearly has nothing to do with the world in which we live. Of course, as fossil stocks are depleted so the price will rise and use be reduced, falling gradually over time. As unrealistic as the asymptotic approach to zero is, the idea that the world will one day be confronted with a sudden transition from extensive to zero use of fossil fuels.

19 For fuller discussion see O'Connor (1993), and Proops (1985, 1987).

20 This is the title of a non-specialist book about the thermodynamics of far-from-equilibrium systems: Prigogine and Stengers (1984).

21 This number is taken from Chapman and Roberts (1983), Chapter six, where there is a more thorough examination of the limits to the efficiency of energy transformations.

22 The discussion here is based on Chapman and Roberts (1983), where more detail can be found.

23 This estimate is from Ramage (1983). Differing estimates can be found in the literature. Clearly, one important factor is where in the world one considers the solar system to be. This estimate is said to be for the sunniest part of the world. For further analysis and estimates, see, for example, Hall et al. (1992).

24 The original article is Costanza (1980). The rejection of the claim is Huettner (1982), which is immediately followed in the journal by a reply from Costanza. See also Hall et al. (1992).

25 An example of the former claim is Hannon (1975): 'In the long run we must adopt energy as a standard of value'. A representative exposition of the latter claim is Gilliland (1975).

26 These data are taken from Georgescu-Roegen (1975) and Ramage (1983). One Quad is 1.055 ExaJoules, i.e. 1.055×10^{18} Joules.

27 See, for example, Webb and Pearce in Thomas (1977).

28 This is the essence of the argument advanced for net energy analysis by Gilliland (1975).

29 These quotations are taken from Young (1993), which contains several other statements culled from international agreements and declarations. See also Cameron and Abouchar (1991).

30 See Perrings (1989), Costanza and Perrings (1990), and Perrings (1991). These bonds are an updating and a generalisation of earlier proposals for material user fees: Mills (1972) and Solow (1971). Both can be seen as extensions of the idea of refundable deposits paid on potential waste, such as glass bottles, which have a long history in many countries.

31 It has been convenient to discuss environmental performance bonds in relation to projects and their approval. However, the basic strategy involved could be extended to ongoing activities in production and consumption. See Costanza and Perrings (1990).

32 A partial analogy is the posting of damage bonds by persons renting accommodation. Here, however, the size of the bond is set at the expected

amount of damage rather than the maximum conceivable amount of damage. There is, in this case, previous experience on which to assess probabilities of different amounts of damage.

33 The references on environmental bonds cited thus far have all been concerned to argue their merits. Shogren et al. (1993) raise some potential problems attending their use.

34 This definition is attributed to Haeckel who coined the term 'ecology' in the nineteenth century. A more modern definition is from Krebs (1972): 'Ecology is the scientific study of the interactions that determine the distribution and abundance of organisms'.

35 This might be taken to imply that ecological economics began with the formation of the society and the first issue of the journal. As several of the contributions to that issue make clear, this is not the case. Martinez-Alier (1987) surveys the work of a number of writers in the nineteenth and early twentieth centuries who approached human affairs from an energetic perspective.

36 Norgaard (1989) argues that the discipline must embrace methodological pluralism rather than strive for the methodological uniformity characteristic of standard economics.

Chapter 9

1 The idea of sustainability as a contestable concept is taken from Jacobs (1991). Jacobs discusses sustainable development as a contestable concept, arguing that its core meaning comprises three elements: the entrenchment of environmental considerations in economic policy-making; an inescapable commitment to equity; the distinction between economic growth and economic development.

2 This quotation is from Townsend (1979, p.31). Townsend reported the results of a survey in the United Kingdom which used this concept of poverty as opposed to a concept based on the consumption of some basket of commodities taken to be necessary for subsistence. The notion of poverty as relative deprivation has a long history in economics. It goes back to Adam Smith. Smith noted that the Romans and Greeks lived comfortably though they had no linen whereas, 'in the present time, through the greater part of Europe, a creditable day-labourer would be ashamed to appear in public without a linen shirt', and that the necessities of life were 'not only the commodities indispensably necessary for the support of life, but whatever the custom of the country renders it indecent for creditable people, even of the lowest order, to be without'. These remarks from Smith are quoted in Townsend (1985), where some of the subtleties of a distinction between an absolute and relative concept of poverty are raised.

3 Young (1992), Chapter 4, discusses a range of property rights regimes in relation to sustainability objectives, including temporary and conditional private rights.

4 This view is rarely stated explicitly. One notes, however, that many contributions to the sustainability literature have relatively little to say about policy instruments, concentrating rather on stating the nature of the problem and generalised appeals for more enlightened attitudes and behaviour. A notable example is Meadows et al. (1992), which devotes almost no attention to policy instruments for the transition to sustainability.

5 The empirical evidence on this and on the effects of taxation on savings behaviour, is mixed and inconclusive. See Atkinson and Stiglitz (1980).

6 This proposal first appeared in Boulding (1964). See also Daly and Cobb (1989).

7 See, for example, Bernstam (1991). Cairncross (1992) discusses government failure in relation to the environment in western industrial economies, in Chapter 3, especially in regard to energy and agricultural policies.

8 This discussion has not been confined to the academic literature. Nor has advocacy of carbon taxation been confined to the radical fringe. *The Economist* has taken up the cause, and published a number of editorials and articles over the past four years urging the case for carbon/energy as tax base, particularly in relation to the reduction of the US deficit. See, for example, the issues for 21 July 1990 and 12 June 1993. The environment editor for *The Economist* considers green taxes as a source of revenue in Cairncross (1992).

9 The basis for this is an assumed world price of oil of A$25 per barrel. There is already some fossil fuel taxation in place in Australia, but we ignore this here to keep matters simple. This means that the fuel price increases given in Table 9.1 overstate those which purchasers would actually face.

10 The chapter by Barrett in Pearce et al. (1991) gives illustrative calculations of the same sort as those in Table 9.2 here, where the fact that the fossil fuels have differing carbon contents is allowed for. It is then necessary to allow for possible substitutions between the fossil fuels, as well as reduced total fossil fuel use. This means considering cross-price elasticities of demand as well as the own-price elasticities.

11 The methods are described in Common and Salma (1992a) and in Proops et al. (1992).

12 See Fisher and Smith (1982), Hall et al. (1992), and Priest (1984). Useful articles also appear in the *Annual Review of Energy and the Environment.*

13 Common (1985) reports results on the regressive impact of higher energy prices in the United Kingdom, which are summarised in Chapter 7 of Common (1988a).

14 The welfare measure used in this study was household expenditure net of indirect tax payments. The rationale for this measure of household welfare is discussed below in connection with Table 9.7, where it is referred to as effective income.

15 In Australia it was claimed that the Toronto target for carbon dioxide emissions reduction could be met, by energy conservation and fuel switching so as to save, rather than cost, billions of dollars. This claim was vigorously disputed by a number of economists. The debate was never properly resolved, with participants using different tests of such matters as cost effectiveness, and different project appraisal methods. The situation appears similar in other countries. The *Energy Journal* regularly contains articles addressing these issues. In the 1987, 1988 and 1989 volumes there is an exchange between Amory Lovins, a noted proponent of the 'free lunch' case, and an energy economist. Here too the outcome is inconclusive.

16 In a study of the effects of carbon taxation on the Norwegian economy using an applied general equilibrium model, Glomsrod et al. (1990) estimated the environmental benefits, other than carbon dioxide emissions reductions, to amount to some 65 per cent of the national income cost. Benefits on account of reductions in carbon dioxide emissions are extremely difficult to quantify, for reasons to be discussed in the next chapter.

17 Barker and Lewney (1991) report results for the United Kingdom from a dynamic model. Despite the fact that what is considered is the unilateral

adoption of carbon taxation by the United Kingdom, implying a loss of competitiveness in international trade, the results show a negligible impact on the national income growth rate.

18 The model for the United States constructed by Boyd and Uri (1991) distinguishes households at different positions in the distribution of income, and can therefore consider regressivity. For energy taxation, Boyd and Uri find no regressive impact when substitutions in production and consumption are allowed for. This would be expected to carry over to carbon taxation.

19 Studies of the national cost of reducing carbon dioxide emissions by means of carbon taxation vary not only in the nature and numerical specifications of the models used, but also in the scenario modelled. There are two main features of the scenarios. First, the size of the reduction in carbon dioxide emissions targeted, or (equivalently) of the tax imposed. Second, whether they involve the nation acting unilaterally or in concert with others. The cost increases with the target reduction/ tax rate. Unilateral action is usually found to cost more, on account of its effects on competitiveness in international trade. Given the different models and different scenarios, there is a wide range of cost results. The chapter by Winters in Anderson and Blackhurst (1992) summarises the results from a number of studies.

20 Table 9.7 is based on data originally collected on a household basis, so that the quintiles actually refer to household rather than individual incomes. The household data were converted to the per person basis using the figures for the number of persons per household shown in Table 9.7.

21 The proposal actually goes under a variety of names. The most commonly used alternatives are **social dividends** and **guaranteed incomes**. Details of proposals going under one of these three names vary, but each refers to essentially the same thing. A related, but substantially different, proposal is for negative income taxation. Walter (1989) discusses the history of the basic incomes proposal, and differentiates it from the negative income tax proposal. Meade (1975) and Meade (1978) deal with a social dividend proposal in some detail. Daly and Cobb (1989) consider negative income taxation in the context of sustainability.

22 Not all basic incomes advocates recognise this dilemma. Meade (1975) does and resolves it in favour of paying on account of children at the adult rate, arguing that moral suasion type instruments to reduce procreation be employed together with a basic income scheme.

23 Daly and Cobb (1989) see a major threat to sustainability as coming from assertive individualism, which standard economic analysis and policy prescription does much to promote. They argue that what is needed is a greater sense of individuals in communities, and advocate negative income taxation as a means to promoting this. See also Walter (1989).

24 This is emphasised in Johnson (1973), where opportunities for community service are also discussed in relation to the natural environment.

Chapter 10

1 Exposition of the theory of comparative advantage will be found in any introductory economics text: see, for example, Wonnacott and Wonnacott (1979), or Samuelson and Nordhaus (1985). The principle has a long history in economics. It was first expounded by Ricardo in 1817.

2 Daly and Cobb (1989) develop this argument at greater length, from a United States perspective, in Chapter 11.

3 For further discussion on trade and debt in relation to developing nations, see: George (1988), Mendez (1992), United Nations Development Programme (1992), and World Commission on Environmental and Development (1987). See also Chapter 2 here.

4 To provide some perspective, French (1993) notes that in 1991 world seaborne trade used an amount of energy equivalent to that consumed in Brazil and Turkey combined, and that the energy used in air transport was equivalent to consumption by the Philippines.

5 During (1992) discusses international trade in exotic consumption goods. In 1989, 'Americans bought 190 million litres of imported water' (p.73). The trade is not confined to food and drink. 'Even the flowers that decorate the tables of the consumer class come from afar: European winter supplies are flown in from farms in Kenya, while American winter supplies are flown from Columbia' (p.75).

6 The standard economic analysis of trade and the environment is covered in several chapters in Anderson and Blackhurst (1992). In the no spillovers case, one of the simplifying assumptions required to get the results in the text here is that both countries are 'small', that is that they cannot affect the world price of widgets by their own behaviour. The small country assumption is directly analogous to the price-taker assumption for firms. The analysis is more complicated, and outcomes less clear-cut, where countries are not small in this sense.

7 Pearce (1987) provides a useful overview of the nature of the acid rain phenomenon. Mäler (1990) considers international environmental problems and, particularly, the acid rain problem in Europe.

8 Anderson and Blackhurst (1992) report the results of two case studies where it is claimed that trade liberalisation would reduce global environmental damage. The first concerns the abolition of subsidies to coal production, the second the abolition of subsidies to agriculture.

9 Mendez (1992) is an argument for the development of just such an international system.

10 Dicken (1992) p.49. See also a special feature in *The Economist*, 27 March 1993.

11 For fuller accounts see, for examples: Legget (1990), Henderson-Sellers and Blong (1989), Houghton et al. (1990), and Houghton et al. (1992).

12 The existence of the greenhouse effect has been known since the beginning of this century. In 1896, the Swedish chemist Arrhenius published a paper in which he argued that a doubling of the atmospheric concentration of carbon dioxide would lead to an increase in mean surface temperature of $4°$ to $6°C$.

13 See Houghton et al. (1990), or the introductory chapter in Leggett (1990).

14 These models are discussed in simple terms in Henderson-Sellers and Blong (1989), where they are called global climate models, and in Schneider's chapter in Leggett (1990).

15 See the chapter by Leggett in Leggett (1990) for further discussion and references.

16 See also section two of Leggett (1990), especially the chapter by Woodwell.

17 These examples are mainly taken from Schelling (1984), where a similar typology of responses was introduced. Schelling splits prevention policy into two categories, one intended to reduce carbon dioxide generation, the other to reduce atmospheric concentrations.

18 Removing carbon dioxide from smokestacks and dumping it as carbon would appear to be very expensive, and perhaps of problematical long-term effectiveness. Reforestation is discussed, for example, in Sedjo (1989). Read (1993) argues that a global programme to replace fossil fuels with wood as the dominant energy source is feasible, would be cost-effective, and have inequality-reducing benefits.

19 The scenario reported here is taken from the chapter by Kelley in Leggett (1990). See also Houghton et al. (1990).

20 Nordhaus (1991) does not give the figure for carbon dioxide emissions reduction in this case. Inspection of Figure 3 in the published paper suggests a reduction of the order of 20 per cent.

21 A study by Cline (1992), for a temperature increase of 2.5°C, puts the total cost to the United States at 1.1 per cent of national income, plus or minus an unknown range of error.

22 Actually the time preference rate concerns utility levels rather than consumption levels, with utility assumed to be a function of consumption. The consumption discount rate then also depends on a parameter which describes how the marginal utility derived from consumption declines as consumption increases. This is ignored here in the interests of simplicity.

23 For a given quantity of a given fossil fuel – black coal, brown coal, natural gas, oil – the carbon dioxide released on combustion is known within fairly close limits. There is some variation according to combustion conditions and the fuel grade or quality. Hence, such indirect emissions-monitoring would not be exact. However, monitoring actual emissions would be expensive, and given all the uncertainties attending the enhanced greenhouse problem, the inexactitudes involved in indirect monitoring would not be important. Virtually all discussion of carbon dioxide emissions control assumes actual control of fossil fuel combustion.

24 Whalley and Wigle (1991). This model is briefly described in Piggott Whalley and Wigle's chapter in Anderson and Blackhurst (1992).

Postscript

1 The convention does not say this explicitly. For the 'developed country Parties', Commitment 2a refers to 'the return by the end of the present decade to earlier levels', and Commitment 2b to 'their 1990 levels'. This has generally been interpreted as meaning a commitment to return to 1990 levels by 2000. The convention does not specify any penalties for non-compliance, and does not say that account will be taken of the individual circumstances of these Parties.

2 Porter and Brown (1991) is an excellent introduction to global environmental politics, which documents a number of international environmental agreements prior to Rio 1992, and discusses the role of such institutions as the World Bank and the General Agreement on Tariffs and Trade (the GATT). See also Mendez (1992).

References

ABARE, *see* Australian Bureau of Agricultural and Resource Economics.

ABS, *see* Australian Bureau of Statistics.

Ahmad, Y., El Serafy, S. and Lutz, E. (eds) 1989. *Environmental accounting for sustainable development: A UNDP–World Bank Symposium.* Washington D.C.: World Bank.

Anderson, F. J. 1985. *Natural resources in Canada: economic theory and policy.* Toronto: Methuen.

Anderson, V. 1991. *Alternative economic indicators.* London: Routledge.

Anderson, K. and Blackhurst, R. (eds) 1992. *The greening of world trade issues.* New York: Harvester Wheatsheaf.

Anderson, T. L. and Leal, D. R. 1991. *Free market environmentalism.* Boulder: Westview Press.

Argyle, M. 1987. *The psychology of happiness.* London: Methuen.

Arndt, H. W. 1978. *The rise and fall of economic growth: a study in contemporary thought.* Sydney: Longman Cheshire.

Atkinson, A. B. and Stiglitz, J. E. 1980. *Lectures on public economics.* Singapore: McGraw-Hill.

Australian Bureau of Agricultural and Resource Economics 1991. *Projections of energy demand and supply, Australia, 1990–91 to 2004–5.* Canberra: ABARE.

Australian Bureau of Agricultural and Resource Economics 1992. *Natural resource management: an economic perspective.* Canberra: ABARE.

Australian Bureau of Statistics 1990a. *Australian national accounts: input–output tables 1986–87.* Canberra: ABS.

Australian Bureau of Statistics 1990b. *1988–89 Household expenditure survey, Australia: detailed expenditure items.* Canberra: ABS.

Australian Bureau of Statistics 1992. *1990–91 Australian national income accounts: national income and expenditure.* Canberra: ABS.

Australian Bureau of Statistics 1993a. *Year Book Australia 1992.* Canberra: ABS.

Australian Bureau of Statistics 1993b. *1990–91 Australian economic indicators: January/February 1993.* Canberra: ABS.

Balling Jnr, R. C. 1992. *The heated debate: greenhouse prediction versus climate reality.* San Francisco: Pacific Research Institute for Public Policy.

Barbier, E. B. 1989. *Economics natural resource scarcity and development.* London: Earthscan.

Barbier, E. B., Burgess, J. C. and Folke, C. 1994. *Paradise lost? The ecological economics of biodiversity*. London: Earthscan

Barbier, E. B., Burgess, J. C., Swanson, T. M. and Pearce, D. W. 1990. *Elephants economics and ivory*. London: Earthscan.

Barker, T. and Lewney, R. 1991. 'A green scenario for the UK economy', in T. Barker (ed.) *Green futures for economic growth*. Cambridge: Cambridge Econometrics.

Barnett, H. 1979. 'Scarcity and growth revisited', in V. K. Smith (ed.) *Scarcity and growth reconsidered*. Balitmore: Johns Hopkins University Press.

Barnett, H. and Morse, C. 1963. *Scarcity and growth: the economics of natural resource availability*. Baltimore: Johns Hopkins University Press.

Bartelmus, P., Stahmer, C. and Van Tongeren, J. 1989. Integrated environmental and economic accounting, Paper presented to 21st General Conference of the International Association for Research in Income and Wealth, August. Lahnstein.

Baumol, W. J. and Oates, W. E. 1979. *Economics environmental policy and the quality of life*. Englewood Cliffs: Prentice Hall.

Baumol, W. J. and Oates, W. E. 1988. *The theory of environmental policy* (2nd edn). Cambridge: Cambridge University Press.

Bayliss-Smith, T.P. 1982. *The ecology of agricultural systems*. Cambridge: Cambridge University Press.

Beckerman, W. 1972. 'Economists, scientists and environmental catastrophe' *Oxford Economic Papers*, 24: 237–244.

Beckerman, W. 1974. *In defence of economic growth*. London: Jonathan Cape.

Beckerman, W. 1980. *Introduction to national income analysis*. (3rd edn), London: Wiedenfield and Nicolson.

Bennett, J. and Block, W. (eds) 1991. *Reconciling economics and the environment*. Melbourne: Institute of Public Affairs.

Berndt, E. R. and Field, B. C. 1981. *Modelling and measuring natural resource substitution*. Cambridge, Mass: The MIT Press.

Bernstam, M. S. 1991. *The wealth of nations and the environment*. London: Institute of Economic Affairs.

Biancardi, C., Tiezzi, E. and Ulgiati, S. 1993. 'Complete recycling of matter in the frameworks of physics, biology and ecological economics', *Ecological Economics*, 8: 1–5.

Binmore, K. 1992. *Fun and games: A text in game theory*. Lexington: D. C. Heath.

Bishop, R. C. 1978. 'Endangered species and uncertainty: the economics of a safe minimum standard', *American Journal of Agricultural Economics*, 60: 10–18.

Blainey, G. 1975. *Triumph of the nomads: a history of ancient Australia*. Melbourne: Sun Books.

Blamey, R. and Common, M. S. 1994. 'Sustainability and the limits to pseudo-market valuation', in J. C. J. M. van den Bergh and J. van der Straaten (eds) *Concepts methods and policy for sustainable development: critique and new approaches*. Washington D.C.: Island Press.

Blaug, M. 1985. *Economic theory in retrospect* (4th edn). Cambridge: Cambridge University Press.

Bohm, P. and Russell, C. C. 1985. 'Comparative analysis of alternative policy instruments', in A. V. Kneese and J. L. Sweeney (eds) *Handbook of natural resource and energy economics Volume I*. Amsterdam: North-Holland.

Boulding, K. E. 1964. *The meaning of the twentieth century*. New York: Harper & Row.

Bowler, P. J. 1992. *The Fontana history of the environmental sciences.* London: Fontana.

Boyd, R. and Uri, N. D. 1991. 'The impact of a broad based energy tax on the US economy', *Energy Economics,* 13: 258–273.

Boyden, S. 1987. *Western civilization in biological perspective: patterns in biohistory.* Oxford: Oxford University Press.

Boyden, S., Dovers, S. and Shirlow, M. 1990. *Our biosphere under threat: ecological realities and Australia's opportunities.* Melbourne: Oxford University Press.

Brown Jnr, G. M. and Field, B. C. 1978. 'Implications of alternative measures of natural resource scarcity', *Journal of Political Economy,* 86: 229–243.

Buchanan, J. M. and Tullock, G. 1962. *The calculus of consent.* Anne Arbor: University of Michigan Press.

Buchanan, J. M. and Tullock, G. 1980. *Toward a theory of the rent seeking society.* Texas: A & M Press.

Cairncross, F. 1992. *Costing the earth: the challenge for governments, the opportunities for business.* Boston: Harvard Business School.

Cameron, J. and Aboucher, J. 1991. 'The precautionary principle: a fundamental principle of law and policy for the protection of the global environment', *Boston College International and Comparative Law Review,* 14: 1–27.

Carson, R. 1967. *Silent spring.* Harmondsworth: Penguin.

Chapman, P. 1975. *Fuel's paradise: energy options for Britain.* Harmondsworth: Penguin.

Chapman, P. F. and Roberts, F. 1983. *Metal resources and energy.* London: Butterworths.

Cipolla, C. 1962. *The economic history of world population.* London: Penguin.

Ciriacy-Wantrup, S. V. 1968. *Resource conservation: economics and politics.* Los Angeles: University of California.

Clark, C. W. 1976. *Mathematical bioeconomics: the optimal management of bioeconomic resources.* New York: Wiley–Interscience.

Clark, J. and Cole, S. with Curnow, R. and Hopkins, M. 1975. *Global simulation models: a comparative study.* London: John Wiley and Sons.

Cleveland, C. J. 1992. 'Energy quality and energy surplus in the extraction of fossil fuels in the U.S.', *Ecological Economics,* 6: 139–160.

Cleveland, C. J. 1993. 'An exploration of alternative measures of natural resource scarcity: the case of petroleum resources in the U.S.', *Ecological Economics,* 7: 123–157.

Cleveland, C. J., Costanza, R., Hall, C. A. S. and Kaufman, R. 1984. 'Energy and the U.S. economy: A biophysical perspective', *Science,* 225: 890–7.

Cleveland, C. J. and Stern, D. I. 1993. 'Productive and exchange scarcity: an empirical analysis of the US forest products industry', *Canadian Journal of Forest Research,* 23: 1–13.

Cline, W. R. 1992a. *Global warming: the benefits of emission abatement.* Paris: OECD.

Cline, W. R. 1992b. *The economics of global warming.* Washington D.C.: Institute for International Economics.

Coase, R. H. 1960. 'The problem of social cost', *Journal of Law and Economics,* 3: 1–44.

Cohen, M. N. 1977. *The food crisis in prehistory: overpopulation and the origins of agriculture.* New Haven: Yale University Press.

Cole, H. S. D., Freeman, C., Jahoda, M. and Pavitt, K. L. R. (eds) 1973. *Thinking about the future: a critique of the limits to growth.* London: Chatto & Windus.

Common, M. S. 1977. 'A note on the use of taxes to control pollution', *Scandinavian Journal of Economics*, 79: 346–9.

Common, M. S. 1981. 'Implied elasticities in some UK energy projections', *Energy Economics*, 3: 154–9.

Common, M. S. 1983. 'The implications of discounting under varying technological and preference regimes', *International Journal of Environmental Studies*, 21: 87–105.

Common, M. S. 1985. 'The distributional implications of higher energy prices in the UK', *Applied Economics*, 17: 421–36.

Common, M. S. 1988a. *Environmental and resource economics: an introduction.* Harwell: Longman,

Common, M. S. 1988b. 'Poverty and Progress revisited', in D. Collard, D. Pearce, and D. Ulph (eds) *Economic growth and sustainable environments.* Basingstoke: Macmillan.

Common, M. S. 1989. 'The choice of pollution control instruments: why is so little notice taken of economists' recommendations?', *Environment and Planning A*, 21: 1297–1314.

Common, M. S. 1993. 'A cost effective environmentally adjusted economic performance indicator', Discussion Papers in Environmental Economics and Environmental Management, Number 9307, University of York.

Common, M. S., Blamey, R. and Norton, T. 1993. 'Sustainability and environmental valuation', *Environmental Values*, 2: 299–334.

Common, M. S. and Norton, T. 1992. 'Biodiversity: its conservation in Australia; *Ambio*, XXI: 258-65.

Common, M. S. and Norton, T. 1994. 'Biodiversity natural resource accounting and environmental monitoring', in C. Perrings, K-G Mäler, C. Folke, C. S. Holling and B-O. Jansson (eds) *Biodiversity conservation: policy issues and options.* Amsterdam: Kluwer.

Common, M. S. and Perrings, C. 1992. 'Towards an ecological economics of sustainability', *Ecological Economics*, 6: 7–34.

Common, M. S. and Salma, U. 1992a, 'Accounting for Australian carbon dioxide emissions', *The Economic Record*, 68: 31–42.

Common, M. S. and Salma, U. 1992b. *An economic analysis of Australian carbon dioxide emissions and energy use: report to the Energy Research and Development Corporation.* Canberra: Centre for Resource and Environmental Studies.

Commoner, B. 1963. *Science and survival.* New York: Ballantine.

Commoner, B. 1972. *The closing circle.* London: Jonathan Cape.

Conrad, J. M. and Clark, C. W. 1987. *Natural resource economics: notes and problems.* Cambridge: Cambridge University Press.

Conway, G. R. 1985. 'Agroecosystem analysis', *Agricultural Administration*, 20: 31–55.

Conway, G. R. 1987. 'The properties of agroecosystems', *Agricultural Systems*, 24: 95–117.

Costanza, R. 1980. 'Embodied energy and economic valuation', *Science*, 210: 1219–24.

Costanza, R., Farber, S. C. and Maxwell, J. 1989. 'Valuation and management of wetland ecosystems, *Ecological Economics* 1: 335–1.

Costanza, R. and Perrings, C. 1990. 'A flexible assurance bonding system for improved environmental management', *Ecological Economics* 2: 57–75.

Cropper, M. L. and Oates, W. E. 1992. 'Environmental economics: a survey'. *Journal of Economic Literature*, XXX: 675–740.

CSO. 1993. *Economic Trends Annual Supplement*. London: HMSO.

Cummings, R. G., Brookshire, D. S. and Schultze, W. D. (eds) 1986. *Valuing environmental goods: a state of the art assessment of the contingent valuation method*. Totowa: Rowman & Allanheld.

Daly, H. E. (ed.) 1973. *Toward a steady state economy*. San Francisco: W. H. Freeman.

Daly, H. E. and Cobb, J. B. 1989. *For the common good: redirecting the economy toward community, the environment and a sustainable future*. Boston: Beacon.

Dasgupta, P. 1982. *The control of resources*. Oxford: Basil Blackwell.

Deadman, D. and Turner, R. K. (eds) 1988. *Sustainable environmental management: principles and practice*. London: Bellhaven.

Department of Trade and Industry 1993. *Digest of United Kingdom energy statistics 1993*. London: HMSO.

Diamond, J. 1992. *The rise and fall of the third chimpanzee*. London: Vintage Press.

Dicken, P. 1992. *Global shift: the internationalization of economic activity* (Second Edition). London: Paul Chapman.

Dietz, F. J., Simonis, U. E. and van der Straaten, J. (eds) 1993. *Sustainability and environmental policy: restraints and advances*. Berlin: Edition Sigma.

Dingle, T. 1988. *Aboriginal economy*. Fitzroy: McPhee Gribble.

Dornbusch, R. and Fisher, S. 1994. *Macroeconomics* (6th edn). New York: McGraw-Hill.

Downs, A. 1957. *An economic theory of democracy*. New York: Harper & Row.

Durning, A. T. 1992. *How much is enough?: the consumer society and the future of the earth*. London: Earthscan.

Easterlin, R. A. 1974. 'Does Economic Growth Improve the Human Lot? Some Empirical Evidence', in P. A. David and M. W. Reader (eds) *Nations and household in economic growth*. New York: Academic Press.

Edmonds, J. A. and Reilly, J. M. 1983. 'A long-term global energy-economic model of carbon dioxide release from fossil fuel use', *Energy Economics*, April: 74–88.

Ehrlich, P. R. and Dailey, G. C. 1993. 'Population extinction and saving biodiversity', *Ambio*, XXII: 64–68.

Ehrlich, P. R. and Ehrlich, A. E. 1981. *Extinction: the causes and consequences of the disappearance of species*. New York: Random House.

Ehrlich, P. R. and Ehrlich, A. E. 1992. 'The value of biodiversity', *Ambio*, XXI: 219–226.

Ekins, P. and Max-Neef, M. 1992. *Real-life economics: understanding wealth creation*. London: Routledge.

Elton, B. 1993. *This other Eden*. New York: Pocket Books.

Faber, M. and Proops, J. 1991. 'National accounting, time and the environment', in R. Costanza (ed.) *Ecological economics: the science and management of sustainability*. New York: Columbia University Press.

Fisher, A. C. 1981. *Resource and environmental economics*. Cambridge: Cambridge University Press.

Fisher, A. C. and Smith, V. K. 1982. 'Economic evaluation of energy's environmental costs with special reference to air pollution', *Annual Review of Energy*, 7: 1–35.

Forster, B. A. 1975. 'Optimal pollution control with a non-constant exponential decay rate', *Journal of Environmental Economics and Management*, 2: 1–6.

French, H. F. 1993. *Costly tradeoffs: reconciling trade and the environment*. Washington D.C.: Worldwatch Institute.

Friend, A. M. and Rapport, D. J. 1991. 'Evolution of macro-information systems for sustainable development', *Ecological Economics*, 3: 59–76.

Galbraith, J. K. 1967. *The new industrial state*. London: Hamish Hamilton.

Garnaut, R. and Clunies Ross, A. 1975. 'Uncertainty risk aversion and the taxing of natural resource projects, *Economic Journal*, 85: 272–87.

George, S. 1988. *A fate worse than debt*. London: Penguin.

George, S. 1990. *Ill fares the land*. London: Penguin.

Georgescu-Roegen, N. 1971. *The entropy law and the economic process*. Cambridge: Harvard University Press.

Georgescu-Rogen, N. 1976. 'Energy and economic myths', in *Energy and economic myths: institutional and analytical essays*. New York: Pergamon.

Georgescu-Roegen, N. 1979. 'Energy analysis and economic valuation', *Southern Economic Journal*, 45: 1023–58.

Gifford R. M. (ed.) 1976. *Energy in agriculture*. Sydney: Australian and New Zealand Association for the Advancement of Science.

Gilliland, M. W. 1975. 'Energy analysis and public policy', *Science*, 189: 1051–56.

Glomsrod, S., Vennemo, H. and Johnsen, T. 1990. 'Stabilisation of emissions of CO_2: a computable general equilibrium assessment', Discussion Paper No. 48, Central Bureau of Statistics, Oslo.

Goldsmith, E., Allen, R., Allaby, M., Davoll, J. and Lawrence, S. 1972. *A blueprint for survival*. Harmondsworth: Penguin.

Goodin, R. E. 1991. 'A green theory of value', in D. J. Mulvaney (ed.) *The humanities and the Australian environment*. Canberra: Australian Academy of the Humanities.

Grubb, M. 1990a. 'The greenhouse effect: negotiating targets', *International Affairs*, 66: 67–89.

Grubb, M. 1990b. *Energy policies and the greenhouse effect: Volume 1 policy appraisal*. Aldershot: Dartmouth and Royal Insititute of International Affairs.

Hall, C. A. S., Cleveland, C. J. and Kaufmann, R. 1992. *Energy and resource quality: the ecology of the economic process*. Niwot: University of Colorado Press.

Hall, D. C. and Hall, J. V. 1984. 'Concepts and measures of natural resource scarcity with a summary of recent trends', *Journal of Environmental Economics and Management*, 11: 363–79.

Hannon, B. 1975. 'Energy conservation and the consumer', *Science*, 189: 95–102.

Hardin, G. 1968. 'The tragedy of the commons', *Science*, 162: 1243–8.

Hartwick, J. M. 1977. 'Intergenerational equity and the investing of rents from exhaustible resources' *American, Economic Review*, 66: 972–4.

Hartwick, J. M. 1989. *Non-renewable resources extraction programs and markets*. Chur: Harwood.

Hartwick, J .M. and Oliwiler, N. D. 1986. *The economics of natural resource use*. New York: Harper & Row.

Heilbronner, R. L. 1991. *The worldy philosophers: the lives times and ideas of the great economic thinkers*. London: Penguin.

Henderson-Sellers, A. and Blong, R. 1989. *The greenhouse effect: living in a warmer Australia*. Sydney: University of New South Wales.

Hirsch, F. 1977. *Social limits to growth*. London: Routledge & Kegan Paul.

Holister, G. and Porteus, A. 1976. *The environment: a dictionary of the world around us*. London: Arrow.

Holling, C. S. 1973. 'Resilience and stability of ecological systems', *Annual Review of Ecological Systems*, 4: 1–24.

Holling, C. S. 1986. 'The resilience of terrestrial ecosystems: local surprise and global change', in W. C. Clark and R. E. Munn (eds) *Sustainable development of the biosphere*. Cambridge: Cambridge University Press.

Houghton, J. T., Jenkins, G. J. and Ephraums, J. J. (eds) 1990. *Climate change: the IPCC scientfic assessment*. Cambridge: Cambridge University Press, for the Intergovernmental Panel on Climate Change.

Houghton, J. T., Callander, B. A. and Varney, S. K. (eds) 1992. *Climate change 1992: the supplementary report to the IPCC scientific assessment*. Cambridge: Cambridge University Press, for the Intergovernmental Panel on Climate Change.

Huettner, D. A. 1982. 'Economic Values and Embodied Energy', *Science*, 216: 1141-3.

Independent Commission on International Development Issues 1980. *North-south: a programme for survival*. London: Pan.

Industry Commission. 1991. *Costs and benefits of reducing greenhouse gas emissions*. Canberra: Australian Government Publishing Service.

International Union for Conseration of Nature and Natural Resources 1980. *World conservation strategy*. Gland: IUCN/UNEP/WWF.

Intriligator, M. D. 1971. *Mathematical optimization and economic theory*. Englewood Cliffs: Prentice-Hall.

Jacobs, M. 1991. *The green economy: environment sustainable development and the politics of the future*. London: Pluto.

Jaeger, J. 1988. *Developing policies for responding to climatic change*. Washington: World Meteorological Organisaton, WC1P-1, WMO/TD–No. 225.

James, D. 1993. *Australia's experience in using economic instruments for meeting environmental objectives*. Canberra: Department of Environment Sport and Territories.

Johnson, W. A. 1973. 'The guaranteed income as an environmental measure', in H. E. Daly (ed.) *Toward a steady state economy*. San Francisco: W. H. Freeman.

Keynes, J. M. 1931. *Essays in persuasion*. London: Macmillan.

Keynes J. M. 1936. *The general theory of employment interest and money*. London: Macmillan.

Kneese, A. V. 1977. *Economics and the environment*. London: Penguin.

Kneese, A. V., Ayers, R. V. and D'Arge, R. C. 1970. *Economics and the environment: a materials balance approach*. Washington D.C.: Resources for the Future.

Kormondy, E. J. 1969. *Concepts of ecology*. Englewood Cliffs: Prentice Hall.

Kravis, I. B., Kenessey, Z., Heston, A. and Summers, R. 1975. *A system of international comparisons of gross product and purchasing power*. Baltimore: Johns Hopkins University Press.

Krebs, C. J. 1972. *Ecology: the experimental analysis of distribution and abundance*. New York: Harper & Row.

Krutilla, J. and Fisher, A. C. 1975. *The economics of natural environments*. Baltimore: Johns Hopkins University Press.

Lane, R. E. 1991. *The market experience*. Cambridge: Cambridge University Press.

Lawton, J. H. 1973. 'The energy cost of food gathering', in B. Benjamin, P. R. Cox and J. Peel (eds), *Resources and population*. New York: Academic Press.

Layard, P. R. G.and Walters, A. A. 1978. *Microeconomic theory*. New York: McGraw-Hill.

Leach, G. 1975. *Energy and food production*. London: International Institute for Environment and Development.

Lee, R. B. and De Vore, I. (eds) 1968. *Man the hunter.* Chicago: Aldine.

Leggett, J. (ed.) 1990. *Global warming: the Greenpeace report.* Oxford: Oxford University Press.

Lind, R. C. (ed.) 1982. *Discounting for time and risk in energy policy.* Washington D.C.: Resources for the Future.

Lind, R. C. 1990. 'Reassessing the government's discount rate policy in light of new theory and data in a world economy with a high degree of capital mobility', *Journal of Environmental Economics and Management,* 18: 8–28.

Lovelock, J. E. 1979. *Gaia: A new look at life on earth.* Oxford: Oxford University Press.

Lovelock, J. E. 1988. *The ages of Gaia.* New York: Norton.

Lovins, A. B. 1975. *World energy strategies.* New York: Friends of the Earth.

Lovins, A. B. 1979. *Soft energy paths: towards a durable peace.* London: Harper & Row.

Lutz, E. (ed.) 1993. *Toward improved accounting for the environment: an UNSTAT-World Bank Symposium,* Washington D.C.: World Bank.

Lutz, M. A. and Lux, K. 1988. *Humanistic economics: the new challenge.* New York: Bootstrap Press.

McCloskey, D. N. 1985. *The rhetoric of economics.* Madison: University of Wisconsin Press.

McCormick, J. 1989. *The global environmental movement; reclaiming paradise.* London: Bellhaven Press.

Maddison, A. 1991. *Dynamic forces in capitalist development: a long-run comparative view.* Oxford: Oxford University Press.

Maddox, J. 1972. *The doomsday syndrome.* New York: McGraw-Hill.

Mäler, K-G. 1990. 'International environmental problems', *Oxford Review of Economic Policy,* 6: 80–107.

Mäler, K-G. 1991. 'National accounts and environmental resources', *Environmental and Resource Economics,* 1: 1–15.

Martinez-Alier, J. 1987. *Ecological economics.* London: Basil Blackwell.

May, R. M. 1973. *Stability and complexity in model ecosystems.* Princeton: Princeton University Press.

Maynard Smith, J. 1982. *Evolution and the theory of games.* Cambridge: Cambridge University Press.

Meade, J. E. 1975. *The intelligent radical's guide to economic policy: the mixed economy.* London: Allen & Unwin.

Meade, J. E. 1978. *The structure and reform of direct taxation.* London: Institute for Fiscal Studies.

Meadows, D. H., Meadows, D. L., Randers, J. and Behrens, W. W. 1972. *The limits to growth.* New York: Universe Books.

Meadows, D. H., Meadows, D. L. and Randers, J. 1992. *Beyond the limits: global collapse or a sustainable future.* London: Earthscan.

Mendez, R. P. 1992. *International public finance: a new perspective on global relations.* New York: Oxford University Press.

Mills, E. S. 1972. *Urban economics.* Glenview: Scott Foresman.

Mills, E. S. 1978. *The economics of environmental quality.* New York: Norton.

Mishan, E. J. 1967. *The costs of economic growth.* London: Staples Press.

Mishan, E. J. 1975. *Cost-benefit analysis.* London: Allen & Unwin.

Mitchell, R. C. and Carson, R. 1989. *Using surveys to value public goods: the contingent valuation method.* Washington D.C.: Resources for the Future.

Moran, A., Chisholm, A. and Porter, M. 1991. *Markets, resources and the environment.* Sydney: Allen & Unwin.

Musgrave, R. A. 1959. *The theory of public finance.* New York: McGraw-Hill.

Myers, N. 1979. *The sinking ark.* New York: Pergamon.

Myers, N. 1993. 'Biodiversity and the precautionary principle', *Ambio*, XXII: 74–9.

Nelson, R. H. 1987. 'The economics profession and the making of public policy', *Journal of Economic Literature*, XXV: 49–91.

Nordhaus, W. D. 1991. 'To slow or not to slow: the economics of the greenhouse effect', *The Economic Journal*, 101: 920–937.

Norgaard, R. B. 1989. 'The case for methodological pluralism', *Ecological Economics*, 1: 37–57.

Norton, B. G. 1986. 'On the inherent danger of undervaluing species', in B. G. Norton (ed.) *The preservation of species.* Princeton: Princeton University Press.

O'Connor, M. 1993. 'Entropy structure and organisational change', *Ecological Economics*, 3: 95–122.

Opschor, J. B. and Vos, H. B. 1989. *Economic instruments for environmental protection.* Paris: OECD.

Ozdemiroglu, E. 1993. *Measuring natural resource scarcity: a study of the price indicator.* CSERGE Working Paper GEC 93–14. London: Centre for Social and Economic Research on the Global Environment.

Panayotou, T. 1993. 'Empirical tests and policy analysis of environmental degradation at different stages of economic development'. Working Paper WEP 2–22/WP 238. Geneva: International Labour Office.

Parker, J. and Hope, C. 1992. 'The state of the environment: a survey of reports from around the world', *Environment*, 34: 19–21 and 39–44.

Patterson, W. C. 1983. *Nuclear power* (2nd edn). Harmondsworth: Penguin.

Pearce, D. W. (ed.) 1991a. *Blueprint 2: greening the world economy.* London: Earthscan.

Pearce, D. W. 1991b. 'The role of carbon taxes in adjusting to global warming', *The Economic Journal*, 101, 938–948.

Pearce, D. W. 1992. 'Economics, equity and sustainable development', in P. Ekins and M. Max-Neef (eds) *Real life economics: understanding wealth creation.* London: Routledge.

Pearce, D. W. and Atkinson, G. D. 1993. 'Capital theory and the measurement of sustainable development: an indicator of 'weak' sustainability', *Ecological Economics*, 8: 103–8.

Pearce, D. W., Markandya, A. and Barbier, E. B. 1989. *Blueprint for a green economy.* London: Earthscan.

Pearce, D. W. and Nash, C. A. 1981. *The social appraisal of projects: a textbook in cost benefit analysis.* London: Macmillan.

Pearce, D. W. and Turner, R. K. 1990. *Economics of natural resources and the environment.* London: Harvester Wheatsheaf,

Pearce, F. 1987. *Acid rain.* Harmondsworth: Penguin.

Peet, J. 1992. *Energy and the ecological economics of sustainability.* Washington D.C.: Island Press.

Penz, C.P. 1986. *Consumer sovereignty and human interests.* Cambridge: Cambridge University Press.

Perrings, C. 1987. *Economy and environment: a theoretical essay on the interdependence of economic and environmental systems.* Cambridge: Cambridge University Press.

Perrings, C. 1989. 'Environmental bonds and environmental research in innovative activities', *Ecological Economics*, 1: 95–115.

Peskin, H. M. with Lutz, E. 1990. 'A survey of resource and environmental accounting in industrialised countries'. Environmental Working Paper 37. Washington D.C.: World Bank.

Pezzey, J. 1992. 'Sustainability: an interdisciplinary guide', *Environmental Values*, 1: 321–62.

Phillipson, J. 1966. *Ecological energetics*. London: Edward Arnold.

Ponting, C. 1992. *A green history of the world*. London: Penguin.

Porter, G. and Brown, J. W. 1991. *Global environmental politics*. Boulder: Westview Press.

Priest, J. 1984. *Energy: principles problems alternatives* (3rd edn). Reading: Addison-Wesley.

Prigogine, I. and Stengers, I. 1984. *Order out of chaos*. London: Heinemann.

Proops, J. L. R., 1985. 'Thermodynamics and economics: from analogy to physical functioning', in W. van Gool and J. Bruggink (eds), *Energy and time in the economic and physical sciences*. Amsterdam: North-Holland.

Proops, J. L. R. 1987. 'Entropy information and confusion in the soical sciences', *Journal of Interdisciplinary Economics*, 1: 225–242.

Proops, J. L. R., Faber, M. and Wagenhals, G. 1993. *Reducing CO$_2$ emissions: a comparative input–output study for Germany and the UK*. Berlin: Springer-Verlag.

Ramage, J. 1983. *Energy: a guidebook*. Oxford: Oxford University Press.

Randall, A. 1986. 'Human preferences, economics and the preservation of species', in B. G. Norton (ed.) *The preservation of species*. Princeton: Princeton University Press.

Read, P. 1993. *Responding to global warming: the technology economics and politics of sustainable energy*. London: Zed Books.

Reilly, J. M., Edmonds, J. A., Gardner, R. H. and Brenkert, A. L. 1987. 'Uncertainty analysis of the IEA/ORAU CO$_2$ emission model', *The Energy Journal*, 8: 1–29.

Repetto, R., Magrath, W., Wells, M., Beer, C. and Rossini, F. 1989. *Wasting assets: natural resources in the national income accounts*. Washington D.C.: World Resources Institute.

Rogers, A. 1993. *The earth summit: a planetary reckoning*. Los Angeles: Global View Press.

Sagoff, M. 1988. *The economy of the earth*. Cambridge: Cambridge University Press.

Sahlins, M. 1974. *Stone age economics*. London: Routledge & Kegan Paul.

Samuelson, P. and Nordhaus, W. 1985. *Economics* (12th edn). New York: McGraw-Hill.

Schelling, T. 1984. 'Implications for welfare and policy: anticipating climate change', *Environment*, 26: 6–35.

Schor, J. B. 1991. *The overworked American: the unexpected decline of leisure*. New York: Basic Books.

Scitovsky, T. 1976. *The joyless economy*. New York: Oxford University Press.

Scitovsky, T. 1986. *Human desire and economic satisfaction: essays in the frontiers of economics*. Brighton: Wheatsheaf.

Sedjo, R. A. 1989. 'Forests: a tool to moderate global warming?', *Environment*, 31: 14–20.

Shogren, J. F., Herriges, J. A. and Govindasamy, R. 1993. 'Limits to environmental bond', *Ecological Economics*, 8: 109–133.

Simon, J. L. 1981. *The ultimate resource*. Princeton: Princeton University Press.

Simon, J. L. and Wildavsky, A. 1993. *Assessing the empirical basis of the 'biodiversity crisis'*. Washington: Competitive Enterprise Foundation.

Slesser, M. 1978. *Energy in the economy.* London: Macmillan.

Smith, A. 1776. *The wealth of nations.* (Cannan, E. (ed.), 1961) London: Methuen.

Solow, R. 1971.'The economist's approach to pollution and its control', *Science,* 173: 498–503.

Solow, R. 1974. 'Intergenerational equity and exhaustible resources', *Review of Economic Studies,* Symposium: 29–45.

Solow, R. 1986. 'On the intergenerational allocation of natural resources', *Scandinavian Journal of Economics,* 88: 141–9.

Solow, R. 1992. *An almost practical step toward sustainability.* Washington: Resources for the Future.

Stiglitz, J. E. 1986. *Economics of the public sector.* New York: Norton.

Stobaugh, R. 1982. 'World energy to the year 2000', in D. Yergin and M. Hillenbrand (eds), *Global insecurity: a strategy for energy and economic renewal.* Harmondsworth: Penguin.

Sugden, R. and Williams, A. 1978. *The principles of practical cost benefit analysis.* Oxford: Oxford University Press.

Symons, E. J., Proops, J. L. R. and Gay, P. W. 1991. *Carbon taxes, consumer demand and carbon dioxide emissions: a simulation analysis for the UK.* Working Paper No. 91–25, Keele: Department of Economics and Management Science, University of Keele.

Tegart, W. C. McG., Sheldon, G. W. and Griffiths, D. C. (eds) 1990. *Climate change: the IPCC impacts assessment.* Canberra: Australian Government Publishing Service.

Thomas, J. A. G (ed.) 1977. *Energy analysis.* Guildford: IPC Science and Technology.

Tietenberg, T. 1992. *Environmental and natural resource economics* (2nd edn). New York: Harper Collins.

Townsend, P. 1979. *Poverty in the United Kingdom: a survey of household resources and standards of living.* Harmondsworth: Penguin.

Townsend, P. 1985. 'A sociological approach to the measurement of poverty – a rejoinder to Professor Amaya Sen', *Oxford Economic Papers,* 37: 659–668.

United Nations 1990. *SNA handbook on integrated environmental and economic accaounting; preliminary draft of part 1, general concepts.* New York: United Nations Statistical Office.

United Nations 1993: *Earthsummit: Agenda 21, the United Nations programme of action from Rio.* New York: United Nations Department of Public Information.

United Nations Development Programme 1992. *Human development report 1992.* New York: Oxford University Press.

Usher, D. 1980. *The measurement of economic growth.* Oxford: Basil Blackwell.

Vitousek, P. M., Ehrlich, P. R., Ehrlich, A. H. and Matson, P. A. 1986. 'Human appropriation of the products of photosynthesis', *Bioscience,* 36: 368–373.

Vogt, W. 1967. 'Conservation and the guaranteed income', in R. Theobold (ed.) *The guaranteed income: the next step in socioeconomic evolution?.* Garden City: Doubleday Anchor.

Wallace, N. 1992. *Natural resource management: an economic perspective.* Canberra: Australian Bureau of Agricultural and Resource Economics.

Wallace, R. R. and Norton, B. G. 1992. 'Policy implications of Gaian theory', *Ecological Economics,* 6: 103–118.

Walter, T. 1989. *Basic income: freedom from poverty, freedom to work*. London: Marion Boyars.

Watt, K. E. F., 1973. *Principles of environmental science*. New York: McGraw-Hill.

Weintraub, E. R. 1975. *Conflict and cooperation in economics*. London: Macmillan.

Whalley, J. and Wigle, R. 1991. 'The international incidence of carbon taxes', in R. Dornbusch and J. Poterba (eds) *Economic policy responses to global warming*. Cambridge, Mass.: MIT Press.

Wilkinson, R. G. 1973. *Poverty and progress: an ecological model of economic development*. London: Metheun.

Wilkinson, R. G. 1988. 'The english industrial revolution', in D. Worster (ed.) *The ends of the earth: perspectives on modern environmental history*. Cambridge: Cambridge University Press.

Wilson, E. O. and Peter, F. M. (eds) 1988. *Biodiversity*. Washington: National Academy Press.

Wonnacott, P. and Wonnacott, R. 1979. *Economics*. New York: McGraw-Hill.

World Bank 1992. *World development report 1992: development and the environment*. Oxford: Oxford University Press.

World Commission on Environment and Development 1987. *Our common future*. Oxford: Oxford University Press.

Worster, D. 1985. *Nature's enemy: A history of ecological ideas*. Cambridge: Cambridge University Press.

Xenos, N. 1989. *Scarcity and modernity*. London: Macmillan.

Young, M. D. 1990. 'Natural resource accounting', in M. S. Common and S. Dovers (eds) *Moving toward global sutainability: policies and implications for Australia*. Canberra: Centre for Continuing Education, Australian National University.

Young, M. D. 1992. *Sustainable investment and natural resource use: equity environmental integrity and economic efficiency*. Paris: United Nations Education Scientific and Cultural Organisation.

Young, M. D. 1993. *For our children's children: some practical implications of inter-generational equity, the precautionary principle, maintenance of natural capital and the discount rate*. Canberra: CSIRO Division of Wildlife and Ecology.

Zolotas, X. 1981. *Economic growth and declining social welfare*. Athens: Bank of Greece.

Index